Writing the Modern Research Paper

FOURTH EDITION

Robert Dees
Orange Coast College

PEARSON
Longman

New York San Francisco Boston
London Toronto Sydney Tokyo Singapore Madrid
Mexico City Munich Paris Cape Town Hong Kong Montreal

Senior Vice President/Publisher: Joe Opiela
Marketing Manager: Christopher Bennem
Senior Supplements Editor: Donna Campion
Production Manager: Eric Jorgensen
Project Coordination and Electronic Page Makeup: Electronic Publishing
    Services Inc., NYC
Cover Design Manager: John Callahan
Cover Designer: Kay Petronio
Cover Photo: Cover Image by Jerry Blank of Stock Illustration Source
Photo Researcher: Julie Hallett
Manufacturing Buyer: Al Dorsey
Printer and Binder: RR Donnelley & Sons Co.
Cover Printer: Phoenix Color Corp.

Library of Congress Cataloging-in-Publication Data
Dees, Robert.
    Writing the modern research paper / Robert Dees.-4th ed.
        p.   cm.
    Includes bibliographical references (p.) and index.
    ISBN 0-321-10754-3
    1. Report writing. 2. Research. I. Title.

    LB2369 .D44 2003
    808'.02-dc21

                                        2002070224

Please visit our Web site at http://www.ablongman.com

ISBN 0-321-21636-9

Printed in the United States of America

10 9 8 7 6 5 4 3 2 1—DOC— 05   04   03

CONTENTS

5 *Researching beyond the Campus Library*   **89**

PREFACE

The fourth edition of *Writing the Modern Research Paper* continues to provide college students in all disciplines with an up-to-date, step-by-step guide to doing enjoyable, effective research and to writing thorough, well-documented papers. This edition, however, also includes much new material intended to increase the text's usefulness and currency:

■ *Critical thinking:* This edition stresses the importance of critical thinking in every step of the research process. Newly added "Thinking Critically..." boxes appear throughout each chapter to advise students about the need for thoughtful attention to such matters as selecting a research topic; working with primary and secondary sources; researching in a library, onsite, or through the Internet; avoiding plagiarism; evaluating and documenting sources; and effectively completing a written research report. The need for students to think carefully as well as independently about research information is introduced in Chapter 1 and is echoed throughout the text and reemphasized in Chapter 9, "Reasoning Critically about Argument and Evidence." This chapter explains inductive and deductive reasoning, the Toulmin model of argument, types of evidence, and common logical fallacies. It also includes newly added advice on "Thinking Critically about" arguments, hypothetical examples, analogies, and evaluating a source's authority.

■ *Electronic resources and the Internet:* The nature of research processes and opportunities has been significantly changed by the proliferation of information available on compact disk (CD-ROM), on the Internet, and by the accessibility of worldwide databases. The fourth edition discusses these and other new aspects of research with attention to what they mean for students writing college or university research papers. Chapter 6, "Researching on the Internet," has been updated to introduce students to more recent opportunities for using databases and the Internet, in particular. This chapter discusses the latest methods of searching the Internet for information, including using email, listservs, mailing lists, and Usenet or newsgroups. The chapter has also been updated with new listings of online resources and an added number of sequential web page illustrations to show students what they will be working with when researching on the Internet.

■ *Current documentation styles:* Most academic discipline authorities have changed their recommended documentation styles within the past few years to address the use of electronic resources and to streamline traditional practices. In keeping with these changes, Chapters 11 through 13 have been revised to present the most recent documentation forms (including those for electronic sources) recommended by the Modern Language Association (MLA), the American Psychological Association (APA), the Council of Biology Editors (CBE), and *The Chicago Manual of Style.*

■ *Avoiding Plagiarism:* The new title of Chapter 7, "Reading Critically, Recording Information, and Avoiding Plagiarism" reflects the increasing need for students to read and record information with critical understanding and accuracy, as well to understand plagiarism and how to avoid it in a research paper. The chapter includes extensive discussion of reading critically; taking effective, accurate notes; and recording source information. To help students understand and avoid falling into plagiarism, "Thinking Critically..." boxes add to the chapter discussion of how to handle summary, paraphrase, and direct quotation, along with illustrative examples of when these techniques are used correctly and when they are not.

Plan for the Text

My own years of teaching about the research paper have shown me that in order to think critically and creatively during the research process, students need to understand the range of possibilities for conducting research and know how to use those possibilities to their advantage. Chapter 1, "Doing Research and the Research Paper," introduces students to critical thinking and the importance of summary, evaluation, analysis, and synthesis in using researched sources to reach logical and supportable conclusions. The chapter also provides an overview of the research paper and explains the value of framing a research question, planning a research schedule, and keeping a research notebook.

Chapter 2, "Using a Library for Research," continues the introduction to research by discussing the use of libraries and the wealth of resources they have to offer, including computer catalogs, reference sources, online accessibility, and experienced support staff. Techniques for using such resources and ways of narrowing a research topic are covered in Chapter 3, "Planning the Focus of Your Research." Chapter 4, "Researching Library Resources," discusses bibliographies and indexes and explains how to prepare a working bibliography.

Since not everything students need to know about their research topics will necessarily be found in college libraries, Chapter 5, "Researching beyond the Campus Library," leads students past traditional library sources and out into their communities. In addition to encouraging research using primary and secondary materials from public sources, this chapter also explains how to gather information by observing onsite, conducting personal interviews, taking surveys, and utilizing such media as radio and television. Chapter 6, "Researching on the Internet," continues to expand students' awareness of and ability to research independently by discussing how to access the Internet and World Wide Web and how to use databases, search tools, e-mail, listservs, and Usenet.

Chapter 7, "Reading Critically, Recording Information, and Avoiding Plagiarism," discusses the importance of careful reading and notetaking—practical, timesaving skills that can ensure accurate content and source citation later. This chapter presents critical thinking techniques to evaluate sources and discusses how and when to use summary, paraphrase, and quotation in research papers. The importance of citing sources to avoid the problem of plagiarism is addressed as well.

Once students have begun to assemble a quantity of research data, they are often confused about how to begin organizing it and writing their papers. Because of the importance of these activities, they are discussed in three separate but related chapters. Chapter 8, "Planning Your Paper," explains how to formulate and use preliminary and final thesis statements to focus the paper's discussion as well as how to devise an appropriate outline to organize the content. Basic written patterns of development are also reviewed. As mentioned earlier, Chapter 9, "Reasoning Critically about Argument and Evidence," discusses what makes an effective argument and how students can evaluate the arguments made in sources and their own papers. Chapter 10, "Writing Your Paper," explains a variety of ways to write the introduction, body, and conclusion and discusses how to revise, edit, and proofread the final draft.

Three chapters are also devoted to explaining and differentiating among the most common documentation styles used for research papers. Chapters 11 and 12 demonstrate correct forms for intext citations and the Works Cited section of a research paper using the MLA style of documentation. A sample MLA-style research paper is included in Chapter 11. Chapter 13 discusses alternative documentation styles, including the author-date styles followed by the APA and *Chicago* and the name-year and citation-sequence styles followed by the CBE.

Chapter 14, "Preparing the Final Manuscript," addresses the many technical and stylistic matters that often confront students writing research papers. MLA conventions for handling abbreviations, numbers, illustrations, titles, and so forth are explained, as is the meaning of *fair use* according to current copyright law.

To assist writers using documentation styles other than MLA, Appendix A presents two additional sample research papers: the first using APA author-date style and the second using CBE citation-sequence style. Appendix B provides a guide to selected subject reference sources.

Like those in the first edition, each chapter in this new edition of *Writing the Modern Research Paper* concludes with a special Working with Others section, which promotes collaboration among students and takes the loneliness out of the research process. These sections may be used by groups of students working on their own, or they may be assigned by instructors as part of structured classroom activities.

Acknowledgments

As always, I am very grateful to Joe Opiela, Senior Vice President and Publisher at Longman, for his encouragement and advice on this and the previous editions, as well as to his assistant, Julie Hallett, who worked diligently to get this new edition ready for production.

I also wish to thank the reviewers who offered useful suggestions for preparing the fourth edition: Warren Anderson, Judson College; Pamela J. Colbert, Marshalltown Community College; Elizabeth Kirchoff, St. Cloud State University; James McDonald, University of Louisiana at Lafayette; James Stokes, University of Wisconsin–Stevens Point.

And of course, my deepest thanks go to my wife, Van, for her patience and love during a tough year.

CHAPTER 1

Doing Research and the Research Paper

The idea of doing research with a capital R never occurred to me. I was just trying to understand something. What I found over a period of time was that if I thought hard about something, I often understood it better than other people—to the point where I could explain some things to other people. Sometimes I could explain things that nobody had seen before.

—I. M. Singer, Professor of Mathematics, Massachusetts Institute of Technology*

Virtually every human achievement— whether discovering fire, building the pyramids, or creating a vaccine for polio—has been accomplished by someone investigating a topic and thinking critically about it. William Shakespeare's plays grew directly out of his own historical research and creative genius. Albert Einstein discovered relativity by studying, analyzing, and evaluating the works of other mathematicians. Every film produced in Hollywood, each law passed by Congress, and all the products on the grocery shelves are the results of research. *Research* is observation and critical study. It is collecting information in order to make judgments and gain truth.

Research Is Learning

In fact, you should regard writing a research paper as learning how to learn on your own. Your professor will not simply hand you information in the form of a lecture or notes, nor will a textbook or other single source sum up all you need to know and understand about a subject. Your efforts in producing a research paper will educate you in ways to acquire information and give you practice in drawing intelligent conclusions from what you discover. You

*From "Mathematics," *The Joys of Research,* ed. Walter Shropshire (Washington, DC: Smithsonian, 1981) 55.

**THINKING CRITICALLY
ABOUT YOUR ROLE AS A RESEARCHER**

You may not fully realize it, but you have been doing research most of your life. From the first time you asked a parent or teacher where clouds come from or where the sun goes at night, or poked a stick into an anthill to try to find what lay beneath, or read through the rules for a new game, you were doing research. Comparing player statistics from sports cards, mixing together different paints to see what colors will result, even poring over fashion or automotive magazines to spot the latest trends—all of these are, to some extent, forms of research. All involve finding answers to questions that interest you.

The same holds true for the research you will do as a student—except that the questions you pose and the answers you seek will be quite a bit more complex. Still, the questions on which you base your research should be, at least to some degree, relevant to your interests. Even if you are given a fairly narrow research topic, you will need to search within that topic for a question that intrigues or puzzles you—a question you care enough about so that you will actively invest the time and critical attention required to carry out thorough—and, ultimately, satisfying—research. As you have been doing all your life, you learn by asking questions, finding answers, and, finally, making judgments.

---

will come to see that doing research is *learning* in its most fundamental form: the acquisition and interpretation of information.

Perhaps you will enjoy finding out about scientific subjects such as efforts to find a cure for AIDS or the possibility of interstellar travel. Or you may be interested in the advantages and drawbacks of certain professions—say, being a nurse, an athlete, or a teacher. What is happening to the earth's ozone layer? Why is teenage suicide so common? What should be done to stem the spread of drugs in U.S. society? Has television become sleazy? Are abortion laws too lenient? Writing a research paper provides you with the opportunity to learn—really learn—about these and other subjects that you may enjoy.

What Is a Research Paper?

The research paper you write will be a documented report resulting from your thinking critically about the information you examine. Its content will focus upon a topic that your own intellectual curiosity brings you to study. The primary purpose of such a paper is to inform the reader about the research topic and to demonstrate the validity or reasonableness of your conclusions about it. Although it is more objective than a personal essay, keep in mind that a research paper is also an expression of your own understanding of the topic. Your personal values, insights, and experiences will shape your responses throughout the research process, eventually finding expression in what you conclude and how you write about the topic.

The Research Topic

The information you collect for a research paper relates to a research subject or, more accurately, to a particular aspect of it called the *topic*. If you were interested, for example, in researching the subject of space exploration, a possible topic might be the benefits of long-range space probes like *Explorer I* or *Galileo*. Another topic for a paper on space exploration might be the physiological effects upon humans of spending prolonged periods of time in outer space.

Once you have selected a suitable topic for research, you can begin to frame a *research question,* which will become the focus of your research and your paper's discussion. How beneficial are long-range space probes? might be one question to investigate. Should we continue sending long-range probes into space? would shift the focus to a different aspect of the same subject. A topic concerning the effects upon humans of prolonged time in space could generate a research question such as Are prolonged flights in space too dangerous for humans?

Questions like these direct the investigation of sources and focus your notetaking. They ensure that your paper will raise a significant issue and provide thoughtful discussion about the topic.

Length

The amount of discussion needed to support your main point about the research topic will determine your paper's length. In general, you will probably want to select a research topic that can be adequately discussed in 10 to 12 typewritten pages (5,000–6,000 words), the assigned length for most college research papers. Depending upon your topic, the amount of time you have for research, and the expectations of your instructor, your paper may be somewhat shorter or longer.

Organization

A completed research paper includes several major parts, usually arranged in this order:

Title page (optional)*
Outline (optional)
Text

*Many instructors have their own requirements for what a research paper should include and how it should be formatted. Check with your instructor to make sure you understand his or her preferences.

Introduction	Introduction of the topic leading to a statement of the paper's thesis.
Body	Several paragraphs that illustrate and support the thesis through discussion, analysis, and examples; acknowledgment of sources as appropriate.
Conclusion	A summary of major arguments or a final statement and example.
Works Cited or References	A list of sources acknowledged in the paper.

FIGURE 1.1   Simplified diagram of a research paper

Note: Although the major sections are named here, they are not usually identified or included as subheadings in the paper itself.

>   Notes (optional)
>   Works Cited/References
>   Appendix (optional)

The largest part of the paper—the *text,* or content portion—generally consists of three major sections:

1. The *introduction,* which sets forth the paper's *thesis,* or main point
2. The *body,* which illustrates and supports the main point with paragraphs of information and discussion
3. The *conclusion,* which states a final idea or summarizes the paper's major arguments

A research paper also includes *documentation,* the citing of sources in the text of the paper as well as their listing at the end of the paper in a section titled Works Cited or References. Figure 1.1 presents a simplified diagram of a typical research paper.

Doing Research for Your Paper

To "re-search" a subject is literally to see it another way: You gather original information of your own or study the work of others and evaluate it from your own point of view and experience.

Finding Sources

The investigation you do for a research paper may draw upon several kinds of sources. *Primary sources* include original material from such sources as the following:

- Your own experiences
- Field observations
- Interviews
- Laboratory reports
- Diaries
- Letters
- Literary works

Or you may be involved in research that uses information written by others about your subject. These *secondary sources* are those found in most libraries and include materials like these:

- Encyclopedias
- Magazines and journals
- Books
- Newspapers
- Pamphlets
- Indexes
- Online sources, such as websites
- Computer databases
- Government reports

In order to give your paper both depth and breadth in its discussion of the research topic, use both primary and secondary sources as much as possible (see Chapters 4 and 5). You will find the critical thinking techniques of summary, evaluation, analysis, and synthesis helpful in assessing and taking useful notes from each kind of source (see Chapter 5).

Documenting Sources

Regardless of which kinds of sources you use, your paper will include *documentation,* a method of acknowledging where you found your information and giving credit for any ideas that are not your own. Depending upon the kind of paper you write and for which discipline, the documentation may appear within the text of the paper itself, in footnotes, or at the end of the paper in endnotes. As described earlier, your paper will also include a list of all the works cited as documentation in the paper. (See Chapter 13 and Appendix A on documentation forms for various academic disciplines.)

Organizing Your Research

A successful research paper reflects careful planning, not only of the re-search activities themselves but also of the time involved to accomplish them. The due date for your paper limits the time available for research and writing, and it puts pressure on you to finish the paper by a specified date. In order to complete the research process fully and to make sure the paper is finished on time, you will need to plan a reasonable research schedule and do all you can to keep to it.

Planning a Research Schedule

A *research schedule* is a calendar of all the steps necessary for com-pleting a successful research paper on time. Obviously, your schedule will list the paper's due date, but you should also include the major research steps that are described in this text:

1. Investigating one or more potential research subjects
2. Selecting a topic and framing a research question
3. Establishing a preliminary bibliography
4. Reading and taking notes on the topic
5. Devising an outline and tentative thesis statement
6. Writing the paper
7. Listing the works cited
8. Revising and editing

In addition, you should add any steps that are unique to your individual re-search methods and necessary for your particular topic.

Your planning for a successful research paper should begin early. In fact, you ought to start thinking about your subject, available resources, and your time for researching and writing the paper the first day you know about the assignment. Starting early like this will save time later and allow you to collect ideas and resources throughout the term.

Once you actually begin your research assignment in earnest, expect to spend at least four to five weeks of ongoing thinking, researching, and writing. If you are not familiar with using a computer to research online materials, give yourself additional time to learn about and practice using such a valuable research tool. Since writing a good research paper requires allowing enough time to complete all the activities mentioned, you should devise a research schedule that identifies the date for accomplishing each task as well as the turn-in date for your paper.

Figure 1.2 represents student Linda Kastan's research schedule for her paper on Internet addiction. The finished paper—Internet Addiction: Is There a Dark Side to Cyberspace?—is included in Chapter 11 (pages 245–60). Note that Linda's research schedule includes the major steps given in this text as well as several activities required by her topic and her individual way of

Linda Kastan
English 101

RESEARCH PAPER SCHEDULE

Date Due	Step	Completed
February 22	Begin thinking about research subject. Start research notebook.	[ ]
March 15	Select research subject.	[ ]
April 14	Read encyclopedia, and review general sources on possible research topics.	[ ]
*April 17	Make topic decision. Get OK from Professor Nuñez.	[ ]
April 18	Start preliminary reading and notetaking.	[ ]
*April 21	Turn in preliminary bibliography.	[ ]
April 22–May 2	Research in library.	[ ]
April 24	Locate newsgroups, conferences, and chat groups discussing talk shows on the Internet or other online sources.	[ ]
April 28	Meet with psychology professor Robert James. Ask about Internet and addiction.	[ ]
May 3–4	Analyze research notes. Make up outline and preliminary thesis statement.	[ ]
May 5–8	Write first draft of paper.	[ ]
*May 8	First draft due to Professor Nuñez for advice.	[ ]
May 8–10	Write final draft.	[ ]
May 11–12	Revise and edit final draft.	[ ]
May 14	Finish Works Cited list.	[ ]
*May 25	Final research paper due!	[ ]

FIGURE 1.2   Student Linda Kastan's research paper schedule

approaching research. Linda also decided to use asterisks to mark any due dates for various steps in the research process.

Linda became interested in the topic of Internet addiction after first reading essays in her English class about how modern technology has influenced today's culture. Later, she watched a television documentary at home that focused on students whose grades were suffering because they spent too much time conversing in Internet chat rooms and playing interactive games. When Linda discussed the documentary with her friends on campus, they agreed that the lure of the Internet was causing problems for some students—even a few they knew. Linda began with the idea of focusing her paper on the attraction of chat rooms and popular interactive games known as *MUDs (multiuser dungeons)*. But when her early research did not turn up enough sources on these particular uses of the Internet, Linda changed her mind. She decided to shift the focus of her research to Internet addiction in general.

Patterns of Research Progress

The shift in direction that Linda made is not at all unusual for someone who is starting work on a research paper. Her research schedule may look complete, but the fact is that Linda's planning, like her topic, actually changed several times during the assignment period. Even though this book will introduce you to the steps every research paper writer must complete, bear in mind that these steps do not necessarily occur in order or only once during the research effort. Your analysis of what you discover one day about your topic (say, the validity of IQ tests) may lead to new discoveries the next day, then a revision of your first analysis, and so on throughout your research. The book you thought would be of no help when you began your research may suddenly become essential at some later stage.

As Linda Kastan discovered after she changed her research focus, research proceeds more in loops and zigzags than in a direct line. Keep your research efforts on track, but try not to become discouraged by this irregular pattern of progress: Looping and zigzagging is the nature of productive research.

The format for your own research schedule may vary from Linda's, but do not overlook this important planning step in preparing to write a research paper. Your schedule will change along with your research; it will also serve as your planning guide and a source of reassurance about the timeliness of your efforts. As you move progressively further into the research process, you will also find that checking off each completed task provides satisfaction and encouragement as you work to complete the paper.

Keeping a Research Notebook

Most of the thinking for your research paper will occur during times that you have specifically set aside for research and writing. Unfortunately, however, the best ideas and sudden insights do not always occur on schedule. Many useful thoughts will spring up spontaneously, often coming only half formed at unexpected times. Seeing a neighbor who works for the city housing agency, for example, may suddenly remind you that he or she would be an excellent interview source for a paper on people who are homeless. While crossing campus on your way to a morning class, you might recall the magazine article you read yesterday on the cost of space exploration. At that moment, you may start to think about how your paper might use some of those statistics.

To make sure useful ideas like these are not lost, you should write them down in a research notebook. A *research notebook* is any handy-size, spiral-bound notebook that you can literally carry with you everywhere and make a habit of using throughout the research process. You will find such a notebook a useful place to record valuable information, especially the spontaneous pondering that occurs both during and between your planned research activities. The research notebook is also a good place to jot down titles you want to look for later, to pose questions you need answered, or to record your progress.

A research notebook will be most useful to you if you give some thought ahead of time to a few practical considerations. Follow these suggestions as you begin to set up your research notebook:

1. Keep a particular notebook reserved especially for your research notes and writing. Mixing your research material with other kinds of writing or class assignments defeats the purpose of the research notebook, which is to record and organize all of your thinking for the research paper in one easily accessible place.

2. Use pencil or ink to record ideas and information. While you do not need to worry about neatness, write legibly and make complete entries. Nothing is more frustrating than having to retrace your steps to find omitted information or not being able to decipher a hastily written note later.

3. Record names, titles, and other bibliographic data accurately and fully to avoid errors in your final paper. Make a point of later copying all such information about sources onto 3″ × 5″ notecards for easier use.

4. Use as many headings or subtitles in the notebook as necessary to keep your entries organized. Headings like Notes and Ideas, Research Subjects, Topic Choices, Sources to Find, and Questions to Answer will keep your entries accessible and encourage your thinking for each section.

5. Date each entry in the research notebook. This will help you see a pattern to the research as well as provide an occasional nudge when you have ignored something for too long.

The pages in Figure 1.3 are from student Linda Kastan's research notebook and show entries she made while preparing her paper on Internet

Linda Kastan
English 101

                    Research Notebook

Notes and Ideas

February 8:   Professor Nuñez described our research paper assignment today. Ten to fifteen pages on a current issue. Start thinking of what I want to write about.

February 26:   I've been thinking about writing something on the Internet. Is it doing any harm? Some people seem to be so into it—are they addicted? Does hurrying home to your e-mail make you an addict? Is the Internet addictive? Or are people just using it in place of something else?

March 10:   Library research on computers and the Internet. There are a lot of issues revolving around the isolation that people get into when they use the Internet so much.

March 12:   Went to the Internet to see what I could find about computer or Internet addiction—a lot! Took one of the addiction tests; downloaded several articles. Some of the articles deny addiction or make fun of it. Some are posted by ex-Internet junkies. Lots of references to Dr. Kimberly Young's study. Need to investigate this more.

March 24:   Found Young's book on Internet addiction at the library. Also one by Stoll—he thinks the Internet is a big hole that will swallow up our personalities. He could be right.

FIGURE 1.3   Student Linda Kastan's research notebook

Internet Research Topics

1. *Effect of the Internet on college students*
2. *Internet addiction*
3. *Power of Internet service providers*
4. *Pornography on the Internet*
5. *Value of Internet communities*

Research Questions

✓1. *What evidence is there that people are getting addicted to the Internet?*
✓2. *How is <u>addiction</u> defined?*
3. *What types of people are most likely to become addicted to the Internet?*
4. *What value do people find in the Internet?*
5. *How much background information about the Internet, chat rooms, MUDs, etc., do I need to include in my paper?*
6. *How many of my own ideas go into the paper, and how many sources do I need to include?*

Sources to Find

✓*February 15:* *Use Yahoo! or another search engine to locate sources over the Internet.*

February 21: *Find Young's book—<u>Caught in the Net</u>—about Internet addiction.*

February 24: *Check Infotrac for sources. Maybe try Medline on the Internet.*

FIGURE 1.3   Continued

addiction. The entries demonstrate how she used her research notebook to record and organize work on her paper.

As these entries show, a research notebook may contain many kinds of information, from short reminders about library hours to extended thinking about sources. You may decide to use your notebook as a place to record all your research notes and do extensive writing for the research paper, or you may want to use it only as a place to try out ideas in very brief forms.

Notice that Linda Kastan dated each entry. She also made a checkmark next to each task as she completed it (see p. 11). You may want to devise your own way of keeping track of what you accomplish, and you may even prefer using a different format than Linda's for your notebook entries. The most important thing is to utilize your research notebook in a way that is genuinely helpful for preparing your research paper.

While there are no set requirements for what goes into a research notebook, the following kinds of entries are typically the most useful:

■ *Your research schedule:* Having your research schedule readily available will keep your efforts organized and give you direction. Make it the first item you put in your notebook.

■ *Ideas about your research topic:* Jot down spontaneous insights before you forget them. If you find yourself writing a lot, keep going. What you write could become valuable material for the final paper.

■ *Research questions:* Keep track of questions you need to answer for yourself about the paper's topic (What are my city's educational requirements for police personnel?) as well as those questions you will need to ask others (Do I hand in my research notebook with my final paper?).

■ *Sources to follow up on:* Record authors' names, source titles, libraries, data services, and other information you may need for your paper.

Since you never know when an idea or useful information may suddenly become available, make a habit of carrying your notebook with you wherever you go, not just to the library or during research times. Once you start using a research notebook regularly, you will find it an essential aid in researching and writing your paper.

Including Your Own Ideas in the Research Paper

Unfortunately, too many beginning writers make the mistake of letting research content alone dominate their papers. Anxious to demonstrate the hours of research they have devoted to their papers or simply overwhelmed by the amount of material discovered, they end up writing summarizing reports instead of the thoughtful, creative responses to research that their instructors had expected. A work that only summarizes sources, instead of using them to illuminate ideas or support an argument, is not a research paper.

Make sure your paper analyzes, compares, and evaluates information and sources to support your position and clarify your thoughts for the reader. As you go about writing, remember that your own ideas are not only valuable but actually are, in one sense, what the paper is about. If you are writing a paper on the subject of homeless people in the United States, for example, your reader will not only want to know about these people but also what the information you present adds up to. Your presentation and interpretation of the facts, your analysis and comparison of other writers' opinions, and your conclusions about all of these constitute the heart of your research content.

WORKING WITH OTHERS

Make a habit of talking over your research assignment with friends or classmates as early in the term as possible. Begin by discussing the following questions together to get a broad view of research and to be sure you understand the class assignment clearly.

- Discuss a recent film or television program you have seen that required someone to do research for its content or production. What kind of research was done? How was it done and by whom? How important to the success of the production was the research? Cite examples of how research or its results are being carried out in other areas of society.

- Review any previous experience you have had researching information, and discuss the major steps or tasks involved. How did that kind of research differ from that involved in doing the research paper for your current assignment?

- What kinds of research have you done on a computer? Discuss your knowledge and experience with those of one or more of classmates. Find out what computer resources for conducting research are available at your campus. What resources do you have at home?

- Regardless of whether you have had previous experience doing some kind of research, what questions do you now have about research and research papers generally?

- Discuss your current research paper assignment. Do you foresee any major obstacles to your successful completion of the assignment? If so, how will you overcome these obstacles?

- Exchange ideas about potential local resources for research. What primary or secondary resources are available?

- Have you used anything like a research notebook or made up something like a research schedule in the past? Why or why not? How helpful do you feel either of these will be to your completing the current research paper assignment?

- Share any ideas you have for a research subject or topic. What interests you about these issues? How do they fit your current research paper assignment?

Each of the chapters in this book concludes with suggestions for Working with Others on a research paper assignment. Also check with your instructor about any guidelines he or she may have for working together, and take advantage of any opportunities you have to share your ideas and progress. You will find that time spent discussing your research and writing with others is one of the best resources available.

CHAPTER 2

Using a Library for Research

Before you can think clearly and critically about a subject, you must have a good understanding of it and know what others have said or written about it. Thus, whether writing a library-based research paper or one developed fully from your own field or laboratory studies, you will need the resources of a good library. You should use the library to discover what is already known about the research topic, what issues need to be addressed, and what sources exist for you to consider. Most campus libraries and large community libraries can provide the information you will need, first to establish the direction of your research and later to investigate a specific research question in depth.

This chapter will introduce you to academic and public libraries and how to use them, including computer catalogs, citation indexes, and database searches. You will need to understand such libraries and resources in order to make your research both efficient and comprehensive.

Understanding Academic and Public Libraries

It is best to begin your research at the largest library available. Access to numerous resources will ensure success in getting started and give you insight to the limitations and possibilities of the research topic. Once you have a topic and can focus on a potential research question, your goal will be to locate appropriate numbers and types of sources to investigate. Both academic and public libraries will be useful to your research for the different emphases and variety of sources they provide.

**THINKING CRITICALLY
ABOUT USING LIBRARIES FOR RESEARCH**

As this chapter suggests, different libraries may be more or less useful to you depending on the topic of your research. Academic libraries—and, in particular, the special interest libraries within a university library system—will generally offer the most specialized and in-depth materials on topics related to academic study. Public libraries are more likely than academic libraries to house general sources, but they may also provide more sources related to popular culture along with more materials of community interest. As for periodicals, the collections in smaller libraries may be limited in terms of how far back holdings go and so may be less useful for researching, say, a history of how a certain product has been advertised in the popular press.

As you begin research, you will need to determine clearly where the most appropriate sources for your topic are available.

Academic Libraries

College and university libraries are created primarily to serve the study and research needs of students, faculty, and scholars. For this reason, academic libraries are your best resource for general as well as scarce or highly specialized materials. The sheer quantity of books, periodicals, microfilms, and other resources at most academic libraries makes them essential to competent research. (The combined libraries at Harvard University, for example, house over 11,000,000 books.) Since they are intended to serve research, the reference sections as well as the research support services of most academic libraries are also more extensive than those of community or private libraries.

Special Emphasis Libraries. Most colleges and universities also maintain separate libraries for such professional areas as law, medicine, business, and technology. Such discipline libraries often contain specialized resources that you would not readily find in other libraries or at least not in such quantity. If you were researching a topic like AIDS, for example, you would most likely find a reference source such as *Encyclopedia of AIDS: A Social, Political, Cultural, and Scientific Record of the HIV Epidemic*, edited by Raymond A. Smith (Penguin, 2001) only at a college or university medical library. Similarly, you would go to a campus law library for *Index to Legal Periodicals* to locate the numerous legal journals not ordinarily found at the main college or university library. You will find that community college libraries are good resources for general research and especially for trade and vocational subjects.

The general emphasis of a college or university is often a reliable clue to its library's resources. Because of its focus on art and design, the Massachusetts College of Art, for example, has an extensive collection of slides, films, videos, and recordings in addition to a large general library. The library at Northrop University, a private California college emphasizing technology and business, houses over 65,000 books, many of them engineering and airframe maintenance sources that would be unavailable at most other academic or public libraries.

To work in the library at a school you do not attend, you may be restricted to using materials right in the library or checking them out on a community-use basis. You may also be able to check out resources through the interlibrary loan services on your own campus. Access to the libraries of private colleges and universities may be available for a small fee. And if you do visit another school's library, do not overlook the campus bookstore as an additional place to find very recent material on your subject.

Assessing What Is Available.   You should thoroughly investigate your own campus or another academic library and its resources before starting research. Though you may feel that you can research effectively at a nearby community library, you never know what research ideas might be better developed through the facilities of a larger library. Ask your instructor or a librarian what subjects the libraries of nearby universities and colleges emphasize.

Thanks to the Internet, you can access the catalogs of many university and public libraries online. One comprehensive source for accessing library catalogs within the United States and around the world is www.libdex.com, where you can narrow your search first to the United States and then to a specific state to obtain a listing of all libraries in that state with available online catalogs.

Public Libraries

If your research steers you toward topics of community, county, or state importance, you may profit by investigating the holdings of one or more public libraries in your area. Public libraries do not usually offer the extensive general holdings or scholarly reference materials found in academic libraries. Most public libraries, however, carry major encyclopedias; dictionaries; subject bibliographies; indexes to magazine, journal, and newspaper articles; and other standard reference works, which can be of help when you are first starting to research.

Special Focus Materials.   Local libraries also offer resource materials not available at most academic or private libraries. News that has particular local importance—say, the closing of a nearby nuclear atomic power plant or the life and career of a famous area resident—may be more thoroughly covered by the small community newspapers kept on file at the local public library.

In addition, county and city libraries are often the only resources for local or regional historical documents. Because of a particular librarian's personal interest or a patron's donation of items, local city or county libraries may have special collections of materials (such as diaries, letters, scrapbooks, and antiques) not commonly included in academic library holdings. Your local public library may also maintain small informal files of pamphlets, handbills, political advertisements, theater announcements, and other items of community interest. Check with the librarian to see what kinds of special collections may be available and useful for your research.

Locating Public Libraries.   Remember that public libraries vary as much as the communities they serve. Sometimes a brief phone call can tell you whether visiting a city or county library would be worth your time. You can probably locate the nearest public libraries just by looking in the telephone book. For more comprehensive information about the location and particular collection emphases of any academic, public, or private library, consult the *American Library Directory: 2001–02* (2 vols.) (New York: Bowker, 2001).

Do not overlook the value of using public libraries at some stage of your research. Their different emphases may provide ideas about what to research, or if you already have a topic, they may suggest a local angle for the paper to make it more representative of your individual approach. The campus library may be the best place to research the general topic of teenage gangs; however, the local library may help you research a paper focusing on efforts to eliminate a widespread gang problem in your own community.

How Libraries Are Organized

You can save time and avoid a lot of frustration doing research by understanding the general arrangement of materials in a library. Although libraries are not alike in the ways they organize information, the reference, book, and periodical sections are the ones you should be most familiar with in doing your research.

The Reference Area

A library's reference area houses its encyclopedias, dictionaries, bibliographies, directories, atlases, indexes, and almanacs. Information is usually available at a reference desk from which a librarian provides assistance by answering questions or locating items that are difficult to find. The reference desk is also where you can request a librarian-assisted database search for your topic.

Since reference books are generally not allowed to circulate outside the library, plan to complete most of your working bibliography in the reference room itself. To save time and get ideas about what resources are available in the reference area, it is always wise to browse awhile in this section before settling into your research. Many libraries provide printed guides that show the general layout of the reference section and other parts of the library.

The Book Area

Also called *the stacks,* this is the area containing books and the bound volumes of periodicals, including magazines and journals. Depending on the library, the stacks may range in size from many rows of shelved books to several floors of them. Some libraries have a separate *oversize* section for all books that exceed normal height or width.

Access to the stacks varies among libraries. In those with open stacks, you can go among the aisles of books yourself to find what you need. In a library with closed stacks, a staff person brings books to you after you make out a request form.

The Periodicals Room

Unbound issues of current magazines, journals, and newspapers are kept in the library's periodical room. Practice varies, but most libraries keep several back issues of a periodical on the shelf until they are ready to be bound into volumes. Some libraries provide only the current issue of a periodical, making past issues available by request.

Academic libraries seldom allow recently published, unbound periodicals to circulate, and they may not always subscribe to certain popular periodicals. In these cases, public libraries may serve your needs much better, since they subscribe more heavily to popular periodicals and frequently allow recent and unbound issues to circulate.

Other Specialized Areas

In addition to the reference, book, and periodicals areas, your library may also maintain a separate microform section, a government documents desk, a media library, or a special collections library. Make a point of exploring your library and finding out which of these or other specialized areas are available.

Library Classification Systems

Libraries organize their holdings by classifying them into groups and storing items of the same groups together in one place. Each item in a group is marked with a *call number,* a series of numbers and/or letters identifying it and the group to which it belongs. The call number also accompanies the item's description in the library catalog system to indicate where it is located.

Two of the most common methods used to classify a library's holdings in this way are the Dewey Decimal (DD) and the Library of Congress (LC) subject-classification systems. Small libraries favor the DD system because it is simpler and thus fulfills their needs. The LC system is used by large libraries because it is almost infinitely expandable and has more main divisions. Most libraries use either one system or the other, though some may be in transition between the older DD system and the newer LC system. Knowing something about how each system works can make your research more effective in any library.

The Dewey Decimal System

The Dewey Decimal classification system assigns a library book or other resource a call number according to the 10 major subject categories shown in Figure 2.1. By the DD system, a book with any call number in the *300s,* for example, has a subject in the *social sciences,* a major category that includes *group dynamics, law, government, education,* and *economics* as subdivisions. A book with a call number beginning with *342* addresses *constitutional and administrative law,* while one with a call number beginning with *345* treats *criminal law.* Successive numbers and decimal points further classify such books more precisely:

340	Law
345	Criminal law
345.01	Criminal courts
345.05	General criminal procedure
345.052	Criminal investigation and law enforcement
345.056	Rights of suspects
345.06	Evidence

CALL NUMBER	MAIN DIVISION
000–99	General works
100–199	Philosophy
200–299	Religion
300–399	Social sciences
400–499	Languages
500–599	Natural sciences
600–699	Technology and applied sciences
700–799	Fine arts
800–899	Literature
900–999	History and geography

FIGURE 2.1   The Dewey Decimal subject-classification system

The Library of Congress System

The most obvious difference between the Library of Congress and Dewey Decimal systems is that the LC system uses letters instead of numbers to identify subject classifications, as identified in Figure 2.2. Like the DD system, the LC system provides subcategories within each of the main divisions. In the LC system, subdivisions are made by adding a second letter and numbers. For the main division of technology (*T*), for example, works about *motor vehicles, aeronautics,* and *astronautics* are classified under the subdivision *TL*. All books classified under *TL670-723* are about *airplanes*. The call letters *TL721* indicate that a book is about *commercial airplanes,* while *TL723* shows it is about *government airplanes.*

As with the Dewey Decimal system, paying attention to the subject designators of the Library of Congress system can save you valuable time during your research. If you were investigating the *safety of private planes,* for example, you would want to spend your time tracking down books with a *TL685.1* designation, *private airplanes,* rather than *TL685.3, military airplanes.* Careful attention to the LC designator would also keep you from spending time trying to locate a work listed in the library catalog under "airplanes" but designated *QA930, airplane aerodynamics.*

CALL LETTER	MAIN DIVISION
A	General works
B	Philosophy and religion
C	History—Auxiliary sciences
D	History—Topography
E–F	American history—Topography
G	Geography—Anthropology
H	Social sciences
J	Political sciences
K	Law
L	Education
M	Music
N	Fine arts
P	Language—Literature (nonfiction)
Q	Sciences
R	Medicine
S	Agriculture
T	Technology
U	Military science
V	Naval science
Z	Bibliography and library science
P–Z	Literature (fiction)

FIGURE 2.2   The Library of Congress subject-classification system

Working with the Library Catalog

Without the catalog, the collection of materials in any library would be practically inaccessible. Arranged alphabetically by author, title, and subject or a combination of the three, the library catalog tells what books and other materials the library has and where they are located.

While the basic information a library catalog provides is generally standard, the kind of catalog a library uses can vary. Card catalogs, in which information about each item in the library is printed on a small card, are still used in some local library systems, though they are rapidly being replaced by more modern and more efficient online computer catalogs. Book catalogs, microform catalogs, and CD–ROM (Compact Disk–Read-Only Memory) catalogs have their own special uses and are found most often at academic or large public research libraries. Most libraries today use one or more of these kinds of catalogs. You will need to understand how to use each to do effective research in any library.

Using the Card Catalog

A *card catalog* consists of hundreds—or in a large library, possibly thousands—of alphabetized cards, usually filed in rows of small drawers, that list every item in the library. Separate author, title, and subject cards are stored in alphabetical order according to the first important word. The words *a, an,* and *the,* for instance, are dropped from the beginnings of titles and subjects when you want to locate a work. An author's name is reversed, putting the last name first. Thus, if you were looking for a book titled *The Life of a Forest,* you would find it in the "L" section of the card catalog under "Life of a Forest, The." If you looked the book up under its author's name, *William R. Owens,* you would look under "O" in the card catalog until you came to "Owens, William R." The DD or LC call number on the card would tell you where the book is shelved in the library.

The information in most library card catalogs is stored in triplicate, with every resource listed on separate subject, title, and author cards. This system allows you to find any book or other work, regardless of whether you know very much about it.

Subject Cards. Use the subject card catalog to begin compiling the preliminary bibliography or any time you need to know what books are available on any particular subject. Begin by looking in the catalog under the subject or topic you are researching. The subject heading appears at the top of each card, with full information about each book and its location in the library (see Figure 2.3, "Subject Card").

If you cannot locate subject cards for your research subject, you may need to look under a different subject heading. For instance, you may have looked under "Macintosh" and need instead to look under "computers." *"See also" cards* may direct you to other headings in the catalog. If not, you

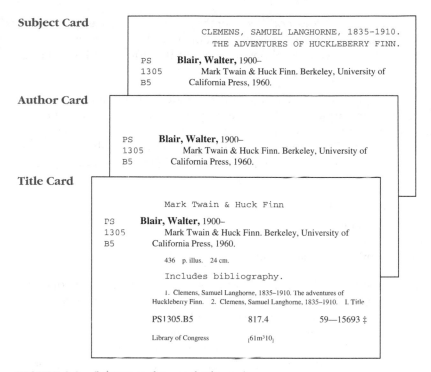

Subject Card

CLEMENS, SAMUEL LANGHORNE, 1835–1910.
THE ADVENTURES OF HUCKLEBERRY FINN.

PS   **Blair, Walter,** 1900–
1305   Mark Twain & Huck Finn. Berkeley, University of
B5   California Press, 1960.

Author Card

PS   **Blair, Walter,** 1900–
1305   Mark Twain & Huck Finn. Berkeley, University of
B5   California Press, 1960.

Title Card

Mark Twain & Huck Finn

PS   **Blair, Walter,** 1900–
1305   Mark Twain & Huck Finn. Berkeley, University of
B5   California Press, 1960.

436   p. illus.   24 cm.

Includes bibliography.

1. Clemens, Samuel Langhorne, 1835–1910. The adventures of
Huckleberry Finn.   2. Clemens, Samuel Langhorne, 1835–1910.   I. Title

PS1305.B5   817.4   59—15693 ‡

Library of Congress   ₁61m³10₁

FIGURE 2.3   Subject, author, and title cards

can find alternative headings by consulting the library's two-volume copy of *Library of Congress Subject Headings,* a list of subject headings and related terms used for all library card catalogs.

Author and Title Cards.   Another way to find sources for your research is to consult the author and title cards of the library catalog. If you know the author of a book or if you want to find the titles of works by a particular authority, consult the author card index. You will find a card for each book by that author filed alphabetically by title under the author's last name (see Figure 2.3, "Author Card").

If you know precisely which book you want, you can locate it most quickly by going right to the title card catalog. Author and title cards give the same information as subject cards. Title cards, however, also have the book's title printed at the top (see Figure 2.3, "Title Card").

Using the Online Catalog

An *online catalog* uses a computer terminal to provide a complete listing of all the items in a library. Such a catalog provides a great deal more than a computerized version of its predecessor, the traditional library card catalog. With an online catalog, not only can you locate books by subject, author, and title, but many systems will also tell you which local libraries have a book if yours does not. Because they can be more easily updated, can provide more information than traditional card catalogs, and can be made available at several locations throughout the library, online catalogs have generally replaced or subordinated other catalog systems.

Locating a Subject.   The tremendous amount of and number of types of information in a modern online catalog system have made research easier as well as more thorough than ever before. For example, many online systems have a browse feature that allows you to begin with a subject like *birds* and alphabetically scan the system's subject catalog in a matter of minutes:

Birds
Birds—Behavior
Birds—Habitats
Birds—History
Birds—Physical characteristics

As the system displays a list of subjects, you simply select the one you want to investigate. The online screen will then display a list of all the available books in the library on your selected subject.

Using an online catalog, you do not even need all the information that would be required if you were using the card catalog to locate a book. You can enter a single term—let's say "college"—and the system will display all titles, subject and author entries, and bibliographic notes in which the term *college* appears. To save time, you can also enter a title code and have the system display only titles with a particular word or combination of words in them. For example, if you know only the first word or two of a title, like *College Entrance Examinations,* you can enter any one or a combination of main words—"college," "entrance examinations," "college entrance," and so on. The online screen will display a list of all books with the words you enter in their titles.

Locating an Author.   You can also enter an author's last name and get a display of all authors with that name. Selecting one author from the displayed list will produce a second display listing all available works by that particular author. Or suppose you are unsure of how to spell an author's last name—like that of *Ernest Hemingway,* for example. Just enter an online code, plus "HEM". The system will display the names of all authors whose names begin with *HEM:*

Hembree, Ron
Hemenway, Joan M.
Heming, William
Hemingway, Ernest
Hemker, H. C.
Hemlon, Marie
Hemmingway, Charles A.

Other Features.   Some online catalog systems allow you to print the information on the display screen as you view it, thereby saving you the work of copying down the information you find. One particular library's online catalog may even be accessible through the system at a neighboring library or on your own home computer through the use of a modem (a device that connects two computers via a telephone line) and payment of a small fee. Since all online catalog systems are not alike in their capabilities or operations, consult a librarian or follow available directions for using the system in your own library.

A word of caution: While online catalogs are wonderful aids to research, they are not everything you need to write a good research paper. As you use your library's computerized online catalog, be careful not to rely on its systems so much that you eliminate your own creative thinking about your research. Browse the bookshelves of the library yourself. Remember that some valuable sources may even be too old to have been entered into the online system. Think of connections between sources and subjects that the system's technology may not have included. Use the online catalog all you can, but remember to approach your research subject with your own individual thinking about it, too.

Using Other Types of Library Catalogs

The most commonly used library catalogs are the card and online computer types, just discussed. Many libraries, however, also use other types of catalogs either as the main cataloging system or as a supplement. You will want to know something about each of these catalogs in order to take advantage of the assistance they can also offer the researcher.

Book Catalogs.   Available in the library reference section, a *book catalog* is, as the name suggests, a book listing all the library's holdings. The pages of a book catalog may be composed of photographed and reduced copies of all the cards in the library's card catalog, or they may contain bound, computer generated lists of all the items in the library collection. Many libraries use a book catalog as a back-up to their online catalog.

Though most online catalogs have information only about local libraries, book catalogs from out-of-area libraries are additionally valuable for researching long distance. A researcher in Tampa, Florida, for example, can use the book catalog from the University of California at Los Angeles (UCLA) to find out what books are at UCLA, to get bibliographic information about resources there, or to obtain a book through interlibrary loan services.

Book-form card catalogs also allow you to scan whole pages of entries at once. Seeing multiple entries allows you to compare several items on the page: publication date, bibliography, number of pages, and so on. If the library allows it, book catalogs also make it possible for you to photocopy the pages themselves as a quick way to record data for several entries at once.

Microform Catalogs.   Library catalogs in microform—or COMCATS (Computer Output Microfilm Catalogs)—are copied at greatly reduced size on cards or sheets of microfilm that must be read at special machines available in the library. Because of the reduced size of its print, a single microform card, for example, can hold up to a thousand pages of regularly printed material. Microfilm, microcards, microfiche, and microprint are all varieties of microforms that differ only in their format (card or sheet) and the amount of reduction they provide.

Because of the small print and the necessity of reading them at a machine, microform catalogs are not as easy to work with as other types of catalogs. Some libraries have machines that can give you a print-out of a microform, but the practice can be time consuming and expensive. In most cases, doing your research through the library's card catalog or online computer catalog will prove more satisfying.

Compact Disk Catalogs.   Rather than working as an online catalog, the CD–ROM (Compact Disk–Read-Only Memory) provides a fixed catalog that library computer terminals read off a single imprinted disk. Similar in size and appearance to a common music compact disk, a CD–ROM disk can store well over a half million words. You read a CD–ROM catalog at a library computer terminal equipped with a monitor, keyboard, and (usually) a printer.

CD–ROM catalog information is generally the same as that given by other catalogs, although information stored on an individual disk cannot be added to or otherwise changed. The catalog is kept current by the addition of new disks as they become available. For this reason, always note the date on the CD–ROM catalog disk you are working with. If it is not current, you may need to go to the online catalog or elsewhere for more recent information.

Library Services and Resources

In order to use any library efficiently, you need to know what assistance it can provide. The services that make life easier for researchers vary with the size and purpose of a library. Naturally, larger libraries can generally give more support than smaller ones, but most libraries can offer more help than you may realize.

Librarian Assistance

Probably the most valuable assistance you can get in the library will come from a librarian. Trained in the resources of a library and the process of research, librarians are also experienced in assisting students with research papers. It is likely that your librarian has helped another student with a topic similar to yours and can tell you what resources to consult or avoid. He or she knows what is available and where to find it in the library as well as how to access materials located elsewhere. Do not underestimate the help a librarian can give you at any stage of your research. You cannot find a better resource.

Information Service

Larger libraries often staff a telephone information service just to answer questions that can be handled with a few minutes of searching by the librarian. Most libraries will gladly answer questions over the telephone, whether you need to know what resources are available or just forgot to write down an author's name. Find out at the start of your research if your library has such an information service.

Search Assistance

A library's search service can locate books or other materials that were not on the shelf when you looked for them. Someone else may have been using a book when you were looking, it may have been at the bindery, or it may have been misshelved. If you cannot locate a book where the catalog says it should be, ask a librarian for a library search request form. You can usually get a search report on the book's status in one or two days.

Interlibrary Loan

You can obtain books and other materials that are unavailable in your own library through interlibrary loan. Your library's online catalog may tell you when a book is located at another local library, or the librarian can use a national library computer network called *OCLC* (Online Computer Library Center) to find where any book is available. Once a work is located, your librarian can arrange to have it sent to you at the library. Be aware that material requested through interlibrary loan may take three to ten days to arrive.

Reserve and Recall

Do not give up on library books or other items you need just because they have been checked out. The library can reserve materials for you, placing a hold on their circulation and notifying you as soon as they have been returned. At academic libraries, where books are often checked out for long periods of time, you can recall items that the original borrower has had out for over two or three weeks.

Nonprint Sources

Many libraries maintain collections of nonprint materials, including audio cassettes, phonograph records, video cassettes, and films. The forms for including such sources in your working bibliography and Works Cited list are addressed in Chapter 12.

Photocopying

Since photocopying has proven so necessary to modern research, most libraries today provide machines for that purpose. A good system of note-taking (see Chapter 7) can reduce the expense of photocopying, but such an aid can be valuable when you need to study noncirculating, lengthy, or complex materials outside the library. Read the copyright restrictions posted on most machines, and avoid plagiarism (discussed in Chapter 7) by crediting any sources from which you borrow.

Computer Facilities

Your library's online catalog and database systems will allow you to search for hundreds of sources in your own and other libraries. If you have a personal computer and a modem, paying a small fee will enable you to link up with your library's catalogs and other databases right at home. For those who prefer to write with a library's resources at hand, most large academic libraries also have computers and word-processing programs available in the library.

W O R K I N G   W I T H   O T H E R S

Use the following suggestions to evaluate local academic and public libraries as well as to gauge your understanding of library resources discussed in this chapter.

- Find out whether your campus library offers orientation tours or special classes for students engaged in research projects. Sign up with a classmate to go on such a tour or to take part in a library research class. If these options are not available, ask a librarian to provide a short orientation for you and a few classmates.

- Discuss your campus library with another student to review what you know of its reference, book, and periodicals collections. If your college has more than one library, also discuss how the others might be useful to your research assignment.

- What local public libraries are available to you, and what kinds of resources might they offer? Consider state, county, and city libraries in your area and how they might differ in the services and resources they provide.

- Compare your own campus library's services with those discussed in this chapter. Which campus library services may be particularly helpful in working on your research project? If you have used any special library services in the past, describe them and their usefulness.

- Find out what kinds of computer research facilities and services are available at your own campus library, and discuss them with a classmate. Also discuss any other library computer resources you are acquainted with and how they may be useful to your research.

CHAPTER **3**

Planning the Focus of Your Research

Getting started on a research paper begins with selecting a suitable topic to investigate and write about in depth. Your goal in selecting such a topic, as well as throughout your research, is continually to refine and narrow the area of investigation in order to make the research and resulting paper significantly specific.

In general, you should start by considering a broad subject of interest to research and then move to a more particular topic within that subject. Preliminary investigation of sources should next lead you to formulate a research question that states what you want to know about the topic. Figure 3.1 illustrates the continual narrowing process of focusing your research in this way. Once you have defined a research question, use it to focus your later investigation of sources and direct notetaking toward a tentative answer, or preliminary thesis, about the topic.

General subject	Topic	Research question
Advertising	Subliminal messages in advertising	Should subliminal messages in advertising be banned?

FIGURE 3.1   Focusing your research

**THINKING CRITICALLY
ABOUT RESEARCH SUBJECTS AND TOPICS**

You will be better able to focus your research efforts if you understand the concepts of a research subject and topic at the beginning of your assignment. A research *subject* is any general area of experience, knowledge, or events that can be studied for more understanding. A *topic* is a more focused area of ideas included within a broader research subject. *AIDS* and *acid rain,* for example, are each research subjects. *AIDS on the college campus* and *the effects of acid rain on human health* are topics included within the subjects *AIDS* and *acid rain,* respectively. A subject is always more general than the topic or topics included within it. Notice how the following subjects for college research papers contain one or several more specific topics:

Subject	*Topics*
Euthanasia	1. Mercy killing and people with AIDS
	2. Euthanasia in the Netherlands
Native Americans	1. Fishing rights of Native Americans
	2. Threats to ancestral burial grounds
	3. Native language use in the classroom
Alcoholism	1. College students and drinking
	2. Pregnancy and alcohol
	3. Television beer commercials
Popular music	1. Sexual violence in popular music
	2. The social power of rap music

Understanding the distinction between a subject and a topic can help you plan your research sooner and more effectively. If you begin the assignment by planning at the subject level, you can compare several potential areas of interest to research before committing to a particular topic. On the other hand, if you begin with a topic already in mind, a sense of its relationship to a broader subject can help you gauge your progress in focusing the research.

Finding a Research Subject and Topic

Several steps described in this chapter for discovering a research subject or topic can work equally well for finding both. Which purpose any of the steps fulfills for you will depend upon how far you have progressed in your planning or actual research. Although the steps are presented sequentially here, they may overlap or occur in different order in actual practice. The

Readers' Guide, for example, is recommended for first discovering a subject; however, you will likely return to it again later for narrowing a subject to a particular topic or to find specific sources to investigate in depth. As you proceed in following the suggestions given here about a subject or topic, keep the overlapping nature of these two elements in mind.

Selecting an Appropriate Research Subject

Unfortunately, many beginning writers have had the frustrating experience of wasting valuable time on subjects or topics that they decided upon too quickly. You can avoid dead-end topics—those that are unsuitable for your interest or resources—with careful planning. The best approach is to consider several possible subjects initially and then to move systematically toward a more particular topic and relevant research question.

Assigned Subjects

If your paper's subject is assigned by your instructor, he or she has already considered its suitability for research as well as your probable level of interest and understanding. It will be your responsibility in an assigned-subject paper to demonstrate a grasp of basic concepts through independent research and thinking. With assigned subjects that are closely related to the course focus, you have the benefit of your class notes, textbook reading, and your instructor's own expertise to draw upon, though you will of course need to do your own research work, as well.

You will find that an assigned subject requires as much original thinking as one you might have chosen for yourself. Try to find an approach that makes your paper different from others on the same subject. This is what Linda Kastan did when her English instructor required that each student write a research paper about how a technological development influences society today. Linda's paper, titled Internet Addiction: Is There a Dark Side to Cyberspace? grew out of her own independent thinking and individual interest in the subject's focus. (See Linda's paper in Chapter 11.)

Free-Choice Subjects

If you are like most students facing a research paper assignment, you will need to select what to write about. This means you may not have the benefit of lectures or class discussions to help you get to know and understand a subject, as you would if it were assigned. When responsible for finding your own research subject, you will need as much time as possible to select the right one.

For this reason, you should start thinking about an appropriate research paper subject from the day you first learn about the assignment. Use the class in which the paper is assigned or other courses you are taking as resources. As you listen to lectures, study your textbooks, or join in class discussions throughout the term, be alert to potential areas for research. The following suggestions will help you discover a research subject that interests you and is appropriate for your assignment.

Reviewing Your Interests

If there were one simple rule for selecting the right research subject, it would be this: *Work with your interests.* As you begin working with a research subject or topic, think critically about those you may be willing to spend time researching. You will recognize more potential topics in a subject you care about than in one you select because it seems impressive or easy to research. In addition to the information you gather from other sources, remember that your research paper should reflect your own insights and opinions.

You will write best on a subject you care about and already have a feeling for. Avoid any that are not part of your general field of interest or that you may be drawn to for the wrong reasons. Though a subject like *uniform commercial code laws* may sound impressive, you will not go very far with it unless you are genuinely interested in laws governing various kinds of commercial transactions. Similarly, *microwave cooking* may sound like an easy subject to write about. Unless you care enough to research and think critically about it, however, such a subject may generate only a tiring exercise for you and a dull paper for your instructor.

Recording Subject Ideas

Begin discovering the right research subject for yourself by using a research notebook (see Chapter 1) to record and later review your general interests. Title a section of the notebook Research Subjects, and use it to explore potential areas of research:

- Take time to think about your hobbies or any clubs and organizations to which you belong. Use your research notebook to discuss events you want to know more about. What controversies need greater examination?
- Consider the subjects of magazines or particular sections of the newspaper you read regularly. What is happening that you have a strong position on? What issues need clarification or updating for an interested and even generally informed audience? Record these subjects in your research notebook.
- Think about your favorite college course, your prospective career, or even the latest book or movie you enjoyed. What subjects do these areas of interest cover? What famous persons or events in these areas intrigue you? List these in the Subjects section of your research notebook.

■ Review the entries of possible subjects you have been keeping in your research notebook. Which subjects seem to interest you most? Which would match your interests and the requirements of your assignment best? Which do you want to learn more about?

Subdividing your interests with questions in this way will put you on the track of potential subjects. Just remember to take your time. Start with a variety of possibilities, and gradually narrow the list to the three or four most suited to your interests and the assignment. Find out more about each of these subjects to select the most promising one for extensive study and research.

Using Library Sources to Find a Research Subject

A library's reference section or book collection contains excellent sources for discovering a potential subject or topic for your paper. Use these sources to discover a research focus or to gauge the potential of possible subjects already listed in your research notebook. Before settling upon any single subject for research, be sure to consult as many such sources as possible. Preliminary investigation of standard library materials will provide important general information as well as specific sources essential to your later research.

Encyclopedias

The articles found in encyclopedias offer excellent, authoritative discussions on nearly every subject known. Written by well-chosen experts who provide reliable facts and informed insights, encyclopedia articles are vital to effective research and writing on any issue. No matter what subject or topic you decide upon, it is wise to begin all your research with a study of relevant encyclopedia articles. You can use what you learn from them to investigate and better understand other sources.

You are probably already familiar with multivolume, comprehensive encyclopedias like *Encyclopedia Americana, Encyclopaedia Britannica,* and *Collier's Encyclopedia.* These references cover hundreds of subjects and include maps, illustrations, and highly useful bibliographies. Entries appear alphabetically by subject, and discussions vary in length from a single paragraph to a dozen or more pages. Most public or campus libraries carry one or more complete editions of such encyclopedias as well as the yearbook supplements intended to keep them up to date. Many encyclopedias, such as *Encyclopaedia Britannica* and the *Academic American Encyclopedia,* are available online at most libraries or through the Internet.

When using encyclopedia articles, keep in mind that they provide intentionally broad introductions to a given subject. More frequently published sources, such as books and periodicals, usually give more detailed or current information. Use encyclopedias to acquaint yourself with fundamental facts about a subject and to understand it in broad terms. It is also wise to consult more than one encyclopedia to begin your research in order to find the most useful information or the most instructive organization of your research subject.

Current Books

Whether written for popular or academic audiences, books are excellent resources in which to discover a direction for your research. Simply browsing through a book's introduction or sampling a few of its chapters can tell you a lot about whether its subject will prove appropriate to your research interests and abilities. Your own textbook for a course may be a good source to begin with, or you can go to the library section for a particular subject and consult several books at one sitting.

A book whose scope is broad and introductory is best for an overview of a possible research subject. (More highly focused books will prove useful when you decide about a specific topic for your research.) As you examine books to investigate possible subjects, keep in mind that your purpose is not to read the books but to get an overview of your potential focus for research.

Using the Table of Contents.   The subject a book covers is outlined by the headings found in its table of contents (see Figure 3.2). You can study the contents to find the major categories of interest for your subject or

CONTENTS

Preface		ix
1	The Nature of Persuasion	1
2	Measuring Attitudes: Scales, Polls, and Samples	21
3	How Attitudes Influence Behavior	43
4	How Actions Influence Attitudes	59
5	Personality and Persuasion	79
6	Social Influence and Group Decision Making	101
7	Persuasion and Political Issues	119
8	Persuasion and Health/Safety Issues	139
9	Persuasion and the Mass Media	159
References		189
Index		195

FIGURE 3.2   A table of contents from a book

to see under what headings it might be discussed. If it helps, skim a particular chapter in order to learn more about the subject. (See Chapter 7 on skimming and close-reading techniques.)

Using the Index.   The index at the end of a book can also be useful for discovering research subjects and their specific subtopics (see Figure 3.3). As you skim the indicated pages for an index entry, take note of additional subjects or topics you may want to pursue for your research. You may find it useful to compare two or more books' index entries to recognize important concepts or compare discussions of the same subject.

The Readers' Guide

Nearly all popular magazine articles are cataloged in one or another of several available indexes. The most well-known of such indexes is the *Readers' Guide to Periodical Literature,* which covers articles and book reviews appearing in nearly 200 popular magazines. (Other magazine indexes are discussed in Chapter 4.)

You can use the *Readers' Guide* to get an overview of a subject as well as to get ideas about major topics within a subject. Figure 3.4 shows a *Readers' Guide* entry for "addictive behavior."

As this sample entry illustrates, the *Readers' Guide* has its own system of listing information. As in other periodical indexes, information about the

ABC. *See* American Broadcasting Corporation (ABC)
absolutist state, 68–69
Adams, Gordon, 122
administration (as element of state), 59–60
Africa, 88, 126, 159, 228. *See also names of specific countries*
African Americans
    Civil Rights Movement and, 55, 106, 188
    nationalism by, 212–213
    political participation by, 63, 136, 148, 150, 200
    representation in Congress by, 139
agenda setting (by mass media), 107–109
Alford, Robert R., 60, 73, 135
American Academy of Arts and Sciences, 94
American Broadcasting Corporation (ABC), 103, 105–106
American Dilemma, An (Myrdal, 1944), 11
American Federation of Labor, 72
American Medical Association, 163
antiestablishment movement (of the 1960s). *See also* Civil
    Rights Movement; Vietnam War
    effect on political sociology, 23–24
    events/issues behind, 52, 149, 181
    political participation and, 149, 150, 152, 181
Argentina, 128, 188, 217
aristocracy, 61, 65, 68
Aristotle, 3, 21, 50, 60–61, 88–89, 136, 218, 220, 221, 225

FIGURE 3.3   An excerpt from an index, showing main topics and subtopics

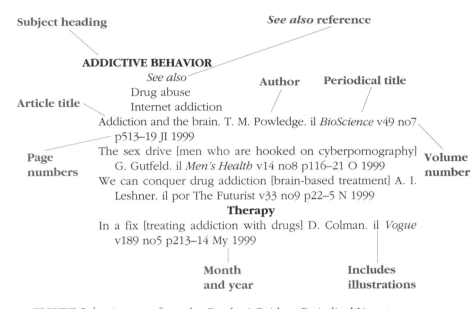

Subject heading   ***See also* reference**

ADDICTIVE BEHAVIOR
       See also   **Author**   **Periodical title**
       Drug abuse

Article title   Internet addiction
     Addiction and the brain. T. M. Powledge. il *BioScience* v49 no7
       p513–19 Jl 1999

Page   The sex drive [men who are hooked on cyberpornography] **Volume**
numbers   G. Gutfeld. il *Men's Health* v14 no8 p116–21 O 1999   **number**
     We can conquer drug addiction [brain-based treatment] A. I.
       Leshner. il por The Futurist v33 no9 p22–5 N 1999

           Therapy
     In a fix [treating addiction with drugs] D. Colman. il *Vogue*
       v189 no5 p213–14 My 1999

       Month   **Includes**
      and year   **illustrations**

FIGURE 3.4   An entry from the *Readers' Guide to Periodical Literature*

Source: Entry from *Readers' Guide to Periodical Literature,* 2000, p. 14. Copyright © 2000 by The H. W. Wilson Company. Reprinted by permission.

magazine's title, date of publication, number of pages, and other useful data are presented. When using the *Readers' Guide* or any periodical index, refer to the front of the volume for an explanation of the symbols and abbreviations used to describe an article entry.

     NOTE: When you are recording source information on your research bibliography cards, remember that the form and data given in the *Readers' Guide* and other indexes are not the same as you will use later in the Works Cited list of your research paper.

The Social Issues Resources Series (SIRS)

     Your library's reference section will no doubt carry several volumes of the *Social Issues Resources Series,* or *SIRS.* With over 30 subjects titled and numbered on the spine, these large, three-ring binders contain hundreds of short, up-to-date articles on dozens of interesting subjects. A Quick Reference Guide lists the subject volumes and indicates which ones contain articles on various major topics. *SIRS* is also available online in many public and university libraries. Those that have *SIRS* online also usually keep the printed and bound copies available on shelves as well. If your library has both, use the most up-to-date version.

     You can use the *SIRS* to find a subject or to learn about a potential topic. Looking over the Quick Reference Guide, for example, may start you thinking about the relationship of *aging* and *divorce,* or you might begin to wonder about *aging* and *civil rights* as possible research interests. A brief search through the subject volume on drugs will turn up such articles as "Addicted Doctors," "The Drug Gangs," "Should Hard Drugs Be Legalized?" and "Cocaine's Children." You can also use the *Index of SIRS Critical Issues* to find out about major issues of national and international importance. Figure 3.5, for example, shows some of the topics listed in the SIRS *Atmosphere Crisis* index. After reading some of these articles, you could decide if one of the topics interested you enough to research it further, or you could turn to a different volume to get ideas about another subject.

E

Earth, Chemical composition
  See Geochemistry
Earth, Orbit, 2
Earth-friendly products
  See Green products
Earth Summit
  See United Nations Conference
   on Environment and Devel-
   opment
Earthwatch, 18
Ecology
  See Coastal ecology: Food
   chains (Ecology)
Education, Environmental
  See Environmental education
El Niño Current, 7, 8
Electric apparatus and appli-
   ances, 5
Emission reduction credits, 9
Emission standards, Automo-
   bile
  See Automobiles, Environmen-
   tal aspects
Energy efficiency, 16
Environment, Effect of man on
  See Man, Influence on nature
Environmental degradation,
   20
Environmental education, 20
Environmental health, 17, 20
  See also Health risk assess-
   ment
Environmental impact
   analysis, 8
Environmental policy, 11
Environmental technology, 4
EPA
  See U.S. Environmental
   Protection Agency (EPA)
Extinct amphibians, 10
Extinction (Biology), 20

FIGURE 3.5 Listing from the Index of *SIRS Critical Issues: The Atmosphere Crisis*

Source: Listing from the Index of *SIRS Critical Issues: The Atmosphere Crisis,* Vol. 3, Articles 1–20. Copyright © 1994 SIRS, Inc., The Knowledge Source. Reprinted with permission.

Moving from a Subject to a Research Topic

Since you cannot read or write meaningfully about everything relevant to the research subject, you will need to narrow your investigation to a more particular topic within it. Because they represent general areas of interest, subjects contain several topics suitable for research (see also Chapter 1). A broad subject like *AIDS,* for example, includes many potential topics:

Subject:	*AIDS*
Topic:	The problem of AIDS on college campuses
Topic:	AIDS education in high schools
Topic:	Mandating AIDS testing for expectant mothers
Topic:	Potential cures for AIDS
Topic:	Support groups for people with AIDS
Topic:	Children with AIDS

Focusing Your Efforts

While considering several possible topics like these during the early research phase may be a good idea (in case one or more prove uninteresting or impractical), you must nevertheless also focus your efforts. A paper attempting to cover all of these topics would be shallow in content, just skimming the surface of each in order to discuss them all. Or it would arbitrarily treat two or three areas and ignore other equally important ones. To avoid producing a scattered, superficial research paper, you will eventually need to select a single topic to investigate at length.

Going Online to Find a Topic

Information available through the Internet or other online resources is highly organized, usually listed by topic and categorized in successively narrower, increasingly focused menus. Once online, you can use these organizational features to discover subjects of interest to you or to help find a related topic for research.

Many of the documents you can read online contain *hypertext,* which is colored or highlighted text, as shown in Figure 3.6. Selecting one of these hypertext words or phrases will take you to an area providing more information or discussion of that particular subject. For instance, if you chose *recognizing Internet addiction* in the hypertext example in Figure 3.6, you would automatically jump to an area discussing this subject and related topics within it. These related topics may also be listed as hypertext, in which case you could then select them and find still more topics to investigate. Using hypertext, you can identify possible topics to investigate and, at the same time, become aware of important concepts that may be relevant to your later research and discussion.

Here you will find a definition of Internet addiction and information on recognizing Internet addiction in friends, co workers, and
family members. You can also explore clinical concepts on what
makes the Internet addictive. Most importantly, you can learn
about identification of the addiction and treatment by the professionals at IIAR. Click on any of the following topics to learn more:

What is Internet addiction?

Recognizing Internet addiction

Problems caused by Internet addiction

What makes the Internet addictive?

Treatment and counseling

FIGURE 3.6   An excerpt from a hypertext document

Source: Reprinted by permission of Illinois Institute for Addiction Recovery at Proctor Hospital
www.addictionrecov.org.

Online search engines can also be useful for discovering a research
topic when you already have a broader subject to work with. Suppose that,
like Linda Kastan, you have been assigned to write a research paper exploring how a current technological development influences society today.
Using a search engine, such as that available through America Online, you
could enter the keywords "effects technology society." A search of these
words would lead you to links for a variety of more or less relevant sites. A
recent such search, for example, led to the website for The Center for the
Study of Technology and Society (http://www.tecsoc.org/). There, one
could click on a variety of topic pages, including "Biotechnology," "Creativity," "Culture," "Education," and "Government and Politics." The "Culture"
topic page provides links to numerous specific newspaper and journal articles with titles like "Internet Addiction a Threat to College Students," "The
Net Could Stifle the Imagination," and "Does the Internet Make Us Lonely?"
The page also offers links to related online organizations, as shown in Figure 3.7, that might also be helpful in finding a topic within the broad subject of the effects of technology on society. (See Chapter 6 for further discussion of how to access and use online search engines.)

A number of other resources about writing a research paper also are
available on the Internet and can be helpful in discovering a research topic.
From the "Idea Directory" under "Society" at *Researchpaper.com,* for example, you could select "Health" as a general interest area, which would link
you with a page listing possible research questions, such as What are the
advantages and disadvantages of plastic surgery? and Are flu shots effective?
At the Internet site for the Electric Library, posing a question such as Is the

Links

Reference

* Cyber Behavior Research Center (CIO.com)
* Johns Hopkins Journal of Technology and Culture
* The Routledge Series in Science, Technology & Culture

Related Sites

* The Center for Research into Innovation, Culture and
  Technology (Brunel University, UK)
* The Marshall McLuhan Program in Technology and Culture
  (University of Toronto)
* NetFuture: Technology and Human Responsibility
* Resource Center for Cyberculture Studies (University of Maryland)

Religion and Technology

* The Institute for Religion, Technology and Culture
* The Society, Religion and Technology Project (Church of
  Scotland)

Internet Addiction

* Addictions and Life: Internet Addictions
* Center for Online Addiction
* Internet Addiction Support Group
* Psychcentral.com Internet Addiction Guide
* University of Albany: Parameters of Internet Addiction

Language

SPECIAL: English: One Language for the New Global Village
(Associated Press)

FIGURE 3.7   Online links provided by The Center for the Study of Technology
and Society on its "Culture" topics page

Source: Reprinted by permission of the Center for the Study of Technology and Society.

Internet harmful? would take you to several pages of recent articles on that
subject. Locating potential topics and sources such as these may help you
find a topic or suggest related subjects that might interest you for research.

Remember to exercise caution when using *any* Internet resource about
writing a research paper. Although many are excellent aids to the research
process, a number offer ineffective advice or outdated information about
documentation styles (discussed in Chapters 11–13). Here are some useful

Internet sites that offer reliable information and can assist your search for an interesting research paper topic:

A+ Research and Writing	http://www.ipli.org/teen/aplus
Electric Library	http://www.elibrary.com
Info Zone	http://www.assd.winnipeg.mbca/ infozone/index.htm
Researchpaper.com	http://www.researchpaper.com
Start Your Research Here	http://www.lib.odu.edu/research/ tutorials/start/

Recording Potential Topics

Under a heading like Research Topics, keep an ongoing list of ideas in your research notebook. Jot down facts, questions, or potential sources as they occur to you. Mark those topics that appear most promising or that you want to discuss with your instructor. You will find that certain entries eventually dominate the list and your interest. These preliminary topics will provide a core of possibilities as you decide which ones to investigate further. The list of potential research topics that Linda Kastan kept in her notebook included the entries shown in Figure 3.8. Notice that some topics are more general than others, but all identify topics of inquiry for research.

Research Topics

* 1. SAT scores and college admissions
  2. Illegal aliens in the U.S.
* 3. Rights of people who are homeless
* 4. The use of force by police
* 5. Television talk shows
* 6. Foreign ownership in the U.S.
  7. The Galileo space discoveries
  8. College athletic programs
  9. Social criticism in popular music
* 10. Internet addiction
  11. Global peace efforts
  12. The war against drugs

FIGURE 3.8   Notebook entries for research topics

Linda did preliminary reading about most of these topics, and she discussed those marked with asterisks with her instructor and a few friends. She began with the idea of discussing how spending a lot of time on the Internet might harm someone's sense of self-esteem and ethics. She considered focusing on the issues of isolation, Internet addiciton, online pornography, and sexism on the Internet. Eventually, Linda chose to write about the problem of Interent addiction and how some people have trouble controlling how much time they spend online. In making this choice, she moved from a broad research subject to a more focused topic for writing. Moreover, thinking about the other topics on her list gave Linda useful back-up options in case she later decided that Internet addiction was not a good topic for her paper.

Using Discovery Techniques to Focus on a Topic

A practical method of deciding what you want to research about any topic is to explore your own understanding of it. You need not follow all the methods described here; rather, use those that will help you focus on a topic that matches your interests with your resources and your assignment.

Freewriting

Freewriting allows you to discuss a subject or topic as freely as necessary to start ideas flowing to a conscious level. You begin by simply writing (with a pen or pencil or at a computer) all your thoughts on a subject, as they occur to you. Do not worry about organization, punctuation, or spelling. The important goal in freewriting is to get your ideas down. Write for about 10 minutes at a time, longer if you suddenly find yourself deeply involved in a discussion on a particular topic.

Figure 3.9 shows the freewriting Linda Kastan did in her research notebook for her paper on Internet addiciton. Notice that this exercise allowed her to identify more clearly the topic she eventually chose for her research and to discover several ideas she would later develop in the paper.

If you have trouble getting started with freewriting, try focusing with introductory phrases that will launch you directly into a discussion of your research subject. Start freewriting with introductory phrases like the following:

One unsettled question about (subject) is . . .

 (Subject) is important today because . . .

 (Subject) should (or should not) be . . .

I am interested in (subject) because . . .

After you finish freewriting, look over the results. Pick out recurring ideas or phrases that indicate a potential topic to discuss at greater length.

Freewriting

May 12

There is a lot of concern about whether people are getting addicted to the Internet, but not even the experts agree so far. A lot of people seem to have a problem with it. Like the woman who beat up her husband because he tossed her computer out the window in order to get her off the Internet for awhile. And the college honors student who flunked out—because she spent so much time in chat rooms every night. But if people are addicted, why? Is it really the Internet, or are they trying to avoid something else in their lives? Do they _have_ lives? Or is the Internet everything to them? Are people addicted because they do something all the time or really enjoy it a lot? Maybe it's just the lure of the Internet. Or the software, all those colors and action games and stuff. Young's study showed that online junkies act like alcoholics trying to quit drinking. The colleges should do more for their students. Maybe block the MUDs and chat rooms so students can't get to them or at least not as much. Why do the experts disagree? It could be that we're all overreacting. Or there really is a big problem, but it's too new to understand yet?

FIGURE 3.9 Freewriting to examine issues

Use such ideas or phrases as the focus of a second freewriting session. You will gradually recognize that you have a lot to say about one or two particular aspects of your subject. These particular aspects are most likely the research topics you have been seeking.

Clustering

Clustering is another useful way to discover a research topic. Begin by writing your research subject in the center of a piece of paper and drawing

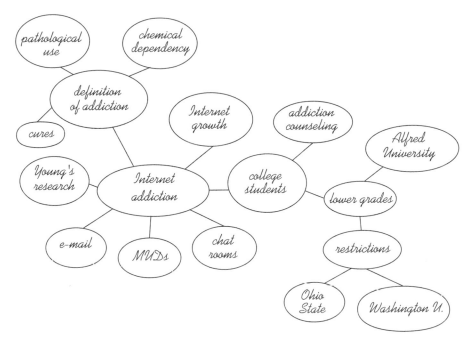

FIGURE 3.10   Clustering to examine issues

a circle around it; then jot down any ideas you associate with the circled subject and connect them to it with lines. Circle each new idea and connect it to other associated concepts, grouping them as you proceed. When you have run out of ideas for one line of thinking, start at the subject circle and begin again with a new connection. Figure 3.10 shows the clustering Linda Kastan did when considering topics for her paper about Internet addiction.

As with freewriting, do not worry about which ideas or associations come to mind as you cluster. Get your ideas down in any order or grouping as they occur. Review and organize your thinking after recording your thoughts.

Narrowing the Focus of the Research Topic

Make any topic you select as specific as possible. Remember that nearly every topic may become increasingly focused as you learn more about it through research. Figure 3.11 demonstrates how continual narrowing of the subject *environmental hazards,* for example, can lead to the general topic of the *decreasing ozone layer,* which, in turn, can be continually narrowed toward even more specific aspects of the original subject.

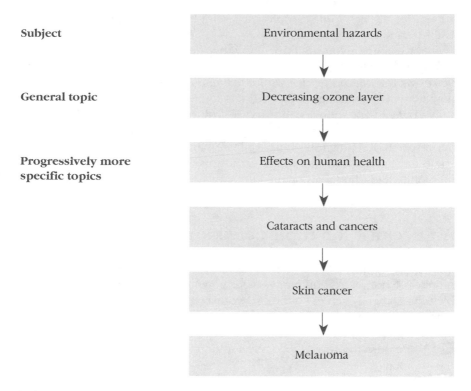

Subject — Environmental hazards

General topic — Decreasing ozone layer

Progressively more specific topics — Effects on human health

Cataracts and cancers

Skin cancer

Melanoma

FIGURE 3.11   Narrowing a topic

A different emphasis or interest on your part, of course, will determine the direction of your narrowing and the choice of topics with which you will work. In the above example, the topic of the ozone layer's general *effects on human health* could also lead to entirely different subtopics, such as *cataracts and cancers*. Whether you would decide to pursue the broader topic of the *decreasing ozone layer* or research its relationship to *skin cancer,* for example, would ultimately depend upon your interests or the availability of resources for one or the other topic.

Working with a Back-Up Topic in Mind

As you explore particular areas for your research paper, consider more than one potential topic, in case your first choice later proves impractical. The unavailability of resources or a lack of time to investigate your first topic thoroughly may make another choice more feasible, or you may later learn enough about an alternate topic to make it a more appealing option. If that happens, you will find that any broad, preliminary thinking about the general subject for the first topic can provide useful background for selecting a related second topic.

For example, you might begin with a general subject like *alternative automobile fuels* and then progress to a narrower topic such as *electric power as an alternative to gasoline.* Preliminary investigation, however, may not uncover enough sources discussing recent developments in electrically powered automobiles. In this case, you could move to a back-up topic such as *gasohol as an alternative to gasoline* and still make use of your earlier research. Keeping a back-up topic in mind as you research will require some mental juggling and a little extra time; however, the precaution will be worthwhile, should an original topic prove unuseful.

A Checklist for Topic Selection

The topic you finally select to research and write about will need to meet a number of criteria. As you narrow your general subject to one or two possible topics, check each of your most promising choices against the following guidelines:

☐ 1. Be sure the topic meets the requirements of your research assignment.

☐ 2. Focus on a topic that you want to learn more about.

☐ 3. Pick a topic for which you can meet an audience's needs and expectations.

☐ 4. Check to see that sufficient resources are available. Depending upon the materials involved, using interlibrary loan or trusting the mail may take more time than you have.

☐ 5. Avoid philosophical topics or those based on personal belief. Topics like *the value of the family* and *why you play sports* rely upon personal opinion and values rather than objective research and discussion.

☐ 6. Avoid strictly biographical topics—*Abraham Lincoln as a father*—that are already discussed fully in book-length studies.

☐ 7. Avoid describing processes such as *how cocaine is sold on the street* or *why getting a suntan may be dangerous.* Such information will not allow for original insight and judgment on your part.

☐ 8. Avoid topics too narrow or too recent for discussion. A paper on *local airport conditions* or *last week's international event* will not allow for adequate use of research materials.

☐ 9. Avoid standard, popular topics commonly chosen for student research papers. Unless recent developments have added new information or conditions, it may be difficult to impress your instructor with yet another paper on the *death penalty* or *animal intelligence.* Besides, all the resources on these topics will be checked out by others when you need them. Pick a topic that shows your individual abilities and interests.

☐ 10. Cease consideration of any topic that you cannot get very far with in terms of an approach or finding resources. If you seem to be meeting a dead end with a topic, ask your instructor or a librarian for help, but recognize that some topics may just not be right for you and your circumstances.

As you approach selecting a research topic, consider yourself part of the paper's audience, someone who will also benefit from its discussion. Through researching and writing, you will discover what you know or do not know about your topic. Writing will allow you to test your ideas and to analyze and evaluate your research data to a far greater extent than before. The topic you select should be one you want to help others, as well as yourself, understand better.

Formulating a Research Question

Even a well-defined research topic presents too broad an area to research and write about by itself. A topic like *women in the Olympics,* for example, needs a more specific focus for the research to promise more than an accumulation of facts. To make your research more effective, formulate a research question about the topic. Questions like the following focus on the topics and the research required for them:

Topic	*Television and race*
Research questions	1. Does television present stereotypes of racial minorities?
	2. Do minority actors have equal opportunities on television?
	3. What does television teach us about race relations?
Topic	*Fan violence and sports*
Research questions	1. What should be done to curb fan violence?
	2. Does the alcohol sold at games contribute to fan violence?

Topic	*Women in magazine advertisements*
Research questions	1. What image of women is conveyed by advertisements in leading national magazines?
	2. Do magazine advertisements over the last 10 years reflect any changes in the way women are presented?
	3. How do women's groups respond to current advertisements for women and women's products?

Remember to regard the answer to any research question as a working hypothesis that your research may confirm or alter significantly. Just asking whether minority actors have equal opportunities in television, for example, implies that they may not. It will be your responsibility to research the question objectively and to demonstrate the validity of your answer in the paper you write.

Recording Research Questions

Which questions you decide to pursue in your research will depend upon several factors, including your own interests, the requirements of your assignment, the available resources, and the needs of your audience. As you begin preliminary research for a topic, keep a section in your research notebook for recording ideas and potential questions about that topic. A section titled Topics and Questions in Linda Kastan's research notebook (see Figure 3.12) contained four entries for various topics she was interested in pursuing.

Linda went on to develop the fourth topic and research question shown here, changing both slightly as her research and further thinking led her to do so. Linda's notebook entry enabled her to identify her own central concerns and led to a research question that could answer them. The other notebook entries gave her useful alternative topic choices and a means of judging what seemed the most interesting and challenging issues to research.

Using Critical Thinking Techniques to Focus on Research

After examining preliminary sources about your subject, you may find that one or more critical thinking approaches will help you identify issues and arrive at a research question or more focused approach to it. If you were in-

Topics and Questions

1. *Television:* How much harm does it really do? Does it do any good? How does TV reinforce social stereotypes regarding race and gender? Too much violence? Too much sex? Is TV news objective, or is it dominated by the ratings race?

2. *Cellular phones:* Some people worry that cell phones give companies and the government just one more way to know what people are doing, since all calls on a cell phone are automatically tracked. There is also a security problem with cell phones—criminals can steal your access code without your even knowing it. Are we too dependent on staying in touch all the time?

3. *Plastic/cosmetic surgery:* It is still very risky in most cases, despite the improvements in techniques and technology. Are people too hung up on their looks? When is cosmetic surgery really justified? Breast implants, liposuction, face lifts—where does it end? Some of these are dangerous, like breast implants and liposuction cases where people have died because of malpractice.

4. *Internet addiction:* Are people really addicted to being online? If so, is there really any harm being done? The documentary I saw showed students who were getting low grades because of spending too much time on the Internet. What do they get out of online chatting, playing MUDs, or sending e-mail? Is any one of these more addictive than the others?

FIGURE 3.12 Entries from a research notebook

vestigating the subject of *subliminal advertising,* for example, the following approaches might be helpful:

1. *Summarize* your preliminary sources to identify and understand different points of view regarding the subject. For example, your sources may each describe several common uses of subliminal advertising, but each has a different opinion about whether these uses are harmful.

2. *Evaluate* the sources in terms of their evidence and the extent to which they may be useful in supporting your own research conclusion. A source that gives weak evidence about the dangers of subliminal advertising may convince you of just the opposite conclusion, or you may think of ways that you could introduce stronger evidence from other sources to better support the same argument.

3. *Analyze* the subject and any conflicting points of view to examine underlying principles and apply them to specific cases or issues. For instance, is it right to allow people, including children, to be unknowingly targeted by such advertising?

4. *Synthesize* the ideas provided by sources to clarify what questions or issues are left unresolved or how they could be incorporated to support your own conclusion. You may find that while most sources claim there is little real evidence of the abuse of subliminal advertising, what evidence exists supports the argument that the use of subliminal ads is unethical and dangerous.

Considering Your Audience

Part of selecting a topic and research question to investigate also involves considering your paper's audience. Naturally, the instructor who assigned the paper is your most immediate audience, though he or she is not the only one you want to think of as you consider a focus for your research.

While your instructor may be your paper's primary reader, his or her reading will have the same criteria that you would want to meet for other readers. When planning the research for your paper, you should assume that the audience is generally knowledgeable about the subject but needs additional information to understand and be convinced of your paper's main point, or thesis. This is the audience you should write for and whom you want to consider when thinking of your research paper.

When considering any topic and research question, assess your readers' needs. Ask yourself what they need to know or what you can discuss to enlighten them further about the topic. What questions do people need to have answered about organically grown foods, for example? What would an audience of chemists want to know? What would a mother of young children want to know? What questions do you need to ask and which audience's needs can your research fulfill?

Because the audience you assume will be generally informed already, avoid topics and research questions that will be so familiar they will offer nothing new. The question of whether cigarette smoking endangers people's health is not likely to interest an already informed audience. Likewise, such an audience is unlikely to find much interest in a paper simply arguing against drug addiction: Why listen to an argument most informed people have already accepted? A good topic and research question stimulates your readers' thinking, drawing upon an assumed interest in the subject to present new perspectives.

Defining the Paper's Purpose

As you determine the focus of your research, you will also need to define your paper's *purpose,* which includes answering the research question and planning your strategy for presenting information. The kind of paper you write and the investigation you do for it will reflect the research question and the paper's purpose.

The Argumentative Paper

Research papers that aim primarily at interpreting information are *argumentative* papers. When you write an argumentative paper, the intention is to lead readers to understand and agree with your analysis of the research topic and your conclusion about the research question.

Argumentative papers are meant to persuade an audience that the writer's perceptions are correct. Such a paper states the author's argument (or *thesis*) and then presents evidence to support it. Argumentative research papers also appear in the form of scholarly articles, scientific essays, legal briefs, business reports, historical studies, and government analyses. In short, writers use an argumentative approach whenever they feel their audience needs or expects comprehensive discussion and reasoned conclusions about a topic.

Because it seeks to persuade readers of her research conclusions, Linda Kastan's paper on Internet addiction has an argumentative purpose. After selecting the Internet as the focus of her research, Linda formulated a research question that addressed what she wanted to answer for herself: Is the Internet really causing harmful addiction? The resulting thesis statement in Linda's paper explains her answer: Evidence is growing that increasing numbers of users are learning too late that connecting online can also become the first step to disconnecting with a healthy lifestyle. After stating this thesis in her introduction, Linda went on to discuss the thesis argument and support it her own research and analysis of the subject (see Chapter 11).

Similarly, Steve Hanner's research paper on emotional intelligence (see Appendix A) is also an argumentative paper. Steve argues that emotional intelligence is indeed important but does not necessarily rival IQ as a measure of overall abilities and a predictor of success in life.

Both Linda's and Steve's research papers grew out of their formulation of *working hypotheses*—possible answers to the questions they posed about their individual topics at the start of their research. After examining sources and thinking extensively about what they had found, each was able to add his or her insight to generate an original response to the topic

As the two resulting sample papers demonstrate, an effective argumentative research paper should demonstrate your ability to gather information and assess it accurately. In discussing any topic, especially a controversial one, present all sides of an issue, not just those that favor your argument. You should acknowledge any facts and opinions that seem to oppose your position, offering counter-arguments or qualifying discussions as you do so. In this way, you are being fair to your audience and to your own understanding of the topic. (See Chapter 9, Reasoning Critically about Argument and Evidence.)

The Informative Paper

Informative research is primarily intended to present information for the reader's benefit. In one sense, of course, all research papers inform their audiences: They offer information to illustrate the writer's ideas and to show how the various parts of the topic relate. Informative research studies, however, minimize expression of the author's viewpoint. Topics for informative research papers are those about which readers need information more than anything else. Although their authors must still argue theses about the topics, research questions for informative papers usually emphasize description, measurable results, or processes, as in these examples:

1. What effect has deforestation in the Amazon had upon already threatened species of wildlife?
2. How are colleges across the United States dealing with the problem of violence on campus?
3. Do students from private schools get better SAT scores than those from public schools?
4. How are other countries coping with the growing problem of waste disposal?

You inform readers when you explain, summarize, report, chart, list, or otherwise make information itself the primary focus of your presentation. Your major role in writing an informative paper is to gather data and organize it in a more clear manner than your readers would otherwise have it. The information you gather to describe may range from entirely new data, such as a report analyzing the impact of an oil spill on local fishing grounds, to a review of the current literature in a field, as was done in the sample paper about alcohol consumption among college students (see Appendix A). If you foresee the need to write an informative paper, remember that it should not be merely a summary of sources or string of quotations from various authorities. Your ability to formulate and answer a significant research question is vital to an effective paper.

Knowing whether you want to write an argumentative or informative research paper will help you decide what to write about and how to shape your ideas for research. As you plan the focus of your research, keep in mind these two major kinds of purposes. You may need to check with your instructor about which kind of paper is required or may be most appropriate for your research assignment.

Working with a Preliminary Thesis

At some point in the initial stages of your investigation, you will undoubtedly begin to perceive a potential answer to the research question you have formulated about the topic. For some writers, such an answer is formed early in the research process. For others, it develops slowly or changes as the focus of the research question itself shifts in response to more information about the topic. Some writers resist forming even a potential answer to the research question until their investigation of sources has been completed.

Guided by a research question, however, most writers find it also helpful to have in mind a preliminary thesis as they work. The *preliminary thesis* is a statement in one or two sentences that summarizes your tentative response to the research question at a particular point in your investigation. Along with the research question, such a thesis statement will direct your research activities toward relevant material, helping you decide what to give close attention to in examining sources.

For example, suppose your research topic is *the effectiveness of anti-youth gang programs in large cities*. An appropriate research question would be: What is required for a successful antigang program? Drawing upon what you know of the topic from your beginning investigation, you might formulate a potential preliminary thesis such as this: The most effective antigang programs include community-based education and employment assistance. Key concepts such as *community-based education* and *employment assistance* can focus your reading. Defining what your paper will mean by *effective* (and its opposite, *ineffective*) can strengthen its content and add breadth to your discussion.

Remember that a preliminary thesis is not intended to be your final opinion on the topic. As you investigate the topic more thoroughly, you will most likely modify the thesis or change it entirely in response to your increased knowledge. You might begin with something like this: The average American's diet is certain suicide. Later, you may decide that the following statement more suitably expresses your ideas: Americans can choose to eat better and live longer. If a preliminary thesis seems helpful at the planning stage, use it with the research question as a way of furthering the focus of your research.

WORKING WITH OTHERS

Discussing your research ideas with others will promote and clarify your own thinking. A five-minute conversation can sometimes eliminate an inappropriate subject from further consideration or make you suddenly enthusiastic over a topic you might not have thought of alone. Use the following suggestions to help you work with others in planning the focus of your research. You will find sharing your ideas and progress acts as a stimulus to your perseverance and thinking for the research paper.

- Meet with a classmate or friend to review the potential subjects listed in your research notebook. What makes each subject particularly appealing to you? Does your friend or classmate have a preference for one subject over another? Why? Discuss each subject and the kinds of resources that might be available for it. What other subjects can you suggest to each other?

- Work with another person to narrow a potential subject toward a particular topic. Try brainstorming together to come up with as many related topics for the subject as you can. What are the major concerns regarding this subject? What questions need to be answered about these concerns? What important research steps might some of these topics require?

- If you used freewriting or clustering to arrive at a topic, share the results. What pattern of ideas or interest is apparent? Does your approach seem to favor an argumentative or informative approach to the discussion? Take turns completing introductory phrases about potential topics, such as "Water conservation is important today because . . ."

- If you are not familiar with using a computer or search tools such as Yahoo! and the Electric Library to find information, ask a classmate or friend to give you a demonstration. Discuss possible topics for research, and explore them together on the Internet or other online resources.

- Once you have some specific topics in mind, use the topic checklist presented earlier (see pp. 46–47) to discuss their merits. Discuss whether each topic seems suitable for the assignment and available resources. Does any particular topic seem too philosophical or too narrow? Will it result in little more than a restatement of well-known and accepted ideas?

- After selecting a suitable topic, your next step will be to investigate specific sources and to take notes. Discuss your general plans with your collaborator, and make arrangements to review your progress together again. If you are working with a classmate, use your research schedules to plan times to meet and begin thoroughly researching sources together.

CHAPTER 4

Researching Library Sources

Having determined an appropriate topic and research question, you will next need to think about locating the information on which to base your research. A large, general library, such as that found at most colleges or universities, will provide the greatest number and variety of resources for you to begin your research.

Organize your search for information by first establishing a *working bibliography*, a list of sources on the research topic. The working bibliography will serve as an ongoing, developing pool of sources to consult throughout your research. You will want to use the full range of standard library resources and reference materials to ensure that the working bibliography, and therefore your research on the topic, is as comprehensive as possible.

Preparing the Working Bibliography

The working bibliography is a *preliminary* list of sources for your paper, one that will change as you add or delete sources throughout the research process. The list is a *bibliography* because it names and provides information about sources on a particular topic. It is a *working* bibliography because it is tentative: You use the working bibliography to record information about available sources, to determine whether there are enough and the right kinds of sources for your research needs, and to locate and work with such sources as you research and write the paper. Sources included in the working bibliography—books, magazines, newspapers, journal articles, interviews, and others—lay the groundwork for the notetaking and organization of data that will come later in your research. Information for all or most of the sources in the Works Cited section of the final paper will also come from your working bibliography.

> **THINKING CRITICALLY**
> **ABOUT LIBRARY SOURCES**
>
> Libraries provide a wide variety of publications suitable for research—books, magazines, journals, newspapers, government documents, and the like. Students sometimes mistakenly believe that because something has been published and included in a library's holdings, it necessarily follows that the information provided is accurate and authoritative. But the fact that an author's work has found its way into print is no guarantee of this. For example, a public library may contain a shelfload of books about UFO sightings, but this doesn't mean that these books would be acceptable as the primary basis of academic research.
>
> On another level, published sources may simply be outdated, superseded by later findings or events; depending on your subject, you'll want to make sure you are working with the most up-to-date sources. More subtly, virtually any piece of writing reflects the biases of its author and, particularly with a periodical, its place of publication. Even some book publishers are more or less devoted to liberal or conservative viewpoints.
>
> So it is important that, as you conduct library research, you read as widely as possible and do everything you can to evaluate and verify the timeliness, authenticity, and potential biases of every source you use. (For more on critically evaluating sources, see Chapter 7, pp. 146–50.)

Listing Sources on Cards or in a Computer File

You will need to devise a consistent means of storing the information you accumulate as you build the working bibliography for your paper. Although researchers vary in how they prefer to do this, storing the working bibliography on index cards, in a computer file, or both is most practical.

Bibliography Cards.   Many library researchers carry packets of *bibliography cards,* usually 3″ × 5″ (or larger) index cards, on which they record information about all their sources as they find them. Such cards offer several advantages for researchers:

1. Cards allow for quick organization and sorting of bibliographic sources.
2. Unwanted cards can be easily discarded and new ones conveniently added.
3. Information from the cards can be easily transferred to a computer file and then serve as a back-up to the file.
4. Because they can be easily shuffled and arranged alphabetically, the cards will later provide bibliographic information in the order needed for preparing the Works Cited list.

Keep a stock of blank bibliography cards handy as you do research in the library, bookstore, or other places that may contain useful sources. Make a habit of jotting down the title and author's name on separate cards every time you come across a possible resource for the paper. If you keep your working bibliography in a computer file, transfer the information from the cards to the file on a regular basis to save time later.

A Computer File.   Another efficient way to list sources for the working bibliography is to enter information about each item into a computer file. Doing so lets you organize the information in different ways—for instance, in categories like *books* and *periodicals* or *primary* and *secondary sources*. Keeping the working bibliography in a computer file also allows you to copy the information to other files or to insert it handily into the draft of the paper once you begin to write. However, since it is unlikely that you will always have a computer on hand for research in libraries or elsewhere, you may still need to use bibliography cards, as well.

It may seem as though transferring the information from your bibliography cards to a computer file creates unnecessary work, but taking this extra step is worth it. Once you begin transferring data from the cards to a file, you will see how handy it is to scroll down your computer screen and assess your research progress from time to time.

Information for the Working Bibliography.   When filling out a bibliography card or adding a source to your computer file, include the information you would need to find the source again or to include it in your paper's Works Cited section. Though you may eventually list many types of sources for your research, it is likely that a majority of them will be books and periodicals.

Book Sources.   In general, record the following information for any book you list in the working bibliography:

1. Library catalog call number
2. Author(s), editor(s), or translator(s)
3. Title (underlined), including the subtitle
4. Place of publication
5. Publisher
6. Publication date (or latest copyright date)
7. Brief note about the book's content or usefulness

Figure 4.1 shows how such information may appear on a bibliography card, using the style followed by the Modern Language Association (MLA). You should follow the form and punctuation you will use in your paper if the form shown here is different. (MLA style is discussed further in Chapter 12. Other bibliographic styles are discussed in Chapter 13.)

PN827.8

73L43

1998

Luchetti, Cathy.

Medicine Women: The Story of Early-American Women Doctors.

New York: Crown, 1998.

— Describes women's roles on the frontier, especially 1840–60.

FIGURE 4.1 A bibliography card for a book (MLA style)

Periodical Sources. Publications that are published at regular intervals are called *periodicals.* The information recorded on a bibliography card about an article from a periodical—such as a magazine, journal, or newspaper—will differ slightly from that for a book. It should include:

1. Author(s)
2. Title (in quotation marks), including the subtitle
3. Periodical name (underlined)
4. Volume number (for professional journals but not popular magazines)*
5. Date of publication
6. Page number(s) the article is found on
7. Brief note about the article's content or usefulness

If no author is given for a periodical article, begin the entry with the article title. Do not use *Anonymous* or *Anon.* in place of an author's name. If you have located the periodical through the *Readers' Guide* or another index, avoid using that source's forms and abbreviations. Either translate them into the bibliographic style of your paper as you write the data on your card, or make a new card when you later locate the periodical. Figure 4.2 shows a typical bibliography card (in MLA style) for a periodical article, but follow the style of your paper's bibliographical form if it is different.

*See also Chapters 12 and 13 regarding issue and series numbers.

Gawande, Atul.
"Cold Comfort."
The New Yorker (Mar. 11, 2002): 42–47.
— Discusses causes of the common cold, how cold viruses are
transmitted among people, and remedies for colds, as well as
how little researchers actually understand about the develop-
ment and spread of cold viruses.

FIGURE 4.2   A bibliography card for a periodical (MLA style)

Gauging the Topic's Feasibility

At the start of your research, the working bibliography serves as an important check against beginning to work at length on an unfruitful topic, If your preliminary search for sources turns up too many—a dozen books and 20 magazine articles on your very topic, let's say—you will need to narrow the topic more or take a different approach to it (see Chapter 3). If you can find only one encyclopedia entry and a few magazine articles that discuss your research question, you will need to broaden your focus or select an alternate topic to research (see Chapter 3). In addition, check the working bibliography against the requirements of your assignment. For example, if your instructor wants you to use particular kinds of primary sources—original materials like diaries or unpublished papers—and none are available, you will need to select another topic.

Expect the working bibliography to change as you delete some works and add others throughout your research. Keep in mind, however, that the working bibliography's completeness is also essential to the success of your research. The more inclusive the working bibliography, the more thoroughly you will be able to study major ideas involved with the research topic. For these reasons, you will also need to understand how libraries organize and store information as well as how to use the resources available in them.

Using Bibliographies to Locate Sources

A list of related books or other written works is called a *bibliography* (hence, the name for the working bibliography). While all bibliographies provide information about each source's title, author, and publication data, they also vary in their emphasis and approach. A bibliography may be *selective* and include only a few works; it may be *descriptive* and provide brief annotations or reviews; it may be *evaluative* and discuss the value of the sources it lists; or it may combine any of these approaches.

The most familiar kinds of bibliographies are those commonly found at the ends of scholarly books or their chapters, at the conclusions of encyclopedia or journal articles, or at the backs of a few popular periodicals like *Smithsonian* and *Scientific American*. These bibliographies are sometimes titled References, Works Cited, or Works Consulted, and they usually list the works that the article authors used to prepare their own discussions of their subjects. The Works Cited list that you will include at the end of your research paper will be such a bibliography.

Some complete reference works, however, are bibliographies only. That is, the entire purpose of a book published *as a bibliography* is to provide a list of sources on a topic. For example, you might go to a work titled *A Bibliography of Jazz,* by Alan P. Merriam, if you wanted a list of published works about jazz. The term *bibliography* is also sometimes referred to as a union catalog or list, a checklist, sourcebook, or index. Thus, G. Thomas Tanselle's *A Checklist of Editions of Moby Dick, 1851–1976* might be a useful bibliography to consult if you were studying that novel's publishing history. Regardless of what they are termed, you will need such whole-work bibliographies, as well as shorter ones listed within other works, to locate sources for your own working bibliography and to establish a larger base of materials to investigate for your research.

Becoming Familiar with General Bibliographies

Probably most helpful to researchers are *general bibliographies,* reference books that tell you about the bibliographies contained in other books.

Bibliographic Index.   One of the most useful general resources is the *Bibliographic Index: A Cumulative Bibliography of Bibliographies.* You can look up an author or subject in this comprehensive work to find other bibliographies that appear in books and periodicals.

As Figure 4.3 shows, an author entry in the *Bibliographic Index* may include bibliographies listed in works *by* an author, *about* an author, as well as *both by and about* an author. In addition to writing down all the usual information about a *Bibliographic Index* source, you should also record where the bibliographies appear in the works cited. This information is given as the page numbers listed at the end of each entry. The bibliography card shown in Figure 4.4 records an entry from the *Bibliographic Index* listing the work by Kimberly S. Young as well as the pages on which the bibliography of works about Internet addiction appears.

Clinton, Bill, 1946–
> Metz, A. Reviews of President Bill Clinton's first two years and second year in office: an annotated bibliography. *Bull Bibliogr* v52 p211–27 S '95
> Metz, A. Reviews of President Bill Clinton's first year in office: an annotated bibliography. *Bull Bibliogr* v51 p355–97 D '94
> **By and about**
> U.S. presidents as orators; a bio-critical sourcebook; edited by Halford Ryan. Greenwood Press 1995 p374–5

FIGURE 4.3   An entry on "Bill Clinton" from the *Bibliographic Index*

Source: From the *Bibliographic Index,* August 1995, p. 196. Copyright © 1995 by The H. W. Wilson Company. Reprinted by permission.

> *Young, Kimberly S.*
> *Caught in the Net: How to Recognize the Signs of Internet Addiction and a Winning Strategy for Recovery.*
> *New York: Wiley, 1998.*
> *Bibliography pp. 240–44*

FIGURE 4.4   A bibliography card for a book cited in the *Bibliographic Index*

Beginning Your Research with Bibliographical Sources.   Begin your search by consulting the *Bibliographic Index* or another general bibliography in your library. Then consult a specialized bibliography such as one of the following:

1. A bibliography of works used by an author to prepare his or her own discussion (those works listed at the end of an encyclopedia article, for example)
2. Bibliographies by or about one author (e.g., *Bibliography of the Works of Rudyard Kipling* or *Emily Dickinson: A Descriptive Bibliography*)

FIGURE 4.5   Moving from a general bibliography to an individual work

3. Bibliographies about one subject or subject field (e.g., *Checklist of Arizona Minerals* or *Bibliography of Mexican American History*)
4. Bibliographies describing materials relating to one country or region (e.g., *Bibliography of Africana*)

From these specific bibliographies, you will proceed to locate individual works by author and title (see Figure 4.5).

Searching Trade Bibliographies for Sources

People in the book trade, mainly librarians and booksellers, use trade bibliographies to buy, sell, and catalog books. You can use trade bibliographies to find out what books exist on your research topic; to get author, title, and publication data; and to find out if a book is still in print.

Subject Guide to Books in Print.   You will find the *Subject Guide to Books in Print* helpful in identifying current sources to include in your preliminary bibliography. Printed yearly, the *Subject Guide* can tell you which books on your research topic are in print. After writing down the information about any works listed, you can seek them out at your local library or ask about borrowing them through interlibrary loan.

Other Guides.   The *Subject Guide to Books in Print* is a version of another trade bibliography, *Books in Print,* which lists works in separate volumes by author, title, and subject. There is also *Paperbound Books in Print,* a good source to go to if you cannot find the hardbound edition of a book in your library and are willing to try the local bookstore instead. *Books in Print* is often available online at college and university libraries, or you can access it from your home computer through some commercial services such as CompuServe. Figure 4.6 shows how the *Subject Guide to Books in Print* lists books under the subject *jury.*

For a listing and publication information about any book published in the English language, consult the *Cumulative Book Index* (*CBI*) for the year in question. If the *CBI* is not available at your library, the *Publisher's Trade List Annual* lists current and past books still in print from over 1,500 publishers.

JURY
see also Grand Jury; Instructions to Juries
ABA, Committee on Jury Standards, et al. Standards
    Relating to Juror Use & Management: Tentative Draft.
    208p. 1982. 11.50 (*0-89656-603-5*, R-069) Natl Ctr St
    Courts.
Abbott, Walter F. Analytic Juror Rater. 142p. 1987. 31.00
    (*0-8318-0588-9*, B588) Am Law Inst.
—Surrogate Juries. LC 90-80485. 265p. 1990. 80.00
    (*0-8318-0607-9*, B607) Am Law Inst.
Abbott, Walter F., et al. Jury Research: A Review &
    Bibliography. LC 90-75867. 346p. 1993. 31.00
    (*0-8318-0638-9*, B638) Am Law Inst.
The Anglo-American Jury: Keystone of Human Rights.
    1993. lib. bdg. 75.00 (*0-8490-8726-0*) Gordon Pr.
Antitrust Civil Jury Instructions (Supplement) LC 80-67740.
    88p. 1986. ring bd. 30.00 (*0-89707-215-4*, 503-0060-01)
    Amer Bar Assn.
Austin, Arthur D. Complex Litigation Confronts the Jury
    System: A Case Study. LC 84-19500. 120p. 1984. text
    ed. 55.00 (*0-313-27009-6*, U7099, Greenwood Pr)
    Greenwood.
Berger, Richic E. & Lane, Frederick S., 3rd. Vermont Jury
    Instructions. 400p. 1993. ring bd. 85.00 (*1-56237-293-8*)
    Michie Butterworth.

FIGURE 4.6   An entry on "jury" from the *Subject Guide to Books in Print*

Source: Reprinted with permission of R. R. Bowker, a Reed Reference Publishing Company, a Division of Reed Elsevier, Inc., from the *Subject Guide to Books in Print™, 1995–1996.* Copyright © 1990–1996, Reed Elsevier, Inc. All rights reserved (p. 5205).

The following trade bibliographies, including those already mentioned, are available at most libraries or bookstores:

American Book Publishing Record. New York: Bowker, 1960–date.
Books in Print. New York: Bowker, 1948–date.
Cumulative Book Index. New York: Wilson, 1898–date.
Paperbound Books in Print. New York: Bowker, 1955–date.
Publisher's Trade List Annual. New York: Bowker, 1873–date.
Subject Guide to Books in Print. New York: Bowker, 1957–date.

Using Indexes to Locate Sources

Bibliographies can tell you what books are published, but they do not list the individual items that may be included within works. Indexes, however, can help you find single works—articles, stories, poems, essays, and other written pieces—located *within* books and periodicals. There are general indexes to periodicals and books as well as specialized indexes to particular kinds of works or subjects.

Periodical Indexes

Publications printed at regular intervals (or periods) are called *periodicals.* These include magazines, journals, and newspapers of every type and description. Because they are published more frequently than encyclopedias or books, periodicals are valuable sources of current information and opinion. Articles appearing in both popular and scholarly periodicals are indexed in a variety of sources. Use these indexes to identify possible areas to explore for research.

Popular Magazines.   In addition to journals and newspapers, periodicals also include popular magazines written for general audiences and usually available at newsstands or the local supermarket. *Newsweek, Ms., Psychology Today, Field and Stream, Penthouse, National Geographic,* and *Rolling Stone* are examples. Popular magazines like these can be useful for exploring a potential research focus and acquiring helpful background information. Because they are aimed at general audiences and vary greatly in their authority, however, articles in magazines may not be suitable for every kind of research. They are best used when you need current, nontechnical information and opinion about a subject. When in doubt about using magazines, consult your instructor.

Magazine Indexes.   You are probably already familiar with the *Readers' Guide to Periodical Literature,* an index to more than 200 of the most popular magazines in the United States. (The *Readers' Guide* and its use are also discussed in Chapter 3.) The format for information in the *Readers' Guide* is representative of that used in most other periodical indexes. Articles are listed alphabetically by author and subject; each entry includes the author's name, article title, name of the periodical, the date and volume number of the periodical, and the page numbers of the article. Figure 4.7 shows a typical entry from the *Readers' Guide.*

While the *Readers' Guide* is no doubt the most comprehensive of the magazine indexes, you should not overlook others that include publica-

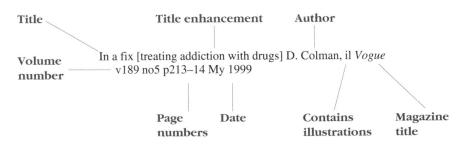

FIGURE 4.7   An excerpt from the *Readers' Guide to Periodical Literature*

Source: From the *Readers' Guide to Periodical Literature,* September 2000. Copyright © 2000 by The H. W. Wilson Company. Reprinted by permission.

tions it does not index. For example, *Access,* issued three times a year, includes 150 or more magazines not included among those indexed in the *Readers' Guide.* Using *Access,* you can find articles printed in such magazines as *Woman's Day, TV Guide, Penthouse,* and *Bicycling,* sources that can provide you with insight to popular taste or current information on well-known individuals.

To find very current articles with slightly different viewpoints than those often found in mainstream publications, you might want to consult the *Popular Periodical Index* and the *Alternative Press Index.* The first of these indexes such magazines as *MacWorld, Playboy, English Journal,* and *Columbia Journalism Review;* the second includes over 200 so-called alternative publications such as *Green Peace, Feminist Studies,* and *Canadian Journal of Political and Social Theory.*

In addition to these print sources, you will find a number of magazine indexes available online or on CD–ROM. Many college and university libraries, for example, provide CD–ROM resources such as *Magazine Article Summaries* or *Magazine Index Plus,* each of which indexes over 400 magazines. In addition, many college and university library computer facilities offer InfoTrac, which includes several popular magazine and newspaper indexes as well as individual newspapers. Commercial services such as America Online, CompuServe, and Prodigy provide online search access to the archives of popular magazines such as *Newsweek, Time, U.S. News & World Report, McClean's,* and a host of others.

For her research paper on Internet addiction, Linda Kastan was able to log onto the online periodicals service ProQuest through her library's website. She used the keywords "Internet addiction" to get the list of possible sources shown in Figure 4.8. From this list, she could click on a particular title and, in most cases, retrieve the full text of the article (in some cases, only an abstract of the article was available). Keep in mind that any such online or CD-ROM periodicals service will give you access only to the periodicals subscribed to by the service; you should search several such services if they are available to you.

While you will obviously want to consider the *Readers' Guide* as your primary index to popular magazines, remember that you can locate useful sources in various other indexes, too. For easy reference later, the following list includes indexes already mentioned as well as others you may wish to consult:

Access, 1975–date (includes only magazines not indexed in the *Reader's Guide*)

Alternative Press Index, 1969–date (covers politically "left" publications)

California Periodicals Index, 1978–date (indexes magazines about California cities and lifestyles)

Catholic Periodical and Literature Index, 1930–date

Children's Magazine Guide: Subject Index to Children's Literature, 1948–date

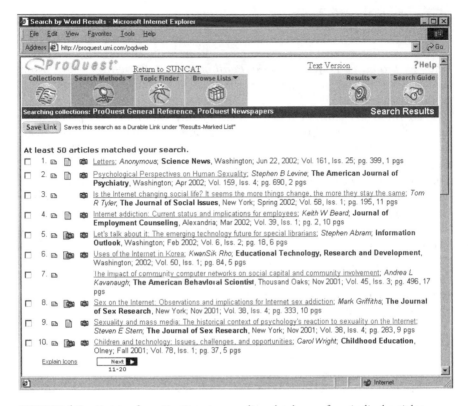

FIGURE 4.8 Entries from ProQuest, an online database of periodical articles

Source: Image produced by ProQuest Information and Learning Company, 300 North Zeeb Road, Ann Arbor, MI 48106-1346 USA. Telephone (734) 761-7400; E-mail: info@il.proquest.com; Web-page: www.il.proquest.com. Further reproduction is prohibited without permission.

Consumer's Index to Product Evaluations and Information Sources, 1973–date

Index to Jewish Periodicals, 1963–date

Index to Periodicals By and About Blacks, 1950–date

Magazine Article Summaries, 1984–date (available on CD–ROM)

Magazine Database Plus, 1980–date (available online through Compu-Serve and at many college and university libraries)

The Magazine Index, 1977–date (appears on microfilm and duplicates the *Reader's Guide* and *Access*)

Magazine Index Plus, 1980–date (available on CD–ROM)

Periodicals Abstracts Ondisc, 1986–date (microfilm)

Physical Education Index, 1978–date (indexes magazines covering nutrition, fitness, and sports)

Physical Education/Sports Index, 1973–date (includes magazines devoted to particular sports)

Popular Periodical Index, 1978–date

Readers' Guide to Periodical Literature, 1900–date (available in print and on CD–ROM)

Resource/One Ondisc, 1986–date (microfilm; available online through DIALOG [File 484] as *Newspapers & Periodicals Abstracts*)

Knowing Which Index to Consult. If you are unsure about which index includes a particular popular magazine, refer to a copy of the magazine itself. The table of contents will often tell you where the magazine is indexed. If it does not, consult one of the following sources, but remember that these publications try not to duplicate each other. You may have to consult more than one before you find the particular magazine you want to know about:

Magazines for Libraries. Ed. Bill Katz and Linda Katz. New York: Bowker, 2000.

Standard Periodical Directory. Detroit: Gale, 2001.

Ulrich's International Periodicals Directory, 2001. New York: Bowker, 2000.

Journals. Periodicals written for scholars or audiences with special expertise in a subject are called *journals*. These periodicals report on current issues, original research, and results of surveys and experiments. They also often include book reviews, which are themselves useful for your research. Journals are written by informed authorities for an audience of similarly informed or interested people. The level of knowledge or experience required to read them easily varies from very accessible ones, like the film journal *Movie Maker*, to more technical ones, like *Accounts of Chemical Research*.

Journal Indexes. Numerous indexes list journal articles covering subjects in nearly every field of study and interest. Four of the most widely used in the social sciences and literature and languages are discussed here.

1. *Social Sciences Index.* Since nearly every subject has implications for social consequences, check general social science indexes on almost any topic you research. A major source to consult in this field is the *Social Sciences Index*, which lists articles in over 250 scholarly journals covering such subjects as anthropology, economics, environmental studies, history, law, philosophy, political science, and sociology. As Figure 4.9 suggests, a check of the *Index* may not only yield sources for research but also suggest new relationships and emphases for you to consider.

2. *Social Sciences Citation Index.* A valuable resource in the behavioral and social sciences is the *Social Sciences Citation Index (SSCI)*. This source indexes approximately 2,000 scholarly journals and is also available through online databases. Citation indexes are useful both for locating published journal articles and identifying authorities who have written on your research subject. Since it is composed of four separate indexes—Citation, Source, Permuterm

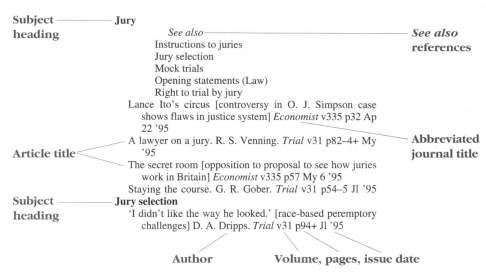

Subject ——————— **Jury**
heading
         See also ————————————————————— *See also*
         Instructions to juries   **references**
         Jury selection
         Mock trials
         Opening statements (Law)
         Right to trial by jury
         Lance Ito's circus [controversy in O. J. Simpson case
           shows flaws in justice system] *Economist* v335 p32 Ap
           22 '95
       A lawyer on a jury. R. S. Venning. *Trial* v31 p82–4+ My   **Abbreviated**
Article title   '95   **journal title**
       The secret room [opposition to proposal to see how juries
         work in Britain] *Economist* v335 p57 My 6 '95
         Staying the course. G. R. Gober. *Trial* v31 p54–5 Jl '95
Subject ——————— **Jury selection**
heading   'I didn't like the way he looked.' [race-based peremptory
         challenges] D. A. Dripps. *Trial* v31 p94+ Jl '95

         Author   **Volume, pages, issue date**

FIGURE 4.9   Entries from the *Social Science Index*

Source: From *Social Science Index,* September 1995, p. 333. Copyright © 1995 by The H. W. Wilson Company. Reprinted by permission.

Subject, and Corporate indexes—this work requires familiarity before it can be consulted efficiently.

  a. The Permuterm Subject Index of *SSCI* is useful at the start of your research, when you need to become acquainted with the key terms related to your subject or need to discover who has written about it. The Permuterm Subject Index lists articles by subject headings, followed by associated terms or subheadings. As Figure 4.10 shows, looking up the subject "television" in the Permuterm Index would yield a large number of more particular subheadings and authors whose journal articles treated them specifically. The entries under "television," for example, show an article on the topic of "adolescents" and television by L. Bernard. By using the Source Index, you could find the title of the source in which Bernard's article appears.

  b. The Source Index provides publication information about each of the authors ("sources") listed in the Permuterm Subject Index and published in periodicals covered by *SSCI*. In addition, it indicates the number of references made to each entry by other authors and lists those authors and where their works appeared. Thus, once you had found L. Bernard's name in the Subject Index under "television—adolescents," you could look him or her up in the Source Index for full information on what he or she had written. The entry would also list other authors who have cited the article. Figure 4.11 shows a complete Source entry for Bernard's article on adolescents and television.

  c. Next, suppose you also wanted to find out more about L. Bernard's work. *SSCI*'s Citation Index will tell you (1) how many

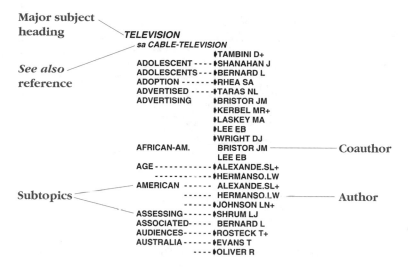

FIGURE 4.10 An excerpt from the Permuterm Subject Index of the *Social Sciences Citation Index*

Source: Reprinted with permission from *Social Sciences Citation Index®*, May–August 1995. Copyright © 1995 by the Institute for Scientific Information®.

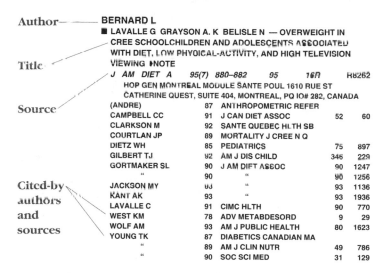

FIGURE 4.11 An author entry from the Source Index of the *Social Sciences Citation Index*

Source: Reprinted with permission from *Social Sciences Citation Index®*, May–August 1995. Copyright © 1995 by the Institute for Scientific Information®.

times and where a particular author has published during the time covered by the index and (2) what authors have made reference to the entries indicated for that author. Note that the Citation Index does not list titles of individual publications by an author. Instead,

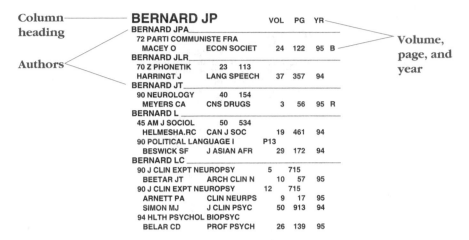

FIGURE 4.12   An author entry from the Citation Index of the *Social Sciences Citation Index*

Source: Reprinted with permission from *Social Sciences Citation Index®*, 1995. Copyright © 1995 by the Institute for Scientific Information®.

it lists the periodical and date when an article appeared (see Figure 4.12).

You should use the Citation Index to gauge an individual author's authority on the subject (indicated by the number of publications and the frequency of citations by other authors). Also use the Citation Index to locate articles by other authors in the field, looking up the names listed there in the Source Index later.

d. The Corporate Author Index of *SSCI* has the same format as the Citation Index. Rather than citing persons, however, this index lists associations, leagues, corporations, and other groups that author publications.

Figure 4.13 summarizes the relationships among the separate indexes that constitute the *Social Sciences Citation Index* and typical citation indexes in other fields of study. In addition to the *SSCI*, the following reference works include source, citation, and Permuterm indexes, as described here:

Arts and Humanities Index, 1977–date
CompuMath Citation Index, 1968–date
Science Citation Index, 1961–date

3. *MLA Bibliography.* If you are researching a topic in languages or literature, consult the Modern Language Association's *MLA International Bibliography of Books and Articles on the Modern Languages and Literature.* This work's title is fully descriptive of its use and focus. Bound as a single, inclusive volume and subtitled *Classified Listings with Author*

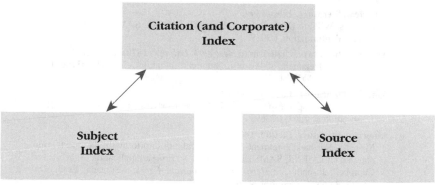

FIGURE 4.13   A summary of indexes included in the *Social Sciences Citation Index*

Index, the *MLA Bibliography* divides articles on languages and literature into five areas:

National literatures (subvolumes I and II)
Linguistics (III)
General literature (IV)
Folklore (V)

Locating an author or work in the *Classified Listings* is a step-by-step procedure:

a. Turn to the appropriate subvolume.
b. Find the section for the appropriate time period of your subject.
c. Find the alphabetical listing for the author or work you seek.

To locate items in the *MLA Bibliography* by subject, you will need to use a second, separate volume, the *Subject Index,* which is organized alphabetically.

Figure 4.14 shows entries from the *Subject Index* of the *MLA Bibliography* on author "Samuel Clemens" (who wrote using the pseudonym "Mark Twain"). Figure 4.15 is an entry from the *MLA Bibliography's Classified Listings with Author Index* on Twain's novel *The Adventures of Huckleberry Finn.*

4. *Humanities Index.* A good source for articles on religion, philosophy, literature, or any of the performing arts—such as dance, television, opera, drama, or film—is the *Humanities Index.* It includes entries from over 200 scholarly journals and follows *Readers' Guide* form in listing information.

CLEMENS, SAMUEL (1835–1910)
See also classified section: 1:7574 ff.
Used for: Twain, Mark.

 American literature. 1800–1899.
 Howells, William Dean. Relationship to CLEMENS, SAMUEL. Includes biographical information. I:7919.

 American literature. Criticism in *New York Tribune* (1870). 1800–1899.
 Hay, John. Treatment of Western American literature; especially Harte, Bret; CLEMENS, SAMUEL. I:7902.

 American literature. Fiction. 1800–1999.
 Treatment of utopia; especially CLEMENS, SAMUEL; London, John Griffith. Dissertation abstract. I:7369.

 American literature. Fiction. 1800–1899.
 Melville, Herman. Treatment of women; relationship to myth; the quest; compared to CLEMENS, SAMUEL; Hemingway, Ernest. Application of theories of Campbell, Joseph: *The Hero with a Thousand Faces;* Neumann, Erich: *Die grosse Mutter.* Dissertation abstract. I:8140.

 American literature. Fiction by Afro-American writers. 1900–1999.
 Point of view compared to CLEMENS, SAMUEL: *The Adventures of Huckleberry Finn* . I:8700.

FIGURE 4.14   An entry on "Samuel Clemens" from the *Subject Index* of the *MLA Bibliography*

Source: Reprinted by permission of the Modern Language Association of America from the *MLA International Bibliography* (Subject Index), 1984, p. G235. Copyright © 1985 by the MLA.

American literature / 1800–1899

CLEMENS, SAMUEL (1835–1910) / *Novel* **/** *The Adventures of Tom Sawyer (1876)*

Novel / The Adventures of Huckleberry Finn (1884)

[7039]   Abderabou, Abdelrahman A. "The Human Dimensions in Multicultural Relations: A Critical Study of Twain's *Huckleberry Finn.*" *JEn* . 1986 Sept.; 14: 1–5. [†Treatment of black-white relations.]

[7040]   Anderson, David D. "Mark Twain, Sherwood Anderson, Saul Bellow, and the Territories of the Spirit." *Midamerica* . 1986; 8: 116–124. [†Treatment of spiritual journey; relationship to American experience compared to Anderson, Sherwood: *Winesburg. Ohio;* Bellow, Saul: *The Adventures of Augie March* .]

[7041]   Barrow, David. "The Ending of *Huckleberry Finn:* Mark Twain's Cryptic Lament." *CCTEP* . 1986 Sept.; 51: 78–84. [†Narrative ending.]

[7042]   Berry, Wendell. "Writer and Region." *HudR* . 1987 Spring; 40(1): 15–30. [†Treatment of place; escape; relationship to community; the individual; society.]

[7043]   Bird, John. " 'These Leather-Faced People': Huck and the Moral Art of Lying." *SAF* . 1987 Spring; 15(1): 71–80. [†Treatment of Finn, Huckleberry (character): relationship to falsehood.]

FIGURE 4.15   An entry from the *Classified Listings with Author Index* from the *MLA Bibliography*

Source: Reprinted by permission of the Modern Language Association of America from the *MLA International Bibliography* (Classified Listings with Author Index), 1987, p. 175. Copyright © 1987 by the MLA.

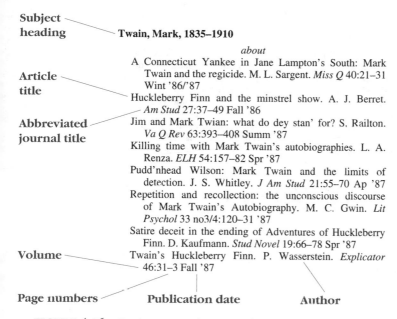

Subject heading — Twain, Mark, 1835–1910

about

Article title — A Connecticut Yankee in Jane Lampton's South: Mark Twain and the regicide. M. L. Sargent. *Miss Q* 40:21–31 Wint '86/'87

Huckleberry Finn and the minstrel show. A. J. Berret. *Am Stud* 27:37–49 Fall '86

Abbreviated journal title — Jim and Mark Twian: what do dey stan' for? S. Railton. *Va Q Rev* 63:393–408 Summ '87

Killing time with Mark Twain's autobiographies. L. A. Renza. *ELH* 54:157–82 Spr '87

Pudd'nhead Wilson: Mark Twain and the limits of detection. J. S. Whitley. *J Am Stud* 21:55–70 Ap '87

Repetition and recollection: the unconscious discourse of Mark Twain's Autobiography. M. C. Gwin. *Lit Psychol* 33 no3/4:120–31 '87

Satire deceit in the ending of Adventures of Huckleberry Finn. D. Kaufmann. *Stud Novel* 19:66–78 Spr '87

Volume — Twain's Huckleberry Finn. P. Wasserstein. *Explicator* 46:31–3 Fall '87

Page numbers — Publication date — Author

FIGURE 4.16 Entries on "Mark Twain" from the *Humanities Index*

Source: From the *Humanities Index,* April 1987–March 1988. Copyright © 1987, 1988 by The H. W. Wilson Company. Reprinted by permission.

Figure 4.16 shows an article entry about "Mark Twain" taken from the *Humanities Index*.

Notice that most of the journals cited are published quarterly rather than monthly. Thus, for the article "Twain's Huckleberry Finn," published in the *Explicator,* a *Fall 1987* publication date is cited rather than the month and year.

Journal Article Abstracts. Journals and the articles they contain are listed for nearly every field of study in a number of specialized indexes. You can often save time by reading an *abstract,* a condensed version of an article, in one of the many abstract references providing such article summaries. Most abstracts are identified by number and indexed according to subject in the abstract source itself. Figure 4.17 shows a summary of an article from *Psychological Abstracts* on *disclosure,* the therapeutic process of revealing private information about oneself. As the example shows, an abstract gives all the information you need—author, title, date, volume, page numbers—to cite the abstract in your Works Cited section or to locate the complete article. If you intend to read both the abstract and the complete article during your research, make a separate working bibliography card or computer file entry for each.

While abstracts are useful for general or background information, they should not serve as major sources for your research paper's discussion.

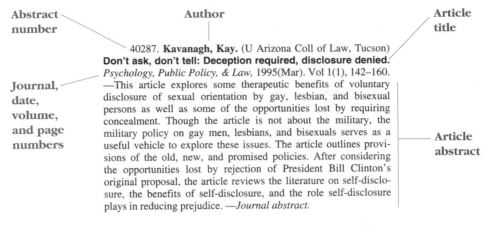

Abstract number

Author

Article title

Journal, date, volume, and page numbers

Article abstract

40287. **Kavanagh, Kay.** (U Arizona Coll of Law, Tucson) **Don't ask, don't tell: Deception required, disclosure denied.** *Psychology, Public Policy, & Law,* 1995(Mar). Vol 1(1), 142–160. —This article explores some therapeutic benefits of voluntary disclosure of sexual orientation by gay, lesbian, and bisexual persons as well as some of the opportunities lost by requiring concealment. Though the article is not about the military, the military policy on gay men, lesbians, and bisexuals serves as a useful vehicle to explore these issues. The article outlines provisions of the old, new, and promised policies. After considering the opportunities lost by rejection of President Bill Clinton's original proposal, the article reviews the literature on self-disclosure, the benefits of self-disclosure, and the role self-disclosure plays in reducing prejudice. —*Journal abstract.*

FIGURE 4.17 An article abstract from *Psychological Abstracts*

Source: From *Psychological Abstracts,* Vol. 82, No. 11, November 1995, p. 82. Copyright © 1995 by the American Psychological Association. Reprinted by permission.

Instead, use a journal abstract to determine whether the original article may be useful enough to seek out and read fully. If it is, use the publication information provided by the abstract to find the article and read it in complete form.

Many specialized journals titled as indexes also include abstracts. Familiarity with the common indexes of your research field will acquaint you with those that do. The following list provides a small sampling of the many indexes and abstracts available at most college and public libraries:

Applied Science & Technology Index, 1913–date (available online)
Art Index, 1929–date (available online)
Art Literature International, 1973–date (available online)
Biological & Agricultural Index, 1913–date
Business Periodicals Index, 1958–date
Child Development Abstracts and Bibliography, 1927–date
Education Index, 1929–date (available online)
Film Literature Index, 1973–date
General Science Index, 1978–date (available online)
Hispanic American Periodicals Index, 1974–date
Historical Abstracts, 1914–date (available online)
Humanities Index, 1974–date (available online)
Index Medicus, 1960–date (available online)
Index to Legal Periodicals, 1908–date (available online)
Index to United States Government Periodicals, 1974–date
Nutrition Abstracts and Reviews, 1931–date

Pollution Abstracts, 1970–date (available online)
Psychological Abstracts, 1927–date (available online)
Public Affairs Information Index, 1915–date
Social Sciences Index, 1974–date [previously part of *Social Sciences and Humanities Index,* 1965–74] (available online)
Women Studies Abstracts, 1972–date

If you need to know if a particular journal is listed in an index or abstract, consult the comprehensive references given in Appendix B or one of these index sources:

Magazines for Libraries: For the General Reader and School, Junior College, College, University, and Public Libraries. Eds. Bill Katz and Linda Sternberg Katz. New York: Bowker, 2000.
Standard Periodical Directory: 2002. New York: Oxbridge, 2001.
Ulrich's International Periodicals Directory 2002. Ed. R. R. Bowker. New York: Bowker, 2001.

Newspaper Indexes

Newspapers report current facts and opinions. While they do not provide the studied or scholarly insights journal or magazine articles offer, newspapers contain valuable current information about such subjects as economics, social trends, politics, sporting events, crime, and fashion. Not all newspapers are indexed, but you can use those that are to find the date of an event. Once you have the date, you can locate information about the event in any nonindexed newspaper.

New York Times Index. You will find the *New York Times Index* (1851–date) available in book form, microfilm, or online at most libraries. As an index to the *New York Times,* it lists news stories by subject and provides summaries of them. Similar to the *Readers' Guide* in its entry format, the *Index* cross references items with *see* and *see also;* indicates whether an article is short (*S*), medium (*M*), or long (*L*); and lists the date, section, and column number for each item.

Other Newspaper Indexes. Like the *New York Times,* other major newspapers—such as the *Chicago Tribune, Christian Science Monitor, Los Angeles Times, Wall Street Journal,* and *Washington Post*—are also individually indexed. You can find and compare articles in several of these and other newspapers at the same time by consulting the following comprehensive general indexes:

Index to Black Newspapers, 1977–date (on microfilm).
National Newspaper Index, 1979–date (carries last 4 years of the *New York Times* and, depending on the library's selection, the *Atlanta*

Constitution, Boston Globe, Chicago Tribune, Christian Science Monitor, Los Angeles Times, Wall Street Journal, and *Washington Post*

Newsbank, 1980–date (indexes articles from over 450 U.S. newspapers; available in print, CD–ROM, and online)

Newspaper Abstracts OnDisc (CD–ROM), 1985–date, monthly (libraries that subscribe get the *New York Times* and select among the *Atlanta Constitution, Boston Globe, Chicago Tribune, Christian Science Monitor, Los Angeles Times, Wall Street Journal,* and *Washington Post;* available online as *Newspaper and Periodical Abstracts*).

Newspaper and Periodical Abstracts, 1985–date, monthly (available online through OCLC FirstSearch; same as *Newspaper and Periodical Abstracts* on CD–ROM, above)

NEXIS, 1977–date (indexes over 50 national newspapers, including the full text of the *New York Times;* available online)

Other newspapers also may be indexed locally. Use the *Gale Directory of Publications and Broadcast Media* (Detroit: Gale, 2001) to locate, by state and then by city, publishers of small and large newspapers nationwide, or check with your library for newspapers you need information about. Almost any newspaper is available by writing to the local library or arranging for a microfilm copy through interlibrary loan.

Many major newspapers allow free online access to full-text articles only for current issues. A subject search of the paper's archives will yield abstracts of pertinent articles, but a fee is often required to access the complete article. Figure 4.18 shows an abstract of a *New York Times* article about Internet dating that was accessed online. If you don't wish to pay the fee to retrieve the full-text article, note the date and page number, then check to see whether the newspaper is available in your library's holdings. Keep in mind that you can also cite the abstract itself in your paper if the full-text article is unavailable. (See pp. 296–99 for listing online sources in the Works Cited section of a paper.)

Newspapers Online

Many newspapers are now online independently, making current and past issues available on the Internet. You can find which newspapers are online and links to their websites at the Internet Public Library—Online Newspapers (www.ipl.org/reading/news/). Here is a sampling of major newspapers and their online addresses:

Boston Globe Online	http://www.boston.com/
Chicago Tribune	http://www.chicagotribune.com/
Detroit Free Press	http://www.freep.com/
Houston Chronicle	http://www.cron.com/

CIRCUITS | January 18, 2001. Thursday
On the Internet, Love Really Is Blind
By JOYCE COHEN (NYT) 1788 words
Late Edition—Final. Section G. Page 1. Column 2

ABSTRACT: Few people find true love over the Internet, and psychologists believe that chat rooms, message boards and especially online dating services may have built-in mechanisms that make any offscreen romance very likely to fail; they say that online correspondence makes people feel they have a strong connection, but that nonverbal communication, with its motion and activity, is essential to discovering a real bond with another person; photo; drawing (M)

FIGURE 4.18   An abstract of a newspaper article accessed online from the *New York Times*
Source: Copyright © 2001 by The New York Times Co. Reprinted by permission.

Los Angeles Times	http://www.latimes.com/
Minneapolis Star Tribune	http://www.startribune.com/
New York Times	http://www.nytimes.com/
Philadelphia Enquirer	http://www.phillynews.com
San Francisco Chronicle	http://www.sfgate.com/
San Jose Mercury News	http://www.sjmercury.com/
USA Today Online	http://www.usatoday.com/
Wall Street Journal	http://interactive.wsj.com/
Washington Post	http://www.washingtonpost.com/

Periodical Files or Serials Lists

Magazines, journals, and newspapers available in your library are listed in a periodicals file or serials list. The list may be in book form, on microfiche, or online at a computer terminal, with each periodical title listed alphabetically. Under the title of the periodical, such lists typically provide publication information, a description of the periodical, its location in the library, and the issues included in the library's collection. Entries without call numbers are shelved alphabetically in the library's periodical section. Figure 4.19 shows an entry from a library serials lists.

```
        Title:    American Health
  Other Title:    A.H.
Dates Covered:    Vol.1, no.1 (Mar./Apr. 1982) -
    Published:    [New York, N.Y. : American Health
                  Partners, c1982-]
  Description:    v. : ill.; 28 cm.
   Subject(s):    Health—periodicals
                  Health—periodicals
        Notes:    Title from cover.
      Library:    BIOMED LIB Call number: W1 AM227
  Library has:    U3N1-3, 5-9 (1984) b4-7 (1985-88)
                  U8N1 (1989)
                  Library has current subscription
```

FIGURE 4.19   A periodical entry from a library serials file

Indexes to Literature in Collections

Most indexes direct you to complete works addressing one major subject almost exclusively. Quite often, however, you need only a certain *part* of a work—say, a brief discussion of a minor subject, a single essay or chapter, or other selection. Fortunately, you do not have to hunt through the indexes of several books to see if the material you want is included. Instead, you can consult subject indexes that locate material within complete works:

Biography Index. New York: Wilson, 1946–date
Essay and General Literature Index. New York: Wilson, 1900–date

The *Biography Index* lists information on people who have been written about in books or in the more than 2,000 popular and scholarly periodicals it cites. The *Biography Index* includes an alphabetized index, giving the date of birth, nationality, and occupation of each person listed in the volume. A second index cites individuals according to occupation. The *Biography Index* is available both in printed form and online as a database. Note that the printed version (see Figure 4.20) provides multiple examples of sources on a topic; however, the online database version (see Figure 4.21) gives only one entry at a time—a factor to consider if you must pay for searching for entries online.

The *Essay and General Literature Index* locates essays and parts of books for which there are no descriptive titles. Suppose you wanted to find some material about the influence that television talk shows have on

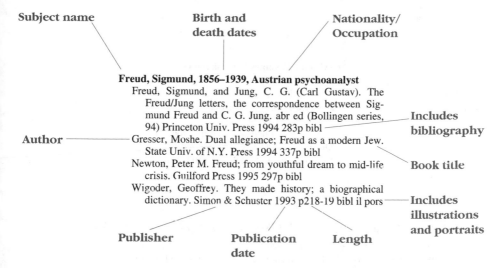

FIGURE 4.20   An entry on "Sigmund Freud" from the *Biography Index*

Source: From the *Biography Index,* September 1986–August 1988, p. 765. Copyright © 1986, 1987, 1988 by The H. W. Wilson Company. Reprinted by permission.

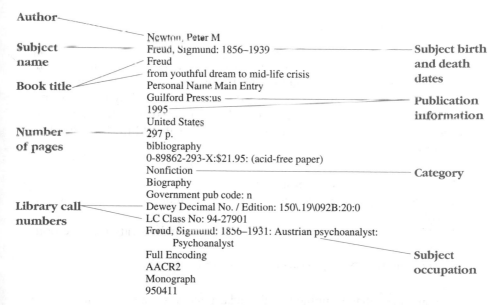

FIGURE 4.21   An entry from the *Biography Index* database

Source: From the *Biography Index* database, 1995. Copyright © 1995 by The H. W. Wilson Company. Reprinted by permission.

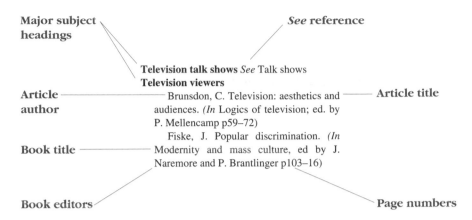

FIGURE 4.22   An excerpt from the *Essay and General Literature Index*

Source: From the *Essay and General Literature Index, 1990–1994*, p. 1633. Copyright © 1990, 1991, 1992, 1993, 1994 by The H. W. Wilson Company. Reprinted by permission.

children. By checking the *Essay and General Literature Index*, you could locate an essay titled "Television: Aesthetics and Audiences" in a work edited by P. Mellencamp, *Logics of Television* (see Figure 4.22).

Pamphlet Indexes

Libraries often maintain collections of pamphlets and other uncataloged printed material in *vertical files* (so named because items in them used to be filed standing upright rather than in file drawers). Pamphlets, flyers, newsletters, and other printed information distributed by local government agencies, clubs, businesses, and individuals are usually filed alphabetically by subject. Used appropriately, pamphlets can add fresh perspective to your research:

1. They can provide current information.
2. They usually discuss local issues or specific minor topics not addressed by other sources.
3. The presentation of technical material is generally written for the nonspecialist.
4. They often reflect opinions not available in other sources.

Remember that pamphlets and similar materials are sometimes written for other purposes than solely reporting information in an objective fashion. Weigh the content, authority, and objectivity of any pamphlet before relying on it too heavily in your research.

Besides investigating the vertical file of your own library, also consult the *Vertical File Index: A Subject Guide to Selected Pamphlet Material* (1935–date). Use this source to identify and order various pamphlets, brochures, and posters directly from their publishers. Figure 4.23 shows an entry from the *Vertical File Index* for a pamphlet on AIDS.

In addition, the United States government also publishes thousands of pamphlets and other small information items every year. Check your library's holdings, or consult the *Monthly Catalog of United States Government Publications* (discussed later in this chapter).

Finally, the most direct means of acquiring pamphlets and other such material is to go directly to places related to your research topic (see Chapter 5). Along with getting a firsthand perspective on your research, you may also discover pamphlet material unavailable in any other way.

Indexes to U.S. Government Publications and Documents

The documents that the United States government prints include reports, bibliographics, dictionaries, guidebooks, maps, posters, pamphlets, directories, magazines, and other resources. Government publications are published and printed by the Government Printing Office, or GPO, which then distributes them to designated depository libraries. There are two such

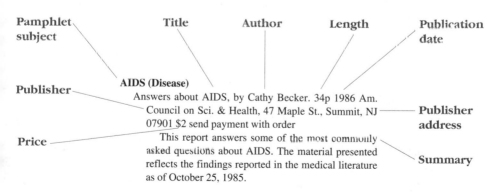

FIGURE 4.23 An entry from the *Vertical File Index*

Source: From the *Vertical File Index,* March 1986. Copyright © 1986 by The H. W. Wilson Company. Reprinted by permission.

depositories per congressional district and several others named in each state according to a range of criteria.

Many state, county, and college libraries serve as depositories for federal publications. Most of these, however, *select* the publications they receive because of the quantity available. Consequently, you may find that your own library either has no government documents available or has only a limited selection. If you know what document you want, ask your library to get it for you (usually in microform) through interlibrary loan. You can also write to this address to order a free copy of any government publication:

> Superintendent of Documents
> Government Printing Office
> Washington, DC 20402

Locating Government Documents in Printed Forms.   The printed forms of United States government documents are not always easy to locate. In most libraries, they are not cataloged with other related material nor are they always shelved in the same areas. Indeed, you will find that the call numbers given for government publications are not those of either the Dewey Decimal or Library of Congress systems. Instead, each documents is assigned what is known as a *Superintendent of Documents (SuDoc)* number and shelved according to the issuing agency, rather than the subject. The first letter in the SuDoc number indicates the government issuing agency (*J = Justice Department, L = Labor Department,* and so forth). The number following the letter is assigned by the Library of Congress for cataloging purposes. Thus, a publication with a SuDoc number such as *S 1.65/3:2734* is produced by the State Department and would be located with the other materials published by that agency.

The nature of this system prevents your browsing to find government material by subject and remains complicated, even for researchers with experience. Until you become familiar with government indexes and documents, you would be wise to work with a librarian to locate what you need.

Commercial as well as government-published guides to federal documents abound. The most comprehensive and generally up to date is:

> *Monthly Catalog of United States Government Publications.* Washington, DC: GPO, 1895–date (annual).

The *MC,* as the *Monthly Catalog* is known, lists the subject, author, title, and complete publishing data, including price, for all publications from United States government agencies. Published monthly, the *MC* supplies information from approximately 2,000 new government publications in each issue.

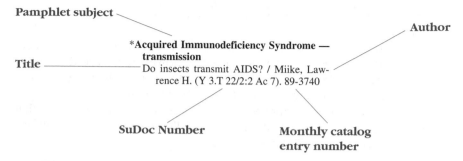

FIGURE 4.24   An entry from the Subject Index of the *Monthly Catalog*

You can locate a publication by first consulting the Subject Index of the *MC* (see Figure 4.24). Then use the entry number given there to find the complete listing in another part of the *Catalog* (see Figure 4.25).

For government documents published since January 1994, you can go to the online Catalog of Government Publications at *www.access.gpo.gov/su_docs/locators/cgp/index.html*. Many records available from government

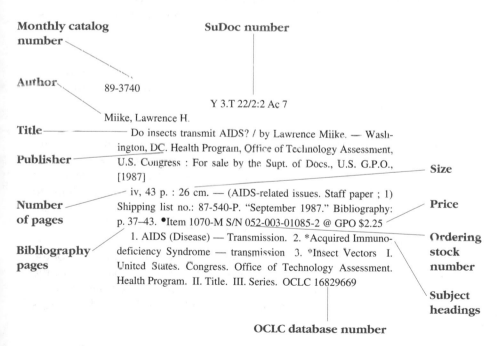

FIGURE 4.25   A pamphlet entry from the *Monthly Catalog*

agency websites are included, with direct links to the electronic text of the document.

Keep in mind that the *MC* is a bibliography; it therefore lists complete works, not the articles they include. You can, however, refer to the subject headings (Figure 4.25) given in the *MC* entry to decide whether the publication contains information that would be useful to you.

For an index to government periodicals and serial publications that does include the articles, consult one of the following, published by Public Affairs Information Service (PAIS):

> *PAIS International,* 1972–date (available on CD–ROM or online as "PAIS")
> *PAIS International in Print,* 1991–date
> *Public Affairs Information Service Bulletin,* 1915–76

Similar to the *Readers' Guide, PAIS* indexes about 1,500 periodicals, books, pamphlets, mimeographed materials, and state and city publications about government and legislation, economics, sociology, and political science.

If your research requires that you examine the reports of congressional committees, testimony of witnesses in congressional hearings, communications from the president to the Senate or House, or committee-prepared background on new legislation, consult the Congressional Information Service (CIS) annual *Index:*

> Congressional Information Service. *Annual Index and Abstracts to Publications of the United States Congress.* Washington, DC: Congressional Information Service, 1970–date.

This useful source appears monthly, with quarterly cumulations and an annual cumulation titled *CIS/Annual.* The *Annual* itself comprises two volumes, *Subjects and Names* and *Abstracts.* Use the first volume to search out a listing for a subject or a person's name; then use the *Abstracts* volume to get full information, including a summary of any report or activities. In addition, the database at *www.access.gpo.gov/congress/* provides access to congressional records published online.

The guides to government documents listed here are only a few of the hundred or more indexes and catalogs available. Every department of the government—from the Agriculture Department to the National Science Foundation to the Veterans Administration—publishes thousands of pages of information yearly. In addition to those sources discussed here, some 2,900 U.S. government publications in 83 subject areas are listed and annotated in:

Bailey, William G. *Guide to Popular U.S. Government Publications*. Littleton, CO: Libraries Unlimited, 1996.

Locating Government Sources Online

State and Local Government Online Resources.   Most city, county, and state governments now provide public records and other important information online through a home page or another accessible form. For example, the home page of the California State Senate at www.sen.ca.gov provides access to state government documents. If you were investigating a topic pertinent to New York City, you could go to the New York City Government Guide at www.ci.nyc.ny.us/ to find statistical or historical information. Contacting the Florida Department of Environmental Protection (www.dep.state.fl.us/default.htm) would be important for any research project relating to Florida's environment.

You should investigate any such online resources whenever you are researching issues related to local government or cities or nationwide topics that may have local impact. Contact a local bookstore for a directory of state or regional online services, or telephone relevant local agencies directly to ask about their online offerings. The Internet directories listed in the following section should also be helpful in finding online addresses for local information.

Federal Government Online Resources.   To reduce paper consumption and to improve the accessibility of public information, more and more federal government information is being placed online each year. Various types of information—ranging from government research data to congressional reports to the names and addresses of members of the House and Senate—are available today through the Internet. You can get information about the president and the White House and read presidential speeches as well as the latest White House press releases at www.whitehouse.gov. You can also go online to read the most recent national census report (www.census.gov).

Online government sources can be used free of charge when accessed directly over the Internet; others can be accessed through commercial providers, who charge fees for their services. You will find that the online

information at FedWorld (http://www.fedworld.gov) provides some of
the best resources and links to information about the federal government.
Here are additional useful online resources for state and federal government
information:

Congressional Quarterly	http://cq.com/
Council of State Governments	http://www.csg.org/
Federal Government Information	http://firstgov.gov
Federal Register	http://www.nara.gov/fedreg/
FedWorld	http://www.fedworld.gov/
GPO Access	http://www.access.gpo.gov/
U.S. Bureau of the Census	http://www.census.gov/
U.S. Congressperson	http://www.congress.org
U.S. House Website	http://www.house.gov/
U.S. Senate Website	http://www.senate.gov/
U.S. Supreme Court	http://www.supremecourtus.gov
U.S. Trade/Exporting/ Business Information	http://www.stat-usa.gov/

In addition to these online resources, a number of widely available
guides and Internet directories are helpful, including the following:

Ernst, Carl R., and Michael Sankey. *Public Records Online: The National Guide to Private & Government Online Sources of Public Records.* New York: Facts on File, 2000.

Hahn, Harley. *Harley Hahn's Internet & Web Yellow Pages 2001.* Berkley, CA: Osborne-McGraw, 2000.

Macmillan Development Team. *New Riders' Official Internet and World Wide Web Yellow Pages.* Indianapolis, IN: New Riders, 1998.

Maxwell, Bruce. *How to Access the Federal Government on the Internet 1999: Washington Online.* Washington, DC: Congressional, 1998.

Reviewing Your Library Search

Before assuming that your search for available library sources is complete,
take the time to review your working bibliography for balance and compre-

hensiveness. You will need sources reflecting a variety of viewpoints and depth of coverage. The number of books, magazines, journals, newspaper articles, or other sources you will need depends upon your topic and the research requirements of your instructor.

Thoroughly review your sources before proceeding too far with any of the activities described in the next chapter. That way, you can better decide how researching beyond campus and community libraries can benefit your research most.

WORKING WITH OTHERS

Establishing a working bibliography will be easier if you share insights and experiences with a classmate along the way. Use the following suggestions to review your understanding of library resources and the working bibliography discussed in this chapter.

- Share your knowledge of the campus library's general bibliographies, indexes, and abstracts with a classmate. Briefly explain the differences among each of these types of reference sources. Does each of you know where these resources are located and how to use them?

- Exchange working bibliographies with a classmate, preferably someone researching a topic related to your own. What differences do you see in the way you are both recording information? Has either of you overlooked a source that should be included in the bibliography?

- Explain citation indexes such as the *Social Sciences Citation Index* or another that you are familiar with. How might you use such indexes in your own research? If you do not understand how to use a citation index, team up with a classmate and ask a campus librarian to show you how to use these useful (but complex) resources.

- Locate the abstract for a published journal article, and compare it to the original. Does the abstract accurately summarize the article's major ideas? Would it make any difference if you read an abstract rather than an original article for your research?

- Located in major cities across the nation, Government Printing Office (GPO) bookstores provide hundreds of government publications, some free and some for sale. Check the local telephone book to see if

there is a GPO bookstore near you. If there is, you will find it reward-
ing to visit the bookstore with a friend to find current sources for research.

■ Exchange working bibliographies from time to time with a classmate to
review each other's list of sources. Are there an adequate number and
variety of sources? Are the sources current enough? Are the sources
varied enough in the points of view they represent?

CHAPTER 5

Researching beyond the Campus Library

As you collect and study materials for the research topic, you will want to broaden your investigations by looking beyond campus and community libraries. Going out in the community to observe sites and activities related to your research topic, for example, is an exceptionally valuable way to understand it more thoroughly. Special library and museum collections can provide scarce primary and secondary sources especially relevant to local and regional subjects. You can also interview experts or people with uncommon opinions and experiences, use surveys and questionnaires to collect original data, listen to radio and television programs, or get firsthand opinions by attending lectures, addresses, and speeches on issues of community and world importance.

Getting more familiar with your research topic in any of these ways provides concrete experiences with which to illustrate and to verify your research. These approaches put you directly in touch with the people, places, events, and objects most closely relevant to your research and understanding of the topic.

Using Primary and Secondary Sources

Going beyond your campus and community libraries also provides opportunities to work with both primary and secondary materials in your research. The majority of books and magazine articles you consult in the library are *secondary* materials, information compiled and interpreted by someone else. Such research sources are valuable in providing information and expert insights that would be unattainable otherwise. For most undergraduate research, secondary materials provide the foundation as well as most of the materials for studying and writing about any subject.

Primary research, on the other hand, results in your discovering your own information and opinions. When you research onsite, interview an authority, conduct a survey, or attend a lecture, your own observations and the materials you examine firsthand are primary sources. You may also do primary research in a library by studying letters, diaries, manuscripts, or literary works or by examining unpublished reports and research collected by others.

For instance, in a marine science course, you might do primary research charting the migration of Atlantic salmon; in a physics lab, you could do primary research measuring air samples to determine local pollution levels. As you can tell from these examples, working with primary materials means getting information directly from original sources and interpreting it on your own. (See also Chapter 1 on primary and secondary sources.)

THINKING CRITICALLY
ABOUT PRIMARY AND SECONDARY SOURCES

Compared to secondary sources, primary sources are often harder to come by, and using them may require more independent judgment in assessing their credibility and value. In fact, *both* kinds of sources will need close critical reading and thinking on your part (see Chapter 7). As you examine such materials, be alert to discrepancies in content or disagreement with other sources, and take care to distinguish between facts and opinions. Keep in mind that your goal in reading both primary and secondary sources is to synthesize their content and gather support for your own conclusions.

Observing Onsite

Reading as much as you can on a subject is essential to knowing it well and being able to make the most of related information. Researching onsite, however, to see and study something firsthand, engages your insight differently. By going to the places and events most directly connected with your topic, you will better understand that topic's importance in other people's lives. While books and articles can tell you about the plight of people who are homeless and living on the streets of America, you will understand their condition far better by visiting local state or federal agencies to talk directly with people trying to assist the homeless. If you are researching the problem the United States faces in disposing of its thousands of tons of trash every week, visit the local city or county dump. The experience may not be wholly pleasant, but you will understand the problem as never before.

Going onsite to explore your research topic more thoroughly will inspire other creative means to gather information for your research. Depending upon your purpose, you may need to make onsite observations to complete your research in several ways:

- *Record behavior:* For example, record social gestures of children at play; describe the actions of police officers making an arrest; test the responses of animals to human and nonhuman sounds.

- *Describe conditions:* Characterize damage from a hurricane; investigate conditions at an animal research laboratory; report on the working environment of air traffic controllers.
- *Examine primary material:* Compare organically and nonorganically grown fruits and vegetables; study a museum painting; examine a historical document; take notes at a lecture or interview.

**THINKING CRITICALLY
ABOUT ONSITE OBSERVATIONS**

Accurate observation and reporting of data are difficult, even for a trained researcher. Remember that your first goal in any onsite observation is to record what you observe *objectively.* As much as possible, come to your subject without expectations about what you will see. Then, as you record your observations, try to refrain from interpreting them or making judgments. Doing so can color and even bias how you perceive and take notes about your subject. Save interpretations until after your observations are complete.

You may later want to return to your site and observe again to confirm your interpretations of what you recorded.

While onsite observation may appear more interesting in some ways than library research, remember that it is not easy to do effectively. Thoughtful preparation before you get onsite can make the difference between conducting a research study and making a tourist visit.

To ensure the effectiveness of your onsite studies, follow these steps for any observation research you do:

1. *Plan your onsite research as early as possible.* List it in your research schedule, along with any arrangements you will need to make for reservations, permissions, tickets, or transportation. For any onsite visit, ask ahead of time about limitations or required authorizations. If you plan to use a camera or tape recorder at the site, find out if such equipment is allowed. In addition, be sure to schedule enough time to complete the objectives of your research visit.

2. *Make a checklist of what you want to observe.* If you will be studying patients in a hospital ward, include the frequency, conditions, and extent of the behaviors to note. If you are making a study of playground equipment at city parks, make a checklist to record the types, conditions, and times of use and nonuse. If you are studying a historical document, list the features you want especially to note. Keep any checklist limited to what you can observe and record with accuracy. It is easy to get so caught up in observing as to forget the purpose of your visit. Once onsite, *use* the checklist to keep your activities focused on the research question you seek to answer. Also add to the checklist as needed.

3. *Take notes during and right after any onsite observation.* Use your research notebook to record factual descriptions of any artifacts or other objects you examine as part of your research study. In an appropriately labeled separate area of the notebook, write down any personal impressions and ideas for later use.

4. *Collect pamphlets, brochures, maps, and other explanatory materials about your topic or about any artifacts you observe at the site.* (Make certain that you never remove any artifacts themselves or other objects that are parts of an exhibit or observation site, however!) You need not bring home a whole library, but collecting available materials can prove valuable later. You might need to review the materials again or draw more extensively upon them than you had originally planned. Make bibliography cards for all such materials if you think you might use them in your paper (see Chapter 4).

The onsite investigation you do now for a research paper will prepare you for the kind of advanced field or laboratory research you may do later for other college courses or a career. It requires training for such observational research to be carried out effectively and for its results to carry any authority. Check with your instructor about your plans before proceeding too far, and exercise careful judgment when you incorporate the results of your investigation in your paper. Done with care and used as a supplement to your other research, any one of the activities described here can enrich the content and individualized approach of your research paper.

Researching Society and Museum Libraries

You can spend an interesting afternoon exploring your city's museum and private society libraries. These facilities may help you discover research ideas and locate primary and secondary resources that might be unavailable at academic and public libraries.

Society Libraries

Local as well as national societies exist in every part of the United States, varying in size as well as purpose. Sometimes called *clubs, lodges, federations, associations,* or *leagues,* such societies are formed by people sharing interests in particular subjects. The libraries they sponsor for their own collecting and research purposes can often provide unusual or hard-to-find primary sources for your research.

Investigate the societal organizations in your local area. You will find groups interested in nearly every subject imaginable: the Civil War, gardening, people with disabilities, bird watching, genealogy, literary topics, the environment, and star gazing, to name just a few examples. Almost every region has at least one local historical society, a good place to start for any topic on a local issue.

The members of such groups range from beginning enthusiasts to informed amateurs and scholars. Any members can provide assistance with your topic or may be willing to serve as the subject for an interview.

A society library may be open only to experienced researchers or perhaps just members; nonmembers may pay a small fee for public use. To locate society libraries near you, consult the telephone book or one of the sources listed later in this chapter (see Finding Special Libraries and Museums).

Museum Libraries

Local museums are excellent sources of information and bibliographic materials on dozens of subjects, including art, history, literature, science, and popular culture. Not only can pamphlets and exhibit materials prove useful primary resources for your research, but the museum's own library may also be available for limited public use.

Check ahead of time with the museum staff about research privileges and the availability of materials for your topic. If you cannot use the materials in the museum library, take advantage of the museum exhibits. You can add available information about them to your list of bibliographic sources. It is also likely that someone on the museum library staff may be able to give you information or direct you to other libraries and resources.

Finding Special Libraries and Museums

The telephone book's Yellow Pages are the handiest reference to societies and museums in your area. In addition to the *American Library Directory* (mentioned in Chapter 2), a number of excellent guides to special libraries and museum collections found nationally are available. Entries from the *Directory of Special Libraries and Information Centers,* for example, indicate the size and type of collection a library has, if it is a government depository, and whether it offers computerized information services (see Figure 5.1). Use such sources as the *Directory of Special Libraries* to locate materials in your local area or to investigate the possibilities of acquiring them in microform or through interlibrary loan. Among the most useful library directories and special collections resources are the following, all published by Gale Research and the R. R. Bowker Company:

American Library Directory, 2001–2002. New York: Bowker, 2001.
International Research Centers Directory. Detroit: Gale, 2001.
Official Museum Directory 2000. New York: Bowker, 1999.
Research Centers Directory. 2 vols. Detroit: Gale, 2001.
Subject Directory of Special Libraries. Detroit: Gale, 2002.

Museums Online.   Thanks to the Internet, you can visit many museums from home. The Smithsonian Institution, in Washington, DC, for example, provides online information about current displays and photographs as

★ **15003** ★
Solano County Library - Special Collections (Rare Book)
1150 Kentucky St.
Fairfield, CA 94533   Phone: (707)421-6510
Founded: 1914.   **Special Collections:** Donovan J. McCune Collection
(printing history, rare books; 1500 volumes); U.S. and state government
documents depository (5000 volumes); local history (500 volumes). **Services:**
Interlibrary loan; copying; collections open to the public; Donovan J.
McCune Collection open to the public by appointment. **Automated
Operations:** Computerized cataloging, acquisitions, and circulation.
Computerized Information Services: DIALOG Information Services;
OnTyme Electronic Message Network Service (electronic mail service).
Performs searches free of charge. **Networks/Consortia:** Member of North
Bay Cooperative Library System (NBCLS). **Remarks:** FAX: (707)421-7474.

FIGURE 5.1   Entry from the *Directory of Special Libraries and Information Centers*

Source: From *Directory of Special Libraries and Information Centers,* 15th Edition, edited by
Janice DeMaggio and Debra M. Kirby. Copyright © 1992 Gale Research, Inc. Reproduced by
permission of The Gale Group.

well as excerpts from museum exhibits (www.si.edu/). You can also visit
the University of California's Museum of Paleontology and WWW Subway
(http://www.ucmp.berkeley.edu/) for a multimedia museum display, paleontology database information, and links to other museums and websites
around the world. Here are some of the many Internet resources for finding
information about museums or for visiting them online:

Art Museum Network	http://www.amn.org/
Musée	http://www.musee-online.org/
Museum Computer Network	http://www.mcn.edu/sitesonline.htm
Museum Links	http://www.pp.iij4u.or.jp/~murai/e.homepage.html
University of California, BerkeleyMuseum Informatics Project	http://www.mip.berkeley.edu/
WWW Virtual Library	http://www.comlab.ox.ac.uk/archive/other/museums.html

Finding Other Sources of Research

Not all useful collections of books, magazines, pamphlets, business reports,
tax ledgers, production schedules, flowcharts, policy statements, consumer
profiles, and case histories are stored in places called *libraries.* Your com-

munity and its surrounding area undoubtedly offer hundreds of places to investigate for research materials. Here are a few of the most common:

- Foreign consulates and embassies provide information covering the education, health care, politics, history, art, and economics of their respective countries.
- Large businesses and corporations maintain collections of data and reference materials pertinent to their operations.
- Hospitals and state and local health departments offer brochures on disease and health care and maintain small libraries for staff research.
- Radio and television stations maintain transcripts of news broadcasts, documentaries, and interviews as well as biography files and reference sources.
- Newspaper offices keep files of past issues that may not be available at libraries.
- Chambers of Commerce provide visitors and interested investors with financial reports, tax schedules, transportation studies, and related business information.

In addition, police departments, social service agencies, water and power departments, zoos, museums, churches, and forestry services all keep records and will provide printed information on a variety of subjects to anyone interested. Your family dentist probably has a small library for his or her own practice, and many of your friends or relatives no doubt have collections of resources about hobbies or special topics. Someone in your family undoubtedly has a scrapbook, a genealogy record, letters, mementos, a diary, or old news clippings that have been stored in a closet or garage for years.

In short, everyone collects information, and libraries are anywhere people store it. Think about and look into all the possible local resources for information as you begin to do your research. Remember to make out a preliminary citation card for any material you investigate in public agencies or business and private collections. Follow the appropriate form for each type, and give the necessary information (see Chapter 4).

Interviews

An *interview* can provide you with current information and personal insights that may not result from consulting other sources. In addition, information from an interview can add a dimension of human interest to a paper that might otherwise be mainly statistical or simply monotonous for other reasons. Taped interviews and those conducted on television or radio allow you to hear from experts and well-known personalities who might otherwise be unavailable to you. The most profitable interviews, however, can be the ones you conduct yourself, directing the questions to focus specifically on the primary information you need for your research paper.

Determining the Purpose

Because of the time required to prepare for and conduct an interview, assess its usefulness and purpose beforehand. Do not include an interview in your research only to add a primary source to your paper's bibliography or just to avoid learning about your topic through more ordinary materials. Instead, use an interview when your critical assessment of the paper's sources indicates a need to strengthen certain areas of your thesis argument or to balance the paper's discussion with other points of view.

An interview will be useful to your research any time it fulfills one or more of the following purposes:

- Provides more current information than other sources
- Samples opinions or viewpoints not usually presented elsewhere
- Answers questions other sources have not sufficiently addressed
- Gives you examples that illustrate and support other research
- Records the responses of a recognized authority to questions specifically focused on your research topic or research question

Selecting the Right Person

People with knowledge about your research subject are probably easier to locate than you might think. You may already know family members or friends who would be valuable subjects. Certainly, the professors on your own college campus are knowledgeable about or directly involved with many types of research topics. City, county, and government employees—from police officers to engineers to social workers—are also informed and usually willing sources to consult. Local societies, associations, hospitals, museums, private businesses, and political organizations are just a few of the many other places you will find people to discuss your research with you. Use your local telephone directory or the Chamber of Commerce to contact businesses in your community. You can also use the *Directory of Special Libraries* (described earlier) to locate individuals with special knowledge or experience in almost any subject.

Scheduling the Appointment

It is usually appropriate to schedule an interview a week or two ahead to allow you and the interviewee time to prepare. Contact the person by telephone or letter, identifying yourself and the purpose of the interview. Establish a few ground rules that you both agree upon concerning permissible subjects, tape recording, approval to quote, and so forth. Be sure to indicate the approximate amount of time you will need (1 to 1-1/2 hours is

> **THINKING CRITICALLY**
> **ABOUT SELECTING INTERVIEW SUBJECTS**
>
> The value of interview research depends significantly upon the choice of the *interviewee*, the person to be interviewed. Remember that not everyone interested in or connected with a research topic qualifies as a good subject to interview. Your neighborhood mechanic may be an expert on the difficulties of repairing or getting parts for certain models of cars, but the local Nissan dealer will know more about consumer trends in auto buying. Your chemistry professor may have some opinions about how his Ford Bronco behaves on mountain roads, but the ideas of a professional test driver will carry a lot more weight in a paper discussing automobile safety standards.

generally long enough). Make your introduction concise and polite, something like this:

> My name is Jeanette Carson, and I'm a student at Bluffs College. I am doing a research paper on air traffic control problems in our area, and I wondered if I could have an hour of your time for an interview. I'd like to find out about conditions at the local airport and what plans there may be for changes there in the future.

Ask the interviewee what day, time, and place would be convenient, and adjust your own activity schedule accordingly.

Preparing for the Interview

Avoid using valuable interview time to ask needless or unfocused questions. Do a sufficient amount of preliminary reading and thinking about the research topic beforehand. Then plan and write out a list of questions focusing on information needed for your research. Use these questions to direct the interview, but do not follow them so strictly that you inhibit the discussion. In order to evoke the interviewee's ideas on the topic, avoid questions that promote only "yes" or "no" responses. Twelve to fifteen questions should allow enough time for you and the interviewee to get acquainted, discuss your topic, and pursue any helpful digressions in detail.

Conducting the Interview

Be on time to the interview, and come equipped with pencils or pens and a notebook (and a tape recorder if the interviewee has agreed to its use). Avoid taking notes or taping the first few questions and answers until your subject gets used to the situation.

Start the interview with a general inquiry about the person's background and interest in the interview topic. Then move on to the questions you have prepared. Maintain a polite, attentive manner while you listen and ask questions. Allow time for the interviewee to complete his or her responses. When clarification or additional information would be helpful, ask follow-up questions, such as "Why do you feel the data are unreliable?" or "I don't know what a tokamak reactor is. Can you explain it to me, please?"

Interview Structures

Some researchers favor a *structured* interview, which restricts responses to interview questions and keeps the discussion closely focused. However, an *unstructured* approach, which allows the discussion to move with the interests of the interviewee, can often generate more useful material. Avoid getting bogged down in clearly irrelevant subjects, but do not worry too much if your interviewee brings up unexpected topics: Brief digressions about an exceptional incident or a personal triumph may yield rich new insights or information for your paper. If the discussion wanders too far afield, return to your prepared questions to bring things back into focus.

Quoting from the Interview

If you do not tape the interview, take careful notes throughout the session. Make a point of quoting authoritative, insightful, or fascinating comments word for word. Because they come from a live interview source, such remarks will add rich authority and interest to your final paper. At the completion of the interview, read aloud any direct quotations you have written down to check their accuracy with the interviewee.

Interview Length

Try to keep to the hour or so you had originally scheduled so the interviewee does not run out of time. That way, you will not have to schedule a second meeting in order to get all of your questions answered.

Before the interview ends, briefly read over or summarize all of your notes for the interviewee to hear and to suggest additions or changes, if necessary. Be sure to thank the person for the interview. Take the time later to send a follow-up note, again expressing your appreciation and indicating how helpful the interview was to your research paper.

Figure 5.2 contains an excerpt from one student's interview with a practicing attorney who also taught at the law school at her campus. To guide the interview, the student used questions she had prepared and typed ahead of time. Notice that she recorded her own summaries and the attorney's words while conducting the interview.

4. As an attorney yourself, do you think you should serve or be allowed to serve on juries?

Yes—sees it as a civic responsibility. Lawyer's presence may not make a big difference. "People will still see the evidence the way they want to." Attorneys could "bring a little extra insight" to their own part of the decision.

5. A lot of people hold a pretty low opinion of juries and the jury process right now. How do you feel about juries?

Trusts juries. They represent the community, or they are supposed to. Admits that juries can be manipulated, but most jury decisions are "the right ones."

FIGURE 5.2   Prepared questions and handwritten notes from a personal interview

Using Telephone or Mail Interviews

A number of factors—including your and the interviewee's schedules and proximity to one another—may make a telephone or mail interview more practical than meeting personally. Because of the cost of telephoning and the limited discussion allowed by mail, however, both types of interviews require more planning than a personal conference might.

Telephone Interviews.   A telephone interview is convenient, but it can also can be expensive. Another drawback is that it forfeits your opportunity to meet directly with the authority you have chosen to interview. Use your best telephone personality to encourage your source to enjoy the discussion enough to talk freely and to volunteer information. To avoid catching the interview subject at an inconvenient time, use the first telephone call to set up a time for the actual interview. Then follow these suggestions while conducting the telephone interview:

1. Prepare a list of well-focused questions ahead of time.
2. At the start of the telephone interview, restate your purpose and set a time limit for the interview. Doing so will ensure that both of you use the time productively.

3. Ask the interviewee to summarize his or her knowledge of or experience with the topic.

4. Ask the interview questions and take notes on the responses. Remember to keep track of time so you avoid a costly bill or take too much of the respondent's time.

5. When the interview ends, thank the respondent and ask if you may call again if you have any further questions. A brief thank-you note or follow-up call when the paper is finished will show your appreciation for the help you received.

Mail Interviews.   Interviews done by mail allow the interviewee to answer your questions more carefully and on his or her own time. In addition, written responses provide accurate notes for your paper and usually give you more details to work with. You can also use mail interviews to correspond with several persons at once, thus getting multiple replies to the same questions.

Of course, a drawback to mail interviews is that, like those done over the telephone, you lose the opportunity of meeting and talking directly with your sources. In addition, people responding to mail interviews may not always do so quickly enough to meet researchers' deadlines. Rather than count on one particular source for an interview, contact more than a single person for mail interviews or be prepared to go forward with your research should a response not arrive soon enough.

If you decide to use a mail interview, follow these suggestions:

1. Contact the person ahead of time by phone or mail. This will ensure that he or she is willing and prepared to respond to your inquiry.

2. Prepare a list of questions to be answered in writing. Keep the questions specific, focused on the research topic, and to a minimum. Ten to twelve well-focused questions is probably enough.

3. Send a cover letter and self-addressed, stamped envelope with the questions. The cover letter should explain the purpose and scope of your research as well as the extent of the answers you expect and the date by which you need a response.

4. Promptly acknowledge any response you receive. A brief follow-up note after the paper is finished will also show your appreciation.

One overall suggestion should be emphasized separately: The interview source will respond more willingly if he or she sees that you are serious enough about your research to write with care. Make necessary revisions to a draft before writing and sending out a final version of any correspondence. Check a dictionary for help with spelling. Consult your college writing handbook for questions about grammar, style, and letter formats.

Online Interviews. Interviewing someone online offers the immediacy of a telephone interview but at a lower cost, usually. Moreover, with an online interview, you have the added convenience of being able to print or download the interview for later review.

You can contact many kinds of experts through Internet newsgroups or special discussion groups, listed in resources such as *New Riders' Official Internet Yellow Pages* or other Internet guides (see Chapter 6). Online services such as CompuServe and America Online often provide opportunities for discussions and interviews with experts or celebrities in a number of fields.

If you know the name of a person you want to interview, you can find out if he or she has an e-mail address through one of the "people-search" functions usually available through Internet search engines. You can also locate experts on a variety of subjects by using an Internet search engine such as Yahoo! or AltaVista. Using such an engine, a search for experts will turn up sites that will connect you with people willing to be interviewed or able to answer questions on your research subject. Here are some examples of sites:

Allexperts	http://www.expertcentral.com/
Ask a Reporter	http://www.nytimes.com/learning/students/ask_reporters/
Experts Database	http://experts.news.wisc.edu/
Go Ask Alice	http://www.goaskalice.columbia.edu/
Mad Science Network	http://www.madsci.org/

As is the case with any interaction over the Internet, always verify the identity of the person you contact and scrutinize the qualifications of anyone you interview.

Documenting the Interview

For any type of interview, make a preliminary citation card ahead of time. If you make use of the interview in your paper, include it in the Works Cited list, following one of the appropriate forms outlined in Chapters 11 and 12. Shown in Figure 5.3 is a sample bibliography card for a personal interview. Other than the identification of the type of interview conducted, information for a telephone or mail interview would be similar.

Robert Curry.

Personal interview. Nov. 24, 2001

FIGURE 5.3   A bibliography card for a personal interview

Surveys

If your research topic calls for characterizing the opinions, behaviors, or conditions of people in your local area, you may want to conduct a survey. A *survey* could provide statistical data for statements like "When asked if they would flirt with a friend's date, nearly two-thirds of the 350 students surveyed answered 'yes.'" You could also use a survey to learn the percentage of people in your city who are satisfied with their personal physicians or to find out how many hours a week students on your campus study. Surveys are also useful when you need to identify trends or make comparisons among groups or individuals (see Figure 5.4).

As with an interview, think ahead of time about the purpose of conducting a survey: What value will the evidence you collect bring to your paper, and how might these results relate to the information provided by other sources? Most importantly, consider how you will use the survey to support your paper's thesis.

Using Published Surveys

When should you use the results of published surveys versus those of surveys you have conducted yourself? Surveys of your own are best done to compare the characteristics of a local population with surveys done on a larger basis by others. For example, you may want to compare local attitudes about hunting with those identified by a national poll. Or you may want to compare the opinions of a certain group with the facts the rest of your research uncovers.

Whenever possible, however, it is generally best to use published surveys. So before you set up your own survey, check the statistical resources in your library. It is very likely that others have already compiled the kind of information you want or can use. The following sources are only a few

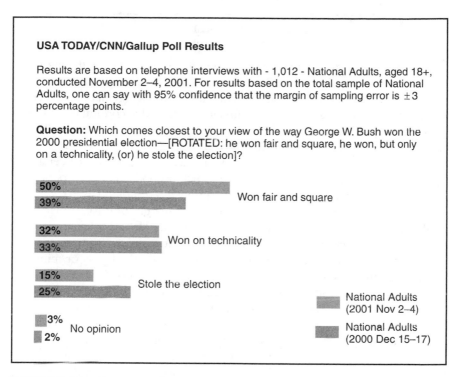

USA TODAY/CNN/Gallup Poll Results

Results are based on telephone interviews with - 1,012 - National Adults, aged 18+, conducted November 2–4, 2001. For results based on the total sample of National Adults, one can say with 95% confidence that the margin of sampling error is ±3 percentage points.

Question: Which comes closest to your view of the way George W. Bush won the 2000 presidential election—[ROTATED: he won fair and square, he won, but only on a technicality, (or) he stole the election]?

- 50% / 39% Won fair and square
- 32% / 33% Won on technicality
- 15% / 25% Stole the election
- 3% / 2% No opinion

National Adults (2001 Nov 2–4)
National Adults (2000 Dec 15–17)

FIGURE 5.4 An illustration of survey results comparing attitudes immediately after the 2000 presidential election and attitudes one year later

Source: From *USA Today,* November 5, 2001. Copyright 2001, USA Today. Reprinted by permission of USA Today and The Gallup Organization (www.gallup.com).

that provide statistical data, rankings, comparisons, and public opinion polls for nearly every subject and locality:

American Statistics Index. Washington, DC: Congressional Information Service, 1973- date.

The Gallup Poll. Princeton, NJ: The Gallup Organization. 1935–date. www.gallup.com

Statistical Reference Index. Washington, DC: Congressional Information Service, 1980–date.

Conducting Your Own Survey

Once you decide to conduct a survey of your own, remember that no survey is ever entirely accurate. A survey with even a fair degree of accuracy requires training to design and conduct. In addition, correctly interpreting a survey's results is usually a job for experts.

For the most part, expect to treat the results of any survey as *supplemental* to your other research. In most cases, it will be more descriptive than conclusive about, let's say, attitudes as to whether the United States should spend more money on fighting drugs through education.

**THINKING CRITICALLY ABOUT
PUBLISHED SURVEYS**

According to a definition attributed to the nineteenth-century British politician Benjamin Disraeli, there are three kinds of untruths; "lies, damned lies, and statistics." While this is an exaggeration, it is certainly true that polls and surveys, unless conducted according to generally accepted standards, can produce highly questionable results. The group of people questioned may not be representative of the general population, questions may be phrased in ways that tend to elicit certain answers, the topic may be one about which a good number of people tend not to answer honestly—these are only a few potential problems. Furthermore, every sampling has a statistical margin of error, a margin that may in some cases make the results meaningless. For example, a poll may put one political candidate's public support at 48% against an opponent's 52%; if the sample has a margin of error of plus or minus 4%, then the candidates' standings might, in fact, be just the opposite.

In general, you can rely at least on the accuracy of surveys conducted by reputable news organizations and well-known polling firms such as Gallup and Yankelovich. Be wary, however, of surveys conducted by advocacy groups or others with a vested interest in certain results. And do not always take statistics at face value—analyze the results for yourself and question any apparent discrepancies or claims that seem too far-reaching for those results. As with any published information, the fact that statistics find their way into print or onto the Internet is no guarantee of their accuracy.

Devising a Questionnaire.   To get started, you will need to devise a questionnaire to poll people about the information you want to know. You will get the best results from a questionnaire that is relatively short, easy to answer, and focused upon a single problem or related issues. The following suggestions will help you design a questionnaire that will be simple to administer and analyze for results:

1. *Define the questionnaire's purpose.* Begin by making a list of the specific information you want to gather. If you were researching the impact of the home video rental craze, you would make a list like this:

I want to know:
- Why people rent video movies
- How often people watch videos
- What kinds of videos they watch
- How they feel about commercials in rental videos
- How they feel about X-rated videos
- How much they pay for video rentals

Having defined what you want to know, you are ready to write your questions.

2. *Decide upon a question-and-answer format.* Frame your questions and their answers to suit the information you seek. Several types of questions and responses are possible.

    a. Open-ended questions allow respondents to answer in whatever way they choose. The variety of responses such questions allow, however, can make answers difficult to interpret and summarize. At the same time, responses to open-ended questions can also provide more details than answers to other types of questions, and they often reveal unexpected, useful information.

        Examples of open-ended questions:

- Why do you think watching movies as videos at home has become such a popular form of entertainment in the United States?
- What do you think the government should do to prevent oil spill disasters from tanker ships in U.S. coastal waters?

Because open-ended questions require more time to answer orally or in writing, you will get better results using no more than five or six per survey.

    b. Controlled-response or multiple-choice questions allow respondents to choose from a limited number of answers.

        Example of a controlled-response question:

- The government should tighten controls on tanker ships transporting oil within 10 miles of any U.S. coastline.
  _____ Agree   _____ Disagree   _____ Undecided

Be careful that each controlled-response question includes an adequate representation of answers. Had the question above allowed only "Agree" and "Disagree" responses, people who were undecided would not be able to answer truthfully or might not answer at all. Yes-or-no questions—like "Do you rent video movies more than three times a month?"—may suit one purpose or reveal some of the information you seek. Giving more choices, however, always provides data for you to make more comparisons among respondents. For example:

- How many times a month do you rent movie videos?
  _____ 1–3 times   _____ 4–7   _____ 8–12
  _____ More than 12   _____ Never

Unlike open-ended questions, controlled-response questions are convenient for respondents to answer quickly, and their results are easy to describe quantitatively.

3. *Word your questions carefully.* The way you ask a question will significantly influence the response it prompts. To prevent biasing answers, keep your language objective. Asking "Do you favor passing stronger laws to protect our valued coastal environments from careless destruction by oil tankers?" unfairly loads the question. Anyone answering "no" may be made to feel he or she does not value the environment and approves of careless destruction. Rephrase the question to be more objective: "Do you favor stronger regulation of oil tanker ships operating in or near the U.S. coast?"

Also avoid asking questions that seem to implicate the respondent. People feel uneasy about admitting their shortcomings or being made to appear in a negative light just because of the way a question is worded. Asking "Do you ever cheat on examinations?" puts respondents immediately on the defensive. Making the question more hypothetical, asking "Would you ever cheat on an examination?" will probably fulfill your research needs and get more accurate responses.

Carefully review the wording of each question in your questionnaire. Consider whether each question is free of bias and offers the respondent a chance to answer accurately. Before administering the questionnaire for research purposes, try it out on yourself and a few friends. Also ask your instructor to look it over and make suggestions. Once you are satisfied that the questionnaire will meet your needs, you are ready to administer it to a representative survey population.

Sampling a Population. In research, the word *population* refers to all the members of a group. A *sample* is a representative portion of the population (see Figure 5.5). When researchers study a group of any kind, they make generalizations about it based upon sampling the population. Sampling is important to research because examining every individual person or item in the group is usually impractical or impossible.

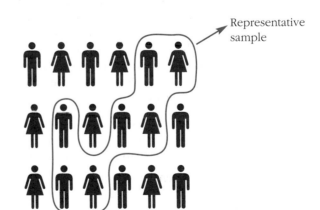

Population:
Long-distance
telephone customers
in Fairview City,
May 2002 (by 100s)

Representative sample

FIGURE 5.5   The population and representative survey sample

Good survey results are derived from an accurate sampling of the research population. You will get the best results from sampling by following these guidelines for a survey:

1. *Define the survey population.* Who gets surveyed and who does not will obviously affect the results of your questionnaire. Begin by carefully defining the population you intend to poll.

If you intend to study the characteristics of inner-city youth gang members, how will you define the population?
- What constitutes a *gang?*
- What kind of gangs will you study?
- Which participants in gang activities are actually members?
- What age range is meant by *youth?*

These and similar kinds of questions show the need for analyzing the population and describing it accurately throughout your research.

2. *Use random sampling.* The more diverse your sample, the more accurate the results. Narrowing your sampling to one kind of group lessens its representativeness. If you want to know how many people think watching television dulls creativity, do not ask only male college students or only those who refuse to watch television at all. A good sampling would include males and females of all ages and educational levels, of varied interests and occupations, and of a range of television-viewing habits.

3. *Take an adequate sample.* Common sense may be your best guide to how large a sample you will need. Since it allows for more variety, a large sample is generally more accurate than a small one. The opinions of 15 people in a population of 1,000 has little practical value. On the other hand, a random sampling of 500 of those individuals represents a significant number for consideration. In general, large populations require proportionally larger samplings, and larger samplings carry more significance than smaller ones.

Polling the Population.   Administer the questionnaire at varied times and places to the population you have identified. Choose a *polling* method that ensures getting a random sample and a good response rate. The results of a recent national telephone survey of married couples were widely challenged because people may have answered in ways to please their spouses (who may have been in the next room listening to the survey response). Another survey to find out what times people wanted college classes offered was criticized because it was done only during the day, while most people who might have preferred night classes were at work.

Almost every survey procedure has drawbacks, but you can safeguard results by consistently considering whether your method leaves out any particular group or overemphasizes the participation of another. If you survey customers at a video store to study their rental habits, include people of various ages and both genders; who come in at all hours of the day on both weekdays and weekends; who are married and single; and so on.

Randall, Steve.

Survey. Oct. 11, 2001.

FIGURE 5.6   A bibliography card for a self-administered survey

Analyzing the Findings.   Having administered the survey question-naire, analyze your findings. Compare the results with other research data you have collected and try to account for any major differences. Review your questions and sampling procedures to check for bias. If you have used the survey to gather statistical data, include information about the various statistical tests (validity, margin of error, and so forth) you have used to verify your results. As you incorporate the survey results in your research paper, include a description of the survey population and the procedures used to administer the questionnaire. Include a copy of the questionnaire in your paper's appendix.

Documenting the Survey

Make a working bibliography card as soon as you decide to conduct a survey. Since in most cases you will not be citing the name of a particular respondent to your survey or questionnaire, list yourself as the author. Figure 5.6 shows the bibliography card for a survey such as you might administer as part of your own research. No separate card is made for the survey questionnaire, since it is part of the survey itself.

NOTE: The information given here on surveys can produce excellent results for the kind of research topics and assignments usually undertaken by college undergraduates. If your research depends heavily upon extensive survey information that you collect yourself, consult a more thorough resource, such as one of the following:

Alreck, Pamela L., and Robert B. Settle. *Survey Research Handbook.* Burr Ridge, IL: Irwin, 1994.
Fink, Arlene. *How to Analyze Survey Data.* Newbury Park, CA: Sage, 1998.
Fink, Arlene. *How to Design Surveys.* Newbury Park, CA: Sage, 1998.
Rosenfeld, Paul, Jack E. Edwards, Marie D. Thomas, and Stephanie Booth-Kewley. *How to Conduct Organizational Surveys: A Step-by-Step Guide.* Newbury Park, CA: Sage, 1999.

Speeches and Lectures

Listening to Community Speakers

One good way to gain more familiarity with your research topic is to listen firsthand to what others have to say about it. Watch local newspapers and community announcements for upcoming events related to your research topic. It is likely that such occasions will feature presentations by recognized authorities or groups of informed spokespersons. If you know of a particular organization that may be sponsoring a conference or public meeting, get its number from the telephone directory and call about future scheduled meetings and speakers.

Use your imagination about where to hear public speakers on your research topic. Remember that public speeches and addresses include everything from your minister's sermon about marriage to a city council member's harangue on taxes.

Attending Campus Lectures

Take advantage of the opportunities presented on your own or neighboring campuses. Consult the campus newspaper and college organizations about visiting scholars, faculty addresses, and club debates. Consult a course syllabus or ask a particular professor when he or she will be lecturing on your research topic. Remember that you may need permission to sit in on lectures for courses you are not enrolled in.

Documenting Speeches and Lectures

Using your research question as a focus, make a checklist of important points to listen for, and take careful notes on any lecture or public address. You may be able to use a tape recorder, or the presentation may be available on video tape later from the sponsoring organization. Check ahead of time about both possibilities.

In addition, be sure to record necessary information for a bibliography card about the event. Include the speaker's name and position and the date, place, and occasion of the presentation. Follow the forms shown in Chapters 11 and 12 if you include the lecture or speech in the Works Cited list of your paper. If the information is not available when you hear a speaker, consult the sponsoring organization later for the documentation details you need.

NOTE: For historic speeches made by well-known individuals, consult the appropriate volume of the *Speech Index* in your library. You can also locate speeches over the Internet by using a search engine such as Yahoo! or HotBot or by visiting any of these resource sites:

Gifts of Speech: Women's   http://gos.sbc.edu/
Speeches from around the World

Good evening.

Just moments ago, I spoke with George W. Bush and congratulated him on becoming the forty-third president of the United States, and I promised him that I wouldn't call him back this time.

I offered to meet with him as soon as possible so that we can start to heal the divisions of the campaign and the contest through which we just passed.

Almost a century and a half ago, Senator Stephen Douglas told Abraham Lincoln, who had just defeated him for the presidency, "Partisan feeling must yield to patriotism. I'm with you, Mr. President, and God bless you."

Well, in that same spirit, I say to President-elect Bush that what remains of partisan rancor must now be put aside, and may God bless his stewardship of this country.

FIGURE 5.7   Excerpt of a speech by Al Gore (December 13, 2000), accessed from an online source

Great Speeches from History	http://www.historyplace.com/speeches/previous.htm
Great Speeches in RealAudio	http://www.chicago-law.net/speeches/speech.html
Historical Speeches Archive	http://www.webcorp.com/sounds/index.htm

Figure 5.7 shows an excerpt from Al Gore's concession speech after the 2000 election; it was accessed through an online source.

Radio and Television

Investigating the Past

Use radio and television programs to put your research in touch with people and events from the past as well as the present. Many early radio and television productions—ranging from the nightly news to old radio dramas like *The Shadow* and popular television comedies like *I Love Lucy*—are commercially available today on tape or video.

One excellent source is the Vanderbilt Television News Archive, an outstanding video tape collection of major news broadcasts and documentaries since 1968. To find out what the archive and other such sources hold, consult your library's copy of the *Television News Index and Abstracts* (Nashville, TN: Vanderbilt Television News Archives, Vanderbilt University, 1972–date [monthly]). You can use taped material to study historical events at the times they were first reported to the world over radio or television.

Researching Current News

Using current radio or television broadcasts as a basis for research requires both alertness and planning. Check the newspapers regularly or scan *TV Guide* or an online source to keep informed about weekly programs related to your research topic. In addition, a brief telephone inquiry to the local radio or television station may yield information about future programs to watch for. Even if you are unsure about a program's content ahead of time, make a checklist of the things you especially want to note for your research. Using a checklist will help you take notes and keep your attention focused.

Taping a Broadcast. A good deal of the time, you will have little or no advance notice of a program airing. In such a case, listen or watch carefully, taking notes throughout the broadcast and checking them during commercial breaks. If you have the equipment, use a tape recorder to record a radio broadcast or a VCR (video cassette recorder) to record a television program while you are tuned in and taking notes. You can review the recordings later, filling out your notes and taking down the bibliographic information for a preliminary citation card. If you cannot get all the information you need during a single broadcast of the program, find out when it may be presented again; check listings for it in the newspaper or, for television broadcasts, consult recent weekly issues of *TV Guide* or an online source.

Using Transcripts. Anytime you miss a radio or television show completely or need to study its contents more closely, you may be able to send for a *transcript,* a printed copy of the broadcast. Transcripts of news broadcasts, documentaries, interviews, talk shows, and even some entertainment programs are often available upon request from major radio and television stations. Issue-oriented television programs—like *60 Minutes, Dateline,* and those produced by the Public Broadcasting Service (PBS)—offer program transcripts on a regular basis. Transcript availability is usually announced during a radio and television broadcast, but you can always call the station to make sure. For transcripts of past radio programs, consult your library's set of *Summary of World Broadcasts by the British Broadcasting Corp.* (microform, 1973–date) or for television, a source like *CBS News*

Television Broadcasts (microform, 1963–date). You can also find radio and television transcripts over the Internet (see Figure 5.7).

Comprehensive information about radio and television stations and programs, as well as sources for audio and videotapes, can be found in the following sources, both usually available at major libraries. Full titles and other bibliographic information is given here to show the range of materials they provide:

> *Gale Directory of Publications and Broadcast Media: An Annual Guide to Publications and Broadcasting Stations, Including News-papers, Magazines, Journals, Radio Stations, and Cable Systems.* 3 vols. Detroit: Gale, 2001.
>
> *Television News Index and Abstracts.* Nashville, TN: Vanderbilt Television News Archives, Vanderbilt University, 1972–date (monthly).

In addition, the Internet provides a number of opportunities for re-searching radio and television programs and history, including these:

The Broadcast Archive	http://www.oldradio.com/
Museum of Moving Images	http://www.bfi.org.uk/museum
Museum of Television and Radio	http://www.mtr.org/
National Museum of Photography, Film, and Television	http://www.nmsi.ac.uk/nmpft/
Radio History Society	http://www.radiohistory.org/
Reel Top 40 Radio Repository	http://www.reelradio.com/
The Television Transcript Project	http://www.geocities.com/tvtranscripts

Others can be found using any Internet search engine.

Documenting Radio and Television Programs

Make out a preliminary citation card for any radio or television pro-gram you intend to include in your research. Figures 5.8 and 5.9 show the information to include for both kinds of sources. If you include a radio or television program in your paper's list of Works Cited, follow the forms suggested in Chapters 11 and 12.

> "*Homo Sapiens Get Smart in Africa*"
> With Christopher Joyce.
> *All Things Considered*
> National Public Radio. KUSC, Los Angeles
> 10 Jan. 2002

FIGURE 5.8   A bibliography card for a radio program

> *Ralph Bunche: An American Odyssey*
> Dir. William Greaves.
> Narr. Sidney Poitier.
> PBS. WETA, Washington, D C
> Feb. 2, 2001

FIGURE 5.9   A bibliography card for a television program

W O R K I N G   W I T H   O T H E R S

Educational research shows that some of the most effective learning takes place among communities of learners. Take advantage of that fact: Let your friends and classmates know when you intend to investigate sources beyond the campus library. More than likely, you will find that they can share in your efforts or at least increase your enthusiasm with their own fresh insights and enjoyment of the topic. If you do team up with a classmate to do research beyond the campus or community library, consider the following suggestions ahead of time.

- Before visiting a research location with someone else, decide about sharing transportation, how long you will stay, and roughly what each of you hopes to accomplish.

- Share the responsibility of finding out about local private libraries, businesses, hospitals, or other sites that may be of value to you and others. Make a list of such places, and divide the work of telephoning or visiting them in person to get information needed before deciding to visit a site together.

- Make checklists of the specific activities each of you expects to accomplish during an onsite visit. Discuss these lists together, checking for any omissions and ensuring that your plans do not conflict.

- If your topics overlap in any way, you may be able to work together on an interview or in conducting a survey. (If your topics do not overlap, it may still be possible to poll people about more than one issue with a single survey instrument.) Work together on setting up and conducting the interview or survey. Formulate questions and analyze results together to make sure that each of you gets the information you need.

- Attend public presentations together or agree ahead of time that one of you will go and take careful notes for both. (Be sure your instructor allows you to use another's notes as part of your own research, however.) You can do the same with radio and television programs by deciding ahead of time who can most conveniently listen to or record a particular broadcast. Prepare a checklist and take good notes for any of these kinds of activities, especially if the notes will be used by someone else.

CHAPTER **6**

Researching on the Internet

Possibly the most significant resource for worldwide communication and research on the planet is the *Internet,* a global communication system composed of thousands of other networks and computers around the world. These individual networks and computers share the information and even the capabilities they have with each other, with the result that anyone using the network has access to all the information and even some of the capabilities of every computer on the Internet.

While it's not the purpose of this chapter to introduce you to everything you need to know about the Internet, being familiar with a few basic concepts will aid your understanding of discussions that follow.

**THINKING CRITICALLY
ABOUT RESEARCHING ON THE INTERNET**

The Internet can provide you with access to many valuable, illuminating sources. But because virtually anyone can post whatever he or she likes to an Internet website, you must treat these sources with particular care. See the section "Evaluating Internet Sources" at the end of this chapter.

Moreover, much important information about many topics is simply not available via the Internet. In particular, only a small portion of what's published in current magazines, periodicals, and newspapers—except for breaking news summaries—can be accessed through the Internet. And while you may find excerpts of recent books online, for a full text you'll need to read their print versions.

For all of these reasons, don't be seduced by the apparent ease of online research. Use the Internet to supplement the kinds of research discussed in Chapters 4 and 5.

Accessing the Internet:
Online Is Onboard

If you are new to using the Internet, you will find that connecting with it can be fairly simple. Using a college's computer network to get to Internet sources, you can generally get started by following the instructions provided on the campus system or by asking a college librarian for help. If you want to access the Internet from your own computer, you will first need to have the necessary software, computer equipment, and services of a commercial Internet service provider such as America Online, Netcom, or Microsoft Network.

Using Internet Addresses

If the computer program you use is set up to connect automatically with the Internet, your research can start as soon as you click on the software link. If not, you will need to enter an Internet *address* for the location you want to contact. You need not be an expert about the Internet or computers to use most addresses comfortably, but understanding some basics about Internet address formats can save time and greatly enhance your research efforts.

Understanding Domain Names.   The thousands of individual computers that make up the Internet are each identified by a unique name, called the *domain name,* consisting of letters or words separated by the symbol . (pronounced "dot"). For example, the domain name for Bookwire, an Internet source about books and publishing, is *www.bookwire.com.*

As with any address, each part of a domain name tells something specific about the computer it designates. In the case of *www.bookwire.com,* the domain name describes a computer that is:

- Part of the World Wide Web—the *www*
- Identified by other computers as *bookwire*
- Operated by a commercial organization—*com*

If Bookwire were not a commercial entity, the domain name for its Internet address would end in different letters, such as *gov, edu, mil, net,* or *org* (for *government, educational, military, Internet network,* or nonprofit *organization,* respectively).

Domain names are useful for identifying Internet sources, but they are not complete addresses. To connect with a particular Internet site, your computer needs to know what communication system that site uses. This is where something called a *URL* comes in.

Understanding URLs.   The complete address for a computer located on the Internet is called a *URL,* for *uniform resource locator,* a term representing a particular communication format used by Internet computers. The URL for the computer at Bookwire, for example, is *http://www.bookwire.com*. This is the address your computer needs to know in order to locate and connect over the Internet with the Bookwire computer.

A URL includes the Internet computer's domain name preceded by what is called a *protocol*—that is, the symbol :// and letters indicating a particular communication format:

URL Protocol   Domain Name

http://www.bookwire.com

The *http* protocol in this example indicates that the Bookwire computer uses *hypertext transfer protocol,* a World Wide Web communications format providing hypertext links, which you can use to jump electronically to or from different Internet locations. A computer with another communications format would require a different URL protocol.

Occasionally during your research, you may run into a complex and lengthy URL that contains more than just a protocol and domain name. Such a URL might look something like *http://www.bookwire.com/rev7?@cri3/t62ju/html*. This kind of URL usually contains additional information—such as *path* and *file* data—telling the Internet computer where specific information is stored among its files and subdirectories. Fortunately, while such data-packed URLs can be useful, you seldom need to work with them: You can use the common, shorter form of the URL to go first to a website's main or home page; from there you can click on a link to the files or subdirectories storing the information you want.

Researching with URLs

The information included in a URL is useful to your research because of what it tells you in advance about an Internet source. As you will learn later in this chapter, sources with, let's say, *www, gov,* or *alt* in their addresses all provide distinct kinds of information, in different formats, and with varying capabilities and limitations. Similarly, you can expect that sources whose addresses include endings such as *com, edu,* or *org,* for example, will all provide different types of information and with varying amounts of authority or expertise. Interpreting an Internet address in these ways beforehand will save time and help you locate the variety of sources and points of view you need for effective research.

The World Wide Web: Worlds within a World

Often written as *WWW* and spoken of as *the web,* the *World Wide Web* is one of the Internet's richest resources and its most popular means of navigation. The web was launched in 1989 in CERN, the European Center for

Particle Physics in Switzerland, by scientists working together to create a global computer system for exchanging research information. The evolutionary leap that made the web what it is today is credited to two scientists at the CERN laboratories, Tim Berners-Lee and Robert Cailliau. Since that time, the rapid development of additional new technologies has made the web one of the world's most important resources for commerce, education, entertainment, and communication.

Search Engines: Workhorses of the Web

If you know the address, or URL, for a particular website, you can access it directly through your computer's *browser.* With more than 80 million web pages and more than 30 million sites on the web, however, you can't possibly know the address of every Internet computer site or information file you may want to research. Enter the *search engine,* the workhorse of the World Wide Web.

Using a Search Engine. A *search engine* is a computer program that hunts for information sites all over the Internet. After you enter one or more *keywords* (called a *string*) about a topic, a search engine scans its own huge database or the Internet and ultimately presents you with a list of possible sources. Although all such Internet search programs are commonly referred to as *search engines,* there are actually two kinds: *directory* programs, which primarily search only their own databases of stored Internet information, and what might be termed *true search engines,* which are programs that actually search the Internet each time you make a request. Both directory and true search engines give such good results that people seldom know or care about the difference between them. But there *is* a difference, and to get the best results from your research efforts, you need some understanding of how each type of search engine works.

Directories. A directory search engine—such as Yahoo, HotBot, and Lycos—doesn't actually search the entire Internet for information sites and files each time it is launched. Instead, a directory searches its own preestablished database—generally, a collection of several hundreds of thousands of preselected Internet files. In response to a keyword request, the directory engine searches its database and then presents successive layers of menu choices listing related topic categories. From this point, you proceed almost intuitively, selecting first one category, then the next related one, and so on—making each selection based on your sense of a category's relevance to your topic. Eventually, you will come to a specific topic and a list of sources from the directory database about it. Figure 6.1 illustrates the way a directory-based search might lead you through several layers of potential, progressively more focused subjects until you eventually arrive at a specific topic to research.

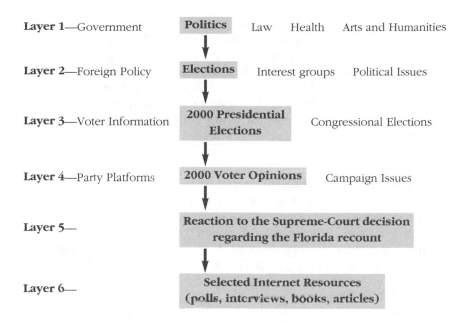

| Layer 1—Government | **Politics** | Law | Health | Arts and Humanities |

| Layer 2—Foreign Policy | **Elections** | Interest groups | Political Issues |

| Layer 3—Voter Information | **2000 Presidential Elections** | Congressional Elections |

| Layer 4—Party Platforms | **2000 Voter Opinions** | Campaign Issues |

| Layer 5— | **Reaction to the Supreme-Court decision regarding the Florida recount** |

| Layer 6— | **Selected Internet Resources (polls, interviews, books, articles)** |

FIGURE 6.1   Menu options for a directory-based search

A directory search can be especially helpful when you first want to explore a potential research topic, discover and examine related issues, or assess the types of resources available for it. You might begin a directory search with no certain idea about a research subject but eventually find several central and related topics for research after working through the directory's layers of categories.

Another plus to a directory search is that it is fast and efficient. You will waste less time hunting for information because most directory databases are large enough to include information on nearly any topic imaginable. So, with a directory-based search, you will not only avoid having empty search results (in most cases), but you will also benefit from having had someone else already screen potential sources for their relevancy and quality.

A small drawback to a directory-based search engine is that, unlike a true search engine, it searches for and finds only items listed in its *own* database. Whatever topics and information files are stored in a directory's database have been previously defined, selected, and categorized according to criteria established by the search site personnel. Thus, if your topic requires that you connect with very recent, offbeat, amateur, or seldom-visited Internet sites, you may have better luck researching with a true search engine.

True Search Engines.   Unlike a directory search program, a true search engine—AltaVista, for example—presents no menu of subject choices to follow. Instead, you simply enter a keyword string, and the search engine finds and presents a list of Internet sources. Because you can't depend on the search engine program to find and narrow a potential topic for you (as you can with a directory search), you need to use very specific keywords to define accurately what you want to investigate and what sources you want the search engine to find. Since several directory-type search engines today also provide for keyword searches of the Internet, you will find understanding such searches useful for researching with both kinds of engines.

Performing Keyword Searches.   When you enter a keyword string in the search box of a true search engine, the program looks through all the websites it knows about to find as many matches with the string as it can. Depending on the particular search engine or the user's instructions, a search might include a comparison of the keywords with the words in a site's URL, document titles, text, a website's own summary of its contents, or all of these.

Although each search engine has its own methods for defining a search, certain conventions are fairly common. For example, search engines are *case insensitive,* meaning they don't distinguish between upper- and lowercase letters; whether you enter *California* or *california* makes no difference. Most engines also have a means of defining a keyword phrase as a group, rather than as separate words, usually by enclosing the phrase in quotation marks, as in *"Civil War."* This is an important technique, since entering the words *Civil War* alone—or even *Civil AND War*—without the quotation marks would yield literally thousands of results for the single word *Civil* and very likely the same number for the word *War.*

A number of special approaches can simplify a keyword search and make it more precise. While few search engines actually provide for *all* the methods described in the following section, acquainting yourself with the possible refinements for a search will help you decide which search engines allow the techniques most helpful to your research.

Refining a Search Engine Query.   A variety of options are available to refine a search query, or keyword string. In fact, many search engines ask you to specify which options you want to use when you enter a keyword string. The following descriptions will help you become acquainted with these options and use them to aid your research:

- *Boolean and other logical operators* limit the terms of a search string to make it more exact. *Boolean operators* are capitalized words and phrases such as *AND, OR, NOT,* and *BUT NOT.* For example, *dolphins BUT NOT bottlenose* would eliminate getting unwanted sources on bottlenose dolphins, a heavily documented species. Many search engines work with a simplified version of Boolean operators or employ other punctuation or devices, such as using + or − signs in front of search terms.

■ *Concept searching* occurs when a search engine runs one or more keywords through its database and then returns with a list of suggested, possibly related sources. If you entered *adolescent* as a keyword, for instance, the search engine would return potential sources using the terms *juvenile, minor,* and *teen.*

■ *Date searching* is a means of limiting a search to web pages that have been posted within a specified period of time. For instance, you could use date searching to ensure getting a list of only those web pages discussing *Seinfeld after* the last original episode had run on television.

■ *Keyword weighting* allows you to define the relative importance of each word in a string by sequencing. When entering a search string such as *Princess Diana AND paparazzi AND Paris,* for instance, you instruct the engine to pay more attention to sources containing references to *Princess Diana* and *paparazzi* than to *Paris.*

■ *Location limiting* allows you to specify a particular web domain or a range of geographical locations. Thus, you could limit a search to include only those sites with *.edu* in their URL or only those located in the *United States* or *France.*

■ *Media searching* allows you to specify a particular type of file, such as one formatted in Java or VRML, or to locate image, audio, or video files specifically.

■ *Natural language queries* define a search in ordinary sentence form, rather than by Boolean or other logical operators or truncated language. Entering *I want to know about national drunk driving rates and insurance costs for drunk drivers,* for instance, would turn up search results regarding the query's key terms, such as *drunk driver, drunk driving,* and *insurance.*

■ *Nesting* is a way of using parentheses in a Boolean-type search to indicate the order in which a search engine should locate material. The string *(american literature AND faulkner OR sound and fury)* directs the engine to locate first any sites using the term *american literature* and then from this list report the ones also using the terms *faulkner* and *sound and fury.*

■ *Proximity searching* locates documents in which two or more search terms appear within 10 words of each other. Thus, *civil AND war NEAR american* will turn up references to *American Civil War* as well as *An American who fought in the Civil War.*

■ *Relevancy ranking* provides for returns ranked according to how often or where in the searched document the search string appears. Sources in which a keyword appears more frequently or in a more central part of a document than in others are ranked higher.

■ *Wildcards* are symbols that tell search engines to substitute letters after a keyword root. For example, to ensure that the engine registers *electrical* and *electrified* when searching for *electric field,* you would use a wildcard such as *electr* field* as the search string.

Using a Metasearch Engine. Rather than hunt through the Internet or even its own database for information sources, a *metasearch engine* goes to several other search engines and returns with the results from all of them listed on a single page. If you used the search engine for Highway 61, for example, it would consult the other engines at Yahoo, Lycos, WebCrawler, Infoseek, and Excite and then return with a list of sources gathered by each. Metasearch engines can be slower in returning with information than other kinds of engines, but you should use them when you can to reach a variety of sources from the Internet and databases—as well as to save time searching.

Finding a Search Engine to Use. You will find search engines available on most campus and public library computer systems as well as on the Internet itself. Figure 6.2 lists some of the most popular search engines and their URLs.

General Search Engines

AltaVista	http://www.altavista.com
About.com	http://www.about.com
Dogpile	http://www.dogpile.com
Excite	http://www.excite.com
Google	http://www.google.com
GoTo	http://www.goto.com
HotBot	http://www.hotbot.com
Lycos	http://www.lycos.com
Mamma	http://www.mamma.com
Northern Light	http://www.nlsearch.com
WebCrawler	http://www.webcrawler.com
Yahoo	http://www.yahoo.com

Metasearch Engines

Galaxy	http://galaxy.einet.net
Highway 61	http://www.highway61.com
Metacrawler	http://www.metacrawler.com
Starting Point	http://www.stpt.com

FIGURE 6.2 World Wide Web search engines and their URLs

A Sample Search: Locating Internet Sources to Narrow a Topic

There are a number of ways to search for information on the Internet. Starting with a web directory can be particularly useful when you have a broad topic in mind but are unsure about what aspect of that topic might interest you or about what resources may be be available.

For example, going to Hotbot.com, you could begin by selecting "Health" from the opening directory page (see Figure 6.3). That selection would take you to a page listing dozens of health-related categories, including "addictions" (see Figure 6.4). Selecting that category would take

FIGURE 6.3   The HotBot home page and directory

Source: HotBot Web pages © Copyright 2002, Lycos, Inc. All Rights Reserved. Lycos® is a registered trademark of Carnegie Mellon University. Reprinted by permission of Lycos, Inc.

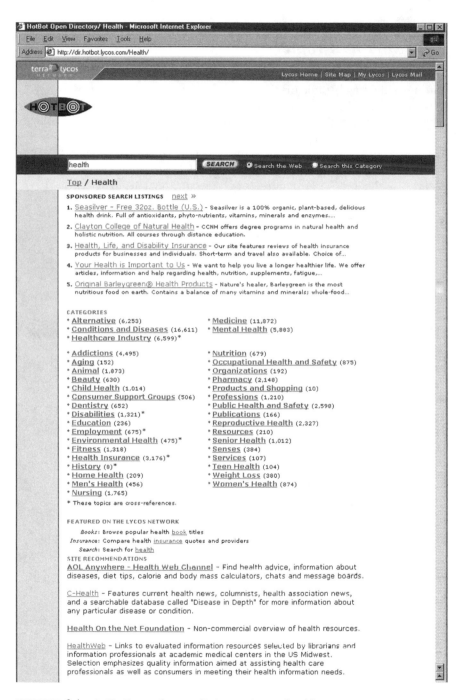

FIGURE 6.4   A HotBot web page listing topics on health

Source: HotBot Web pages © Copyright 2002, Lycos, Inc. All Rights Reserved. Lycos® is a registered trademark of Carnegie Mellon University. Reprinted by permission of Lycos, Inc.

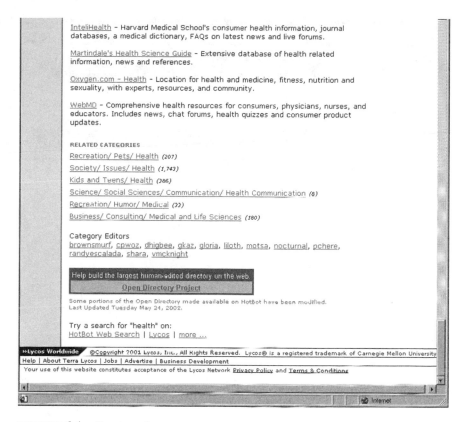

InteliHealth – Harvard Medical School's consumer health information, journal databases, a medical dictionary, FAQs on latest news and live forums.

Martindale's Health Science Guide – Extensive database of health related information, news and references.

Oxygen.com – Health – Location for health and medicine, fitness, nutrition and sexuality, with experts, resources, and community.

WebMD – Comprehensive health resources for consumers, physicians, nurses, and educators. Includes news, chat forums, health quizzes and consumer product updates.

RELATED CATEGORIES
Recreation/ Pets/ Health *(207)*
Society/ Issues/ Health *(1,743)*
Kids and Teens/ Health *(386)*
Science/ Social Sciences/ Communication/ Health Communication *(8)*
Recreation/ Humor/ Medical *(33)*
Business/ Consulting/ Medical and Life Sciences *(180)*

Category Editors
brownsmurf, cpwoz, dhigbee, gkaz, gloria, liloth, motsa, nocturnal, pchere, randyescalada, shara, vmcknight

Help build the largest human-edited directory on the web.
Open Directory Project

Some portions of the Open Directory made available on HotBot have been modified.
Last Updated Tuesday May 24, 2002.

Try a search for "health" on:
HotBot Web Search | Lycos | more ...

»Lycos Worldwide   ©Copyright 2001 Lycos, Inc., All Rights Reserved. Lycos® is a registered trademark of Carnegie Mellon University
Help | About Terra Lycos | Jobs | Advertise | Business Development
Your use of this website constitutes acceptance of the Lycos Network Privacy Policy and Terms & Conditions

FIGURE 6.4   Continued

you to a further page of categories related to addiction, including the category "Internet" (see Figure 6.5). Clicking on "Internet" then leads you to a page listing a number of web sources that discuss the issue of Internet addiction (Figure 6.6). From here you can go directly to any sources that interest you. For example, clicking on "Internet addiction survey" will lead you to a site that offers a questionnaire allowing users to test their tendency to become hooked on Internet use (see Figure 6.7). Many of the sites you access may also provide links that can give you access to other sites pertinent to the subject.

Once you have narrowed a subject, you should search that subject on other search engines as well. Because not all engines will come up with the same list of sites, you'll find accesss to the greatest number of pertinent sites by trying several different engines. Doing a keyword search of "Internet addiction" on Netscape Navigator, for example, produced the list in Figure 6.8, which includes a number of sites not available in the Hotbot listing in Figure 6.6.

FIGURE 6.5   A HotBot web page listing categories of addiction topics

Source: HotBot Web pages © Copyright 2002, Lycos, Inc. All Rights Reserved. Lycos® is a registered trademark of Carnegie Mellon University. Reprinted by permission of Lycos, Inc.

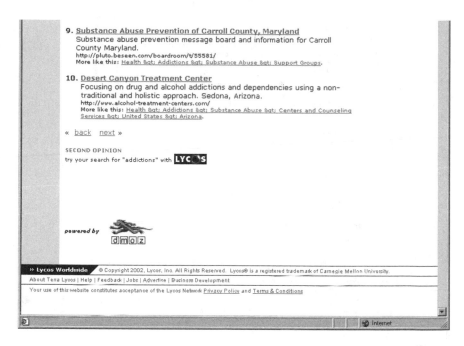

FIGURE 6.5 Continued

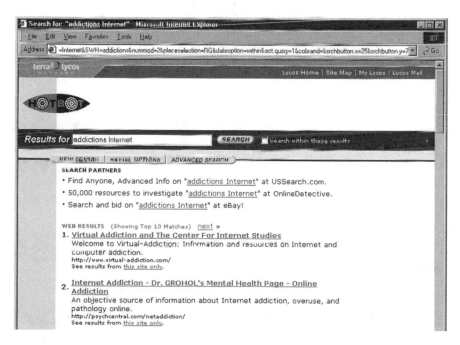

FIGURE 6.6 A HotBot web page listing resources on the topic "Internet addiction"

Source: HotBot Web pages © Copyright 2002, Lycos, Inc. All Rights Reserved. Lycos® is a registered trademark of Carnegie Mellon University. Reprinted by permission of Lycos, Inc.

(continues on next page)

3. Warning: Internet Addiction
While no one WE know is addicted to the internet, in the interest of public awareness, we are making public these symptoms to point out to our members some of the sure signs of Internet Addiction. You
http://www.westward.com/club/cl05004.htm
See results from this site only.

4. Internet Addiction - Is the Internet Addictive, or Are Addicts Using the Internet ?
Internet Addiction Disorder, Review of research
http://www.concentric.net/~Astorm/iad.html
See results from this site only.

5. Center for Online and Internet Addiction - Help and Resource for Internet Addicts, Healthcare Professionals, and...
Welcome to Netaddiction.com and the Center for Online Addiction - Resources for therapists and families, tips on Cyber-wellness, and Personal Therapy
http://www.netaddiction.com/
See results from this site only.

6. Symptoms and Information on Internet Addiction
Symptoms of Internet Addiction 2) Loosing track of time after making a connection. 3) Goes out less and less. 4) Spending less and less time on meals at home or at work, and eats in front of the monit
http://www.addictions.com/internet.htm
See results from this site only.

7. Nurseweek/Healthweek | Internet addiction?
August 8, 1997 Early in 1995, New York psychiatrist Ivan Goldberg, MD, announced the appearance of a new addiction: people abandoning their family obligations to sit gazing into their computer monitor
http://www.nurseweek.com/features/97-8/iadct.html
See results from this site only.

8. Internet Addiction
InternetAddiction.ca: Internet Addiction Help Site
http://www.internetaddiction.ca/
See results from this site only.

9. Help! Were addicted to the Internet!
You know you're addicted to the internet when: 1. You turn off your computer and go watch your Web TV. 2. You see something funny and scream, "LOL, LOL." 3. You meet the mailman at the curb and swear
http://thefunnypage.com/addiction/signs.htm
See results from this site only.

10. Ivan Goldberg discusses Internet Addiction
JUST CLICK NO Some doctors, like Thomas Hodgkin, are celebrated for identifying a disease; others, like Jonas Salk for defeating one. But Dr. Ivan K. Goldberg may be the first in his field to gain not
http://www.psycom.net/iasg.html
See results from this site only.

1 - 10   next »

RELATED CATEGORIES   (Showing Results 1 - 1 of 1 Match)

1. Health / Addictions / Internet

SECOND OPINION
try your search for "addictions Internet" with LYC S

FIGURE 6.6   Continued

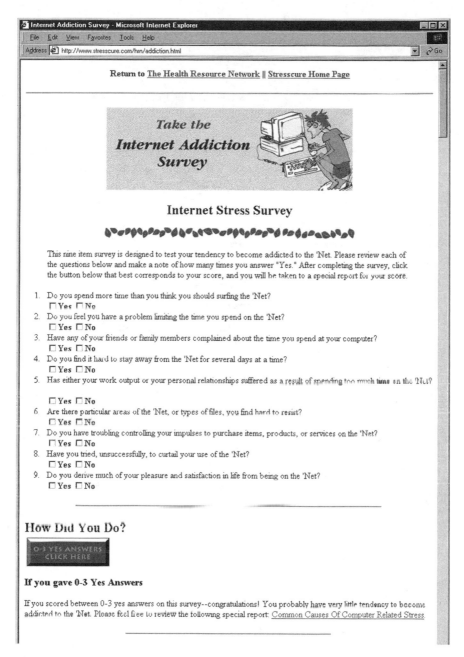

FIGURE 6.7 Part of an Internet addiction survey from the Health Resource Network's Stresscure site

Source: Internet addiction survey from the Health Resource Network's Stresscure site. Reprinted by permission of Morton C. Orman, M.D., author, and the Health Resource Network, Inc. (www.stresscure.com).

(continues on next page)

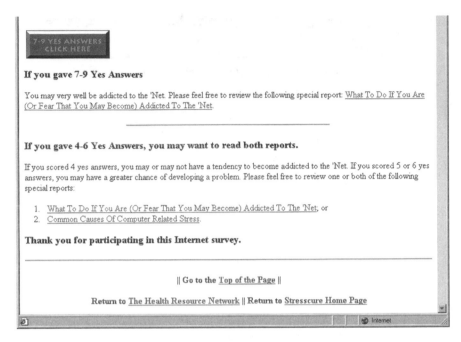

FIGURE 6.7 Continued

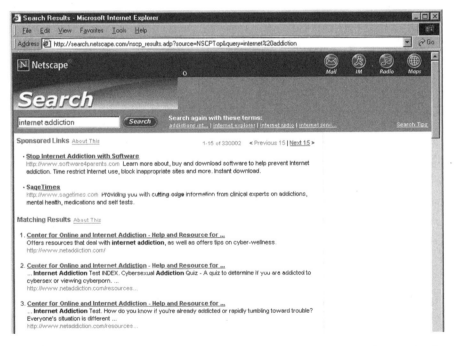

FIGURE 6.8 A page from Netscape Navigator showing the results of a search of the keywords "Internet addiction"

Source: Netscape website © 2002 Netscape Communications Corporation. Screenshot used with permission.

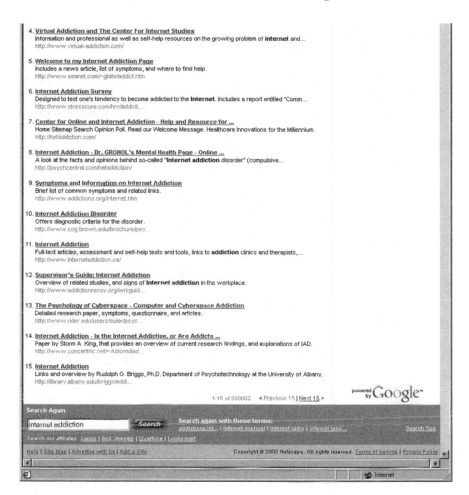

FIGURE 6.8　Continued

E-Mail: Electronic Letters

"Have you checked your e-mail today?" is a common question asked across campuses, at home, at work, and around the world. *E-mail,* a means by which you can send and receive electronic messages, is probably the most widely used feature of the Internet and one with which millions of people are already familiar.

Accessing E-Mail.　If you don't have an e-mail account, you may want to investigate getting one, both as an aid to your current research project and as a way to communicate on a daily basis with others in your community and around the globe. Many college campuses offer e-mail free to their students, or you can sign up for free e-mail service from national systems such as Juno. By paying a small monthly fee, you can also get e-mail and other Internet services from commercial providers like America Online, Prodigy, and the Microsoft Network.

Researching with E-Mail. Besides the communication conveniences e-mail provides, the fact that so many people have e-mail today makes it a useful tool for research. You can use e-mail to find and ask questions of specialists, query libraries about sources, conduct interviews, check source authorities, send and receive files, subscribe to online magazines and newspapers, and even get help with Internet access.

If you know the name of an authority who might be willing to talk with you about your research subject but don't know how to contact him or her, you can try looking for an e-mail address through search systems available from most search engine sites or a free service such as *Four11* (*http://www.four11.com/*), which lists over 1.5 million names and e-mail addresses of people who have voluntarily provided the information. If you find an e-mail address, send a polite, brief message about your research subject and the questions you would like answered.

Two other popular uses of e-mail—Internet mailing lists and Usenet news-groups—can be especially helpful to your research.

Listservs and Mailing Lists: Group E-Mail

"How big is your conference table?" is a question posed by an Internet site that indexes mailing lists, worldwide addresses of thousands of people who receive and send e-mail about a wide variety of subjects. A mailing-list service is commonly referred to as a *listserv* (for "list service"), a term derived from the name of the best-known mail-list program. *Listserv* has become an informally used generic term for all Internet e-mail systems, although other programs, such as *listproc* and *majordomo,* are also widely used.

Some listservs use e-mail only to disseminate information, but most use it to allow for ongoing group discussions on topics ranging from *Phenfen* (a controversial diet medication) to *gender communication* or the music group known as *The Police.* Several thousand listservs exist already, and more are started daily. Some last no more than a week or two; others are well established. Although listserv sites are often operated by and sometimes moderated by the individuals who begin them, many are also automated, so that e-mailing takes place via a computerized program.

Joining a Mailing List.   To join a mailing list, you might start by accessing a comprehensive Internet directory called the *PAML* (publicly accessible mailing lists). You can get to the PAML at *http://www.paml.net.* Once you find a mailing list that focuses on your research topic, you can subscribe to it (and later unsubscribe, if you wish) by sending an e-mail to the list's subscription address. Once you have subscribed, you will receive the e-mail address where you can begin sending messages.

Researching with Mailing Lists. At the start of your research efforts, mailing lists can be a good way to learn about a topic and some of the major issues surrounding it. Later in your research, becoming part of a mailing list can also provide you with an informal forum for questions and an opportunity to discuss ideas and resources with others. In some cases, the list may become a means for you to conduct an interview or survey about your research topic. As you participate in a mailing list, keep in mind that your audience will range from individuals only mildly interested in and knowledgeable about your research subject to experienced or recognized experts. Avoid being judgmental, but do exercise a critical attitude about any respondents' authority on a subject and what you decide to include in your research paper. The guidelines given later in this chapter for evaluating Internet sources should help in this regard (see pp. 135–138).

Usenet/Newsgroups: Posting Information

Like mailing lists, *Usenet* groups (also known as *newsgroups*) are conferencelike, e-mail-based discussions on practically every subject you can imagine. Currently, more than 10,000 Usenet groups around the world communicate in a variety of languages on topics as serious as *women's rights* and *euthanasia* to some as lighthearted as *whether American cooking is as good as French cuisine.*

Understanding Usenet Postings. Usenet differs from a mailing list in the way information is shared. Whereas a mailing-list system routinely sends each e-mail message received to every subscriber in a group, Usenet participants send messages—variously called *posts, postings,* and *articles*—to a central Internet site for others to read and respond to. The postings are listed and numbered in the order they are received, which means you need to keep up with or read several postings on a topic to follow and respond to the ongoing flow of responses (called a *thread*). Also, unlike a listserv, there are no subscribers in a Usenet group; individuals participate by simply accessing a newsgroup site and then reading and responding to what's posted there.

Given the number and variety of newsgroups, software programs called *newsreaders* are a necessity. Newsreaders can be configured to collect information only from those newsgroups that are of interest, thereby relieving you of having to keep track of existing and new groups on the Internet. Newsreaders are available commercially and included in popular browser software such as Netscape Navigator and Microsoft Explorer. Commercial providers like America Online and CompuServe offer Usenet connections as well.

Accessing Usenet. Addresses for Usenet groups and their postings follow a standard hierarchical naming system, which makes them similar to but not the same as Internet URLs. A typical address begins with a hierarchy category such as *alt.* (for "alternative"), *sci.* (for "science"), and *misc.* (for "miscellaneous"), followed by the various subjects discussed in a successively narrowing order. For example, *alt.rec.sport.paintball.rules* specifies a site listing discussion about the *rules of paintball.* Addresses such as *misc.writing, biz.stocks.dj,* and *sci.photosyn.orchids* indicate Usenet discussions about *miscellaneous/writing topics, business/Dow-Jones stocks,* and *science/photosynthesis in orchids,* respectively. Several search engines, such as Hotbot.com and Excite.com, link to Usenet postings; however, the most comprehensive of these engines is Google.com *(http://www. google.com/),* which provides a searchable database where you can locate current newsgroups as well as past Usenet postings by topic.

Researching with Usenet. The majority of information in Usenet postings is in the form of an informal opinion. Used carefully, such postings can provide you with information you may not be able to find in more usual sources. You might go to a Usenet discussion to ask for information or about sources on a particularly current topic or obscure hobby, to find someone who has experience with your research topic, or just to get a sense of people's attitudes. You might consult similar discussions for ideas about a topic or to learn about other sources of information available through the Internet or elsewhere. You can even consult Usenet postings for advice about writing in general, as shown by the excerpt from a Usenet web page in Figure 6.9.

Date	Thread Subject	Most Recent Poster
26 Mar 2002	song lyrics (11 articles)	CyberCypher
25 Mar 2002	To speak a more fluent English (1 article)	Denis Morissette
25 Mar 2002	commas in a list (8 articles)	Dave Swindell
25 Mar 2002	Format of formal English letter (3 articles)	Mailman
24 Mar 2002	Spoken english to improve pronunciation (1 article)	Marco Rinaudo
23 Mar 2002	Change to formal one (2 articles)	boytum
23 Mar 2002	Curso de Ingles en Internet Gratis (1 article)	La Mansion del Ingles
23 Mar 2002	Acceptable syntax or wrong position of verb? (7 articles)	Andreas

FIGURE 6.9   Web page listing of Usenet postings

Keep in mind that Usenet postings vary widely in terms of accuracy and reliability and that assessing the authority of anyone who posts to a Usenet listing can be quite difficult because the forums allow for anonymity. More often that not, treat such postings as personal opinion rather than as primary sources for a research paper.

Evaluating Internet Resources: Whom Can You Trust?

Many people naively believe that if something appears in print, it must be true. In fact, it might not be. As a critical reader, you should *always* consider the source of information as a primary factor in determining its value. Ask yourself these questions: What agenda does this person or group have? and How reliable is the source in terms of providing complete and accurate information?

Information found at many Internet sites is intended to represent a particular point of view or to promote a cause. Although such sites may support worthwhile causes, they are frequently highly selective about the information they provide or otherwise biased in the ways they present material. Figure 6.10 shows a web page titled "McCruelty to Go," for example, depicting a well-known character from McDonald's Corporation's commercials behind bars. Although the page's content describes a recent agreement between McDonald's and the site's sponsor, the page's URL ("meatstinks.com"), its title, and the depiction of the McDonald's character behind bars are clearly intended to prejudice the reader. The site's content explains the success People for the Ethical Treatment of Animals (PETA), the sponsoring organization, has had in negotiating with McDonald's and the reasons for their dispute with the Corporation, but no information representing McDonald's point of view is included. Another web page, shown in Figure 6.11, uses loaded language—*murder, innocent, tortured, cruel*—as well as the gruesome image (in color) of a skinned animal to persuade readers to accept its point of view about fur products sold by the Macy's Company.

As web pages such as these demonstrate, you need to be especially alert to—even completely mistrusting of, in some cases—Internet sources that demonstrate a one-sided, biased approach to an issue. Approach such sources with a critical attitude that includes consciously evaluating their authority, questioning the origins and intention of the information provided, and being alert to strategies intended to bias your understanding of what is presented.

The Range of Internet Content

A critical mindset is essential for anyone conducting effective research on the Internet, considering the vast number of people posting information and expressing ideas on it. You will find that much of the information available

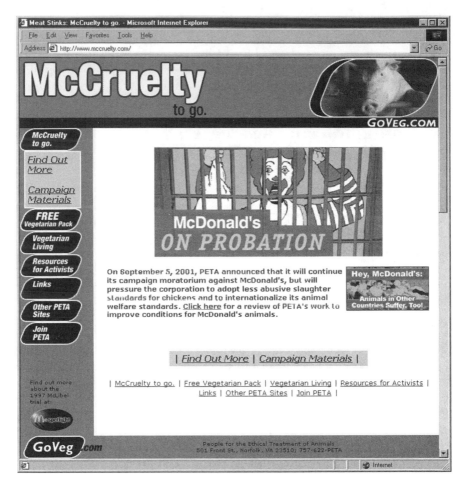

FIGURE 6.10   Meatstinks: McCruelty to Go. A web page sponsored by People for the Ethical Treatment of Animals (PETA)

Source: From www.meatstinks.com. Reprinted by permission of PETA (People for the Ethical Treatment of Animals).

over the Internet is commercial in nature, which raises the obvious possibility that it's biased—presented to sell a product or at least emphasize certain characteristics over others. Further, because it is democratic and essentially unrestricted, Internet content often lacks the usual information-filtering mechanisms, such as competition, academic review, financial and legal concerns, and even matter-of-fact judgments about whether something is worth circulating. As a result, you can find on the Internet everyone with an idea, every group with a cause, everything and anything someone thinks is important, needed, or valuable to someone else. These conditions account for much of

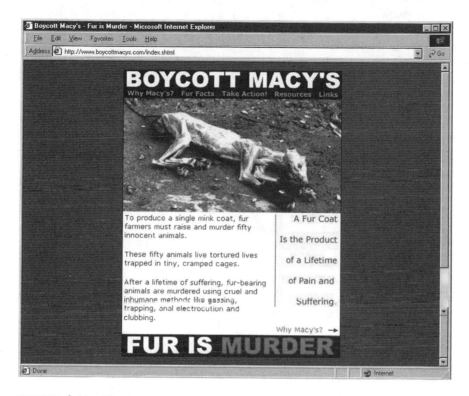

FIGURE 6.11   The Boycott Macy's-Fur Is Murder web page

Source: From www.boycottmacys.com

the Internet's great value, of course, but they also mean there's a lot of junk out there. It's *your* job to sort through it.

A Reliability Checklist for Internet Sources

None of what's said here should diminish your enjoyment of the Internet and your use of its resources for your research. Just keep in mind that you should continue to apply the same critical assessment to Internet sources and content that you would to traditional library sources, but with a sense of the differences between the two. Although there are no certain criteria for evaluating Internet sources, the following checklist may guide you to think critically about your research on the Internet.

Content

☐   1. *Currency:* Does the material appear to be current, and is there an indication of how often it is updated?

☐ 2. *Fairness:* Does the material demonstrate the author's knowledge and consideration of other viewpoints as well as current research by others that may be relevant? Is the tone reasonable and temperate?

☐ 3. *Evidence:* Does the content provide statistics, examples, or anecdotal evidence to support the author's position? Are the examples and other evidence presented fairly, and do they reflect current data? Is there a clear separation of fact and opinion?

☐ 4. *Research:* Is there evidence of credible research, such as a description of methodology or a bibliography? Are links to other sites with established credibility listed?

☐ 5. *Credibility:* Would the content of the document be considered credible in the non-Internet world? If so, why and with whom?

Authority

☐ 6. *Identity:* Does the author of the material or the person responsible for posting it include an e-mail address, URL, or other means of being contacted for comments and questions about the Internet site and its contents?

☐ 7. *Qualifications:* Does the author include or express willingness to provide information about his or her qualifications on the subject?

☐ 8. *Reputation:* Is the author or organization responsible for the content known and commonly accepted as credible? Does other information speak to credibility, such as education, employment, publications, awards, experience, or other verifiable qualifications?

☐ 9. *Other postings:* Has the author posted other kinds of entries on the Internet? If so, what kinds? How do they compare with the current document?

☐ 10. *Credibility:* Would the author of this document be considered credibile in the non-Internet world? If so, why and with whom?

Other Resources

Most campus libraries have information and designated staff to assist individuals who have questions about using computers to search available databases or access the Internet. As with other library resources, use them when you need help.

In addition, bookstores today abound with Internet directories and how-to books about getting the most out of the web, using search tools, and simply accessing the entire potential of the Internet. The following titles are representative of the books available, but also check your local campus bookstore and others for current resources that may match your needs:

Hock, Randolph. *The Extreme Searcher's Guide to Internet Research.* Medford, NJ: Cyberage Books, 2001.

Glossbrenner, Emily, and Alfred Glossbrenner. *Search Engines for the World Wide Web.* Berkeley, CA: Peachpit Press, 2001.

Sherman, Chris, and Gary Price. *The Invisible Web: Uncovering Information Sources Search Engines Can't See.* Chicago: Independent Publishers Group, 2001.

WORKING WITH OTHERS

Begin immediately with your classmates to share information about using the library's resources on campus or exploring the Internet or other online resources from your own home-based computer. Although researching via computer may seem a little scary at first, your confidence and expertise will grow with each new effort. Explore the web, search databases through CompuServe or America Online, chat with experts from across the United States, e-mail classmates about research questions, or download files from other universities. You will find that researching online and sharing your experiences with others will make your efforts not only more effective but more enjoyable as well.

- With a friend or classmate, find out what computer facilities and services are available at your campus library and which databases can be accessed using them. Discuss each other's knowledge of or experience in accessing such databases.

- If you are not familiar with the types of online or Internet search tools described in this chapter, ask your campus librarian about participating in introductory sessions that explain these resources. You may also be able to share some of your research time working alongside a classmate who has experience in using the library's online programs.

- Find out if any of your classmates subscribe to commercial services such as Prodigy, CompuServe, and America Online. Compare your experiences with such services, and discuss how they may be of use to your research projects. Consider how you might utilize chat groups, e-mail, database searches, Internet access, or other services to aid your research. If you do not subscribe to a commercial service and have a modem on your home computer, ask your classmates to recommend one to get started with. You may want to investigate the free trial periods offered by many of the leading commercial providers.

- Use e-mail or another form of online communication to share your daily or weekly research results with a classmate. Use such communication as an opportunity to ask questions, try out ideas, or share resources with one another. You will find that sharing in these ways will keep your enthusiasm going and help you finish your research paper on time.

■ Join one or more of your classmates to browse campus or local bookstores for online or Internet guides that may contain information helpful to your research. Look through Internet directories, for example, to see what resources may be available on your research topic. Or if you are unsure about how to access or use the Internet, browse through some sources that provide this information. Discuss these sources with your classmates to see if they have recommendations or can perhaps lend you resources of their own. Remember, too, that you may be able to check out such materials from your campus or city library rather than purchase them.

Most colleges offer introductory, short-term classes about using computers or the Internet. If you are not experienced in such matters or want to strengthen your knowledge, investigate these courses and enroll in one or more as soon as you can. Doing so will prove useful for more than one semester's research assignment. For added enjoyment, ask a friend or classmate to take a class with you so you can share experiences.

CHAPTER 7

Reading Critically, Recording Information, and Avoiding Plagiarism

An accurate understanding and interpretation of sources is integral to the value of your research paper's content. Conduct your research to make the most efficient use of your own time and the resources available. Careful reading, accurate notetaking, and thoughtful evaluation as you examine a source will ensure good results.

THINKING CRITICALLY
WHEN PLANNING YOUR READING

Avoid putting the time and thinking about your topic at the mercy of haphazard reading. Once you have established a working bibliography, take the time to use the source's title, publication information, author's name, and length to estimate its place in your research needs. Naturally, you cannot always know in advance what a source contains, but thinking about your source materials before you begin to read can help you focus on which are likely to be most important and productive in this stage of your research process.

Planning Your Reading

The following suggestions will help you plan an efficient use of reading time:

1. Review the working bibliography to consult general sources first: magazine articles, histories, and other broad discussions. This will allow you to organize your research of available materials.

2. When selecting sources to read, consider their intended audience as well as your own purposes. Popular magazines will be your best resources when you need general ideas, current opinions, or recent developments; turn to more scholarly journals and books for detailed studies and recognized authorities on the topic.

3. Once familiar with a topic through reading general sources, move next to those sources that treat the topic specifically or in detail. It is best to work in such sources as soon as you can do so comfortably. This way, you avoid having to read through general ideas that are repeated throughout several sources.

4. Plan your reading to examine no more than one or two related aspects at a time. This will organize notetaking and focus your thinking on the material. For example, student Linda Kastan made a point to read first a journal article and then a book that specifically addressed people's problems with spending too much time online. Take care to keep your bibliography and your reading balanced. Consulting different viewpoints will enhance your understanding of the topic and allow for comparing opinions as you read.

5. Finally, you can waste a lot of valuable time and energy running back and forth from the periodicals room to the book stacks or from one campus library to another. When possible, organize your reading activities around types of sources and their locations. This will prevent your omitting a potentially valuable source because you do not have time to go back for it.

Types of Reading

Skimming

Skimming is a way of reading quickly to find out what is said. Rather than read everything in a selection, look for key words, main ideas, subheadings, illustrations, and other features related to your research question. The goal in skimming a source is not to read it thoroughly. Rather, find out if it has the kind of information you seek, and if it does, determine what to read more closely.

Skimming Books.   Before spending time on a close reading, first skim a book to evaluate its possible usefulness. Use the book's major components to determine its contents and scope:

1. *Start with the title.* A main title alone may be too general to indicate a book's subject, or it may not accurately reflect the book's focus. Main titles such as *Lucy's Child* or *Verdict for Justice,* for example, give no hint of the books' respective contents. The full titles of these works, however, more completely suggest their subjects:

> *Lucy's Child: The Discovery of a Human Ancestor*
> *Verdict for Justice: The American Jury System on Trial*

Attention to a complete title can tell you if a particular book is something you want to examine more closely, put off reading until later, or ignore altogether.

2. *Consult the table of contents.* Here, you will find a list of the chapters included in the book and the pages on which they begin. A quick examination of the table of contents and of any promising chapters will tell you whether to return to the book later for more detailed study.

Let's say, for example, that you were interested in researching the topic *animal intelligence.* A general bibliographic source, such as the *Essay and General Literature Index,* might refer you to a work titled *Through a Window,* anthropologist Jane Goodall's account of her studies of chimpanzees in the Gombe region of East Africa. The table of contents (see Figure 7.1) for Goodall's book lists at least one especially relevant chapter, "The Mind of the Chimpanzee." You would skim this chapter first to assess its usefulness and then examine others whose titles also suggest they might address your topic or research question. If your skimming indicated any chapters

Contents

FIGURE 7.1 A table of contents listing the chapters in a book

that merited further study, you would make out a bibliography card for the book so you could return to it later.

3. *Search the index.* In case small segments of information on your topic also appear in other places than the chapters you consult, turn next to the index located at the back of the book. A nonfiction book usually includes an index, an alphabetical list of the topics, subtopics, ideas, places, and names mentioned in it. The page numbers after each entry tell where to find it in the book. In addition to looking for a topic by name in the index, also search for it under a major term. In Jane Goodall's book on chimpanzees, for example, the index lists *mind, brain, intelligence, 12–23, 206–9* under the term *chimpanzees.*

Sometimes you need to look for a topic under a synonym or closely related term. If you found no entries in a book's index under *alcoholism,* for instance, you should next look under related terms, such as *substance abuse, addiction, drinking,* or *encounter group.*

In addition to skimming a book's table of contents and index, look for other useful features:

- The *preface* or *introduction* to a book may give an overview of the subject or suggest that particular book's approach to it.
- An *appendix* (plural *appendices* or *appendixes*) provides additional information on topics discussed in the book and may include maps, graphs, charts, or other helpful material.
- A *glossary* lists special terms and their definitions as they relate to the book's subject.
- A *bibliography* may guide you to other books or resources.

If you do not read closely and take notes from a book when you first skim it, use the working bibliography card to record the author and title as well as a brief note on what you found and the relevant page numbers. Return to the book later when you know more about what you need from it.

Skimming Periodical Articles.   You can usually skim articles in magazines, journals, and newspapers more quickly than those in books. Titles of periodical articles are usually more specific than book titles, and they often include subheadings to label and organize content for readers. Articles in most scholarly science journals, such as *Journal of Marine Research* and *Journal of Applied Psychology,* are organized according to guidelines recommended by the American Psychological Association (APA). Articles in APA form are often divided into major sections boldly labeled as Abstract, Introduction, Method, Results, Discussion, and References. Use these headings to skim such journal articles for the information you seek as well as to organize and label any notes.

To skim a periodical article, scan it quickly, paying attention to features such as boldfaced headings, subsections, and illustrations. Skim the first sentence of each paragraph or subsection to identify its main idea. You may want to read the last paragraph or two closely to understand the author's conclusions. If you think the article is worth reading more thoroughly later, make a note on the back of the bibliography card to review it.

Close Reading

Close reading requires careful attention to all the words and sentences in a selection to understand its full meaning. After you have skimmed a source and decided to read all or part of it closely, you read carefully to comprehend ideas and record information. While these two purposes can undoubtedly overlap, awareness of them as separate activities will help focus your notetaking and organize your thinking as you read.

Reading for Meaning. Reading to comprehend meaning involves recognizing main ideas as well as making inferences about what you read. As you read any material, pay attention to key ideas and statements that support an overall point.

The Thesis or Summary Statement. In most articles or chapters in books, you will recognize a thesis or summary statement that explains the author's major point. (Review the discussion of thesis statements in Chapter 3.) The main point usually appears near the beginning of a discussion but not necessarily. Wherever it occurs, the main point dominates the text. All the other ideas, sentences, paragraphs, and examples relate to it. Make a habit of identifying the main point of any material you read. As you read and take notes, consciously relate the main point to the other ideas in the text.

Topic Sentences. The topic sentence contains the paragraph's major idea, the concept that all other elements in the paragraph support or explain. Supporting ideas for a thesis may occur as the topic sentence stated at the beginning, middle, or end of a paragraph. In the following paragraph, the topic sentence is the first sentence. Notice how all other sentences help build upon the idea stated in the topic sentence:

Topic sentence	Regular cocaine users put up with many unpleasant drug effects. Restlessness, irritability and apprehension are common.
Examples support the topic sentence	Users tend to become suspicious and even display paranoid symptoms—frequently changing locks and phone numbers, doubting friends and showing inappropriate anger or jealousy. All this derives from cocaine's impact on the sympathetic nervous system—the network that controls "flight or fight" responses to fright. In addition, even at fairly low doses
Transition word signals *additional* details	cocaine may cause tremors, cold sweats, and grinding of teeth. At higher doses, vomiting and nausea may result, along

with muscle pains, a disoriented feeling and dizziness—followed, in some cases, by life-threatening seizures.

—Ira Mothner and Alan Weitz, *How to Get Off Drugs: Everything You Should Know to Help Someone You Love Get Off—and Stay Off—Drugs, Including When to Seek Help and Where to Find It* (New York: Simon and Schuster, 1984) 75.

When reading this paragraph for ideas, note particularly the main idea stated as the topic sentence. Use the main idea to focus your attention on the examples and details that develop the topic sentence further.

Implied Topic Sentences.   Sometimes the main idea in a paragraph is implied rather than stated directly. In these cases, the author feels that the point of the paragraph is obvious, and it is up to the reader to understand the central meaning. This paragraph by Annie Dillard, for example, avoids stating in an outright topic sentence that a jungle is crowded with unusual and somewhat threatening varieties of life:

Unseen in the jungle, but present, are tapirs, jaguars, many species of snake and lizard, ocelots, armadillos, marmosets, howler monkeys, toucans and macaws and a hundred other birds, deer, bats, peccaries, capybaras, agoutis, and sloths. Also present in this jungle, but variously distant, are Texaco derricks and pipelines, and some of the wildest Indians in the world, blowgun-using Indians, who killed missionaries in 1956 and ate them.

—Annie Dillard, "In the Jungle," *Teaching a Stone to Talk: Expeditions and Encounters* (New York: Perennial-Harper, 1988) 57.

You should read such a paragraph as you would any other, paying attention to how the ideas and information fit together to present an overall picture or main idea. When reading paragraphs with implied main ideas, always sum up the main point in your own words, and make it a part of your notes.

Developing Critical Judgment

In part, your judgment of a source's authority and value to your research will develop out of your own reading in the field. The more you learn about your subject, the more perceptive you will become about sources. Some that were impressive at the start of your research may eventually seem inadequate; the importance of others will emerge only as your research becomes more complete.

To gauge the reliability of an individual author's work, critically assess it in terms of its overall effectiveness in areas such as these:

■ *Fairness:* Does the author demonstrate knowledge and consideration of other viewpoints and research in the field? Is there discussion of opposing viewpoints as well as application and citation of other works or authorities?

THINKING CRITICALLY
TO EVALUATE SOURCES

The critical evaluation of source materials will continue throughout your research. As your understanding of your topic changes, so, too, will your estimation of your sources. In turn, your opinion of each source's value or authority will shape the way you think about the topic and read or take notes.

Consequently, evaluation of sources should not come only after your research has been completed but before and during your reading as well. This is because in thinking judgmentally about a source, you also think critically about its content. You may decide not to bother reading a source at all or to take entirely different kinds of notes because of what you decide about its value. By consulting the opinions of others about sources, you can learn which ideas are considered important or what others have found controversial. You can study sources more efficiently because you know what to look for as you read and take notes.

- *Logic:* Has the author supported his or her ideas with valid evidence? Is the presentation logical, and has the author avoided bias and common fallacies of logic?
- *Evidence:* Do the examples and other evidence presented fairly reflect current data? Is there a clear separation of fact and opinion?
- *Authority:* Does the author refer to qualified experts or establish his or her own credentials to speak with authority on the subject?

You should apply these and other similar criteria as you begin to take notes from research sources and also when you begin writing your paper and integrating source material into the text. Give extra consideration to how you use information from a source that appears unreliable in any of the areas described above.

Consulting Other Opinions

Because you cannot read everything written on your research topic, you will want to consult those sources who have the greatest authority or whose ideas are most valuable to your discussion. While your own broad reading on a topic will help judge the expertise and usefulness of some sources, you may also need opinions from others more familiar with the field. After locating a particular source, such as a book or a scholarly journal article, use your library's general reference sources to find out how others reacted to it.

Using Book Reviews.   Critical discussions like those published in the *New York Times Book Review,* the *Times Literary Supplement,* and scholarly journals give you the opinions of experts about a work's strengths and weaknesses. Book reviews can help you learn more about a topic as well as about the book and its author's standing in the field.

The most useful resource for general book reviews is *Book Review Digest (BRD)* (New York: H. W. Wilson, 1905–date). Drawing upon reviews published in nearly one hundred general periodicals and scholarly journals, *BRD* summarizes a book and any reviews written about it (see Figure 7.2). Because *BRD* usually includes several reviews for each work listed, use it to avoid having to consult multiple sources to learn about a book or its author. If you need more information than summarized versions provide, use *BRD* to locate the complete reviews in their original publications. Note that *BRD* is also available online (1983–date) through DIALOG or CompuServe's IQuest.

In addition to *Book Review Digest,* reviews of scholarly books and articles are available in most of the specialized indexes discussed in Chapter 3. The following indexes are also useful for general and scholarly works:

Book Review Index. New York: H. W. Wilson, 1905–date.
Current Book Review Citations. New York: H. W. Wilson, 1976–date.
Index to Book Reviews in the Humanities. Williamston, MI: Thomson, 1960–date.
Technical Book Review Index. New York: Willis, 1961–date.

Using Citation Indexes.   The number of times an author has published in a field, which journals have carried his or her work, and how oth-

---

PRESTON, RICHARD. The hot zone. 300p il $23/Can$31
    1994 Random House
        614.5   1. Ebola virus 2. Epidemiology 3. Animal experimentation
        ISBN 0-679-43094-6   LC 94-13415

SUMMARY: This volume focuses on the viruses Ebola and Marburg, named "for the places where they were first detected, [and] classified as 'Biosafety Level 4' because they are more lethal than HIV but also highly contagious. This is the story of their recent escape from the . . . African rainforest to big centres of human population via modern roads and planes. . . . Ebola and Marburg are filoviruses or thread viruses. . . . [Preston argues] that these viruses have 'jumped species' from monkeys to humans at precisely the time when human activity is threatening the habitat and survival of other primates." (New Sci) Glossary.

FIGURE 7.2   A sample entry from *Book Review Digest*

Source: From *Book Review Digest,* Vol. 91, No. 5, August 1995, p. 438. Copyright © 1995 by The H. W. Wilson Company. Reprinted with permission.

ers have valued it are all important considerations in evaluating a source. Computer-produced periodical indexes such as *Arts & Humanities Citation Index, Science Citation Index,* and *Social Science Citation Index* provide information such as the following:

- What other current and past work an individual has authored
- What other authors have cited the work, as well as where and when
- Where a work has been reviewed
- Where follow-up studies, corrections, or applications have been described
- Where the article is summarized as an abstract in the major journals for the field

Available in print or online, citation indexes can supply information to help judge a work's originality, authority, and application. Citation indexes list mainly journal articles, but some books are included as well. Remember that citation indexes are usually organized as three volumes: *permuterm index, source index,* and *citation index.* Using keywords from a work's title or the name of an author, you can use any one of the indexes to locate information. (See Chapter 4 on citation indexes and how to use them.)

Evaluation Criteria

While it is essential to consult the work of recognized authorities in order to integrate their ideas with your own thinking, not all your research information will come with identifiable credentials. In general, a source will be useful to your research if it meets one or more of the following criteria:

1. It was written by a reliable authority whose methods and reasoning appear valid. Not everything you use in your research has to (or should) be written by someone with a PhD, but the author's education, experience with the topic, and reputation should play a major part in your evaluation and use of a work.

2. It offers facts and ideas other sources do not.

3. It sets forth facts and ideas that do not contradict known concepts or other works without good evidence.

4. It demonstrates knowledge and consideration of other viewpoints and research in the field. Look for discussion of opposing ideas and also the application and citation of others' works.

5. It is current in terms of both publication date and information. Remember that knowledge changes more rapidly in some fields than others. Ideas in the humanities, for example, tend to remain consistent longer than those in the sciences, where constant research and new technology change existing knowledge daily.

Apply these criteria both when you begin to take notes from your research sources and when you begin writing your paper and integrating source material into the text.

Taking Effective Notes

You will need to take good written notes on all the information collected during your research. The notes will help organize your thinking about what you investigate as well as provide general ideas, quotations from authorities, and specific data when you write the paper. Since you cannot remember everything you discover about a topic, develop and follow a consistent system of notetaking that will help you select, organize, and record information.

What to Take Notes About

Your research notes will be more useful if you recognize in advance what to record from your reading. Certain information needs to be written down each time you take any kind of notes about a source:

1. The title and author of the source (You will also need to include the publisher's name, as well as the place and date of publication, if you have not made a working bibliography card for each source consulted during your research.)
2. The page number(s) from which the material is taken
3. The content you want to record

In general, the content of your notes should reflect your close, critical evaluation and analysis of the source. Summarizing the source is a valuable way to ensure your own understanding. Doing so also provides a reference that will be useful later, whether as a reminder as to what the source is about or to provide the documentation needed in your Works Cited list. As you evaluate a source, make notes about the author's authority on the subject, the use and kinds of evidence presented, and your overall impression of the author's effectiveness. Consider these questions:

- What facts or opinions seem to contradict those you found in other sources?
- What ideas agree with those of other writers and with your own conclusions about the topic?

As with the answers to these and similar questions, focus your notes upon content that will assist you in thinking critically about the source and its use in your research paper.

Note Format

Arrange note information any way that is convenient and makes for easy reference. Consistency in the way you record page numbers, identify direct quotations, and add your own commentary is essential for accurate interpretation of the notes later.

Figure 7.3 shows a typical arrangement of essential note material on one of Linda Kastan's notecards. She labeled the card with the heading Problems with Online Addiction and used it for notes on an article titled "Hooked Online." Notice that only the source's author, identified by a first

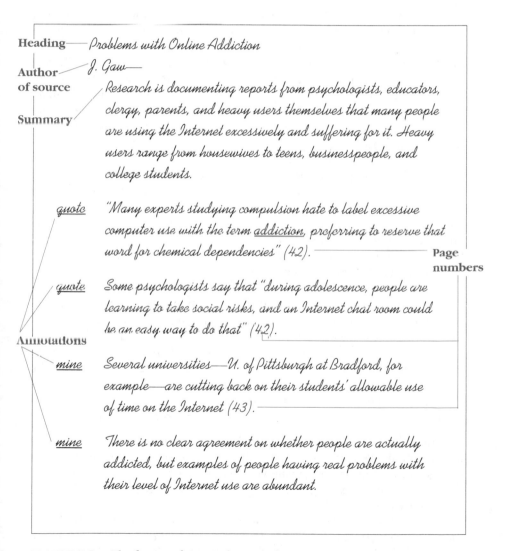

Heading — Problems with Online Addiction

Author — J. Gaw —
of source

Summary — Research is documenting reports from psychologists, educators, clergy, parents, and heavy users themselves that many people are using the Internet excessively and suffering for it. Heavy users range from housewives to teens, businesspeople, and college students.

quote — "Many experts studying compulsion hate to label excessive computer use with the term *addiction*, preferring to reserve that word for chemical dependencies" (42). — **Page numbers**

quote — Some psychologists say that "during adolescence, people are learning to take social risks, and an Internet chat room could be an easy way to do that" (42).

Annotations

mine — Several universities — U. of Pittsburgh at Bradford, for example — are cutting back on their students' allowable use of time on the Internet (43).

mine — There is no clear agreement on whether people are actually addicted, but examples of people having real problems with their level of Internet use are abundant.

FIGURE 7.3 The format of a typical notecard

initial and last name, is needed on the notecard. Linda had previously recorded the author's complete name, the full title of the source, and all relevant publishing information on a separate bibliography card. In order to make her notes clearly understandable later, she punctuated each section of quoted material clearly and added the notation *quote* next to it in the margin. She also indicated her own analysis with the notation *mine* and used parentheses to separate and identify page numbers.

Note Content

Using your research question as a guide, you will find that a good deal of your notetaking will be based on evolving intuition: As a preliminary thesis or response to the research question begins to form from your reading, you will start to recognize what things to record in your notes. Taking more notes, you will also begin to recognize how the pieces of collected information fit together to support one or more major ideas that may form an answer to the research question or seve as the basis of a preliminary thesis for the paper. The further you progress in your research, the more you will recognize with increasing certainty what material to record.

Before starting research, review the sample papers in Chapter 11 and Appendix A. Examine them to acquaint yourself with the kinds of ideas and information that make up a research paper. Naturally, you will not know all the information needed from your research sources until you begin writing the paper; however, your increasing sense of what you will eventually say about the topic should help identify material for notes. Depending upon your topic and your own knowledge of the subject, the contents of the notes will include a wide variety of information:

1. Take notes to record background information that you need to understand the research topic better. If you are investigating welfare fraud, you may first need to learn about the extent of the problem, existing laws, facts about the history of state assistance programs, or the legal definitions of terms. Eventually, your reading and notes on such material will supply the broad understanding necessary to research and write effectively on the topic. Expect the background notes on any subject to decrease as you learn more about it and begin focusing on supporting a preliminary thesis.

2. Take notes to summarize general ideas supporting your preliminary thesis statement. Your preliminary thesis will probably shift in focus or change completely as you pursue your research. Groups of major ideas will emerge from your reading, changing your thinking or the emphasis of the preliminary thesis.

You will find it easier to organize your notes on such ideas by listing them under subtopic headings. As Linda Kastan did her reading research on Internet addiction, for example, she recorded her notes under headings such as Problems with Online Addiction, Defining Addiction, and How People Get Hooked. As Linda gathered additional ideas about her topic, she added more headings, discontinued a few, and eventually merged others under new headings. In doing so, she found a way to organize her notes and to begin identifying categories of ideas to include in her paper (see Figure 7.4).

3. Take notes on explanatory information such as histories, definitions of terms, plot summaries, biographical data, and other material that you may need to provide for your readers. For a paper about former Soviet President Mikhail Gorbachev, you may need notes about the form of the Soviet government, background on the 1991 coup attempt, or information about the highlights of his political career. A paper on cocaine use would need notes for defining terms such as *crack* and *freebasing,* for example.

4. Take notes to record quotations, examples, and anecdotes that will illustrate or support your ideas in the paper. Quoting an eloquently stated opinion or the words of a recognized expert lends interest as well as authority to your own discussion (see Using Quotations, Chapter 10). For instance, in a paper on computer viruses, you could use specific examples from an interview with an expert on the subject. A paper on problems faced by new U.S. immigrants might include an anecdote about someone's first attempt to register for school or to apply for a job.

Physiological and Psychological Addiction Signs.

Young's study—

<u>mine</u>   *The dependent users got a positive feeling from being online but developed a tolerance after they got used to the technology ("Internet").*

<u>quote</u>   *Dependent users "felt unable to live without the Internet for an extended period of time" ("Internet").*

<u>quote</u>   *"Dependents explained that these cravings felt so intense that they reestablished their Internet service, bought a new modem, or set up their computer again to obtain an 'Internet fix.'" ("Internet").*

FIGURE 7.4 Notes used in writing the paper (see paragraph on p. 155)

5. Take notes on little-known facts or questionable and controversial ideas about your topic. Even if accurate, facts and opinions that are not commonly known or may seem questionable to your paper's reader need to be carefully recorded and supported by documentation. For instance, selected research may suggest people can actually lose weight by *thinking* themselves thin, but your readers may not accept this assertion or may believe you have misunderstood the facts. To prevent losing credibility, take good notes to describe the research fully and indicate an authoritative source for it in your paper. (See Chapters 11–13 on citing such sources.)

6. Take notes to record statistical figures, such as percentages, weights, amounts of money, ratios, and dates that are not commonly known, as well as the sources in which you found them. Your readers may need to know that Americans throw away 160 million tons of trash each year or that 55% of American women in 1993 worked outside the home. Figures like these can add precision to your paper's discussion and also convincingly support and illustrate your ideas. Take notes on all such figures related to your research question. The frequency with which you come across such statistics in your research will determine whether they are commonly known or need to be documented. (See Chapter 11 about documenting figures.)

The notes from material such as that mentioned here will shape your thinking during the research stage. Expect to take more notes than you will actually need, and do not hesitate to write down anything you think may be of importance later. Eventually, you will combine the material from your notes with your own ideas as well as those of others you cite in the research paper.

Figure 7.4 shows one of Linda Kastan's notecards for a discussion of the physiological and psychological characteristics of Internet addiction. Notice how Linda used her notes on the original source material to illustrate and support the main idea of a paragraph in her paper:

Original from source   Dependents developed a tolerance as subjects reported they gradually needed periods of time on-line to achieve the desired effect. . . . Dependents were unable to restrict their usage to the prescribed time limits. When time limits failed, Dependents cancelled their Internet service, threw out their modems, or completely dismantled their computers to keep themselves from using the Internet. Dependents felt unable to live without the Internet for an extended period of time. They reported developing a preoccupation with being on-line, which they compared to "cravings" that smokers feel when they have gone a length of time without a cigarette. Dependents explained that these cravings felt so intense that they reestablished their Internet service, bought a new modem, or set up their computer again to obtain an "Internet fix."

—Kimberly S. Young, "Internet Addiction: The Emergence of a New Clinical Disorder"

Notes as used in the paper   Although the need to go online may not fit the clinical definition of <u>addiction</u>, evidence exists that the high most heavy users get from being online can be as physiologically and psychologically inducing as that from any drug. Young's subjects, for example, demonstrated a variety of symptoms usually associated with chemical addiction, including a heightened sense of pleasure when online, eventual increased tolerance and a need for more time online to feel stimulated, and withdrawl-like symptoms whenever they were not online for prolonged periods of time ("Internet").

Where to Record Notes

While everyone has his or her own method for taking notes, some are more useful for preparing a research paper than others. Again, *consistency* is the key to any successful notetaking. Decide early on a system that you will follow. A regular routine for storing notes and registering information will keep them from getting lost and prevent omissions that may cause extra work later.

Record your notes in a legible and accurate fashion. It is easy to become confused later about note contents. Be consistent about listing or marking bibliographic data, source summaries, quotations, page numbers, and your own comments. (See Chapter 10 on how to punctuate quotations and quote accurately.) Mark your notes in a way that clearly separates and identifies each. As mentioned earlier, notations such as *mine, quote, summary,* and the like can keep note content clearly identified (see Figure 7.3).

Decide how or on what you want to store your notes. There are plenty of options. Notecards, a notebook, photocopies, or a computer are common preferences. You will probably vary your method from time to time to suit certain kinds of information, but using one medium throughout your research is most efficient. In general, the best method is one that consistently fits your work habits and meets the needs of your research materials.

Notecards.   Keeping your notes on cards offers the greatest flexibility and convenience. Notecards can be arranged or shuffled to suit any order you need, and you can easily add or take out cards as your research progresses. Use cards big enough to record plenty of information. Large 5″ × 8″ cards provide ample space for recording notes, commentary, and bibliographic information. Use a separate card for each source. Include subtopic headings to categorize your notes (see Figures 7.3 and 7.4) and to group cards in the same categories later. Keep the cards bound with a rubber band, and carry them with you when doing research.

A Research Notebook.   For some topics, especially those requiring extensive notes or columns of figures, recording all your research ideas in a single notebook is also a good idea. Notebook pages allow plenty of room for adding your own extensive commentary or other remarks to your notes, and a bound notebook keeps all your work together for easy use. If you have been keeping a research notebook, use a major part of it to record reading notes. This will make other research material (research schedule, observations, survey questions, etc.) more accessible for review when working with your notes or their sources. You can cut and paste various sections of the notebook pages together for easy reference when you start to write your paper.

Photocopies.   Photocopied materials are not notes but the basis for notes. Nonetheless, considerations of length, complexity, availability, or your need for precise data may make it necessary to photocopy portions of printed research sources. Photocopying is a valuable aid to any researcher, though overreliance on it can become expensive and doubly time consuming: You will still have to reread the contents of photocopied material and make notes on it before writing your paper.

Figure 7.5 shows the kind of notes Linda Kastan made on a photocopy of material about Internet addiction. She decided to photocopy the page rather than record notes from it because of the quotes it included and her uncertainty about whether she might want to use them later for her paper. In this way, Linda used the photocopied material to supplement her note-taking, not replace it.

On Computer.   Computers can make storing and using research notes both easier and more difficult. On the positive side, storing research notes on a computer allows you to revise them with follow-up commentary, to reorganize them according to developing subtopics, and to merge them once you get to the writing stage. A separate file for sources listed in the working bibliography is also a good idea: You can update and alphabetize the list as you need, adding it to the paper when you have finished writing the text. If your computer software program has outlining features, you can use the topic headings from notecards to create a working outline.

There are also some drawbacks to keeping your notes on computer. Unless you have regular access to a computer and are in the habit of working consistently with one for your academic needs, you may need to use an additional method of notetaking as well. Remember that you will not always have a computer available wherever you do research, and you will

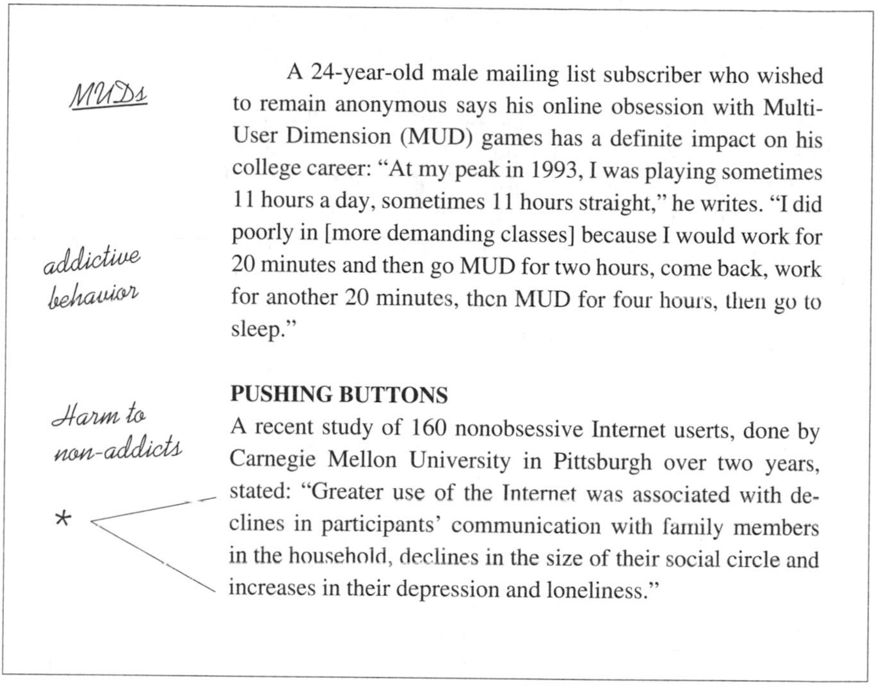

MUDs

A 24-year-old male mailing list subscriber who wished to remain anonymous says his online obsession with Multi-User Dimension (MUD) games has a definite impact on his college career: "At my peak in 1993, I was playing sometimes 11 hours a day, sometimes 11 hours straight," he writes. "I did poorly in [more demanding classes] because I would work for 20 minutes and then go MUD for two hours, come back, work for another 20 minutes, then MUD for four hours, then go to sleep."

addictive behavior

Harm to non-addicts

*

PUSHING BUTTONS
A recent study of 160 nonobsessive Internet userts, done by Carnegie Mellon University in Pittsburgh over two years, stated: "Greater use of the Internet was associated with declines in participants' communication with family members in the household, declines in the size of their social circle and increases in their depression and loneliness."

FIGURE 7.5   A photocopy on which notes have been added in the margin
Source: From "Internet Addiction" by R. W. Greene. Copyright © 1998 COMPUTERWORLD, Inc. Reprinted with permission of *Computer World Magazine*.

have to transcribe handwritten notes and other collected data into the computer almost daily. Unless your computer program does it for you, you will also need to make back-up copies of all your material on a regular basis to prevent loss due to a machine or program malfunction.

Too many methods of storing information result in misplacing notes and wasting time trying to consolidate results. For all your notetaking, avoid using loose sheets of paper, more than one notebook, or too great a mixture of ways to store your research notes. Choose a means of storing notes that prevents loss while still allowing flexibility, organization, and ease of use.

Types of Notes

Your notes are a literal record of what you learn about the research topic. In addition to recording your findings, taking notes prompts you to read sources critically. In the act of reading and taking notes, you organize and reinterpret information for yourself, thereby understanding it better. (A drawback to photocopying materials is that it postpones this important critical process.)

Different research sources and your individual responses to them will require varying kinds of notes. Though books and periodicals will supply the majority of your note content, notetaking will also be important for recording what you learn from other kinds of sources: Onsite observations; pamphlets and other literature; responses to interview questions; films, radio, and television broadcasts; and public speeches or lectures will also require good written notes. While your way of recording information will vary with each kind of source, the following methods are basic to all notetaking:

- Summary
- Paraphrase
- Direct quotation
- Combination notes

As this lists suggests, the majority of your notes will represent a condensation of information. You should know the differences among these major kinds of notes and how to use them effectively in your research, including giving proper acknowledgment to your sources.

**THINKING CRITICALLY
ABOUT WHEN TO SUMMARIZE, PARAPHRASE,
OR QUOTE DIRECTLY**

The most important decision you will need to make in the course of your notetaking is whether to summarize, paraphrase, quote, or use a combination of these in recording source information. The following discussion of each type of note will provide more detailed guidelines, but in general *summarize* when what's important is the gist of a passage, particularly a lengthy one; *paraphrase* when you feel you can—or should—restate a relatively brief passage in your own words; and *quote directly* only when you feel a passage or an element of a passage would lose something in paraphrase.

Summary.   In writing a summary, you reduce what was originally said in a source by restating it more briefly in your own words. You summarize original material by eliminating unimportant ideas and condensing essential ones to a single statement or two. Since your goal is to reduce without distorting meaning, you must understand the original well before attempting to summarize it.

How much you summarize from a source depends upon your purpose. You may summarize large portions of a work, such as the action of a novel, the development of a scientific theory, or the content of a journal article. To summarize large amounts of content, read the whole piece closely at least twice. Take notes as you read, looking for main ideas or subdivisions of the content (see Close Reading, earlier in this chapter). Then combine your notes by reducing their content into a few sentences that summarize the whole. Read your summary carefully several times. Add or delete content until you have condensed the original without distorting or leaving out important parts.

In summarizing any entire work or large portions of it, your aim is to reduce the whole piece by including only the main ideas. Smaller portions of a work are summarized in much the same way, though you can be more selective about what you summarize. In most research notetaking, you need to condense and record only the information most relevant to your topic, research question, or thesis. This could mean summarizing only a few sentences or a single paragraph, if that is all the information relevant to your research.

Linda Kastan used such selective notetaking to summarize information from one of the sources she read for her paper on Internet addiction. The following excerpt from that source provided a statistical example of the problem she was writing about:

> Middle-aged women, the unemployed, and Internet "newbies" are most prone to Internet addiction, says Kimberly Young, a University of Pittsburgh psychologist who presented a study of 496 Net users at the convention. "Addicts" in her study spent 38 hours per week online for nonwork purposes. (Normal users average eight hours per week.) Students may also be at risk; one third know someone with social or academic problems traceable to heavy Net use, according to a study of 1,200 undergraduates by psychologist Keith Anderson of Rensselaer Polytechnic Institute.
>
> —"But Can It Lead to the Harder Stuff?" *U.S News & World Report*, 1 Sept. 1997: 12.

Linda recorded her summary of this paragraph onto a notecard with the heading College Students. Notice that in writing her paper, she used the examples from the source selectively and incorporated part of the original language in her own sentence form:

> Although other researchers have found fault with the methodology of Young's study,[1] few disagree with her conclusion that something widespread and potentially harmful is going on with Internet use.
> A recent New York survey, for example, reported that 17% of the male respondents said they spend more than 40 hours a week online ("Over-Use"), and in a survey of 1,200 undergraduates, one-third

reported they know someone with "social or academic problems" stemming from heavy Internet use ("But Can It Lead").

Like Linda, you may occasionally want to summarize information using fragmentary phrases—such as "social or academic problems"—or your own shorthand for reducing language. It is best, however, to write summaries in complete sentences. Doing so will help you better grasp the content as you record it and ensure that you will be able to understand it later.

Paraphrase.   A good paraphrase clarifies a source's content by recasting it into your own words. Whereas a summary seeks to condense or eliminate length, a paraphrase restates the original almost line by line. The result is that a paraphrase is usually about the same length as the original, but the words are your own. Remember that proper citation of the source must always accompany any paraphrase.

You should paraphrase whenever the language or content of the original cannot be adequately summarized. This often happens with technical and scientific material, in which the detailed content or language may be unsuitable for condensing to notes or for use in your paper. At other times, you may paraphrase by combining original details and language with your own wording in order to shorten the content. In general, paraphrase whenever doing so will make your notes more useful and the information clearer to your paper's readers.

The following excerpt demonstrates material suitable for paraphrase. The example is from an article published in *TESOL Quarterly,* a journal written for linguists and (as the title acronym indicates) Teachers of English to Speakers of Other Languages (TESOL). The paragraph summarizes research on the relationship between notetaking and learning by students who are native and nonnative speakers of English:

> There appears, in other words, to be a need to rehearse information noted down rather than just to take notes on information imparted via lecture format. Incorporating a review-of-notes condition into the present design might have yielded quite different results and might have tested the delayed effect, not just the immediate effect, of the encoding hypothesis. In sum, results of the present study suggest that note taking without opportunity for review of notes is of questionable utility for either American or international lecture attendees.
>
> —Patricia Dunkel, Shitala Mishra, and David Berliner, "Effects of Note Taking, Memory, and Language Proficiency on Lecture Learning for Native and Nonnative Speakers of English," *TESOL Quarterly* 23 (1989): 547.

The language and content in this excerpt may be appropriate for the author's intentions and the journal's audience. For the purposes of notetaking, however, and for better understanding by your paper's readers, the passage should be paraphrased.

A good paraphrase effectively recasts original language for better clarity and readability. A poor paraphrase simply changes the words of the original or mixes the original with rephrased material. Compare the following paraphrase with the original paragraph above:

A poor paraphrase

There seems, then, to be a necessity for rehearsing note content instead of just taking notes on lecture information. Including a note review in the current plan may have given different results and tested not only the immediate effect but also the delayed effect of the encoding hypothesis. In summary, the findings of this study suggest that taking notes without the chance to review them has questionable usefulness for American or foreign lecture students ("Effects of Note Taking" 547).

This is a poor paraphrase because it merely substitutes new words for the language of the original. A good paraphrase, on the other hand, translates the *meaning* of the original by effectively recasting its language into clearer form:

A good paraphrase

Students need to review lecture notes rather than simply write down information presented in lecture. If this research study had included the practice of reviewing notes, the delayed as well as the immediate effect of notetaking on learning might have been tested. Overall, however, it seems that notetaking alone, without the practice of reviewing notes, may have little value for any lecture student, whether native or nonnative speaking ("Effects of Note Taking" 547).

Because you are adding your own wording and using your own sentence structures, a good paraphrase should sound like your own writing. This does not mean that you should take credit for the paraphrased material, however. Notice that the preceding paraphrase correctly cites the title (shortened for convenience) and page number of the original source. Be sure to record the page number of any paraphrased original on your notecard, and cite the source for any paraphrase when it appears in your paper.

Direct Quotation.   Use a quotation when you need to record a source's precise language, whether spoken or written. The emphasis here is on *need:* You should quote because the original language is necessary or the sense cannot be conveyed by other words. You may need to use quotations for the following purposes:

1. *To capture individual authority or interest:* An authority, a well-known person, or another individual should be quoted when his or her own words would be more important or more interesting to your reader. For example:

> Hillary Rodham Clinton probably spoke for all working mothers when she asked, "What power wouldn't I trade for a little more time with my family?" (Carlson 36).

> Dr. Robert Webber, head of research for the New York Cancer Institute, says a person's attitude "can influence susceptibility to disease more than most of us realize" (102).

> "I got my father to let me ride the mule to school one day. As I came over the hill toward the schoolhouse, a cub black bear came out of the bushes behind us. The mule turned and saw the bear, gave a sort of loud snort, and took off! I could hardly hold on, but I did. The next thing I knew, the mule and me had raced through the front door of the schoolhouse and landed smack in the middle of a geography lesson" (Satler 129).

Used in appropriate amounts to illustrate points or demonstrate character, direct quotations from individuals add liveliness and credibility to your paper's discussion.

2. *To ensure accuracy:* Exact language is often needed to define special terms, describe conditions, or report results. The precise language that scientific, medical, and technical sources rely upon for accuracy cannot always be preserved in a summary or paraphrase. In these cases, it is usually best to use direct quotations:

> A complex number in trigonometry can be represented on a two-dimensional diagram: "The horizontal axis is the real axis and the vertical axis is the imaginary axis. The number $\underline{a + bi}$ is represented by a point drawn $\underline{a}$ units to the right of the origin and $\underline{b}$ units up" (Glenn 82).

"Ibuprofen is one of several nonsteroid anti-inflammatory drugs used to reduce inflammation, relieve pain, or reduce fever. All nonsteroid anti-inflammatory drugs share the same side effects and may be used by patients who cannot tolerate Aspirin" (Simon and Silverman 317).

Legal discussions may require quotations to ensure strict interpretation or accurate description of a given law:

> Our Constitution states that "No person shall be convicted of treason unless on the testimony of two witnesses to the same overt act, or on confession in open court" (III, 3).
> —U.S. Constitution, Art. III, Sect. 3.

> The court decreed that, in cases of divorce, an indignity is any "affront to the personality of another or a lack of reverence for the personality of one's spouse" (Gifis 284).
> —Steven H. Gifis, *Law Dictionary* (New York: Barton's, 1984) 284.

In instances such as these, you may need quotations to ensure precise meaning or to emphasize the accuracy of your own understanding of the material.

3. *To illustrate unique language:* Sometimes language is more important for its uniqueness or emotional power than its ability to convey meaning. In discussing a literary work, for instance, a quotation demonstrates the author's use of language to create meaning and tone. You might quote an example like the following from John Steinbeck's *The Grapes of Wrath* to illustrate how he describes the onset of the great drought that created the "dust bowl" conditions of his novel's setting:

> "The dawn came, but no day. In the gray sky a red sun appeared, a dim circle that gave a little light, like dusk; and as that day advanced, the dusk slipped back toward darkness, and the wind cried and whimpered over the fallen corn" (Steinbeck 2-3).
> —John Steinbeck, *The Grapes of Wrath* (New York: Viking, 1939) 2–3.

In other instances, a memorable phrase or a particularly telling remark can often reveal more than any paraphrase could capture:

> Those of us who are well fed may find it difficult to understand that people who are homeless are grateful for whatever is available. As Benjamin Franklin once said, "Hunger never saw bad bread" (40).
> —Benjamin Franklin, *Poor Richard's Almanac, 1773* (Philadelphia: Rosenbach, 1977) 40.

As government cutbacks in social and educational programs increase, the need for volunteers becomes even greater. We should remember the words of John F. Kennedy, who said, "Ask not what your country can do for you—ask what you can do for your country."
—John F. Kennedy, Inaugural Address, Washington, DC, 21 Jan. 1961.

Who had the right to sign memos for the president in his absence? "Everybody and nobody," according to one White House source (Miller 91).

These examples demonstrate situations in which the use of direct quotations is appropriate and effective. Remember, however, that too many quotations will dilute the quality of your discussion. By depending on quotation instead of paraphrase, you will decrease your analysis of the material during notetaking. Furthermore, by including too many quotations in your paper, you may bury your own ideas and make your readers do all the thinking. Avoid excessive quotation by summarizing and paraphrasing whenever possible. If a quotation adds something that a paraphrase or summary cannot, be sure it fits one of the situations described here.

Whenever you use a quotation, be sure to quote all words and punctuation *exactly as they appear in the original.* Mark your notecard clearly to indicate that the material is a direct quotation and to show all necessary punctuation and page numbers. Notice that each of the examples given earlier cites the source for the quoted material. Such citation is an absolute requirement any time you use a quotation in your paper.

Combination Notes.   Combining summary, paraphrase, and quotation in your notes or the paper itself allows for adapting source material to your own style and fitting it into a discussion. When combining notetaking methods, take care to identify for yourself which notes are summary, paraphrase, or quotation so as not to misrepresent the material later in your paper.

Avoiding Plagiarism

Plagiarism—that is, including in a paper another person's language or ideas as if they were your own—is the worst form of academic and intellectual dishonesty. Whether plagiarism is entirely deliberate or essentially unintentional, it is—purely and simply—an act of theft, and consequences for student writers who plagiarize may range from a failing grade on the paper to a failing grade in the course to expulsion from college. In the professional world, writers who are discovered to have plagiarized may lose their jobs or face serious lawsuits. You should do everything you can to avoid even the appearance of plagiarism in your writing.

By the time they reach college, most students clearly recognize what constitutes deliberate plagiarism. It may involve submitting under one's own name a paper written by another student or a paper purchased through a local, mail-order, or online service. It may involve a writer borrowing heavily from a single source throughout a paper without adequately acknowledging his or her dependence on that source—documenting direct quotations, for example, but consciously not documenting paraphrases and other uses of the original author's ideas. In some instances—particularly in assignments, such as literary analyses, where student writers are expected to offer their own interpretations and insights—it may involve stitching together quotations and paraphrases from published authors with no acknowledgment whatsoever. Deliberate plagiarism is a blatant form of academic cheating and need not be discussed here in more detail.

Some plagiarism, however, results from borrowing from a source and either forgetting or otherwise neglecting to acknowledge its author in the paper. To avoid committing such plagiarism, make sure as you read through potential sources that you take notes for any information you might ultimately use in your paper, that any notes you take are complete and accurate, that direct quotations are clearly indicated as such in your notes, and that you have provided yourself with enough information about the source itself so you will be able to acknowledge it later. (A paraphrase that too closely resembles the original source—as discussed on page 161 and below—may also be considered plagiarism.) As you write the paper, remember that any time you use someone else's words, expressions, or ways of thinking about something—as well as any information from a source that may not be considered common knowledge (see pp. 152–55; 162–64)—you must give credit to the source. Otherwise, you will be committing plagiarism.

Following are some examples of plagiarism.

ORIGINAL SOURCE

In medicine, there has long been a conflict between the imperative to give patients the best possible care and the need to provide novices with experience. Residencies attempt to mitigate potential harm through supervision and graduated responsiblity. . . . But there is still no avoiding those first few unsteady times a young physician tries to put in a central line, remove a breast cancer, or sew together two segments of colon. No matter how many protections are in place, on average these cases go less well with the novice than with someone experienced. (Gawande, Atul. "The Learning Curve." New Yorker 28 Jan. 2002: 57-58)

Plagiarism: Failure to acknowledge a direct quotation
According to surgeon Atul Gawande, while hospital residency programs do what they can to make sure patients are well cared for, when a student doctor first <u>tries to put in a central line, remove a breast cancer, or sew together two segments of colon, on average these cases go less well with the novice than with someone experienced</u> (57-58).

Corrected with quotation marks
According to surgeon Atul Gawande, while hospital residency programs do what they can to make sure patients are well cared for, when a student doctor first <u>"tries to put in a central line, remove a breast cancer, or sew together two segments of colon, [. . .] on average these cases go less well with the novice than with someone experienced"</u> (57-58).

Corrected by paraphrasing
According to surgeon Atul Gawande, while hospital residency programs do what they can to make sure patients are well cared for, when a student doctor first <u>attempts a procedure on a patient, the results are usually not as successful as when the procedure is performed by an experienced surgeon</u> (57-58).

Plagiarism: Too close to the original source
In the world of medicine, there has always been a tension between the desire to offer patients the highest-quality care and the need to supply experience to new doctors. Residencies try to limit possible harm through oversight and slowly increasing responsibility (Gawande 57).

Here the writer has simply substituted synonyms for the original language while maintaining the original's phrasing and sentence structure.

Corrected by paraphrasing and limited direct quotation
Doctors have always faced the problem of balancing high-quality patient care with the need for physicians in training to receive hands-on experience, a problem residency programs have dealt with by supervising residents and providing them with "graduated responsibility" (Gawande 57).

Plagiarism: Writer's use of source not clear
Residency programs "attempt to mitigate potential harm through supervision and graduated responsibility" (Gawande 57). Still, patients

may not always receive optimal care when student doctors are performing a procedure for the first time.

While the direct quotation in the first sentence is clearly attributed to the original source, the paraphrase in the second sentence is not.

Corrected: Attribution clarified

According to surgeon Atul Gawande, while residency programs "attempt to mitigate potential harm through supervision and graduated responsibility," patients may still not always receive optimal care when student doctors are performing a procedure for the first time (57-58).

Acknowledging a Source.   To acknowledge a source, name it at the same time you present its words or ideas in your paper. Whether the language presented is your own or the source's makes no difference. The idea is as important as the words used to express it. Notice how sources are named directly within the text in each of these examples:

MLA (Modern Language Association) Style

The first life forms probably began appearing about 3,000 million years ago in a kind of "prebiotic soup of organic molecules" (Gregory 233).

People who argue for legalizing drugs believe that they are not really as dangerous as we think or that truly unsafe drugs would never be widely used (Nadelmann 56).

APA (American Psychological Association) Style

While classification of children's drawings shows some similarity among individuals (Kellog, 1996), Golomb (1998) emphasizes the difficulty of interpreting development by comparisons with models.

Number-Reference Style

If we assume that phobic neuroses can be effectively treated by desensitization,[1] there still remains the problem of treating multiple afflictions. Roth's work in this area suggests several useful approaches.[2]

(See Chapters 11–13 for instruction on documentation following these various styles.)

Guidelines for Avoiding Plagiarism.   Because of the ethical and practical seriousness of plagiarism, give scrupulous attention to avoiding it throughout your research. Following these guidelines will keep you from making mistakes that might result in unintentional plagiarism:

1. *Understand and use correct notetaking methods.* Know the differences among summary, paraphrase, and quotation as well as when and how to use them correctly. (See the preceding discussion for the proper uses of these methods.)

2. *Take accurate and legible notes.* Record page numbers clearly for any material you summarize, paraphrase, or quote as well as for any figures or uncommonly known facts you borrow. Annotate your notes by adding comments such as *my words, quoted, summary, her idea,* and so forth (see Figure 7.3). Remember that faint periods and ambiguous quotation marks will later be easily overlooked or misread. Use heavy, bold punctuation, especially for quotation marks and any punctuation included within quotations.

3. *Know what to document.* You must cite in your paper's text and document in the Works Cited or References page(s) the source for any words, expressions, ideas, organization of ideas, facts, or lines of thinking you borrow or adapt. This means that your notes will always need to include the title, author's name, and publication facts about the source as well as specific page number(s) for any information you record. (See Chapter 4 on what to record on bibliography cards for books and magazines.)

Whenever you quote directly, for example, or even paraphrase what another writer has said, you must cite the source for that material. Similarly, if you state in your paper that "three-fourths of the American public favor raising the tax on cigarettes," tell where you got such information. If you rely particularly upon one source for your extended description, let's say, of how a typical nuclear power plant operates, give credit to that source. In each of these cases, make sure that your notes include specific page numbers and other documentation information you will need in the paper. (Chapters 11–13 describe necessary documentation information and forms for various kinds of sources.)

Your paper will not need to document information that is *common knowledge*—ideas or facts that are generally well known or basic to a field of study. Understandably, you may not be able to judge what information is considered common until you have done a fair amount of research on your topic. Thus, when beginning research on *dinosaurs,* for example, you may not know that they lived during what is called the Mesozoic Era. Similarly, when first investigating the topic *heroin,* you may not know that the main effects of this narcotic occur in both the nervous and digestive systems. After you have consulted three or four sources on your topic, however, you will be able to recognize what information is common knowledge.

It is always a good idea, of course, to record complete documentation for any information you find. Do so during initial reading and notetaking until you have a sense of what is common knowledge for your subject. As you later write the paper, however, remember that you should not cite sources for commonly known facts and ideas.

4. *Make a bibliographic card for every note source.* You cannot give credit to a source if you lack the information to do so. Fill out a bibliography card for each source you take notes from, and *consistently* record the title, author's name, publishing date, and other data necessary to acknowledge the work in your paper. (See Chapter 4 on what to record for various sources.)

5. *Be particularly careful about text and any other information you download from the Internet.* Because it is so easy to download material from the Internet and then copy and paste this material into a word-processing document, student writers—deliberately or not—may fall into the trap of failing to acknowledge Internet sources. Remember that it is just as important to acknowledge Internet sources used in a paper as it is to acknowledge print sources.

In general, unless you wish to quote directly from such sources and plan to make it clear within the paper that you are doing so, avoid copying and pasting downloaded material directly into your document. If you revise downloaded material within your document—even if you acknowledge the original source—your revision will likely be far too similar to the original not to count as plagiarism. Rather, print out downloaded source material— or the sections that are pertinent to your work—and then treat the printout pages as you would photocopies of a print source. Use them as the basis for your own summary or paraphrase, which you then may incorporate into your paper (again, being sure to acknowledge the source).

Keep in mind that any downloaded graphics you include in a paper— charts, illustrations, artwork, and the like—must also be clearly and accurately documented.

In order to document Internet sources fully and accurately on your Works Cited or Reference pages, be sure to record all the information required for the format you are using (you will find samples of these formats in Chapters 11–13). Such information includes the author or sponsoring organization, the title, the date of posting (if available), the date you accessed the online source, and the complete web address.

6. *Acknowledge sources in your paper.* Follow the correct form for citing sources in the body of your paper as well as for listing them on the Works Cited or References pages (see Chapters 11–13).

A final word. Savvy instructors are alert to any potential instances of plagiarism in student papers. Often they can spot plagiarism because the material simply doesn't read like a student's work. Moreover, a number of online resources and services now offer instructors the ability to check for plagiarism in a far more systematic way than has previously been possible. Do not underestimate the potential problem of plagiarism.

That said, do not let the threat of plagiarism distort your perception of the research paper. You are encouraged to use and to build on the work of others, when properly acknowledged. If you remember that the point of a research paper is, first of all, for you to develop your *own* ideas on a topic—buttressed and supplemented by information discovered over the course of your research—you should never fall into inadvertent plagiarism.

W O R K I N G   W I T H   O T H E R S

The diligence required for reading and taking notes can seem less demanding when you share your progress and results with others. As often as possible during this period, take time to discuss your work with a friend, or compare your reading and notetaking with those of a classmate. Telling others about what you have read will give you a better perspective on what you have done so far. Consider these suggestions as you share your research reading and notetaking with another.

- Compare your techniques for skimming and close reading with those used by a classmate. What differences can you identify that may suggest ways to improve your own approaches? Can you provide the other person with any tips?

- Discuss the notes you take and compare your method of notetaking with that of your classmate. Does a comparison reveal you are taking the right kinds of notes? Are you taking too few? Too many?

- Find out how someone else stores his or her research notes. Can you suggest any ways to improve upon your friend's method or your own? What problems have you each had with notetaking? Were you able to solve them?

- Show the person you are working with a sample of how you record a quotation or paraphrase in your notes. Does your method seem adequate? Discuss the concept of plagiarism. Do you both understand what it means? What has your instructor said about it?

- Compare your evaluations of the sources from which you have both read and taken notes. Have you used the same criteria to evaluate such sources? Are there others that would also be useful?

- Using *Book Review Digest* or library citation indexes can be difficult. Discuss these sources with your collaborator to make sure you both understand their benefits and how to use them.

Sharing your thoughts about your reading will help you to understand and to evaluate your sources more thoroughly than thinking about them alone. Continue discussing these and any other aspects of your research with a classmate or friend.

8

Planning Your Paper

You should no sooner write a research paper without having a plan than you should build a house without having a blueprint. Depending upon your writing skills and the way you prefer to work, a plan can range from a rough sketch of your major ideas to a detailed outline. Planning the paper will get you started writing and help direct your efforts any time you are unsure of how next to proceed.

**THINKING CRITICALLY
ABOUT PLANNING YOUR PAPER**

Rather than simply plunge into the act of writing your paper, take the time beforehand to think carefully about the research materials you have collected, the purpose you wish to pursue, and the way you can shape your essay to best suit that purpose. In this planning stage, however, realize that you need not lock yourself into concrete decisions. While you want to develop a thesis statement that can clearly guide your eventual drafting, bear in mind that any thesis can be modified to better reflect the ideas expressed in the draft. Similarly, you want to map an organizational structure that will allow you to progress from point to point, but that structure may need to be modified in the process of drafting and, particularly, revising.

A plan is crucial for any writer at this stage, but be careful not to treat this plan too rigidly. Flexibility is the key.

Using Your Research Notes

Plan your paper by first reviewing notes you recorded from library materials and other research sources. Your goal at this point is to get an overall view of your topic, as represented in the notes. Reviewing the notes will also show what you have to work with in terms of ideas and information for the paper.

Arranging and Studying Your Notes

Read carefully through the notes several times, studying the contents and observing subheadings and other clusters of information. Relate the contents of each set of notes to the information in other sets as you proceed. The goal here is to see how your notes—all the pieces of information you have collected—fit together. What picture do they make in terms of answering the research question?

You may find it useful to merge groups of notes with different subheadings or to arrange the notes in a particular order, such as a chronological or cause-effect sequence. (Having notes on cards makes such rearranging easy, as does having them on computer. If you use a notebook to record notes, cut out each section so you can rearrange the notes as needed.) In your review of the notes, look for examples, anecdotes, quotations, and statistics that appear particularly useful or striking. Consider how these and other content relate to your research question or a preliminary thesis statement.

Reviewing the Research Question

Although the planning stage is not the place to begin a new research topic, you may need to modify the focus of your research question and its answer before proceeding further (see Chapter 3). After reviewing your research notes, take time to consider the research question and the answer that the notes best support. If you began your research by asking What effect does early fame have upon the adult lives of child stars? a review of your notes may suggest a different approach: What factors contribute to successful adult lives for child stars? A slight change such as this may promote fuller use of your research material and help you frame a more precise final thesis statement.

Reviewing the Preliminary Thesis Statement

The preliminary thesis statement you devised earlier to guide your research may still be sufficient, or it may need to be revised to reflect your note material and any modification in the original research question (see Chapter 3). Write the research question and thesis statement at the top of a notebook page or other sheet of paper. Underneath, list the topic headings from your notecards. As you do so, include under the various headings the major ideas or examples that should be part of the paper. Do not worry too much whether you list information in some final order or if it will indeed be part of your paper. At this stage, you simply want to see how major ideas relate and how accurately the thesis statement describes the note material. As you compare the research question, note material, and preliminary thesis, consider the extent to which they relate. Modify the preliminary thesis as needed to match the research question as well as the ideas and information on the notecards.

Devising a Final Thesis Statement

The thesis statement asserts the main idea controlling your paper's content and organization. In turn, every part of the paper's content supports the thesis statement by explaining it further or offering evidence and examples that show it is accurate. Your thesis will grow out of the thinking you do about the research topic and from deciding on a focus for the information collected from your sources.

A good thesis statement is not devised quickly. It will probably be revised several times before and during the writing of the paper so that it conforms to the evolving content. You may also need to add or delete content during the writing stage in order to support the thesis statement more closely. Good planning of the thesis before you write can help you avoid making too many alterations later.

Writing an Effective Thesis Statement

State the thesis statement as a single sentence, perhaps as two, if necessary. Your goal is to convey your main point concisely but fully. That will help the reader recognize the relationship among ideas and the emphasis of your paper.

Most thesis statements are expressed as *claims,* argumentative assertions about which people will disagree. There are three types of claims:

1. Claims about *facts* argue that something exists, causes something else, or is defined in a particular way:

> Alien beings are making routine flights over the United States.
>
> TV talk shows are corrupting Americans' morals.
>
> Freedom of the press means complete freedom to print any information of interest to the public.

2. Claims about *value* make subjective statements about the worth of something:

> The Internet will have a profound impact on education.
>
> Billy Budd remains the finest example of Melville's sense of justice.
>
> Current research about the causes of Alzheimer's disease will benefit future generations.

3. Claims about *policy* state what action should be taken:

> Limits should be imposed on congressional terms of office.
>
> Americans should be encouraged to carpool.

Additional funding needs to be provided for early childhood education programs.

Like any effective argument, a claim needs to be supported by evidence and a clear pattern of reasoning that logically connects the evidence to the claim. If your claim has developed with your research and notetaking, you will have this support.

THINKING CRITICALLY
ABOUT THESIS STATEMENTS

Remember that a good thesis (or claim) invites readers' interest. Rather than state the obvious, the thesis should promise a discussion worthy of the time needed to read the paper. Avoid weak thesis statements that only summarize known facts and conditions, that are too general to state clear arguments about topics, or that state intentions:

Weak (summarizes known facts)	AIDS is a usually fatal disease in which the body's immune system fails to resist infection.
Better	People with AIDS should have legal access to promising new drugs without having to wait for their approval by the U.S. Food and Drug Administration.
Weak (too general)	The drug problem is something we need to solve.
Better	Antidrug campaigns are most effective when designed and targeted for specific local populations.
Weak (intention only)	This paper will show that the moral content of children's cartoons is too ambiguous to present acceptable behavior models.
Better	The moral content of children's cartoons is too ambiguous to present acceptable behavior models.

As the "Better" examples above demonstrate, a good thesis statement focuses the paper's discussion on a central idea. In most cases, you will need to experiment several times to find the exact wording for the thesis, and you may need to reword it again during or after writing the paper. The more focused you can make the thesis when planning the paper, the easier writing the body of the paper will be.

Reviewing Your Paper's Purpose

The overall purpose of your paper is determined by what you plan to tell your audience and your strategy for presenting information on the topic. A research paper that primarily intends to persuade the reader of the author's viewpoint about a topic has an *argumentative* purpose; one that minimizes expression of the author's ideas and seeks mainly to present information for the reader's benefit is *informative*. In order to organize your discussion material effectively, you should plan your paper with one of these two major purposes in mind.

An Argumentative Purpose. In an argumentative paper, remember to keep your position on the topic consistent and clearly related to the thesis throughout. Your thesis *statement,* or a form of it, should appear more than once in the introduction and perhaps only once again in the conclusion of the paper. The thesis *idea,* expressed in varying ways to match the context, should be a continuous concept that runs more or less explicitly through each section of the argumentative paper. An argumentative paper about the challenges of raising an adopted child, for example, would emphasize the thesis throughout the discussion:

Introduction leads into thesis	[. . .] Raising an adopted child can pose unexpected problems for even the most loving of parents.
Topic sentence restates thesis idea	One difficulty adoptive parents have to overcome is an often unrecognized desire that the adopted child is actually theirs. "I feel like she is one of my own" is a warm expression of closeness, but it may also reflect the wish that the adopted child _had_ been born into the family. [. . .]
Successive paragraphs develop thesis further	Raising a child of another race presents adoptive parents with additional and sometimes overwhelming challenges. Experts, in fact, are divided over the wisdom of interracial adoptions. [. . .]
	Becoming the parent of an adopted child can get even more difficult when there are other biologically parented children in the family. [. . .]
Thesis statement idea is continued	The difficulties of raising an adopted child are certainly real, but they are not insurmountable. When parents learn ahead of time [. . .].

An Informative Purpose. In an informative paper, the thesis will receive less emphasis than the information you provide the reader. Keep the content focused on information rather than issues, and maintain a reasonable balance in the material you provide about each subject discussed. To avoid stuffing an informative paper with unneeded material, create topic sentences that control the content and focus of all paragraphs.

Notice how the following discussion blurs its informative purpose by introducing facts and issues (here, shown boldfaced) not related to the topic sentence or the writer's purpose:

Informative topic sentence	Several studies document sustained changes in sexual behavior within the gay male population residing in
Irrelevant facts and issues	various U.S. cities. **Researchers had difficulty gathering certain kinds of data because some gay men are hesitant to share information or identify themselves as gay, evidence that social disapproval is still a concern for many gay males in American society.** Anti-AIDS programs seem to be working, as shown by contrasting the results of a 1984 study of San Francisco men with those found more recently in a New York study showing an even greater decline in risk-related activity.

THINKING CRITICALLY
ABOUT WHICH PURPOSE IS APPROPRIATE

Deciding whether your paper's purpose is argumentative or informative depends upon your research assignment, your research material, and how important your own interpretation, viewpoint, or evaluation is to the discussion. Your research material will determine, for example, whether you are prepared to argue for or against allowing females to serve in U.S. combat forces (argumentative paper) or should instead report on the growth of opportunities for women in the armed services today (informative paper).

Comparing the Purposes
of Sample Papers

Because Linda Kastan's paper on Internet addiction seeks to persuade readers of her research conclusions, it has an argumentative purpose (see her paper in Chapter 11). Similarly, Steve Hanner's paper on emotional intelligence is argumentative in that he demonstrates how important understanding and controlling our emotions has become in U.S. society (see Appendix A). Both of these writers recognized that their topics provided enough unsettled questions or controversy to call for further discussion and reasoned conclusions.

Linda Nguyen's research paper reviewing the current literature on alcohol and college students, on the other hand, is an informative paper (see Appendix A). She seeks to inform her readers more than convince them of any particular viewpoint (see Appendix A).

Using Your Paper's Purpose for Planning

Unless your assignment requires a particular purpose, decide whether it will be more effective as an argumentative or an informative paper. Keep your purpose in mind as you construct an outline for the paper.

Working with an Outline

An *outline* is a tool to assist you in organizing and writing the paper. You will understand and appreciate the use of an outline best by keeping certain principles in mind:

- An outline assists you by organizing material and providing a pattern to follow as you write. It gives your reader an overview of the paper's discussion and major ideas.

- There are two general types of outlines: informal and formal. You may wish to use the informal type for your own writing needs, perhaps using it later to create a formal outline of the paper. A formal outline is more effective for planning a paper, especially a longer one, but it also takes more preparation.

- Some writers work best by drafting a working plan or outline before they write and making changes as needed. Others prefer to complete the outline after the paper is finished, using it as a means to check the paper's organization and emphases. You should follow the practice that works best for you.

- Since writing is a creative and recursive process, the outline and the paper's content will necessarily change at times to consistently reflect each other.

Both informal and formal outlines are discussed in the following pages. Which type you work with depends upon your writing preferences and the requirements of your research assignment.

An Informal Outline

If you are not required to make a formal outline for your research paper, you may want to work from an informal one. Though such an outline is informal and intended for your use only, it still requires careful planning to be useful.

Begin by writing your paper's title at the top of a work page, with the final thesis right below it for easy reference. After reviewing your notecards, list the major categories of ideas for the paper in a logical sequence, perhaps under headings such as Introduction, Body, and Conclusion to get started or until more specific major headings occur to you. It will probably help if you number the categories and leave enough space between them to add supporting material from notes later.

Since the informal outline is solely for your own use, make notations, additions, or deletions as you need to while organizing and writing the paper. Under the proper subheadings, include important facts, dates, and examples that you want to include in the paper. Feel free to write full sentences: At some point, you may want to add them directly to the paper.

Figure 8.1 shows the informal outline for Linda Kastan's paper on Internet addiction. Though Linda was required to submit a formal outline with her paper, she felt more comfortable beginning with her own loosely structured plan. She followed her informal outline to write most of the paper and then used it later to construct a formal topic outline (see later in this chapter). Linda found her informal outline helpful to her writing, but she also recognized that the form and structure required by a formal topic outline better demonstrated the organization of ideas in the paper. In fact, she used the formal topic outline as a guide when she revised her paper's first draft. A comparison of the informal outline in Figure 8.1 with the final topic outline (see the Appendix to Chapter 11) shows the changes, additions, and deletions Linda made when she wrote the paper.

A Formal Outline

A formal outline differs from an informal one by following a standard format and organization. The formal outline subdivides categories of information, designating each category by different letters and numbers and by separate headings. The degree of importance or inclusiveness of each heading is shown in the outline by successive indentation; that is, the less important a category, the more it is indented under more significant categories:

I. Major heading
   A. Minor heading
      1. Detail heading
         a. Example heading

Internet Addiction:
Is There a Dark Side to Cyberspace?

Thesis: While not everyone agrees that the Internet itself is the source of the problem, evidence is growing that increasing numbers of users are learning too late that connecting online can also become the first step to disconnecting with a healthy lifestyle.

Introduction
- - Internet use is increasing, and so are the addiction problems attributed to it.

Body
1. Young's study shows that addiction-like behavior exists
2. Other studies show that all types of people are being addicted to the Internet
    - - New York study; University of Maryland
    - - College students are most exposed to overuse; Alfred University example
3. What are schools doing?
    - - Ohio State and U. of Washington have limited students' time online
    - - Other campuses have put in online addiction centers
4   Problems with definition
    - - Experts don't agree about whether dependent Internet behavior is addiction
    - - Some say anything in extreme is addiction; others treat it like a joke
5. Some Internet addicts have shown physiological and physical dependence
    - - Cannot quit or reduce their time online
    - - Get high from being online, depressed when offline
    - - Chat rooms and MUDs are biggest problems
6. Is there a cure?
    - - Users need to recognize their problem

Conclusion
- - Going online does have consequences, even addictive-like ones for many people.

FIGURE 8.1   Linda Kastan's informal research paper outline

    b. Example heading
      (1) Minor example heading
      (2) Minor example heading
  2. Detail heading
B. Minor heading
  1. Detail heading
  2. Detail heading
C. Minor heading, etc.

Subdivisions within headings can continue even further than shown here, though most rarely need to go beyond the level of example headings (*a, b,* etc.).

As the above example demonstrates, the headings within a formal outline are each part of a whole. If you subdivide a topic heading, it must have at least two parts. Thus, every *I* will have at least a *II,* every *A* a *B,* every *1* a *2,* and so on:

I. National parks
  A. Size
    1. Public-use areas
    2. Primitive areas
  B. Types
    1. Recreation
    2. Preservation
II. State parks

Outlines for papers and articles written for the sciences or business may use a decimal outline, in which decimal divisions indicate successive headings:

1. Major heading
  1.1 Minor heading
    1.1.1 Detail heading
    1.1.2 Detail heading
      1.1.2.1 Example heading
      1.1.2.2 Example heading
  1.2 Minor heading
    1.2.1 Detail heading
    1.2.2 Detail heading
2. Major heading, etc.

Types of Outlines

A Topic Outline. Each heading in a topic outline is worded as a noun (e.g., "College") or nounlike phrase (e.g., "Applying for Admission," "To Enroll in Classes"). Keep all headings brief and clearly related to the major heading.

A topic outline can appear easy to compose, but be aware that its level of generality can cover up weaknesses in organization or content. The advantage to a topic outline is that it is brief and identifies the main points of discussion quickly:

  I. Reduction of the rain forests
     A. Questionable benefits
         1. Increased farm land
             a. Cleared forest
             b. New farmers
         2. Timber for export
         3. Intracontinent trade
         4. Modernization
             a. New roads
             b. Hydroelectric dams
     B. Environmental effects
         1. Failure of land to support farming
         2. Loss of plant and animal species
             a. Numbers
             b. Potential uses
         3. Extermination of primitive cultures
             a. Relocation
             b. Modernization
             c. Disease
         4. Disruption of major rivers
         5. Increase in the greenhouse effect
 II. International response

A Sentence Outline. A sentence outline requires more planning and writing than a topic outline, but its completeness will prove more useful when you begin to write the paper. You can incorporate complete sentences from the outline into the paper as topic sentences for successive paragraphs:

  I. Despite progress in utilizing the Amazon more productively, development is producing disastrous results with worldwide consequences.

A. The eight nations through which the Amazon runs have had high expectations that its development would prove beneficial.

   1. The Amazon forest has been cleared to provide increased farm land.

      a. Some 20% of the state of Rondonia is under development.

      b. Farmers receive free land.

   2. The exportation of rare hardwoods has increased since restrictions have been removed.

   3. The building of roads and clearing of the Amazon River have increased the possibility for intracontinent travel and trade throughout Amazonia.

   4. The changes have helped modernize many primitive areas of the Amazon.

      a. Dams and roads are making it possible for Amazon people to reach new areas to live.

      b. Electricity has improved living conditions.

B. Attempts to utilize the Amazon's rich forest and land, however, are having devastating effects on the region.

   1. The nutrient-poor soil will not support farm crops.

   2. Hundreds, perhaps thousands, of valuable plant and animal species have already been lost because of development.

      a. A four-mile area of forest may support over 1,500 species.

      b. Many of these have valuable uses in medicine or industry.

A Paragraph Outline.   A paragraph outline provides a summary of the main parts of the outline. You should be careful to develop each paragraph fully as a unit. Remember, however, that since each paragraph in such an outline represents an entire section, it is not developed enough to fit directly into the paper:

I. Reduction of the rain forest

   A. The elimination of millions of acres of Amazon rain forest has provided many Amazonians with the opportunity of clearing and owning their own farms. In the western state of Rondonia, some 20% of the land has been cleared to provide new farm land for those who will settle there. Exports of hardwood have increased significantly from the massive reduction of the forest, and modern roads have allowed increased travel and trade. New hydroelectric dams provide electricity for hospitals and other modern advantages.

B. Attempts to utilize the Amazon's rich forest and land, however, are having devastating effects upon the region. Since the nutrient-poor soil will not sustain crops, clearing millions of acres of forest to provide new farm land has proven dismally unsuccessful. Worse yet, hundreds, perhaps thousands, of valuable plant and animal species have already been lost because of development. A four-mile area of forest may support over 1,500 species, many of which have valuable uses in medicine or industry.

Creating Your Own Outline

To begin the outline for your paper, start by arranging your notecards or other materials into main categories, assigning each a major heading designation indicated by a roman numeral. For example, an outline from notecards for a paper on current research findings about drug addiction might begin this way:

    I. Definition   **Major headings**
   II. Causes
  III. Effects
  IV. Treatment

Next, review the note material included in each major heading category. If you have enough material for at least two minor categories, add them as subdivisions. The number or letter identifier of each new level of subdivision should align with the text portion of the preceding level. Note that the *A* below aligns on the preceding entry, *Definition*. Follow this style:

    I. Definition
       A. Problem of defining   **Minor headings**
       B. Use and abuse
       C. Prevalent types

II. Causes
   A. Social factors   **Minor headings**
   B. Psychological needs
   C. Genetic origins
III. Effects
   A. Physiological   **Minor headings**
   B. Psychological
   C. Societal
IV. Treatment
   A. Chemical substitutes   **Minor headings**
   B. Clinical therapy
   C. Support groups

Now examine the note material included within each of the minor categories to determine whether you have enough material to subdivide into at least two detail headings. If so, include them in the outline, using Arabic numerals (*1, 2, 3,* etc.) and aligning them on the appropriate indent (as explained earlier):

I. Definition
   A. Problem of defining
      1. APA definition   **Detail headings**
      2. WHO definition
   B. Use and abuse
      1. Stable addiction   **Detail headings**
      2. Unstable addiction
   C. Prevalent types
      1. Physiological   **Detail headings**
      2. Psychological
II. Causes
   A. Social factors
      1. Alienation   **Detail headings**
      2. Drug availability
   B. Psychological needs
      1. Personality disorders **Detail headings**
      2. Stress and trauma
   C. Genetic origins
      1. Neurologic vulnerability **Detail headings**
      2. Alcoholism

Most outlines do not require extensive enough development to need example headings. If you wish to include them, however, repeat the processes described above, using small letters (*a, b, c*):

II. Causes
　　A. Social factors
　　　　1. Alienation
　　　　　　a. Familial　　　　　　**Example headings**
　　　　　　b. Economic
　　　　2. Drug availability
　　　　　　a. Cocaine　　　　　　**Example headings**
　　　　　　b. Alcohol
　　B. Psychological needs
　　　　1. Personality disorders
　　　　　　a. Antisocial behavior　　**Example headings**
　　　　　　b. Low self-esteem
　　　　2. Stress and trauma
　　　　　　a. Overachievers　　　　**Example headings**
　　　　　　b. War veterans, etc.

Guidelines for the Formal Outline

■ Although not always necessary, it is a good idea to include the thesis statement at the top of the outline for a research paper. (See the outline for the sample research paper in Chapter 11.)

■ Align each new level of subentry below the previous-level entry (see last section and examples).

■ Align headings of the same level on the same indent. Do so by aligning the periods following the number or letter identifiers:

　　I. _____
　　　A. _____
　　　　1. _____
　　　　2. _____
　　　B. _____
　　II. _____
　　　A. _____ , etc.

■ Word your headings to maintain the same parallel forms, generally as noun phrases (Addiction) or nounlike phrases such as gerund phrases (Treating addiction) or infinitive phrases (To treat addiction). Which form you use will depend upon the grammatical parallelism of your outline:

Unparallel headings

   I. Defining addiction

      A. Difficult to define

      B. Some uses and abuses

      C. Prevailing types

  II. Causes of addiction

      A. Societal

      B. Your own personality

      C. Genes also contribute

Parallel headings

   I. Definition

      A. Problem of defining

      B. Use and abuse

      C. Prevalent types

  II. Causes

      A. Social factors

      B. Psychological needs

      C. Genetic origins

Once you have completed a satisfactory outline for the paper, write your final thesis statement at the beginning of the outline, as well. The thesis statement and outline will direct your writing and help to keep the content and main idea consistent.

A Review of Basic Patterns of Development

Planning the organization and exposition of your paper's content should include considering the standard patterns that underlie most people's thinking about a subject. Writers employ these patterns to provide a structure for their ideas and for developing a discussion. Narration, description, definition, and analogy are minor patterns that can sustain brief discussions or whole paragraphs in long works. The major patterns—argumentation, comparison-and-contrast, classification, and cause-and-effect—are useful structures for longer compositions like the research paper. These four major patterns can support a paper's purpose by providing logical methods for organization, development, and expression.

The patterns of development described in the following sections may be used as outline structures for your research paper or combined with other outline models. They may also serve as development patterns for smaller sections of the outline and the paper.

Argumentation

Arguing a position requires presenting opposing viewpoints and refuting or qualifying each reason for opposition to your argument. The structure for arguing a position is often determined by the nature of the pro and con arguments discussed. The following outline demonstrates a typical argument pattern:

   I. Thesis
      A. Background
      B. Thesis position
  II. Ideas opposing thesis
      A. First reason
      B. Second reason
 III. Support for thesis (refutation)
      A. First reason
      B. Second reason
 IV. Conclusion

Another argumentation pattern might take this form:

   I. Introduction
      A. Background to the problem
      B. Thesis statement
  II. Body
      A. Opposing viewpoint
         1 Reason
         2. Reason
      B. Thesis position (refutation)
         1. Reason
         2. Reason
      C. Solution proposal
 III. Conclusion

Comparison-and-Contrast

Although it is possible to write an entire paper that either compares or contrasts two or more things, a more common practice is to combine the two approaches into a comparison-and-contrast pattern.

One method of comparison-and-contrast examines each subject separately in terms of selected features:

I. Japanese education	**Subject 1**
A. Levels	**Feature 1**
B. Access	**Feature 2**
C. Standards	**Feature 3**
II. U.S. education	**Subject 2**
A. Levels	**Feature 1**
B. Access	**Feature 2**
C. Standards	**Feature 3**
III. Conclusion	

A second method compares and contrasts subjects directly by examining the same features:

I. Education levels	**Feature 1**
A. Japan	**Subject 1**
B. U.S.	**Subject 2**
II. Access	**Feature 2**
A. Japan	**Subject 1**
B. U.S.	**Subject 2**
III. Standards	**Feature 3**
A. Japan	**Subject 1**
B. U.S.	**Subject 2**
IV. Conclusion	

Classification

The process of classification is similar to that of comparing and contrasting: identifying the qualities that put things into the same category or distinguish one category from another (e.g., drug therapy programs: behavior versus encounter). Begin by identifying the principle by which items will be classified (e.g., types of children's toys, kinds of legal statutes, ways to purchase a car). Next, designate the categories to which the items belong. Then describe the items in such a way as to differentiate them from other items and categories:

   I. Principle of classification: Types of therapy
  II. Categories of classification
      A. Behavior therapy
         1. History
         2. Examples
      B. Encounter therapy
         1. History
         2. Examples
      C. Gestalt therapy
         1. History
         2. Examples
      D. Interactional approach
         1. History
         2. Examples
 III. Conclusion

Cause-and-Effect

Cause-and-effect patterns are useful for showing how one event or circumstance causes another event or circumstance. Direct and indirect causes may be discussed as well as recommendations for any problem or condition they have created. For example, a paper discussing the problem of decreasing numbers of insect pollinators (such as bees, moths, and butterflies) might develop from a cause-effect outline such as the following:

   I. Problem or condition: Severe reductions in insect pollinators
  II. Causes
      A. Direct: Loss of habitat
      B. Direct: Use of pesticides
      C. Indirect: Increased human population
 III. Effects
      A. Direct: Loss of natural vegetation
      B. Direct: Declines in commercial crop production
      C. Indirect: Loss of species diversity

    D. Indirect: Threats to human health

  IV. Solution (recommendation)

A paper following the guidelines of the American Psychological Association (APA) or one discussing research, methodology, and conclusions for a scientific study may be organized as follows:

     I. Introduction

    II. Methodology

   III. Results

   IV. Discussion

    V. References

Creating a Title

Many writers prefer to create a title after the paper is finished so that it accurately reflects the content and focus. Others create the title along with the thesis statement and outline as an additional reminder to themselves of the paper's focus during the writing stage. Whichever you prefer, take the time to devise a title that indicates (1) what the paper is about and (2) what approach you have taken toward the subject. The following titles meet these criteria:

A Critical View of Tax Shelters

Why New York Is America's Best-Loved City

Families: Do They Really Exist Anymore?

Use a subtitle (added after a colon) when it provides additional focus:

Teen Music: Can Mean Lyrics Hurt You?

Sleaze T.V.: Viewers Are Saying No

Avoid vague, high-sounding, or cute titles that hide the paper's content and approach:

Vague   Youths at Risk

Overblown   A Brief Examination of the Cause-and-Effect
Relationship of Lower-Than-Average Grades among
College Transfer Students

Cute   The "Purrrfect" Pet: Cats as Support Animals

Remember: Do not underline or use quotation marks around the title
of your own paper, unless it is named in your text. (See Chapter 14 for
guidelines on placement and spacing when typing the title.)

W O R K I N G   W I T H   O T H E R S

The more completely you plan the research paper at this point, the more
smoothly you will proceed with writing it. Planning the paper with the help
of a friend or classmate will ensure that you are actually ready to write and
that the logic of the paper's organization is apparent to others. Take the
time to share your research material and to discuss the following major
points from this chapter with someone else.

- Review the research question and your notes with another person to
  be sure you have enough material to support a thesis statement. Point
  out the examples you intend to include in the paper.

- Does your friend or classmate feel there are enough examples in the
  notes to support your thesis? Discuss any quotations you plan to include in the paper as well as your reasons for doing so.

- Ask the person you are working with to state the final thesis statement
  in his or her own words. How could the thesis be stated more effectively?

- Ask whether the paper seems to be informative or argumentative in its
  purpose. Can the other person offer any advice on which one of these
  approaches might work best for your paper? If you are working with a
  classmate, what purpose will his or her paper support?

- Look over the outline for the paper together. Does it meet the requirements of the assignment? Does the proposed content support the
  thesis? Is the organization of material logical and effective? Should any
  headings be changed, moved, or deleted? Is the form for the outline
  correct?

- What pattern of development is best for this paper? Briefly summarize the approach the paper will take. Decide together whether that approach seems appropriate for your thesis and purpose.

- Evaluate the proposed title for the paper. Does it clearly indicate the paper's subject and the author's position? Can the two of you think up any other appropriate titles together?

If possible, share your writing preparation with more than just one person, especially if you have lingering questions about any particular aspects of the paper. Be sure to ask others to review their plans with you, also. You will find that discussing another's plans for writing the research paper will provide valuable insights about your own readiness.

CHAPTER 9

Reasoning Critically about Argument and Evidence

The effectiveness of your research effort—and the paper that results from it—will depend greatly upon your critical understanding of *argument,* a carefully considered set of reasons or evidence offered in support of a conclusion.

**THINKING CRITICALLY
ABOUT ARGUMENTS**

Your research sources will present arguments and opinions rang-ing from simple to complex as well as from erroneous to valid. While taking notes on such sources, you will need to assess their arguments critically, paying attention to the logic of the conclusions offered and the reliability of their evidence As you write your paper, you should also assess your own arguments critically, ensuring that the thesis statement and other conclusions you offer are reasonable and logi-cally supported by evidence.

The discussions of argument and evidence in this chapter will make you better able to present both.

Logical Reasoning

To think critically about an argument, you must understand *logical reason-ing,* a way of thinking in which your consideration of one or more facts leads you to a reasonable conclusion. The following argument represents logical reasoning because the conclusion expressed reasonably derives from the evidence:

Evidence	Records show that sales increase whenever the price of home computers drops. Since prices for home computers are dropping,
Conclusion	we can expect sales to increase.

The two most common kinds of logical reasoning are *induction* and *deduction,* two ways of thinking that occur any time people express ideas. You will need to understand both as you analyze the arguments of your research sources and state your own conclusions in your research paper.

Inductive Reasoning

Inductive reasoning first examines specific examples and then draws a conclusion or states a generalization based upon those examples (see Figure 9.1). A research biologist, for instance, might use inductive reasoning as she first gathers information about a dramatic drop in the local frog population and then draws a conclusion about the cause of the decline. Her line of inductive reasoning might proceed as follows:

Problem:	Local frog populations have declined in numbers and reproductive levels.
Fact:	Each of the populations suffers from severe multiple invasions of known amphibian viruses.
Fact:	These viruses are usually nonlethal when occurring separately.
Fact:	Other research has shown that natural defense mechanisms in frogs fail when there is an infection by more than one kind of bacteria.
Fact:	There is no other evidence of an unusual environmental or physiological threat to these populations.
Conclusion:	The increased decline in these frog populations probably results from multiple invasions by otherwise nonlethal viruses.

Notice that this conclusion is qualified by the word *probably.* No matter how much information or examples you gather, you can never have *all* the facts about a situation. So a conclusion that is stated in absolute terms would, in fact, be unfounded. The research biologist may correctly conclude that severe invasion by multiple viruses has caused the decline among frog populations; however, that does not mean that viral infections are the *only*

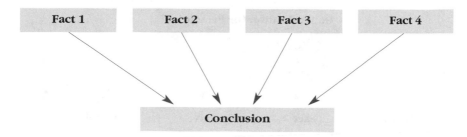

FIGURE 9.1   Inductive reasoning

cause of declining frog populations. Other causes—such as the effects of pollution or the loss of a food source—may have yet to be discovered.

Because the results of inductive reasoning are, at best, only *highly probable,* make sure to qualify most inductive conclusions with terms such as *most, many, apparently, probably,* and *evidence suggests.* Doing so allows for further consideration of additional data when they become available and usually makes an argument more acceptable to an audience.

Deductive Reasoning

Deductive reasoning works just the opposite of its inductive counterpart: Instead of beginning with separate facts, as induction does, deduction begins with a general principle that serves as the basis for interpreting or drawing a conclusion about specific instances (see Figure 9.2). For example, when an astronomer views a new, orange-colored star in a faraway galaxy, he can conclude immediately that it is both cooler and less massive than the star nearest the earth, the sun. How does he know this? His conclusion is based upon the general principle that *Stars more massive and hotter than the sun appear blue or white; those less massive and cooler are typically orange or red.* By using deduction to apply this principle to the new star, the astronomer gains an almost immediate understanding of its basic physical properties.

Syllogisms.   The astronomer in the previous example uses a form of reasoning formally known as a *syllogism*—an argument that contains two statements and a conclusion. Logicians call the beginning statement (or general principle) of a syllogism the *major premise* and the statement about other information the *minor premise:*

Major premise: Stars with less mass and heat than the sun appear orange.

Minor premise: This star appears orange.

Conclusion: Therefore, this star has less mass and heat than the sun.

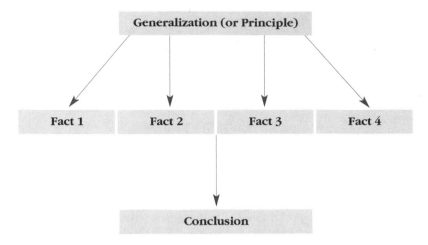

FIGURE 9.2   Deductive reasoning

The validity of a syllogism's conclusion rests upon the truth of both premises. If the premises are true, the conclusion must also be true. Since no other conclusion could logically follow from the two premises stated, the astronomer's conclusion about the new star may be considered both valid and true.

When a syllogism contains a false major premise, however, the conclusion will also be false:

Major premise: Only criminals carry guns.

Minor premise: This man is carrying a gun.

Conclusion: This man is a criminal.

This argument is false because the major premise is untrue (i.e., people other than criminals carry guns).

A syllogistic argument will also be unsound if there is no relation between the major and minor premises:

Major premise: All horses are mammals.

Minor premise: Humans are mammals.

Conclusion: All horses are humans.

This conclusion is absurd, of course, but the example demonstrates the importance of paying close attention to the premises on which you base your conclusions.

Arguments with Unstated Premises.   Not all deductive arguments are stated in the form of explicit, recognizable syllogisms. When either of the premises or the conclusion of a deductive argument is unstated, the argument is called an *enthymeme* (from a Greek word meaning "to hold in mind"). The assertion that *Since Bill is studying hard for this test, he will do well on it* is an enthymeme most people would accept because they undoubtedly understand the complete argument, which includes an unstated major premise:

(Unstated)
Major premise: People who study hard do well on tests like this.

Minor premise: Bill is studying hard for this test.

Conclusion: Bill will do well on this test.

The effectiveness of an enthymeme-based argument depends upon the audience's understanding or acceptance of the assumed, unstated premise or conclusion. A statement such as *Praxy should be regulated like other dangerous drugs* assumes at least one unstated premise: *Praxy is a dangerous drug.* It is possible, however, that not every audience would recognize or agree with the unstated premise. For the argument to be convincing for any audience, the author would also need first to assert that Praxy is a dangerous drug and then provide evidence that it is.

The Toulmin Method of Argument

Although inductive and deductive reasoning are enormously valuable for analyzing the structure of arguments, such logical methods are not always useful for creating an argument that can effectively persuade an audience. Partly for these reasons, logician Stephen Toulmin devised a slightly different approach to logic during the 1950s that centered upon three basic elements that make arguments both valid and convincing to an audience.

The Three Parts of a Toulmin Argument

According to Toulmin, every argument has three parts:

1. A *claim* is a conclusion based upon evidence; like the thesis of your research paper, it is an assertion you make and then defend.
2. The *evidence* for a claim includes the facts, statistics, expert opinions, and other information that supports or leads to a conclusion.
3. The *warrant* is the rationale behind the argument; it is an assumption or belief that you and your audience share.

In making the *claim* that the United States needs stronger laws against drug dealing, for example, the *evidence* may be in the form of research showing a correlation between decreased drug abuse and increased penalties for sellers. The claim's *warrant*—a belief shared by the arguer and the audience—is that drug use is harmful and should be decreased whenever possible.

An Example Argument

To get a fuller idea of how a Toulmin argument works, consider an example. Suppose that you have decided your friend Tom is a good rock climber. To reach this conclusion, you probably reasoned as follows:

> Tom is a very good rock climber. After all, he successfully climbed both Sawtooth and Pinnacle last year.

The claim in this case is the statement *Tom is a very good rock climber.* The evidence is the fact that *He successfully climbed both Sawtooth and Pinnacle last year.* The warrant—or unstated assumption you believe the audience understands and agrees with—is something like this:

> Only someone who is a good rock climber could climb Sawtooth and Pinnacle.

While your thinking may seem sound to you at this point, you need to consider how convincing it might appear to others. After all, it is possible that Tom had help in making his climb. Maybe he was just lucky. Or perhaps Sawtooth and Pinnacle are not adequate tests of a climber's skills. What can you do to make your argument more convincing?

Qualifying Arguments.   Since it is rare that we can state any opinion with absolute certainty (and rarer still that we can think of every possible exception to an argument), Toulmin logic calls for adding a *qualifier*—such as *some, probably,* or *most*—that limits the claim and makes it more reasonable to an audience. To clarify the argument and to make sure your audience accepts the unstated warrant, you may also decide to provide additional *backing*—that is, reasons the warrant is true.

In the Toulmin model for argument, then, the reasoning for a claim about Tom's climbing skills might look something like this:

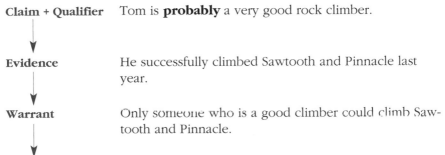

Claim + Qualifier   Tom is **probably** a very good rock climber.

Evidence   He successfully climbed Sawtooth and Pinnacle last year.

Warrant   Only someone who is a good climber could climb Sawtooth and Pinnacle.

Backing
1. Sawtooth and Pinnacle present extremely difficult climbing conditions.
2. Most people who attempt to climb Sawtooth and Pinnacle fail.

Stated and Unstated Parts of an Argument. The claim and evidence for an argument must be stated explictly. However, whether you need to state the warrant explicitly—or provide supportive backing—depends upon the complexity of the claim and the degree of resistance an audience might have to it. In arguing for stronger enforcement of restaurant health codes, for example, you could likely assume that most audiences readily understand and agree with the unstated warrant that *Restaurants should be safe, healthy places in which to eat.* But suppose you are arguing a more controversial position, such as that *Because of the effects of second-hand smoke, restaurants should not allow smoking.* In this case, you may need to strengthen your argument by explicitly explaining (or insisting upon) the warrant that *Restaurants should be safe, healthy places in which to eat*—for smokers and nonsmokers alike. Stating the warrant in this way ensures the audience will understand its importance and influences their reception of other evidence, both pro and con.

Putting the Toulmin Model to Use

You may find the Toulmin model for argument useful in judging the arguments made in research sources and for assessing whether those you make in your paper are sufficient. Think of your paper's thesis as your claim and your research data as the evidence supporting the thesis, for example. Remember, too, that since the Toulmin model for argument does not require any specific pattern in which the claim, evidence, and warrant are stated, you can include these elements in your paper in the order in which they are most effective. You may begin by stating the claim at the beginning of the paper or perhaps toward the end, after you have discussed the evidence and warrant. Or you may decide to begin the paper by stating the warrant and then discussing the claim and evidence.

Looking Critically at the Evidence

Evidence provides the grounds on which an argument is justified. In an inductive argument, the evidence leads logically to the conclusion; in a deductive argument, the evidence is stated in the premises. In the Toulmin model, the evidence supports the claim. For any argument to be effective, the evidence must be convincing enough to counter opposing data and arguments. Since not all evidence is alike or of equal weight in a given situation, you should consider carefully the evidence provided by each of your sources and the evidence you include in your research paper. Examples and authority are the most common kinds of evidence you will need to deal with in completing your research assignment.

Examples

Examples provide specific details—such as facts, statistics, or authoritative opinion—to illustrate and support a writer's claims. Asserting that *Lifting weights provides a number of health benefits for women,* for instance, remains only an unsupported, vague generalization when stated without examples. Describing how women who work out with weights increase needed bone mass, improve their posture and balance, develop better eating habits, and increase their self-esteem provides examples that make the claim understandable as well as reasonable to an audience.

How Many Examples?   An effective argument includes enough examples to justify the conclusion. Examples should be numerous enough to demonstrate the extent and variety of cases that support the conclusion, and they should be typical, not the results of special circumstances. Keep in mind that one example is almost never enough to support a claim, even if the claim is qualified. Thus, the argument that *Tattoo artists should be formally trained and licensed* needs more evidence than the single example of unsafe practices by the tattoo artists at Bayside Tattoo. To be convincing, the argument needs to include examples of malpractice by other tattoo artists from other tattoo parlors.

What Types of Examples?   Think about when each of the following kinds of examples might be useful:

■ *Statistical examples:* Statistics provide quantitative examples in the forms of numbers, graphs, and charts. Since numerical data can be interpreted in any of several ways, you should regard any statistics with care. Be sure the statistics you use come from unbiased sources, are current, and represent adequate samplings.

Although statistical examples can provide impressive evidence, they are not necessarily easy to interpret nor do they always justify the conclusion they are intended to support. Suppose a news article reports that the average cost of renting an apartment in a certain city has risen 25% in the last three years. Does this mean that renting an apartment has therefore become excessively expensive? Before reaching a conclusion, you should ask who conducted the study and which apartment locations were included. Were preexisting rental costs relatively low and consequently due for an increase? Does the increase include optional costs, such as paid utilities? How does the jump in rent compare with the general increase in the local cost of living?

Statistics cannot present all the relevant issues in a case, and they can be easily misused or misunderstood. As you study sources and use statistics in your research paper, make sure that you understand them fully and use them fairly and accurately.

■ *Hypothetical examples:* An invented instance in the form of a hypothetical example can sometimes illustrate the basic principles of an argument better than a real example. Hypothetical cases are particularly useful when actual examples are not available, as may be the case in arguing about a future event or a proposed action—for example, *If we do pass this law against loitering near a school, let's say a parent is waiting for her child* [. . .]. Invented cases are also useful in providing examples that are free of personal associations and general enough to avoid an audience's biases. When trying to convince teenage drivers of the need for laws restricting when they can drive and with whom, for instance, a hypothetical example can help this audience think beyond concern for their own driving privileges—*Suppose you had a teenage son or daughter. Wouldn't you want laws that could protect them from driving under unsafe conditions?*

THINKING CRITICALLY
ABOUT HYPOTHETICAL EXAMPLES

You should regard hypothetical examples with care. While an invented case can help illustrate a complex point or provide another way of looking at an issue, remember that it is not the same as *actual evidence.* Made-up examples may not be as convincing as concrete evidence for some audiences, and invented instances cannot replace the actual facts needed to support an inductive conclusion. Keep in mind, too, that hypothetical examples should be relevant and realistic enough to be logically convincing. When a hypothetical case is exaggerated or becomes too fanciful—for instance, *Suppose we lost a whole generation of young people to auto accidents because we failed to restrict teenage drivers*—the argument appears unsound and the author loses credibility with the audience.

■ *Examples by analogy:* An *analogy* is an extended comparison in which something unfamiliar or abstract is made understandable by comparing it, point by point, to something more familiar. Like a hypothetical case, an example by analogy can help illustrate an argument and clarify an audience's understanding of the issues. Someone arguing that the city should provide free shelter and food for people who are homeless, for instance, might offer the analogy that a city is like a large family: *Everyone lives together and shares certain resources, and the well-being of each person affects the quality of life shared by everyone else.*

An analogy may help sway an audience's acceptance of an argument, but it is not the same as factual evidence, which, when well documented, is usually not refutable. Do not regard an analogy as evidence. Thus, any analogies that appear in your research sources—as well as any you include in your research paper—must be backed up with concrete evidence and examples to support the arguments completely.

**THINKING CRITICALLY
ABOUT ANALOGIES**

Although an analogy often provides appealing evidence in an argument, it should logically carry very little weight. Most analogies cannot stand up to extended examination, and they can usually be nullified by counter-analogies. The previous example comparing the provision of food and shelter for homeless people to providing for the members of one's family household may be useful in illustrating a point; however, homeless persons are not members of people's immediate families, and a city is actually vastly different from a family household. A counter-argument, moreover, could offer a negative analogy that would essentially negate the first. Someone could argue, for example, that *Homeless people are like parasites, sustaining themselves at the expense of their host and contributing little or nothing to the host's well-being.*

Authority

Much of the evidence for your research conclusions will come from authorities with special insight or knowledge about your topic. An *authority* is someone qualified to offer an opinion or make a statement on a topic. The extent to which someone qualifies as an authority depends upon the topic and the individual's background and experience. A medical doctor qualifies as an authority when talking about the health risks involved with piercing one's navel to accommodate body jewelry; however, the same doctor is not an authority on the reasons that young people are so fond of this trend. That opinion should come from someone with more background on the topic, such as an authority on culture or a researcher who has interviewed a number of teenagers about navel piercing.

You will find most authorities agree about factual evidence, but they may disagree about larger and more intangible issues. Make sure you consult authorities on each side of an issue during your research, and discuss any conflicting points of view as you set forth your own conclusions in the research paper. (Refer to pp. 135–38 about evaluating evidence and authority in sources found on the Internet.)

Being Aware of Logical Fallacies

Logical fallacies represent errors in thinking. Most of them reflect overvaluing or ignoring certain evidence; others use language that distorts the basis of an argument. Since the conclusions derived from such fallacies are usu-

---

**THINKING CRITICALLY
TO EVALUATE A SOURCE'S AUTHORITY**

You should judge the authority of a source by a variety of criteria. In addition to an individual's background and experience, weigh factors such as the following in determining a source's level of credibility or expertise:

☐ 1. If the source's qualifications are not immediately clear, is there an adequate explanation of them?

☐ 2. Does the source demonstrate knowledge of the topic and an awareness of recent issues, research, and opinion?

☐ 3. Is the source recognized and cited by others who address the topic?

☐ 4. Is the source current?

☐ 5. Does the source acknowledge information and opinions from others?

☐ 6. Do the information and opinions offered appear in a reliable publication or other type of trusted source?

☐ 7. Is the source unbiased in presenting his or her own ideas and the ideas of others?

---

ally stated in ways that make them sound logical, they are frequently popularized and accepted as common sense.

Because logical fallacies are common in popular attitudes and arguments, you need to be aware of them in your own thinking and in the arguments of your research sources. Following are brief descriptions of some of the most common logical fallacies (traditional terms for some of the better-known fallacies are given in parentheses):

■ *Against the person (ad hominem):* Confusing the validity of an argument with the character of the person who makes it. Rather than address the argument itself, an attack against the person focuses on an opponent's appearance, personal habits, or character. *We can't trust the testimony of a DNA scientist who once declared bankruptcy and has been divorced twice, can we?* is an example of an argument against the person.

■ *Appeal to authority:* Assuming that the authority or reputation of an individual is evidence for the truth of his or her views. While the views an authority expresses may be validated by other evidence, the fact that someone is an Oscar-winning movie star, for example, is not a sufficient reason to buy the brand of car he or she is advertising.

■ *Appeal to ignorance (ad ignorantiam):* Arguing that a claim must be true simply because no one has shown that it is false. *The abominable snowman must exist. After all, no one has shown it doesn't* is an appeal to ignorance resulting from an illogical inference. While an audience might agree with the premise that the abominable snowman *could* exist, it does not logically follow that it therefore *does.*

■ *Appeal to pity (ad misericodiam):* Attempting to persuade by arousing pity instead of addressing the real issue. *But I still think my paper should get a passing grade, Professor Harper. I missed work yesterday and stayed up all night to get it finished on time* is an appeal-to-pity argument all too familiar to English teachers!

■ *Appeal to the people, or bandwagon (ad populum):* Arguing that something is right or best because many others think it is. Complaining to one's parents that *All our friends have QuickConnect online service. We should, too* ignores any evidence for or against QuickConnect's services. The argument assumes QuickConnect must provide good service solely on the evidence that others are using it. *Everybody else is doing it* is not a logical reason or excuse for doing anything.

■ *Circular definition, or begging the question:* Restating an assumption as part of its proof. Arguments using circular definition simply repeat their initial proposition in different words. *A man's gotta do what he's gotta do* and *Pornography is dangerous because it harms lives* are circular arguments that beg, or put off, the question they raise by actually ignoring the issue at hand.

■ *Equivocation:* Shifting the meanings of the terms used in an argument. For instance: *You claim whales are intelligent. But if whales are intelligent, why do we have to protect them? Can't intelligent creatures take care of themselves?* Such reasoning may seem plausible, but it is not: The speaker has changed the meaning of *intelligent* from "capable of understanding" to something different than was meant in the opponent's original claim.

■ *False analogy:* Using a comparison in which the differences between two things are greater than their similarities or in which the similarities are irrelevant to the argument being made. Referring to television as the *plug-in drug,* for example, overlooks major differences between the varied causes of habitual television watching and those of life-destroying, addictive drugs.

■ *False cause (post hoc, ergo propter hoc):* Assuming a cause-effect relationship because two events are related in time. The fallacy of false cause is also known as *post hoc* reasoning, from the Latin phrase *post hoc, ergo propter hoc,* meaning "after this, therefore because of this." False-cause reasoning assumes that because one thing happened at the same time as another, the first caused the second. Such reasoning is often the basis for superstition, as when a person has bad luck after breaking a mirror and concludes, wrongly, that the accident with the mirror caused the bad luck.

■ *False dilemma, or either-or:* Arguing for a conclusion as if there are only two alternatives. The alternative in a false dilemma is generally more attractive than the initial proposal. For example, *Either learn to play golf or forget about getting that job as vice president* presents a false dilemma that ignores the fact that someone may advance in a career for many other reasons than being the boss's golf partner.

■ *Hasty generalization:* Drawing a conclusion based on inadequate evidence. Arguing that Professor Tolmas's examinations are easy at a point when you have taken only one is a hasty generalization. You do not have enough examples of his tests to reasonably draw such a conclusion; indeed, the one test you have taken may have been an exception. The error of making judgments based on inadequate evidence can lead to stereotyping and prejudice, both the results of erroneously generalizing about a group on the basis of one or two pieces of evidence. Just because someone in Rome stole your wallet is not justification to call all Romans thieves.

■ *Poisoning the well:* Using loaded language to discourage discussion of an argument before examining it. Saying that *No one who cares about children will hesitate to support this law* intimidates would-be opponents and discourages them from responding. To argue against the law might mean being viewed as not caring about children or having to defend oneself against such a charge.

■ *Red herring:* Diverting discussion of an issue by introducing another, unrelated topic. The term *red herring* derives from the fact that smoked herring is strong smelling and used to divert hunting dogs from a trail. Similarly, most red-herring issues are controversial or interesting enough to get an audience's attention and make them forget about the issue at hand. *Yes, we may need to look at this city's use of landfills, but isn't the problem of illiteracy among our high school graduates more important?* is an example of a red-herring technique.

■ *Slippery slope:* Claiming that an action should not be taken because doing so will lead to a chain of undesirable events. Slippery-slope reasoning assumes one action will inevitably lead to the next, then the next, and so on until a calamitous point is reached. Those who oppose banning the sale or import of assault weapons, for example, often fall back on slippery-slope arguments: *Once assault weapons are banned,* they reason, *other automatic weapons will be banned next, then handguns, and so on until all guns are banned.* The fallacy behind such arguments is in presuming that the same reasons for the first action would necessarily lead to the second, the third, and so on.

W O R K I N G   W I T H   O T H E R S

Your understanding of argument will be vital to the success of your research effort and the resulting research paper. To understand what makes an effective argument, you must be able to reason logically—to consider one or more facts and come to a reasonable conclusion. As you complete your research and fine-tune the plan for your paper, discuss these points with someone else.

- Review several of your sources to look for examples of deductive and inductive reasoning. Consider what makes each approach effective or ineffective in these sources. Do a rough outline of the argument presented in one source, showing either the deductive or inductive pattern of reasoning.

- Review several of your sources to look for examples of Toulmin's three-part argument: claim, evidence, and warrant. In addition, look for examples of claim qualifiers and backing for warrants. Pick one source and use the Toulmin model to judge how effectively the argument is presented.

- Look for the basic two types of evidence in your sources: examples and authority. Where do examples provide the most convincing evidence? Where does authority provide the most convincing evidence? Explain why in each case.

- Examine your thesis. What claim, or argument, are you making? Is it valid and reasonable? Evaluate your thesis using the criteria for a good argument presented in this chapter. Revise your thesis, as needed.

- Now examine your outline. Does it provide ample evidence to support your argument, as stated in your thesis? Specifically, do you have enough evidence? Do you present the right kinds of evidence to convince an audience? Identify any weak areas for which you might need to provide more or better evidence. Revise your outline, as needed.

- Go through the notes you have taken from your sources to look for logical fallacies. If you discover any such errors in reasoning, discard the information from your notes. Also look for conflicting information from sources, and determine how best to present it in your paper. Finally, consider whether you are making any reasoning errors in planning the argument for your paper.

If you can, discuss these points with more than one person, particularly if you are unsure of the validity of your argument. Get feedback about your argument and the evidence you plan to provide in support of it. Be sure to give feedback to others, too, pointing out strengths and weaknesses in their claims and evidence. Remember that your goal in writing this research paper is to convince an audience of your viewpoint. Find out while still in the planning stage whether you are on the right track.

CHAPTER **10**

Writing Your Paper

Once you have completed a carefully planned outline, writing your paper should proceed fairly smoothly. Plan to write the paper over several days, expecting to make changes, to run up against writer's block for short periods, or even to make another visit to the library. But do not despair: Such hurdles are always overcome. They rarely prevent a paper from getting written if the author has been working diligently up to this point.

Reviewing Your Preparation for Writing

Before actually starting to write, take time to review what you have prepared so far to support the composing process:

- A final thesis statement
- A clear purpose (argumentative or informative)
- Notecard material
- An outline of the projected paper

You will need to draw upon all of these as you write the paper. Keeping your purpose, thesis, outline, and notecards nearby as you work will help generate ideas and keep the paper organized.

Preparing to Write

Progressing in Stages

Your paper will undoubtedly go through several versions before it is completed. It is usually helpful to work from successive drafts, though writers vary in the way they like to proceed with any paper.

**THINKING CRITICALLY
ABOUT YOUR RESEARCH NOTES**

You can often speed the drafting process by carefully evaluating your research notes before you begin. If several of your sources make essentially the same point, decide in advance which source seems to make that point most emphatically or authoritatively. This is the source you should probably refer to in your paper, so you can pull out the notecards that simply repeat this material. You can also pull out any notecards that, given the thesis and purpose you have decided on, are probably no longer pertinent to your paper. (Do not discard these, of course; save them in case you need to refer to them later.)

At the same time as you mentally project the development of your paper, consider areas where your research at this point seems incomplete. If such a gap seems to exist, add a placeholder notecard appropriately within your sequence that poses the question you feel you may still need an answer to or that indicates the information you feel you still need to supply. When you come to that point as you draft, you can then insert this note to yourself and replace it with the needed information after completing additional research.

Revising as You Write. Some writers prefer to write, revise, and finalize each part of the paper fairly thoroughly before moving on to the next part. This system works well when you have a strong outline and need to have a sense of completing one part of the paper before moving on to the next. A drawback is that you can get bogged down finetuning a single section: You may spend so much time trying to get one part just right that you lose momentum for writing.

Revising a Whole Draft. A more practical method of writing is to create the paper in three draft stages, usually in rough, revised, and final forms:

1. In the *rough draft,* aim to get as much of the paper's content written down as you can. Do not worry much about spelling, copying whole quotations, or even fully documenting sources.
2. In the *revised draft,* review the writing style, make improvements in the order of ideas, add supporting details, and check to see that you have fully developed and supported the thesis statement.
3. For the *final draft,* check spelling and punctuation closely, make sure all documentation is accurate in form and content, and generally check the paper to see that it conforms to the standards of the research paper assignment.

Whether you revise as you write, prefer to work with whole drafts, or use a combination of approaches is really up to you. The important thing is to write consistently, following the outline you prepared or changing it when necessary to maintain organization and focus in the paper.

Determining an Appropriate Style

Before you begin to write, decide how you want to sound to your paper's audience. The semiformal style and language you use for most college papers is also appropriate for the research paper; however, because the research paper is not a personal essay, pay particular attention to matters of voice and tone, qualities that influence how your writing affects the reader.

Voice.   Avoid using the personal pronoun *I*, since in most cases, the paper is not about you but about your research findings and conclusions. Avoid saying *I think . . .* or *I found that . . .* unless you are reporting your own efforts and they are relevant to the immediate subject under discussion. For instance:

Though Cranston and others have argued for changing the law,
I found most police personnel in favor of the current statute.

In most cases, express your ideas in a third-person voice that remains objective and allows focus on the subject:

Though Cranston and others have argued for changing the law, **most police** personnel favor the current statute.

Tone.   Throughout the paper, write in a tone that is consistent with the paper's purpose, subject, and audience. *Tone* is the writer's attitude toward the subject and the audience. It can be formal, serious, humorous, sarcastic, ironic, or any other quality evoked by the language and style of expression. The tone you adopt for your paper will depend upon the subject and your attitude toward it. Obviously, some subjects require a certain tone just because of their nature. The subject *AIDS* would undoubtedly require a serious tone, for example. A sarcastic or humorous tone would be unusual for a research paper, though some subjects might be effectively handled in one of these ways (a paper about *designer clothing for pets,* for example).

Considering the Audience

Since most readers will not share your familiarity with the paper's topic, anticipate what they will need to understand to follow the paper's discussion most easily. Be alert as you write to include necessary information and definitions that will assure the clarity and effectiveness of your discussion.

Defining Unfamiliar Terms.   Review your topic to identify unfamiliar names, terms, and concepts that you should define for the reader. Make sure you understand such items yourself, and be prepared to define them for your audience. Unless it is the subject of your discussion, you normally will not define a common term (e.g., *nuclear reactor, Pentagon, dolphin*). Brief mentions of well-known individuals seldom require further identification, but explain any persons, terms, or concepts that may be unfamiliar to your reader:

Individual identified	At this point, Madison turned to his friend Elbridge Gerry for support. Gerry was also a member of the Democratic-Republican Party, and he later became Madison's vice-president. Madison had hoped . . .
Major term defined	The <u>Electra complex</u>, which Sigmund Freud first identified, is today defined as a normal emotional crisis in females resulting, at an early stage of psychosexual development, from sexual impulses toward the father and jealousy of the mother (Heber 112). This is the Electra complex that Sylvia Plath once stated the speaker of her poem "Daddy" was attempting to resolve . . .

Note that in the second example, *Sigmund Freud* is not identified, since readers would likely be familiar enough with his name to understand this brief mention. The same is not true for *Elbridge Gerry,* mentioned in the first example.

Using Appositives.   When possible, keep definitions and explanations from interrupting the text by using *appositives,* which are descriptive words or phrases that qualify or rename the terms that precede them. Notice that an appositive is usually connected by a comma to the term it identifies (shown in bold in the following examples):

> At this point, Madison turned for support to his friend Elbridge Gerry, **also a Democratic-Republican and later Madison's vice-president.**

> The poem can be understood in the context of Freud's theory of an Electra complex, **a normal emotional crisis in females resulting, at an early stage of psychosexual development, from sexual impulses toward the father and jealousy of the mother** (Heber 112).

Simplifying Difficult Terms.   Avoid overdefining terms or defining those that may be simply sophisticated or unfamiliar to you. Use a simple term when possible, especially if a more complex term is going to show up only once in the paper. Thus, rather than burden the reader with a term like *microcom networking protocol* when discussing computer functions, use instead *a method for detecting and correcting errors in data transmissions.* Your reader will also probably follow a discussion about the human immune system more easily if you refer to *erythrocytes,* for example, simply as *red blood cells.*

Explaining Special Uses of Common Terms.   Familiar terms that

you use with special meanings in the paper or that are used synonymously with other familiar terms may require clarification. For instance, one student writing about the responses of black readers to Mark Twain's *The Adventures of Huckleberry Finn* realized that the term *black* had several popular definitions and could carry special implications for many readers. Since the student decided to use *black* to denote what several of her sources called by various other names—*African American, Black,* and *Negro*—she included the following note near the end of her paper to define what she meant by the term and why she preferred to use it:

> [1]For consistency and to reflect the most common usage today, I
> have throughout this paper used the term <u>black </u>to refer to the people
> several of my sources have called <u>African American, Black</u>, and <u>Negro</u>.
> As Jane Carson has observed in her essay "Words and Culture,"
> <u>black</u> remains the most recognized and consistently used term
> among different races in U.S. society (67).

In general, sensitive consideration of your audience will help you decide which terms need defining and which do not. As you prepare to write the paper, be sure to have on hand the information you may need to provide any necessary definitions or explanations.

Writing the Paper

The Introduction

The introduction announces the paper's topic, presents the thesis statement, and engages the reader's interest in what the paper will say. There are no rules as to how long an introductory section should be. An overly lengthy introduction, however, can lose the paper's focus and eventually cause the reader to wonder what you are getting at. How you go about introducing the paper's topic and thesis will depend upon your own writing preferences and the material you need to include before moving to the body of the paper.

Starting with an Anecdote.   Introduce the paper with an anecdote

(a brief account of an incident) when it helps to illustrate or lead into the topic. Notice how this introduction leads into a statement of the author's thesis (which is boldfaced in all the following examples):

> When David Prentice answered the knock at his apartment door one
> evening last July, three men rushed him, threw him to the floor, placed

duct tape over his mouth, and handcuffed him. Though Prentice fought all he could, the men soon carried him out of the apartment and threw him into the trunk of a waiting car. They then drove to a police station, where they announced they were licensed bounty hunters with a wanted bank robber in the car's trunk. The police investigated, and four hours later, the terrified and confused Prentice was released--the victim, apparently, of mistaken identity ("Police"). In reality, however, Prentice was the victim of inadequate and misused laws, those that license and regulate the actions of bounty hunters, individuals legally authorized to hunt down and arrest wanted felons. As Prentice's case demonstrates, **laws empowering bounty hunters are in need of serious and immediate revision.**

Introducing the Topic's Significance.   Point out the importance of a topic by demonstrating its widespread effect or important consequences:

The crack and cocaine epidemic in the United States has gone beyond killing the users to addicting children even before they are born. All across the United States today, doctors are delivering babies whose symptoms range from all-out dependency on crack or heroin to major brain and organ damage due to the mother's use of drugs. The problem is so great that next year, more babies born in the United States will die from drug addiction than in any other country in the world (Keeler 23). **Though federal and state programs to educate the young have reduced their numbers, drug-dependent pregnancies seem destined to continue in this country for some time.**

Offering Statistics.   Statistics provide a quick and concrete way to interest a reader in the topic:

Americans today throw away 160 million tons of garbage and trash a year, roughly 3.5 pounds a day apiece. That is enough to spread 30 stories high over 1,000 football fields. The average family of three sends 29 bags of trash to the dump every month, but in five years, one-third of our present landfills will be full ("Buried" 57). The question facing the United States today is: Where will we bury all the mountains of garbage and trash in the future? Right now, no one has an answer, but **states are scrambling to resolve a problem that, if not settled soon, literally threatens to bury us in trash.**

Quoting an Authority.   Quoting an authority allows you to agree or disagree with the opinion expressed, or the quotation can emphasize the importance of the paper's topic. A paper on Mark Twain could open with this quotation by another author, Nobel Prize winner Ernest Hemingway:

> "All modern literature comes from one book by Mark Twain called Huckleberry Finn," wrote Ernest Hemingway in 1935. "It's the best book we've had" (22). Although most literary critics and scholars, as well as the general reading public, would agree with Hemingway's assessment, Mark Twain's The Adventures of Huckleberry Finn is also one of the most controversial classics on American bookshelves. Indeed, Huckleberry Finn has borne a long history of staunch criticism and debate, first over what white audiences viewed as its common vulgarity and, increasingly in this century, over what many perceive as its racist and demeaning portrayal of black characters. **The result has been a concerned, often outraged black response to Huckleberry Finn that centers not only upon the work's language and characterization but upon its consequent value as literature, as well.**

Reviewing a Controversy.   If your paper is taking a position on or examining a controversy, you may want to review general issues before discussing the major arguments in depth:

> The American public's long-standing debate over gun control has taken on new urgency of late because of the widespread availability and use of assault-style weapons. Gun-control advocates fear that awesome, rapid-fire weapons like the Uzi and AK-47 are giving drug lords and other criminals the ability to outgun the police. They want these kinds of weapons banned, but gun enthusiasts say that would mean the end of their right to own such guns, too. Pro-gun advocates argue that the Constitution guarantees them the right to bear arms, including Uzis and AK-47s. **The recent debate has set off a flurry of political reactions that seem to have upset everyone but the criminals it originally centered upon.**

Summarizing the Literature.   A summary of the recent literature presents an overview of issues related to the paper's topic. The introductory summary below focuses on the positions of black critics on the issue of the literary value of *The Adventures of Huckleberry Finn* and the question of banning the novel:

> Black critics of Mark Twain's <u>The Adventures of Huckleberry Finn</u> continue to define the novel's strengths and weaknesses along both literary and racial lines. Kenny J. Williams, for example, recognizes several flaws in characterization and plot but ends by calling the novel a "classic." Richard K. Barksdale sees the novel as great because of its ironic rather than simply positive view of black and white friendships. **The one point on which both of these critics agree, however, is that Twain's <u>The Adventures of Huckleberry Finn</u> is too important a book to go unread by any generation of Americans.**

Providing Background Information.   Set the stage for a discussion by providing the reader with background information on the topic:

> Though the first airplane flight by the Wright brothers in 1903, as well as the early rocket experiments of Dr. Robert Goddard, certainly laid the foundations for space flight today, the real leap in progress came in 1957 when the Soviet Union launched the first orbiting satellite. That success was followed by several more Soviet firsts: the first long space flight, the first man in space, the first woman in space, and the first walk in space. The United States began catching up to the Soviets in the early 1960s with President John F. Kennedy's promise to land a man on the moon before the end of the decade. **When the first moon landing did take place in 1969, it changed the United States's commitment to space exploration in ways no one had expected.**

Defining a Key Term.   Define a central term, and explain its relationship to the discussion:

> The <u>Electra complex</u>, which Sigmund Freud first identified, is today defined as a normal emotional crisis in females resulting, at an early stage of psychosexual development, from sexual impulses toward the father and jealousy of the mother (Heber 112). This is the Electra complex that Sylvia Plath once stated the speaker of her poem "Daddy" was attempting to resolve. **An examination of the Electra complex**

theory, in fact, reveals the psychosexual sources for the basic structure and major images of Plath's remarkable poem.

The Body

The body of the paper develops the thesis statement according to the sequence of ideas planned in the outline. You should write the body of the paper as if it were an unfolding discussion, advancing one major idea at a time. Each paragraph should state a main idea, which is developed by supporting discussion and examples and followed by the next logical point for development. Your goal is to examine the topic fully while integrating your research material to support and develop the thesis statement.

Writing Effective Paragraphs. As you compose the body of the paper, avoid writing paragraphs that amount to little more than a collection of other writers' ideas and examples. Each paragraph in the paper should contain at least one idea of your own, usually expressed as the topic sentence. The paragraph should gain development from further discussion and supporting examples, with your own analyses and commentary weaving the various parts together.

Transitions show the relationship between words, sentences, and paragraphs. Use transitions (boldfaced in the following example) to give your writing *coherence,* which is the logical flow and connection of ideas:

> We cannot blame the activities of humans entirely for acid rain, **however.** Volcanic eruptions and forest fires, **for example,** release substantial amounts of sulfur and nitrogen compounds into the air. **In addition,** microbial processes in oceans and coastal mud flats the world over generate constant amounts of gaseous sulfur compounds. **Finally,** nitrogen oxides in the air result not only from the action of soil bacteria but also from the heat produced by lightning. Studies indicate, **in fact,** that natural emissions of sulfur and nitrogen are roughly equal to those produced by humans (Cordova 258).

The above paragraph also demonstrates *unity* because the content relates to the single idea expressed in the topic sentence: We cannot blame the activities of humans entirely for acid rain. Everything in the paragraph's examples and discussion directly relates to the topic sentence.

Writing in the Appropriate Tense. In discussing a work of literature, use the present tense to write about what is said or to describe actions or events occurring within the context of the work:

> As the hero of the book <u>The Great Gatsby</u>, Jay Gatsby projects an ambiguous greatness that is as much owed to his idealism as his past.

When Nick reminds Gatsby that he cannot repeat the past, Gatsby responds, "Why of course you can!" (115). Following this comment, Nick describes Gatsby as looking intently around him, as if the past itself were just out of reach.

In discussing other kinds of subjects, use the tense appropriate to the event described. Note how the tense shifts in this paragraph as the discussion moves from the past to the present:

Three years ago, the small, economically depressed town of Blytheville wanted a Japanese steel firm to build its new 500-acre steel mill there instead of elsewhere. To convince the Japanese of the town's potential, citizens invited corporate officials to visit, even hosting dinners and community sports events in their honor ("Blytheville"). In a similar manner, American-owned microchip manufacturers are today busily courting Sony, Hitachi, NEC, and Mitsubishi in hopes of gaining much-needed Japanese assistance in technology and production costs.

Integrating Sources.   The paper's content is a discussion of what your research has led you to understand about the topic. You will need to draw upon your research sources for examples, authority, certain kinds of facts, and effective expressions. Rather than simply add these to the paper, however, you should blend your research into the discussion as part of your own way of understanding the topic. The research material should fit logically and linguistically into the paper's discussion. Irrelevant material, no matter how interesting or otherwise important, should be omitted.

The following discussion uses source material without integration, preventing the voice of the paper's author from coming through:

Though such analyses may amount to little more than posttrial hindsight, the advice of jury consultants in the O. J. Simpson case appears to have been credible. Decision Quest, Inc., a consulting firm for the defense, guaranteed seating a jury with a low educational level by advising Simpson's attorneys to reject anyone who read a newspaper regularly:

Use of colon isolates quotation from the writer's discussion

Only two of the jurors graduated from college, and most said they derived their information from tabloid TV, a factor Decision Quest found correlated directly with the belief that Simpson was not guilty.

Overquoting obscures writer's point

One declared that she read nothing at all "except the horse sheet." The jurors eventually tuned out during the weeklong interrogation of the state's hapless LAPD criminalist Dennis Fung. (Miller 39)

In the opinion of some lawyers, "Simpson's defense team took a giant step toward his acquittal the day the jury was seated" (Greenburg).

Overuse of sources

"The defense built the kind of jury they wanted and the state had to sit and let them do it," said one trial analyst (Lord 24). "They got what they paid the consultants for," said another

Sources not integrated

(Jordan). According to Paul Lisneck, a Chicago-based trial consultant, the O. J. Simpson case "was over with the jury pick" (Greenburg).

The following version shows a better integration of sources and clearer expression of the writer's own ideas:

Use of selected quotations and paraphrase condenses material and keeps writer's ideas prominent

Though such analyses may amount to little more than posttrial hindsight, the advice of jury consultants in the O. J. Simpson case appears to have been credible. Decision Quest, Inc., a consulting firm for the defense, guaranteed seating a jury with a low educational level by advising Simpson's attorneys to reject anyone who read a newspaper regularly. While one juror said that she read nothing at all "except the horse sheet" (Miller 30), the majority of jurors selected said they derived their information about national and world events from tabloid TV, "a factor Decision Quest found correlated

Source material condensed

directly with the belief that Simpson was not guilty" (Miller 39). So effective was the defense strategy in using peremptory challenges to eliminate better-educated jurors that, according to Paul Lisneck, a Chicago-based trial consultant, the O. J. Simpson case "was over with the jury pick" (Greenburg).

As this second example demonstrates, you should weave source material into your own commentary and explanation, pruning quotations to highlight important ideas.

Using Quotations. Use direct quotations to give examples and lend authority or whenever a summary would forfeit precision or lose the effectiveness of the original. Except as explained below, maintain the exact wording, spelling, and punctuation of the original any time you quote.

Quotation Marks. Quotation marks separate your own words from those of another. In general, include all quoted words, phrases, and sentences of less than four lines between quotation marks. The following example demonstrates the integration and clear indication of quoted material with the writer's own sentences:

> The speaker in Plath's "Daddy," for example, expresses her seething bitterness over the men in her life who have failed to return her love. Thus, she claims her father is "a devil" and her husband "a vampire" who "drank my blood." Though the speaker says at the end of the poem that she is "through" with anguishing over her father's death and lost affection, her words seem more insistent than certain. As Carol Langer points out, "The poem's intensity of tone and imagery suggest there is yet more grief than has found words" (45).

Note that titles of short poems such as "Daddy" are also included between quotation marks.

Selection. Since few statements from your sources will require full presentation, omit unnecessary words when you quote. Rather than quote a whole sentence, integrate fragments of the original into your own sentence:

Original	"A book so clearly great, yet with such evident defects, poses a difficult critical problem."
	—Henry Nash Smith, Introduction, *Adventures of Huckleberry Finn* by Mark Twain (Boston: Houghton-Riverside, 1958) v.
Integrated quotation	Almost since its first appearance, readers have been divided over the work literary historian Henry Nash Smith describes as "a book so clearly great, yet with such evident defects" (v).
Original	"The genesis of speech is not to be found in the prosaic, but in the poetic side of life: the source of speech is not gloomy seriousness, but merry play and youthful harmony."
	—Otto Jespersen, *Language: Its Nature, Development and Origin* (London: Allen and Unwin, 1922) 154.

Integrated quotation	Though Jespersen holds that the origins of speech are "not to be found in the prosaic" or in "gloomy seriousness" (154), language is nonetheless a practical medium before it is anything else.

Exceptions to Quoting Exactly.   In most cases, a quotation must reproduce words, phrases, and sentences exactly as they appear in the original. Occasionally, however, a quotation may be made clearer or used more effectively with slight alteration of grammar or wording. While some changes are permissible, remember that they must be made in accordance with accepted practices as well as with care not to distort the original meaning of the quotation. Follow these guidelines:

■ *Initial capital letters:* If you incorporate a quotation that is a complete sentence into a sentence of your own, you must maintain the capitalization of the original or show any changes in brackets:

Original	"War is the father of all." (Heraclitus)
Original sentence and capitalization	It was Heraclitus who said, "War is the father of all."
Quotation integrated, capitalization changed	Heraclitus believed that "[w]ar is the father of all."

Clearly, the use of brackets in the above sentence is awkward. To avoid the need for brackets, quote only part of the original sentence, when possible:

Heraclitus believed that war is "the father of all."

■ *Ending punctuation:* You may change or omit the ending punctuation of the original when you add the quoted material to your own sentence:

Heraclitus said, "War is the father of all," but I disagree.

or

Although Heraclitus believed that war is "the father of all," we cannot let that point of view lead us into war.

Though the original sentence ended with a period after *all,* it is understood that the punctuation in these examples may have been changed to fit grammatically with the second writer's own sentence structure.

Other than the two cases discussed here and following, you must indicate all other changes in the original material with the use of brackets or ellipses.

■ *Brackets:* Square brackets may be used to change or add to the original wording of a quotation. If your typewriter or computer does not have square brackets, leave spaces for them as you type the paper and add them later in ink. Do not confuse brackets [ ] with parentheses ( ).

As with ellipses (discussed in the following section), alter original wording sparingly to avoid interrupting your text with cumbersome punctuation or explanatory material. Use brackets only as needed for the following purposes:

1. To alter a quotation for grammatical accuracy:

   Original   "Herst finally realized he was not familiar with those types of locks" (Gross 21).

   Quotation altered   According to Gross, it was only then that "Herst finally realized he [Houdini] was not familiar with those types of locks" (21).

2. To enclose the term *sic* (meaning "thus" or "so") to reassure the reader that you have quoted accurately despite an error in the source:

   Bruner claims that Elizabethan drama "went idle and then died with Shakespeare's death in 1621 [sic] and the advance of the Great Plague in 1665" (117).

   William Shakespeare died in 1616, not 1621. The addition of *sic* in square brackets following the erroneous date acknowledges the error in the original without altering it.

3. To clarify a quotation's meaning:

   As Alan Shears argues in <u>The Dollar Abroad</u>, "These fluctuations [in the value of the dollar] are not just economically important. They can make or break world peace efforts" (34).

4. To add material between parentheses:

   Yates manages to tell us a number of intriguing details about the members of Sylvia Plath's family (e.g., "Otto [Sylvia's father] grew up speaking German and Polish" [126]).

5. To explain added emphasis:

   Williams argues that the greatness of Hemingway's style lies in its "<u>integrity of form and level of detail</u> [emphasis added], not in its romanticism" (74).

An alternate method that avoids interrupting the text is to follow the quotation with an explanation of the change, placed in parentheses (following the page number):

Williams argues that the greatness of Hemingway's style lies in its "integrity of form and level of detail," not in its romanticism" (74; emphasis added).

■ *Ellipses:* Omit unnecessary material from a quotation or show that it is part of another sentence in the original with the use of three spaced periods (. . .), called *ellipsis points: He insisted that "the original work . . . was not completed until after the revolution" (Hagg, 23).* Note that ellipses can indicate the omission of words, phrases, or even sentences. However, their use should never misrepresent the meaning or context of the original material.

If you wish, or if your instructor prefers, you may place square brackets around ellipsis points you have added whenever it is necessary to distinguish between your own and ellipsis points that appear in the original: *As Langley points out, "When commercial computer users upgrade to newer versions, [. . .] even the trash bin is no longer an option for the old models" 60.* If you include square brackets in this way, use them consistently throughout your paper whenever you add ellipsis points to a quotation.

The guidelines below demonstrate different uses of ellipses to quote from the following sample passage:

When commercial computer users upgrade to newer versions, they soon discover that even the trash bin is no longer an option for the old models. The heavy metal content of computers qualifies them as hazardous waste. The cost of disposing of old computers can grow to be a problem even for the big companies.

—John Langley, "Old Computers Die Hard," *Time* 23 June 1998: 39–41.

1. To omit material from within a sentence:

   As Langley points out, "When commercial computer users upgrade to newer versions, . . . even the trash bin is no longer an option for the old models" (60).

2. To omit beginning material:

   Although the recycling of such technology is on the increase, the sheer expense involved in ". . . disposing of old computers can grow to be a problem even for the big companies" (Langley 60).

Though the above method is acceptable, avoid cluttering your sentences with unnecessary ellipses. Instead, introduce the quoted material using the word *that,* with no punctuation between it and the quotation:

Although the recycling of such technology is on the increase, the sheer expense involved is so great that "disposing of old computers can grow to be a problem even for the big companies" (Langley 60).

3. To place omitted material at the end of a sentence:

Langley (60) points out that even for companies such as IBM, the "cost of disposing of old computers can grow to a be a problem . . . ."

Note that in this situation, with the source page citation included *before* the quotation, three spaced periods are required for the ellipsis and a fourth period is needed to end the sentence. Another method is to give the source page citation *after* the quotation. The period goes after the final parenthesis:

Langley points out that even for companies such as IBM, the "cost of disposing of old computers can grow to a be a problem . . ." (60).

4. To omit sentences in the middle of a quotation:

Langley has shown that when "commercial computer users upgrade to newer versions, they soon discover that even the trash bin is no longer an option for the old models. . . . The cost of disposing of old computers can grow to a be a problem even for the big companies" (60).

Note that there is no space before the period ending the first sentence, but there are spaces before and after the ellipsis points that follow it.

5. To omit paragraphs from a long quotation, using a continuous line of spaced periods to indicate the ellipsis:

When commercial computer users upgrade to newer versions, they soon discover that even the trash bin is no longer an option for the old models. The heavy metal content of computers qualifies them as hazardous waste. The cost of disposing of old computers can grow to be a problem even for the big companies.

. . . .

Many of the recycling efforts were led by computer companies who saw in doing so the opportunity to solve their own and their customers' problems. The winners in this situation appear to be third world countries anxious to get their hands on anything even close to an old 386 model. A side business has consequently sprung up of parts and repair middlemen who see to it that the machines are ready to sell and operate. (Langley 60)

Do not indent the first line of a single paragraph when you quote it, even though it may have been indented in the original. But note that when quoting *two or more* paragraphs that were indented in the original, you must indent the first line of each paragraph three spaces, as shown in the previous example.

6. To omit lines of poetry from a quotation:

You stand at the blackboard, daddy,
In the picture I have of you,

. . . .

I was ten when they buried you.
At twenty I tried to get back, back to you.
I thought even the bones would do. (Plath 53)

—Excerpt from "Daddy" from *Ariel* by Sylvia Plath. Copyright © 1963 by Ted Hughes. Copyright Renewed. Reprinted by permission of HarperCollins Publishers, Inc., and Faber and Faber, Ltd.

Long Quotations.   Any quotation that is longer than four typed lines should be set off as a block and indented ten spaces from the left margin. Introduce the quotation with a complete sentence and a colon (unless the context calls for some other kind of structure and punctuation):

It is difficult to enforce these rules, and they say nothing about eliminating individuals whose education or experience might make it difficult for attorneys to control a jury. One experienced trial attorney expresses the matter this way:

> All potential jurors . . . inevitably bring with them the views and biases built into their race, religion, age, and gender. These preconceptions supposedly influence the eventual verdict as much, if not more than, the evidence presented at trial. The task of the lawyer, therefore, is to outsmart the system. (Abramson 143)

The Conclusion

The conclusion to your research paper is as important as every other part, possibly even more so. Here is where you will summarize, evaluate, restate for emphasis, place in perspective, and finally drive home the major ideas and lasting impressions you want a reader to take away from the paper. Do not disappoint your audience with an ending that does no more than restate what has already been said. Make the conclusion of your paper as interesting and insightful as possible, something worth the reader's further consideration.

Devising an Effective Conclusion. While there is no single way to conclude any research paper effectively, two guidelines should be observed:

1. Reemphasize the thesis statement without repeating it word for word.
2. Be sure the last paragraph clearly signals a conclusion about what has been said.

Avoid the temptation to introduce new issues or list unanswered questions in the conclusion. Instead, offer your reader content that brings the discussion to a logical close.

The following examples demonstrate common approaches to concluding a research paper discussion. You will notice that some closings combine more than one approach.

Reemphasizing the Thesis Statement. Make certain your reader grasps the main point of your paper by emphasizing the thesis again in the conclusion. Rather than simply repeating the thesis statement word for word, emphasize key words and concepts that represent the thesis in the context of the conclusion itself. The final paragraph of one student's paper on television talk shows, for example, echoed the paper's thesis that such programs have offended or alienated too many people to survive in their present form:

> In providing such opportunity, the talk shows have indeed gone too far, for they have moved into realities which, once examined, cannot remain entertaining. As we watch the lives held up for examination and exposed on our screens, our better judgment tells us they deserve another kind of forum than <u>Jerry Springer</u> or <u>Ricki Lake</u> provide. It is for this reason that as talk shows change, as they surely must to survive at all, their alteration will result less from mere matters of taste than from an overruling, collective conscience as to what is fair and decent.

Presenting a Quotation. An eloquent or particularly striking comment by a voice other than your own can effectively sum up your position or significantly affect your reader's awareness. The writer of a paper on *The Adventures of Huckleberry Finn,* for example, felt she wanted her readers to recognize that the conflicting concerns surrounding the novel were rooted in its power as a great literary work. For this reason, her conclusion returned to the quotation from Ernest Hemingway that appeared at the beginning of the paper:

> Huckleberry Finn has come a long way from what made it the "veriest of trash" for white audiences in the nineteenth century. Today, the book acts for black as well as white readers as what another black writer, David L. Smith, calls "a trigger to outrage" (5), a classic work of art that stirs reflection and humanity in all of us. In this sense, The Adventures of Huckleberry Finn is perhaps, after all, just what Ernest Hemingway insisted, "The best book we've had" (Hemingway 22).

Providing Direction or Offering Solutions.   If your paper has explored a problem or traced its effects, provide your audience with a direction for action or point out realistic solutions. For instance, an informative paper dealing with new developments in the treatment of AIDS might conclude with the following suggestions for further action:

> As actress Whoopi Goldberg said, we can all learn to do something about AIDS: "If you're a carpenter, you could build a ramp that would allow more mobility for someone in a wheelchair. A good cook could provide hot meals for someone living nearby" (43). What can you and I do to help? Start by finding out about state-sponsored AIDS projects or other concerned groups in your community. Join them. Take part. You'll find you have more to offer in the war against AIDS than you ever thought possible.

Evaluating Results.   Use the conclusion of your paper to evaluate significant effects or to describe and analyze results. A research report on experiments to identify color preferences among different ethnic groups, for example, might conclude with an analysis of major problems encountered and their influences on the project results. The following paragraph concluded a research paper discussing attempts by world governments to preserve threatened species and environments through international agreements:

> As these cases demonstrate, international treaties alone cannot overcome worldwide threats to fragile ecosystems and endangered species. The Third World countries in which threatened entities are found are often too debt ridden to enforce agreements, preserving instead what are referred to as "paper parks" that exist only in writing (Golob and Brus 349). Written global agreements to save wetlands

or threatened plants and animals will never be enough, however, without the recognition of people everywhere that nature is neither ours to control nor to destroy. Without such recognition, human beings themselves may become the most endangered species on the planet.

Providing a Broader Perspective.   Just as the paper's introduction has led your reader to a closer examination of the topic, so, too, should the conclusion lead away from it to a broader perspective. An examination of a historical event, for example, would conclude by discussing its relationship to later events or its relative significance today. In a literary study, move from discussing the work itself to seeing it in the context of the author's life or other works:

> Sylvia Plath was nearing her thirtieth birthday in the month that she composed "Daddy" and several other of her strongest poems. As her marriage to poet Ted Hughes began falling apart during this time, Plath used her anger and pain as catalysts to transform her earlier dependency on male authority figures into spiteful, creative independence. It is no surprise that "The Jailer," "Fever 103°," "Ariel," and "Lady Lazarus" all echo "Daddy" in their vivid images of rebirth and purification mixed with angry renunciation of males. The speaker of "Lady Lazarus" rises "out of the ash" the way the poet's genius itself seemed to rise out of her own suffering and spiritual rebirth. Plath's suicide four months after writing "Daddy" and these other late poems only adds a further, harsh validity to the psychological and spiritual complexity of all her work.

Other Backmatter

The concluding section of your research paper will be followed by a separate page(s) of content notes (see Chapter 11) and a separate Works Cited page(s) (see Chapter 12), in that order. Documentation of sources cited in the paper (see Chapter 11) will appear both in the body of the text and in the Works Cited page(s).

Preparing a Final Draft

By now, your research paper should have a well-developed introduction, body, and conclusion followed by any necessary content notes or footnotes and the Works Cited page(s). What you have written at this point will most likely represent 95% or more of the paper's final content. Any remaining material will come through performing three important last steps: revising, editing, and proofreading. These steps understandably often overlap during the process of revision. Conscientiously following through on each of them, however, will ensure that nothing is left out of your paper and that everything you have done so far is in its most effective and final form.

Revising

Few papers can be written thoroughly with only a first draft. You will undoubtedly need to make revisions in the arrangement of the paper's major parts to ensure its general readability, to be certain that it forms a whole, and to know that everything is in the right order. Since up to now, you have no doubt been deeply engrossed in the act of writing the paper, set it aside for another day or two. When you return to it, you will read it through with a fresh eye.

**THINKING CRITICALLY
ABOUT YOUR FIRST DRAFT**

Begin your revision by looking at the overall paper as an investigation and discussion of the research subject. Does the content develop a smoothly connected *discussion* rather than an assemblage of quotation and paraphrase? Does the paper exhibit unity and coherence as a whole and in the development of its paragraphs? Look for transitions that make the writing clear and flowing.

Review each part of the paper as follows:

1. Reread the *introduction.* A good introduction will arouse a reader's interest in the subject and the discussion that follows. The thesis statement should be clearly stated and follow logically from the introductory material itself.

2. Is the *body* of the paper developed sufficiently? Is there a logical progression of ideas among individual paragraphs? Remember that the thesis statement idea should be prominent throughout the paper. Check each paragraph for its relationship to the thesis.

3. The *conclusion* should be worth reading. Make sure it offers sufficient content without beginning or alluding to a new subject of discussion. The paper's thesis statement should be emphasized again in the conclusion, but avoid repeating it word for word.

Revise the paper by rearranging large parts of the content as needed. You can accomplish this by drawing arrows or making notes on the draft itself, or you can cut and paste various parts in the desired order. If you are writing on a computer, use the "copy" and "move" functions of your software to rearrange text. How much you need to revise will depend upon what you recognize is needed, but do not fall into the trap of starting the paper all over again. If you have followed your outline and provided logical connections between major parts of the paper, rearranging some parts or editing others should be sufficient to prepare for the final typing.

Editing

Editing involves making changes to the text in order to strengthen the content and writing style. This is when you will need to improve the paper's language or edit sentences and paragraphs for weak style or development. Edit for these purposes:

1. *Reread each paragraph to see that it has a topic sentence related to the paper's thesis.* Be alert to noticeably long paragraphs that may need trimming or division. Paragraphs that are surprisingly short may need to be combined with others or developed with more examples. At the same time, check for paragraphs that may be "stuffed" with research information irrelevant to the thesis. Edit such paragraphs out of the paper, or revise them as needed. Be sure that each paragraph offers examples and that they support or explain the topic sentence.

2. *Edit the paper's language to sharpen vocabulary.* Be sure that all central terms are defined for the reader and that any complex terms are used only when necessary. Avoid the passive voice where possible, and use strong, active verbs in place of weaker constructions. Vary your paper's style and vocabulary to avoid repetition and to add precision; weave paraphrase and quotation into your own sentence structures:

> As Brewer **points out,** "Though certainly admirable, Twain's stylistic versatility could sometimes become a major weakness" (66).

> Brewer (66) **says** that Twain's versatility was at times also a great weakness.

> Brewer **has argued** that Twain's versatility was at times also a great weakness (66).

> Other critics **agree** with Brewer (66) that Twain's versatility was at times also a great weakness.

A dictionary or thesaurus can provide alternatives for any words that may be frequently repeated in the paper. If you are editing on computer, these references are likely available with your software. Also use the "find" function to locate words or phrases you tend to overuse.

3. *Edit to avoid sexist language.* Eliminate wording that discriminates against males or females by inaccurately portraying them in stereotypical ways. The following sentence, for example, demonstrates erroneous sexual stereotyping of male and female roles:

> A nurse's salary can improve a great deal once she has two or three
>
> years of experience. A doctor, however, has to complete his residency
>
> requirement in a hospital before he sees much increase in income.

Language such as this is sexually biased because it implies that all nurses are female and all doctors are male. Using *he or she* in place of the single pronouns may eliminate some of the bias, but such use can sound awkward if repeated. A better way is to construct sentences using plural nouns and pronouns:

> Salaries for **nurses** can improve a great deal once **they** have two or three
>
> years of experience. **Doctors,** however, have to complete **their** residency
>
> requirements in a hospital before **they** see much increase in income.

Another way to avoid bias is to omit the use of pronouns altogether:

> Salaries for nurses with two or three years' experience can improve a
>
> great deal. Doctors, however, have to complete residency requirements
>
> in a hospital before seeing much increase in income.

Also edit to remove language that discriminates against groups of various ages, ethnicities, sexual preferences, exceptionalities, and so on.

Proofreading

Proofread your paper several times to make minor corrections in spelling, punctuation, and typing. Do not make the mistake of relying upon others to proofread for you. Even if someone else has typed the final version, you will find that your own acquaintance with the research material is an essential safeguard against misspellings or omissions of content.

If you have written your paper on a computer, make use of its "spellcheck" function. Depending on what software you use, you will be able to check for misspelled words and perhaps repeated words, as well. Do not rely on the computer, however, as your only means of proofreading. Keep in mind that a "spellcheck" will identify only words that are misspelled, not those that are used incorrectly (e.g., *form* vs. *from* and *county* vs. *country*). You will still need to read the paper.

Correct small typing mistakes and other errors neatly by hand, using correcting fluid and ink. If there are very many such corrections, however, preserve the paper's neatness by retyping and reprinting some pages. After you have carefully read the final version several times and made necessary corrections, share the paper with others who can proofread it again for you with a fresh view of the language and content.

W O R K I N G   W I T H   O T H E R S

Rather than wait until the entire paper is completed, discuss your efforts with others throughout the planning and writing stages. If it helps, set up a regular meeting time at two- or three-day intervals to discuss your progress. Such a pattern will help to keep your writing on schedule.

You will find that talking over your progress with others during the writing stage of the research paper can help you get over writer's block and test the paper's effectiveness as you work. Having someone else review the final draft of the paper for revision and editing purposes is always a good idea.

After you have proofread the paper yourself, ask a friend or classmate to look it over, too. Listen carefully as he or she responds to these or any additional concerns about which you have questions or would value responses.

- Often another person's immediate reaction or interest in a paper can be a measure of how well it is written. Ask your friend or classmate how he or she responds to the paper. Is it readable? Is the discussion interesting?

- How effective does your reader feel the paper's introduction, body, and conclusion are? What areas are particularly strong? Do any weak parts need more development or revision?

- Does the paper have a clear, logical organization? Is the thesis supported throughout?

- Proofread the paper together. If you are working with a classmate, take turns reading each other's papers. Indicate any mistakes with small checks in pencil in the paper's margin. Discuss the checked places together to be sure about any changes needed in the paper.

- Next to your instructor, a classmate is probably the best judge of the paper's use of sources and their proper citations. Ask his or her opinion on these matters, and be prepared to follow through with any you feel are important to the paper's total effectiveness.

As you discuss your paper with others during the writing and revision stages, listen carefully and take notes whenever you can. Try not to hurry this important sharing session. The more time you spend reviewing each other's papers, the more confident you can be of your own paper's strengths. While working with other classmates during this time, remember to offer the same serious attention to their papers as you have asked them to give yours.

CHAPTER **11**

Acknowledging Sources

Intext Citation and Content Notes (MLA Style)

In addition to the discussion of the research topic, your completed paper will also include documentation of the sources you have cited and, in some cases, content notes that provide further information about your research. You must always give credit in the paper for any ideas and language you borrow directly or adapt from other sources, although you should not cite sources for information that is common knowledge. (See the discussion of plagiarism and common knowledge in Chapter 7 on pp.164–70.)

Following a Standard Documentation Format

Generally speaking, entries in the Works Cited section at the end of the paper tell the reader what sources you have consulted in writing the paper's content. Such general acknowledgments, however, do not tell the reader precisely what was taken from a source and where, or show how it was used in the paper's discussion. Consequently, documentation formats used in writing for various disciplines also include either intext citation of sources or endnotes or footnotes to convey this kind of precise acknowledgment of sources.

This chapter describes the methods of documentation recommended by the Modern Language Association (MLA), a nationwide association of teachers and scholars that sets standards for publishing papers about literature and modern and classical languages. Documentation formats used by writers in other disciplines are discussed in Chapter 13.

**THINKING CRITICALLY
ABOUT ACKNOWLEDGING SOURCES**

All writers have an obligation to note the source of any ideas or information that they have gathered through research. In most popular writing—that in newspapers and magazines, for example—it is necessary only for the writer to name his or her sources within the body of the text. In academic writing, however, the requirements for acknowledging sources are quite a bit stricter. Sources must be referred to and identified in such a way that readers can, if they wish, find any source for themselves to verify its authenticity or read it more fully. To provide such complete information within the text would be cumbersome and awkward for both writers and readers; consequently, academic research papers generally offer just enough in-text information about each source referred to that readers can easily find full information about it on the Works Cited page at the end of the paper.

As you acknowledge your sources within the body of your paper, keep two things in mind:

1. Integrate source acknowledgments into your paper smoothly so they do not interrupt or detract from the flow of your writing. In general, provide only the information required to allow readers to find the full source information on your Works Cited page.

2. Be sure to provide enough intext information so that readers can find *exactly* what you are referring to in the sources you cite. This means always including page numbers for published sources.

MLA Documentation

MLA documentation style requires up to three methods of acknowledging sources in a research paper: (1) parenthetical intext citation of sources, (2) full documentation in the Works Cited page(s), and, when appropriate to the paper, (3) content notes. All sources cited in text or mentioned in the content notes must also appear in the Works Cited page(s). These methods of documentation are preferred by the MLA, though some schools and journals still use footnotes or endnotes. Which documentation method you use may depend upon your subject and the format your instructor wants you to follow.

Using Intext Citation

Intext citation (also called *parenthetical documentation*) means identifying the source of any borrowed material immediately as it appears, right in the text of the paper. (An intext citation is only the first such acknowledgment you will give each of your sources; the Works Cited section of your paper will list each source again, giving complete publication information.) Intext citation requires the minimum information a reader would need to find the item in the Works Cited page(s) of your paper or in the cited material itself. In most cases, this means giving the author and page number(s) for the source you are crediting:

Author

> According to Berman, adopted children "want to be connected with a past heritage or a genealogical history"
> **Page number** (119).

This example demonstrates intext citation form for a single author. Note, however, that no citation is needed when you refer to an author's entire work, rather than a part of it:

> Alice Walker's The Color Purple examines people's hopes and dreams with great sensitivity.

For citing authors, titles, and other kinds of information, follow the guidelines given in the following sections:

1. PLACEMENT OF ITEMS

When the identity of an author is important for purposes of clarity, emphasis, or authority, include the name in your text as you introduce a quotation or paraphrase. Place the page number(s) of the source in parentheses at the end of the borrowed material:

Author cited with quotation

> Donald R. Griffin, author of Animal Minds, points out that "Darwin and many others have been impressed with the fact that sleeping dogs sometimes move and vocalize in ways that suggest they are dreaming" (258).

Author cited in paraphrase

> Donald R. Griffin, author of Animal Minds, points out that many scientists have interpreted the movements and sounds of sleeping dogs as evidence that they dream (258).

When your major emphasis is on the content of the borrowed material, however, include the author's name in parentheses with the page number(s):

> Many scientists, including Charles Darwin, have "been impressed with the fact that sleeping dogs sometimes move and vocalize in ways that suggest they are dreaming" (Griffin 258).

Many scientists, including Charles Darwin, have interpreted the movements and sounds of sleeping dogs as evidence that they dream (Griffin 258).

NOTE: Be certain that you do *not* place a comma between the author's name and the page number(s). MLA citation form calls for listing the author's name and the page numbers *without punctuation,* as in the preceding examples. In addition, never use *p.* or *pg.* before the page number(s).

An author's name should appear only once in any intext acknowledgment. Include the author's name in the text or in the parentheses following, but not in both:

Incorrect: Author named in both text and parenthetic citation	Ex-ambassador to Japan Mike Mansfield believes that the relationship between Japan and the United States "holds the promise of well-being for nations and peoples around the world" (Mansfield A12).

2. CITING AN AUTHOR, EDITOR, OR CORPORATION

In general, treat individuals, editors, corporate authors, and others who would normally be considered responsible for producing a work as its author. Note that the intext citation form for an author and editor does not distinguish between their roles. In the Works Cited section of the paper, however, the designation *ed.* (for "editor") differentiates between them for your reader. The following examples demonstrate alternative techniques for placement of author names:

Single author	During the American Revolution, Native Americans were more likely to side with the British than with the colonists, although most native factions attempted to remain neutral (Richter 220–21).
Single editor	As Robert J. Slater insists, "If we can't learn from the younger generation, it's because we don't really want to" (77).
Corporate author	A report by Western Trends, Inc., showed that more than fifty percent of those surveyed distrusted the current jury system ("Survey").
	The U.S. Department of Health and Safety reports that death from ATVs (all-terrain vehicles) has increased by over 15% a year since 1987 (76).

In a case such as the last one, in which the name of the source is long or perhaps similar to that of another source, the MLA suggests citing the name in the text discussion rather than within a parenthetical citation. Long intext citations, as well as other parenthetical material, break up the content and impair the reader's concentration.

3. CITING MORE THAN ONE AUTHOR

Cite all authors by their last names if there are two or three. If there are more than three authors, cite only the first author's last name followed by *et al.* ("and others"):

For Two Authors:

Authors introduced in text	Naisbitt and Aburdene claim we are approaching the day when "virtually all women will work except for a few months or years when they are raising children full-time" (7).
Parenthetical citation of authors	We are approaching the day when "virtually all women will work except for a few months or years when they are raising children full-time" (Naisbitt and Aburdene 7).

For More Than Three Authors:

Authors introduced in text	According to studies by Johnson et al., a "significant association" exists between the number of hours adolescents spend viewing television and aggressive behavior on their part later in life (468).
Parenthetical citation of authors	One series of studies has shown a "significant association" between the number of hours adolescents spend viewing television and aggressive behavior on their part later in life (Johnson et al., 468).

(You can also cite all the authors' last names in a parenthetical citation, but doing so in text would be awkward.)

4. CITING MULTIPLE WORKS BY THE SAME AUTHOR

When listing more than one source by the same author in the Works Cited page(s), give the author's name in the citation, followed by a comma, followed by the name of the source and the page number(s):

Plath's poetry has long been recognized as exhibiting a "good deal of disturbance with proportionately little fuss" (Alvarez, "Poetry" 26).

Entries for Alvarez's work would appear in alphabetical order by title in the Works Cited page(s). After the first entry, additional works listed would show three unspaced hyphens for the author's name:

> Alvarez, A. "Poetry in Extremism." <u>The Observer</u> 14
>   March 1963: 26-33.
> - - -."Sylvia Plath." <u>Tri-Quarterly</u> 7 (1966): 65-74.

5. CITING TITLES

Cite titles of sources only when (a) no author's name is provided or (b) you need to distinguish between one source and another by the same author—for example, *The Sun Also Rises* and *The Old Man and the Sea,* by Ernest Hemingway. In both cases, use recognizable, shortened versions of the titles when they are cited: *Sun* for *The Sun Also Rises; Huck Finn* for *The Adventures of Huckleberry Finn;* and so on. (See Chapter 14 for common abbreviations for literary titles.)

Examples within this text follow the current MLA preference for using underlining, rather than italics, for titles of published works. The text also explains, however, that either option is acceptable for research papers and that students should check with their instructors if they wish to use italics.

Also follow these guidelines in citing titles:

- If there is no author to cite, describe the issuing magazine, newspaper, agency, or other authority when you introduce the borrowed material:

  A survey published in <u>Consumer Reports</u> in 2001 found that only slightly more than half of respondents had home computers connected to the Internet ("Exploring").

  A survey by a respected consumer advocacy organization found that in 2001 only slightly more than half of respondents had home computers connected to the Internet ("Exploring").

  The Works Cited entry for either form would look like this:

  "Exploring the Digital Divide." <u>Consumer Reports</u> Feb. 2001: 6.

- To distinguish between material taken from different sources by the same author, cite page number(s) and shortened titles in parentheses, as follows:

  The strongest of Hemingway's male characters embrace rituals of disciplined courage as a part of their roles in life. We see this in the fine, respectful precision of the great Belmonte when he enters the

"territory of the bull" (<u>Sun</u> 135) and again when the old fisherman
vows to "be worthy of the great [Joe] DiMaggio who does all things
perfectly even with the pain of the bone spur in his heel" (<u>Old Man</u> 68).

6. CITING INDIRECT SOURCES

Though it is always best to consult a source directly for any material
you adapt from it, you may not always be able to do so. In a case in which
you cannot locate the original source of a quotation, cite the source you
have, preceding it with *qtd. in* ("quoted in"):

> A July 2001 report from the Carnegie Endowment's Information
> Revolution and World Politics Project found that within authoritarian
> nations such as China and Cuba "effective control of the Internet is
> much more prevalent than conventional wisdom would suggest" (qtd.
> in "Mama" 14).

The inclusion of *qtd. in* with the source citation indicates that the writer
did not take the quotation from the actual *Foreign Policy* article but instead
got it from an article with the shortened title "Mama." The Works Cited entry
for this citation would include only the indirect source, not the Carnegie En-
dowment's report:

> "Mama Sees You." <u>Foreign Policy</u> Sep./Oct. 2001: 14-15.

7. CITING MULTIPLE SOURCES

If you borrow an idea mentioned in more than one source, give credit
in the paper to all sources. Always cite multiple sources parenthetically.
Separate the sources with semicolons:

> Social researchers and defenders of television talk shows say that, in
> providing such opportunities for otherwise silent or misunderstood
> individuals to be heard, the programs perform a valuable outlet and a
> needed service to society (Priest 73-91; Cabot 19).

Each source would then appear in the paper's Works Cited section in
the normal manner.

NOTE: Citing multiple sources parenthetically in the text is cumbersome and may interfere with your reader's concentration. Given this, you
should cite multiple sources sparingly in the text and only when necessary.
If you need to list more than three sources, cite them in a note, rather than
parenthetically in the text (see Using Content Notes later in this chapter).

8. CITING VOLUME AND PAGE NUMBERS

For a work in more than one volume, cite the volume number, followed by a colon, followed by a space and the page number(s):

> Freud believed in a process he called <u>free association</u> to uncover the hidden meanings of dreams (5: 221).

9. CITING PAGE NUMBERS OF CLASSIC WORKS

A classic work remains in demand long after its author's death. Once its copyright has expired, such a work may be published in several editions by different publishing houses. Classic works such as *The Adventures of Huckleberry Finn* and *The Scarlet Letter,* for example, appear in several editions, each published by a different publisher and each bearing the same material but on differently numbered pages. Since your reader may have an edition with a different pagination than yours, give the page number for your source, followed by a semicolon and the chapter, book, section, or other parts abbreviated and numbered, as well:

> Twain satirizes monarchies by having Huck give Jim a brief lesson about kings and dukes (130; ch. 22).

> The main character in Dostoyevsky's <u>Crime and Punishment</u> tries to convince himself that he has "killed a principle" rather than another human being (271; pt. 3; sec. 6).

When discussing a classic poem such as *Paradise Lost* or *Canterbury Tales,* line numbers will also be more useful to your reader than page numbers of an edition he or she may not have. Omit page numbers, and cite the work by divisions such as canto, book, part, line(s), scene, or act. Use abbreviated or shortened titles (see Chapter 14) followed by numbers separated with periods to represent the work's divisions. Thus, *"PL* 2.428–29" would indicate "part 2, lines 428–29," of John Milton's *Paradise Lost:*

Reference to a poem	Milton's Satan exhibits "monarchal pride/Conscious of highest worth" (<u>PL</u> 2.428-29) when speaking early in the poem. Later, however, he is described as "Squat like a toad, close at the ear of Eve" (4.799-800).

Similarly, discuss a drama (such as Shakespeare's *Macbeth*) by providing line, scene, and act numbers: *"Mac.* 3.2.25–38." Roman numerals, instead of arabic (as shown here and above), are acceptable if they appear in the source or if your instructor prefers them. (See Chapter 14 on numbers.)

10. CITING NONPRINT SOURCES

Nonprint sources such as interviews, recordings, and television and radio speeches have no page numbers. Cite each of these kinds of sources by giving the author's name in the text or parenthetically. The author's name in the Works Cited list will key your reader to the type of work referred to:

Text entry	Governor Barrington said he would be sorry to see opponents of the bill "use the law to fight against justice."
Works Cited entry	Barrington, Alan. Personal interview. 18 Oct. 2002.
Text entry	As one critic complained, "It's not certain that Shakespeare knew what he was doing at the end of Hamlet, so why should we?" (Carter).
Works Cited entry	Carter, Andrew R. "What Hamlet Cannot Tell Us-- And What It Can." National American Literature Conference. Boston, 20 May 2002.

11. CITING MULTIPLE PAGE REFERENCES
TO THE SAME WORK

When discussing a short story, novel, long poem, or play throughout the paper, do not repeat the author's name for each reference. In general, name the author and title once, and cite only page numbers after that:

> In The Old Man and the Sea, Hemingway's fisherman believes firmly in his own courage, of being "worthy of the great DiMaggio" (68). He recalls days when, much younger, he felt he could "beat anyone if he had to" (70). Though he eventually loses his great fish, the old man insists that "man is not made for defeat" (103), and the novel ends with his "dreaming about the lions" (127).

When discussing any written work, omit the author's name after the first page citation:

> The old fisherman believes firmly in his own courage, of being "worthy of the great DiMaggio" (Hemingway 68). He recalls days when, much younger, he felt he could "beat anyone if he had to" (70).

To allow a reader to find quoted material in any edition of a prose work, include the chapter number after the page number, separated by a semicolon:

> The old fisherman believes firmly in his own courage, of being "worthy of the great DiMaggio" (Hemingway 68; ch. 4).

Using Content Notes

Content notes differ from the documentation appearing in footnotes or the Works Cited page(s) of your paper. You may find such notes helpful in providing additional commentary or explanations that are not immediately relevant to your paper's discussion. Be aware, however, that you should use such notes sparingly. Make a point to include important material in the main text of your paper. Reserve content notes for adding *necessary* qualifications or explanations when including them in the main text would otherwise interrupt your discussion.

To include content notes in your paper, follow these guidelines:

1. Refer your paper's reader to a content note by means of a superscript numeral, a raised arabic number immediately following the material to which the note refers:

Superscript numeral in text refers to numbered content note

> According to a 1986 U.S. Supreme Court decision, lawyers are not supposed to eliminate potential jurors because of race or gender. It is difficult, however, to enforce this rule, and it says nothing about eliminating those whose education or experience might be the cause of their dismissal.[2] One experienced trial attorney [. . .].

The following content note refers to the correspondingly numbered material in the preceding paragraph:

Content note

> [2]Judges can also dismiss jurors for a variety of reasons, ranging from health matters to violations of court restrictions. In the O. J. Simpson case, Judge Ito removed a juror because he believed she was meeting with a literary agent and intending to write a book about the trial (Gleick, "Disorder"). As Rubank has noted, jurors in high-profile trials often see this experience as "their 15 minutes of fame" (24).

2. Type superscript numerals—such as the numeral ² shown here—by turning the typewriter roller up so that the typed number appears about a half space above the text, usually at the end of the sentence to which it refers, as here.² If you are writing on a computer, type the superscript numeral by using the appropriate function keys or commands in your word-processing program.

3. Do not space between the superscript number and any word or punctuation that precedes it.

4. Remember that superscript numbers for content notes should appear in numerical sequence throughout the text, regardless of what pages they appear on.

5. Place all content notes on a separate page(s) following the text of your paper; type the centered title Notes at the top of the page. (See the Notes page of the sample research paper at the end of this chapter.) Content note entries should appear immediately below the title, each preceded by a raised number indicating the text material to which it corresponds (see the preceding example).

6. Any source you mention in a content note must also appear with complete documentation in the Works Cited page(s) of the paper. For instance, you would need to include the authors mentioned in the preceding example (*Gleick* and *Rubank*) in the Work Cited page(s), even if you did not also cite them in the paper's text.

Content notes can be used for a variety of purposes:

1. TO ELABORATE ON MATTERS NOT STRICTLY RELEVANT TO THE TEXT DISCUSSION

[1]Oprah Winfrey made talk show history in 1985 when she disclosed on her own program that she had experienced repeated acquaintance rapes throughout her life (Priest 3). The disclosure was hailed by thousands of women who needed Oprah's example to confront their own victimization and to begin to heal their pain from it.

[2]Sacks (149) points out that there has also been a parallel shift in the public's attitude toward people who are deaf. He claims the change from perceiving these individuals as pathetic victims to viewing them as uniquely empowered is demonstrated in two earlier films: <u>The Heart Is a Lonely Hunter</u> (1975) and <u>Children of a Lesser God</u> (1986).

2. TO ADD CLARIFICATION

[3]Not all the New York critics were as lavish in their praise of The Glass Menagerie. Joseph Wood Krutch, while calling the work "remarkable," also noted that "good writing and very bad writing have seldom been as conspicuous in the script of one play" and pointed to its "fuzzy haze of pretentious, sentimental, pseudo-poetic verbiage" (357). The most powerful critic of the day, George Jean Nathan, termed the play "a freakish experiment [. . .] deficient in any touch of humor" (qtd. in Leverich 586).

[4]This is not to say that Asians and Europeans consider all U.S. exports inferior. American-made clothing--especially denim jeans--and Hollywood films are still top-rated exports everywhere (Dorn 33).

3. TO EVALUATE OR COMPARE SOURCES

[5]Conducted over twenty-five years and involving some 707 subjects, the Children in the Community study offers the most comprehensive longitudinal examination of the relationship between television viewing among adolescents and young adults and a tendency toward violent behavior.

[6]Keeler's study of underachieving college students is based on interviews with college students and professors. A more persuasive viewpoint is expressed in Mike Rose's Lives on the Boundary (New York: Macmillan, 1989). Rose tells of his own underprivileged education and its relevance to his teaching and working with struggling minority students at UCLA.

4. TO PROVIDE STATISTICS

[7]A recent survey by U.S. News & World Report of 696 college seniors found that 95% could name Mark Twain as the author of The Adventures of Huckleberry Finn, while only 62% could name Geoffrey Chaucer as the author of the next best-known work, Canterbury Tales ("Reader's Block" 89).

[8]Laboratory results over a six-week period showed a loss of 3.05 mg of potassium, with a corresponding 9% decrease in fluid volume. Density measurements were not recorded during the first cycle of testing but were found during the second cycle to be 0.07% higher.

5. TO EXPLAIN METHODS OR PROCEDURES

[9]I interviewed Robert Nelson with the assistance of an interpreter, who conveyed my questions to him in American Sign Language (ASL), translating his responses orally to me. Nelson's words, as quoted in this paper, are the verbatim answers provided to me and recorded on tape by the interpreter, Louise Ibarra.

[10]Researchers induced three types of naturally occurring fungi--penicillium, acremonium, and uloclabium--into selenium-contaminated soil through addition of humus, regular aeration, and irrigation between 1983 and 1985. The fungi converted selenium to the less toxic gases dimethylselenide and dimethyldiselenide. See Golub and Brus (369).

6. TO CITE ADDITIONAL SOURCES

[11]For more information on Einstein's religious thinking, see Calder (143); Hoff (326-27); and Gamow (187). Einstein's argument with Niels Bohr on the origin of matter is recounted in Jason M. Collier's "Discussions of Genius," New Mexico Journal of the Physical Sciences 21 (1994): 4-11.

[12]See also Sacks (12), Luria and Yudovich (121), and Church (63).

7. TO SHORTEN MAJOR SOURCE CITATIONS

[13]All references and citations for this discussion of Darwin's early life are to Charles Darwin: A Biography (New York: Knopf, 1995), by Janet Browne.

[14]Ernest Hemingway, The Old Man and the Sea. Future citations in the text will be to page numbers only.

8. TO DEFINE IMPORTANT TERMS

[15]The term phantasmal voices refers to the sense of actually hearing speech, which people who are postlingually deaf may experience when they read lips. They do not, of course, actually hear speech. They instead translate the visual experience into an auditory correlate based on their memory of sound, as they knew it before becoming deaf. See Sacks (6).

The sample research papers in the appendix to this chapter and in Appendix A demonstrate the use of content notes to clarify and add information pertinent to the author's discussion. As you examine these papers, note how sources are used and given proper intext citation throughout.

WORKING WITH OTHERS

Check the accuracy of your paper's documentation by sharing the final draft with others. Seek advice about the effectiveness of any content notes, and encourage readers to make suggestions. The following suggestions may also be helpful.

- Ask your reader to note the placement and accompanying punctuation for each intext citation as it appears in the paper. Check for complete parentheses and the use of a period following the closed parenthesis whenever a citation appears at the end of a sentence. Be sure that no comma separates the author's name and the page number citation, as in this correct example: *(Smith 65)*.

- Point out any unusual intext citations that you want your reader's opinions about. For example, look especially at multiple-author entries, works cited only by title, and citations of different authors with the same last name. Are these cited correctly in the paper?

- Discuss your rationale for each of the paper's content notes. Does your reader feel each note serves a useful purpose? Should any be reduced or rewritten?

- Use the sample paper that follows to compare your own and your reader's final drafts. Discuss major differences as well as any intext citations or content notes you have questions about.

APPENDIX

A sample student research paper follows on pages 245–60. Review the annotations throughout for guidelines on a variety of subjects. Consult the cross-references given for more information.

Also be sure to follow any guidelines your instructor has provided about formatting requirements, which may or may not be the same as MLA style. For instance, many instructors require that a title page and outline be included with the research paper, though MLA style does not.

Center paper's title, your name, and course information on title page

Internet Addiction:

Is There a Dark Side to Cyberspace?

by

Linda Kastan

English 101

Professor Nuñez

May 10, 2002

Outline

Write thesis at beginning of outline

Thesis: While not everyone agrees that the Internet itself is the source of the problem, evidence is growing that increasing numbers of users are learning too late that connecting online can also be the first step to disconnecting with a healthy lifestyle.

Use standard outline form

I. Introduction: Internet use and online addiction

II. Dr. Kimberly Young's study of Internet addicts

III. Evidence of widespread Internet addiction

    A. Among the general population

    B. Among college and university students

Outline is organized by topics

IV. Resistance to the idea of Internet addiction

    A. Definition of <u>addiction</u>

    B. Mocking of the addiction concept

        1. Internet jokes

        2. "Internet Addiction Disorder"

V. Going online and addiction

    A. Parallels to chemical addiction

    B. Difficulty of changing behavior

    C. Motivating problems of excessive online use

        1. Preexisting illnesses

        2. Resulting states of unhappiness

VI. Entrapping Internet areas

    A. Chat rooms

    B. MUDs

VII. Treatment of Internet dependency

    A. Recognition of dependency

    B. Professional support

    C. Online support

Use your last name and page number in running head; use lowercase roman numerals for preliminary pages and arabic numerals for text pages

Kastan 1

Internet Addiction:

Is There a Dark Side to Cyberspace?

Access to the Internet at home, work, and school
has grown so rapidly in the United States that,
according to one respected research organization, some
111 million people regularly spend time online (Pew).
While such findings may be good news for America
Online and other Internet service providers, they
also support the likelihood that 5% to 10% (Greene)
of those 111 million are victims of a disorder described
variously in the media as "Internetomania," "Internet
Addiction Disorder," "Pathological Internet Use," or just
plain "Internet Addiction." Regardless of its name,
dependent overuse of the Internet is blamed for people
losing their jobs, getting lower grades or failing college,
sacrificing their marriages, missing out on close
relationships with others, and simply lessening their
general well-being--all because they are hooked on the
Internet. People who spend excessive time on the
Internet can be divided into four categories: those who
pursue online relationships--even adulterous ones--to
the detriment of family relationships; those who
compulsively play games, gamble, shop, or trade stocks;
those who surf incessantly for often trivial information;
and those whose obsession is with pornography on the
web (Komando). While not everyone agrees that the
Internet itself is the source of the problem, evidence is
growing that increasing numbers of users are learning
too late that connecting online can also become the first
step to disconnecting with a healthy lifestyle.

**Repeat title
on first
page**

**Cite sources
parenthetically
in text**

**Consistently
spell out
or use
numerals for
percentages**

**Thesis
concludes
introductory
section**

Kastan 2

Although the Internet has been around since the World Wide Web was first established in the late 1980s, its potential as a source for addiction became a subject of study only in the mid-1990s. The most widely publicized evidence of Internet abuse has come from a 1996 online study by Dr. Kimberly Young, a psychologist at the University of Pittsburgh. Studying 396 self-described "dependent" users of the Internet and 100 nondependent users, Young found that those she classified as "Internet addicts" averaged 38 hours a week (<u>Caught</u> 54) and suffered from what she found to be moderate to severe impairments to their academic, professional, personal, interpersonal, or financial lives (<u>Caught</u> 6-9).

Author named in text

The men and women Young studied included Internet users of all ages and occupations, "on-lineaholics" as she termed them, who spent so much time with e-mail, newsgroups, cybersex, chat groups, online pornography, or interactive games over the Internet that their lives were falling apart as a result. Though the backgrounds and reasons for hooking up to the Internet varied among those Young studied, they all had one thing in common: their seemingly insatiable need to be online. There was, for example, the construction worker who habitually stayed online 50 hours at a time with the help of caffeine pills (<u>Caught</u> 54); the college student who watched her 3.5 grade point sink to 1.8 as she spent her nights chatting on the Internet (<u>Caught</u> 55); and the woman whose online habit got as high as $800 a month (<u>Caught</u> 56).

Cite multiple works by same author by author's name, brief title, and page number (but omit name if already mentioned in text)

Examples illustrate discussion

Kastan 3

At the conclusion of her study, Young described her work at a meeting of the American Psychological Association, wrote a book about her findings, and established a popular website called <u>Center for On-Line Addiction</u>. Based upon her study and the ensuing success of her website, Young concluded that she had "tapped into a potential epidemic" (<u>Caught</u> 5).

Quotation incorporated within text

Although other researchers have found fault with the methodology of Young's study,[1] few disagree with her conclusion that something widespread and potentially harmful is going on with Internet use. One New York survey, for example, reported that 17% of the male respondents said they spend more than 40 hours a week online ("Over-Use"), while another found that Internet users are increasingly giving up other activites, such as exercising and seeing films, to spend time online (Steinert-Threkeld). In a survey of 1,200 undergraduates, one-third reported they know someone they believe is addicted to the Internet ("But Can It Lead"). Johnathon Kandell, a research psychologist who leads an Internet addiction support group at the University of Maryland, estimates that as many as 5% of all Internet users are addicts. According to Kandell, "The Internet is so engaging that people will substitute [online] activities for real activities, get involved in chat rooms and lose their skills in dealing with people. If someone gets obsessed with this kind of behavior, it can ruin their life" (qtd. in Smith).

Use superscript number to refer reader to endnote

Cite work with no author by title

Use brackets to indicate content inserted within quotation

It is not hard to find the damage done by excessive Internet use. At one of the numerous online sites for addicts and their loved ones, a woman named Rachel

Use *qtd. in* to show one source quoted within another

Kastan 4

Use single quotation marks within double for material already quoted in original

writes, "My marriage is 'breaking up' because of my husband's addiction, which seems to have destroyed not only our marriage but my husband's personality, his values, his morals, his behavior, his parenting. . . . I had no idea what the potential for destruction was" (Greene). In Cincinnati, a woman was charged with child neglect after leaving her child alone for 12 or more hours a day so she could surf the net (Smith). And in New York, the vice president of a communications firm found himself out of a job after running up $400 a month in bills and missing work because of surfing the net 30 to 40 hours a week (Egger and Routerberg). In another case, a wife beat her husband because he threw her computer out a window to keep her from spending so much time online (Greene).

Use ellipsis to show content omitted within quotation

For source with two authors, give both names separated by *and*

Because of college students' encouraged exposure to the Internet for educational purposes and the potential amount of free time available to them, these individuals may be the most at-risk population for excessive, dependent online behavior. As University of Maryland's Kandell points out, "Use of the Internet on college and university campuses has shown explosive growth in the last few years, paralleling, if not outpacing, the strong advances in the society at large" (qtd. in Fryer, Piro, and Shoufani). "Students from 18-22 are at particular risk," he says, "because they face serious developmental challenges as they leave home, solidify their identities, and form intimate relationships" (qtd. in Wirth).

Perhaps not unexpectedly, then, many campuses are discovering that the explosion in Internet use for

Kastan 5

learning has also led to a parallel, potentially harmful
increase in its overuse (Young, "Surfing"). A study of
failing students at Alfred University, for example, shows
a strong correlation between Internet use and a more
than doubled rate of academic dismissals at the campus
(Young, <u>Caught</u> 176). Other campuses have responded
to their students' heavy Internet use and consequent
grade problems with new regulations and increased
counseling. Both Ohio State and the University of
Washington have begun to limit the amount of time
their students can spend online each day, and the
University of Pittsburgh at Bradford has established
a Center for Online Addiction for students with
online-use problems. Three other universities--
Maryland at College Park, Texas at Austin, and
Marquette--have instituted similar counseling centers
("Over-Use"). Still, counselors at relatively few colleges
are trained to recognize the signs of Internet addiction
in troubled students (Young, "Surfing").

Although referring to excessive online use as an
"addiction" is common among laypeople and is even
used informally by some professionals, experts resist
labeling such behavior an "addiction," preferring to
view immoderate use as a manifestation of other
more common problems. Many people, they argue,
overindulge, making habits of food, video games, sex,
soap operas, exercise, work, sports, and the like without
experiencing life-threatening problems and without
being labeled as "addicts" ("Over-Use"). John Grohol, a
clinical psychologist and director of Mental Health Net,
a nonprofit collection of online mental health resources,

Give author's name, brief title, and page number for multiple works by same author

Use double-hyphen to indicate abrupt addition or change of thought

Kastan 6

says, "I don't see how [anyone] can see the Internet as a
disorder, but not look at a bookworm who reads 10
hours a day and not say he is a book addict. Anything
taken to an extreme is a disorder, but we don't go
around coining everything taken to an extreme as an
addiction" (qtd. in Smith).

The very idea of Internet addiction strikes some
people as downright ludicrous, as evidenced by the
numerous Internet sites devoted to parodies and
jokes about its symptoms.[2] Even Ivan Goldberg, a
psychologist who originated one of the current popular
terms for heavy online dependency, "Internet Addiction
Disorder," says he did so only to parody the DSM-IV's
classification of compulsive illnesses. "There's no
such thing as Internet addiction," says Goldberg. "The
Internet is about as addictive as work: Sure, there are
workaholics, but they're simply working to avoid other
problems in their lives" (qtd. in "Over-Use").

Although excessive use of the Internet may
not qualify as a true addiction, evidence exists that
it can be seen as a serious behavioral disorder related
to addiction. A three-year study published in the
Journal of Affective Disorders by University of
Florida and University of Cincinnati researchers
found that subjects who went online for more than
30 hours a week were likely to miss sleep, neglect
their families, and perform poorly at work. These
subjects exhibited many behaviors characteristic
of what is clinically labelled an "impulse control
disorder," the overriding, even compulsive,
need to carry out some activity in order to

**Underline
titles of
periodicals**

Kastan 7

Cite single-
page source
without page
number

achieve a sense of relief (Holliday). Kimberly S. Young's
subjects described feeling more stimulated when online
and suffering from withdrawal symptoms when they
were not. Dependent users felt they were "unable to
live without the Internet" and needed a periodic
"Internet fix" by getting back online after being away
for a time (Young, "Internet"). In a survey about
excessive online use, researchers report that 22 out of
100 respondents said they experience a cocainelike
"rush" as they get online and that chat lines help them
relax (Egger and Rauterberg).

Like addicts, Internet overusers find that quitting
completely or even cutting back on the amount of time
they spend online is difficult, if not impossible. For
example, nearly half of 531 students surveyed at the
University of Texas at Austin said they had tried to cut
down their time online but could not. Even more
disturbing is the fact that over one-third of these students
reported having social, academic, and employment
problems resulting from their overuse of the Internet
(Greene). As a 23-year-old, self-described ex-Internet
junkie expressed the problem of online dependency,

Use ellipsis
to show
content
omitted

". . . where the Internet is concerned, once you're in it,
you're really in it" (Young, <u>Caught</u> 215).

Unfortunately, those who are deeply "in it"
may not even be enjoying their time on the Internet.
Consciously or not, many of those trapped in online
dependency become caught up in a cycle of using the
Internet to cope with preexisting feelings of loneliness,
low self-esteem, and other unhealthy states, only to
have such feelings reinforced by their online habits.

Kastan 8

Young's research and a study at the University of
Cincinnati found that many people who get hooked on the
Internet also suffer from underlying but treatable diseases
such as manic depression, anxiety disorder, and substance
abuse (Young, "Internet"; Seaman). As a two-year, $2.3
million study by Carnegie Mellon University in Pittsburgh
concluded, even those with initially healthy mental states
are also at risk online. The study showed that the more
hours people spent on the Internet, the more depressed,
stressed, and lonely they became, even when they spent
most of their time communicating online with other people
in chat rooms or exchanging e-mail (Greene).

Separate multiple sources with semicolons

The most bewitching areas of the Internet for most
heavy users are chat rooms--Internet sites at which
users communicate back and forth online--and MUDs
(Multiuser Dungeons)--interactive, ongoing, fantasy
game worlds in which a player assumes and lives out
the life of an online character. Such online activities
offer many users levels of acceptance they are unable
to achieve in the offline world and that they find
increasingly compelling. One ex-chataholic who says
she was never good at making friends, for example, first
started going to chat rooms only a few hours a week.
Eventually, however, that changed, as she describes:
"The people I seemed to know best and who cared
about me most were those I talked to online. I started
spending all my time chatting. When my online bill hit
$600 one month, I knew I was in trouble but vowed to
cut down. It was really hard" ("Over-Use").

Define abbreviations in parentheses

MUDs are equally entrapping, perhaps even more
so for those whose lives lack personal fulfillment.

Kastan 9

Players act out complex fantasies, usually of power and
sex, that the real world denies them. One excessive
player explained his fascination for MUDs as follows:
"MUDs are like religion to me, and I am a god there. . . .
My character Chameleon is a legend, and I identify with
him" (Young, <u>Caught</u> 69). Because MUDs are
continuous, ongoing games, players must be almost
constantly online to advance their characters and
keep up with the online action. A former student
says:

**Use ellipsis
to indicate
omitted
sentence**

> At my peak, in 1993, I was playing sometimes
> 11 hours a day, sometimes 11 hours straight.
> I did poorly in [more demanding classes]
> because I would work for 20 minutes and
> then go MUD for two hours, come back, work
> for another 20 minutes, then MUD for four
> hours, then go to sleep. (Greene)

**Indent long
quotations
10 spaces
from left
margin**

**Cite source
for indented
quotation
at end
following
period**

Is there a cure for such behavior as this? According
to Goldberg, "You rid yourself of this addiction by working
out a better solution to the problem. The first step is to
recognize that you're involved with an avoidance
activity" (qtd. in Stoll 92). Such recognition is not always easy,
especially since heavy Internet users tend more often
to think of others they know, rather than themselves,
as being online too much (Stoll 94). For those who do
recognize or suspect a problem with their Internet habits,
a number of self-administered Internet addiction tests
are around, many of them variations on Young's original
survey and available on the Internet itself.[3] Most
psychologists agree that counseling, improved time
management, and self-discipline are the keys to

Kastan 10

overcoming a compulsive Internet behavior problem.
In addition, medical centers such as McClean's Hospital
in Belmont, Massachusetts, and Proctor Hospital in Peoria,
Illinois, have established clinics specifically designed to
treat such disorders (Young, <u>Caught</u> 223-32).

For inclusive page numbers cite only last two digits of second number

Ironically, perhaps, some of the most readily
available help is online. There is, for example, Kimberly
S. Young's own "Center for On-Line Addiction" on
the Internet as well as sites by a number of other
researchers and therapists. A variety of self-help groups
with names such as "Webaholics," "Internetters
Anonymous," and "Internet Addiction Support Group"
also provide support, information, links, and self-
administered tests for online addiction. Such resources
can be helpful, but Young and others remind those they
counsel that "responsibility for regaining control lies
in [their] own hands" (Young, <u>Caught</u> 232).

Conclusion summarizes thesis and general content

While it is evident that today's Internet can
provide enormous opportunities for learning and
human communication, it is equally evident that
many who go online do so at risk. Growing numbers
of individuals are discovering too late that the virtual
reality offered by the Internet comes to some at a great
price, that the Internet does indeed have a dark side.
In his 1995 best-seller, <u>Silicon Snake Oil: Second
Thoughts on the Information Highway</u>, author
Clifford Stoll warned of the online world's then-
unrecognized potential for harm. Stoll was not against
computers, but he understood the power of technology
as well as the vulnerability of the human psyche.
His advice to those who would venture onto the

Underline titles of books

Kastan 11

Internet remains disturbingly wise: "You're entering a
nonexistent world. Consider the consequences" (4).
Fortunately, we are--and not at all too soon.

Kastan 12

Notes

Begin section on new page; center title

Note clarifies or adds information that would interrupt text

[1]Young's study was criticized primarily because it was based on volunteers who were self-described heavy Internet users, rather than a randomly selected population. Young has conceded that the study had significant limitations. See Greene.

Indent superscript number and first line of note 5 spaces

[2]One current website, for example, asks: "How do you know when you're addicted to the Internet?" Answer: "When your wife says communication is important in a marriage, and you buy another computer and a phone line so the two of you can chat." See Greene.

Refers reader to source listed in Works Cited

[3]The Internet sites Young and others sponsor provide a variety of self-administered Internet addiction surveys, most of which ask essentially similar questions like the following: (a) Do you stay online longer than you intend? (b) Do others complain about the amount of time you spend online? (c) Do you find yourself trying to hide the amount of time you spend online? (d) Do you find it difficult to reduce the amount of time you spend online? (e) Is your time online interfering with work, school, or relationships with family members and friends? See Young, <u>Caught</u>, 3-4; Egger and Rauterberg.

Use semicolon to separate multiple sources

Kastan 13

Works Cited

"But Can It Lead to Harder Stuff?" <u>U.S. News & World Report</u> 1 Sept. 1997: 12.

Egger, O., and M. Rauterberg. "Internet Behaviour and Addiction." 10 Aug. 1996. 12 Apr 2002 <http://www.ifap.bepr.ethz.ch/~egger/ibq/res.htm>.

Fryer, Toba, Andrea Piro, and Sandra Shoufani. "Internet Addiction." 24 Nov. 1997. 10 Apr 2002 <http://www.fis.utoronto.ca/~piro/addict.htm>.

Greene, R. W. "Internet Addiction: Excessive Internet Use Causes Social Dysfunction, Depression." <u>Computerworld</u> 21 Sept. 1998: 78.

Holliday, Heather. "Hooked on the 'Net." <u>Psychology Today</u> August 2000: 10.

Komando, Kim. "Tips for Fighting Internet Addiction." <u>USA Today Online</u> 6 Feb. 2002. 3 Apr. 2002 <http://www.usatoday.com/life/cyber/ccarch/2001-04-23-komando.htm>.

"Over-Use of the Internet as Addictive Behavior." 4 Apr. 2002 <http://www.interuse.com/ja/txtall.html>.

Pew Internet and American Life Project. 15 Apr. 2002 http://www.pewinternet.org/reports/chart.asp?img=Internet_Activities.jpg

Seaman, Debbie. "Hooked Online." <u>Time</u> 12 Oct. 1998: 22.

Smith, Michael. "Psychiatrists Study the Internet." 1 June 1998. 7 Apr 2002 <http://www.medserv.dk/health/0698/story1.htm>.

Marginal annotations:

Alphabetize entries by authors' last names or works' titles, if no author given

Article in monthly magazine

When necessary, divide online address at period or slash

Place online address within angle brackets

Begin section on new page; center title

Work with two authors

Online source with three authors; no page numbers given

Show posting and access dates for online sources

Article in weekly magazine

Steinert-Threkeld, Thomas. "The New Social Disorder."

eWeek 29 Jan. 2001. 3 Apr. 2002

<http://www.eweek.com/print_article/0,3668,a=

10458,00.asp>.

Underline titles of books

Stoll, Clifford. Silicon Snake Oil: Second Thoughts

on the Information Highway. New York: Anchor,

1995.

Wirth, John. "Colleges Say Students Can't Live Without

Their Internet Connection." Chronicle of Higher

Education 10 April 1998: A20.

Newspaper article

Young, Kimberly S. Caught in the Net: How to

Recognize the Signs of Internet Addiction--and a

Winning Strategy for Recovery. New York: Wiley,

1998.

For multiple works by same author, use three hyphens for author's name after first entry

---. "Internet Addiction: The Emergence of a New

Clinical Disorder." 8 Apr. 2002 <http://www.pitt.

edu/~ksy/apa.html>.

---"Surfing Not Studying. Dealing with Internet

Addiction on Campus." Student Affairs On-Line 2.1

(2001). 4 Apr. 2002 <http://www.studentaffairs.com/

ejournal/Winter2001/addiction.html>.

CHAPTER 12

Documenting Sources

The Works Cited List (MLA Style)

The Works Cited list follows your paper's Notes section (or the paper's text, if there are no notes), its pages numbered consecutively with those preceding it. Although often informally referred to as a *bibliography* (which is a broad list of *available works* on a subject), the Works Cited section is actually more precise: It is a summary listing each of the *sources named in the text*. For this reason, the Works Cited section of the paper reflects the focus and breadth of your discussion, and it serves as an aid to the research others may do on the subject.

What to Include

When compiling the list of sources for the Works Cited page(s), be certain to include every source you have mentioned in the paper but no others. List each source from which you (1) borrowed ideas or (2) quoted material or that you (3) named in a note. Sources included in the first two categories will also have previously been cited parenthetically in the text. Works mentioned in your paper's Notes will have received previous citation there as well. Only works included in the text or Notes should appear under the heading Works Cited.

This undoubtedly means some, perhaps several, works that contributed background information or common knowledge to your research will not be listed on the Works Cited page. You may have consulted 50 sources during your research and ended up paraphrasing, quoting, or naming only 10 of them in your research paper. Only those 10 sources will be listed under Works Cited.

Works Cited Entries

The Works Cited section should provide the paper's reader with enough information to locate any of the works listed. The three basic units of information included for any kind of source are *author, title,* and *publication facts,* in that order. Some sources require additional information or may be cited with a special focus. In order to save the reader time and to ensure accuracy, follow the standard forms and abbreviations recommended for the discipline in which you are writing. (See Chapter 13 on documentation forms for other disciplines.) The discussion and examples that follow in this chapter conform to the documentation guidelines of the Modern Language Association, or MLA, and its publication *MLA Handbook for Writers of Research Papers,* 6th edition, by Joseph Gibaldi (New York: MLA, 2003).

Listing Works Cited Entries

In keeping with the MLA format, sources named on the Works Cited page should be listed alphabetically by the author's surname or, if no author is given, by the first word of the work's title. (If the title begins with the word *A, An,* or *The,* alphabetize by the second word in the title.) When listing more than one work by the same author, cite each work alphabetically by title, using three hyphens in place of the author's name after the first entry. (See the examples for *McWhorter* in Figure 12.1.)

To prepare the list of entries, it is easiest to sort your bibliography cards into the desired order and then work directly from them. If you have entered the bibliography sources into a computer file, you may be able to utilize a "sort" function to alphabetize the list for you.

Formatting the Works Cited Page

To type the initial Works Cited page, center the title *Works Cited* one inch down from the top of the paper. Begin the first line for each entry flush with the left margin. Indent the second and all other lines for each entry five spaces from the left margin. Double-space throughout, including between entries (see Figure 12.1).

General Guidelines

The Works Cited entries for most sources will follow the standard order of author, title, and publication information. Note that the second and following lines of information for an entry are indented five additional spaces:

Book entry form   Wilson, Edward O. <u>The Future of Life</u>. New York:

Knopf, 2002.

Martin 14

Works Cited

Abate, Frank R., ed. <u>The New Oxford American</u>
 <u>Dictionary</u>. New York: Oxford UP, 2001.

<u>Britannica Online</u>. Vers. 97.1.1. Mar. 1997. Encyclopaedia
 Britannica. 24 Nov. 1998 <http://www.eb.com/
 language/>.

Calvin, William H. "The Emergence of Intelligence."
 <u>Scientific American</u> Oct. 1994: 100-07.

Lighter, J. E. <u>Random House Historical Dictionary of</u>
 <u>American Slang</u>. Vol. 1. New York: Random, 1995.

McWhorter, John H. <u>The Power of Babel: A Natural</u>
 <u>History of Language</u>. New York: Freeman, 2002.

- - - . <u>The Word on the Street: Fact and Fable about</u>
 <u>American English</u>. Cambridge, MA: Perseus, 1998.

Moore, Bob, and Maxine Moore. <u>NTC's Dictionary of</u>
 <u>Latin and Greek Origins</u>. Lincolnwood, IL: NTC,
 1997.

Otter, Jane. "The First Noun and the Second Verb."
 <u>New Language Journal</u> 11 (1998): 177-83.

Quinion, Michael. "How Many Words?" <u>World Wide</u>
 <u>Words</u>. 11 Apr. 2002. <http://www.
 worldwidewords.org>.

"Synonyms Live Up to Their Names." <u>New York Times</u>
 6 April 1998: B2.

Washington, Patrick D., et al., eds. <u>Language for Our</u>
 <u>Times: Essays on Communication</u>. New York:
 Appletree, 1998.

FIGURE 12.1 Sample Works Cited page: MLA style

Gawande, Atul. "The Learning Curve." <u>New Yorker</u>
                      28 Jan. 2002: 52-61.

When the entry for a source requires additional kinds of information,
follow these sequences, as applicable:

For a Book
1. Author(s)
2. Title of section of the book (in quotation marks)
3. Title of the book (underlined or italicized—see p. 267)
4. Editor, translator, or compiler
5. Edition
6. Volume number of this book
7. Series title or number
8. Place, publisher, and date published
9. Page numbers for the part cited from this book (#2 above)
10. Number of volumes

These elements would appear as follows in the Works Cited entry for a
book:

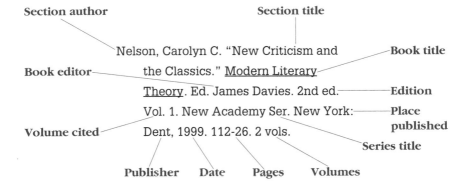

For a Periodical
1. Author(s)
2. Title of the article (in quotation marks)
3. Title of the periodical (underlined or italicized—see p. XXX)
4. Series title or number
5. Volume number (and issue number, if there is one)
6. Date of publication
7. Page numbers of the article cited

These elements would appear as follows in the Works Cited entry for a periodical article:

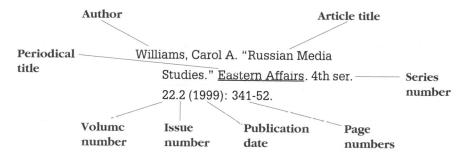

Author   **Article title**

Periodical title   Williams, Carol A. "Russian Media

Studies." <u>Eastern Affairs</u>. 4th ser.   **Series number**

22.2 (1999): 341-52.

Volume number   **Issue number**   **Publication date**   **Page numbers**

Authors' Names. A book, periodical, or other type of source may be written by one or several authors or an organization or group of some kind, or it may be the product of an editor, translator, or other type of compiler. Any one of these individuals or groups may be listed in the Works Cited section as the "author" of the work.

To list a source in the paper's Works Cited section, follow these general practices:

1. Cite the work alphabetically by the author's last name. If no author is given for a source, list it under the first word of its title (see the entry for "Pyramids Repaired," below, and the section on Titles, p. 267):

> Bauval, Robert, and Adrian Gilbert. <u>The Orion Mystery: Unlocking the Secrets of the Pyramids</u>. New York: Crown, 1995.
>
> Cairo Historical Foundation. <u>Policies for Exploration and Excavation, 1991-93</u>. Cairo, Egypt: 1998.
>
> Hamblin, Dora Jane. "A Unique Approach to Unraveling the Secrets of the Great Pyramids." <u>Smithsonian</u> Apr. 1986: 39-42.
>
> "Pyramids Repaired." <u>Archaeology</u> Feb. 1993: 23.
>
> Verner, Miroslav. <u>The Pyramids: The Mystery, Culture, and Science of Egypt's Great Monuments</u>. Trans. Steven Randall. New York: Grove, 2001.

The Works Cited example in Figure 12.1 (see p. 263) also shows entries listed in alphabetical order by their authors' last names or by the first words of their titles.

2. Provide the author's name exactly as it is stated on the book's title page. Do not substitute initials for names when names are given (not *R. L.*

Atwood instead of *Robert L. Atwood*). Do not omit initials when they are given (not *Carolyn Maitland* instead of *Carolyn M. Maitland*). Omit titles, positions, and degrees, such as *PhD* and *MD*, but include suffixes that are essential parts of names, such as *Jr.:*

> Cook, William J. "Updating the Obelisk." U.S. News & World Report 25 Jan. 1999: 60.
>
> Coetzee, J. M. Stranger Stories: Literary Essays. New York: Viking, 2001.
>
> Gates, Henry Louis, Jr. Colored People: A Memoir. New York: Vintage-Random, 1995.

Editors, Compilers, and Translators of Books.   A work that is an anthology or collection is usually the product of an editor or compiler. List such persons alphabetically by their last names, followed by the abbreviation *ed.* (plural *eds.*) or *comp.:*

> Carrigan, Robert C., comp. Astronomy Abstracts, 1994-95. Creeley, MA: American, 1995.
>
> Jones, Steve, Robert Martin, and David Philbeam, eds. The Cambridge Encyclopedia of Human Evolution. New York: Cambridge UP, 1992.
>
> Mathieson, Kenny, ed. Celtic Music. San Francisco: Backbeat, 2001.
>
> Nicholson, Colin, and John Orr, eds. Cinema and Fiction: New Modes of Adapting. New York: Columbia UP, 1992.

For the editor or translator of another writer's work, cite the person first whose work you are focusing upon in your paper:

Emphasis upon editor or translator	Bruccoli, Matthew J., ed. The Short Stories of F. Scott Fitzgerald. New York: Scribner-Simon, 1989. MacAdam, Alfred, trans. The Campaign. By Carlos Fuentes. New York: Harper Perennial, 1990.
Emphasis upon original author	Fitzgerald, F. Scott. The Short Stories of F. Scott Fitzgerald. Ed. Matthew J. Bruccoli. New York: Scribner-Simon, 1989. Fuentes, Carlos. The Campaign. Trans. Alfred MacAdam. New York: Harper Perennial, 1990.

(For citing the writer of an introduction, foreword, preface, or afterword, see section 29 later in this chapter.)

Titles.   List the title of a work exactly as it appears on the work itself. For a book, consult the title page, and include a subtitle if one is given. For the title of a periodical article, locate the first page of the article itself or check the periodical's table of contents for the exact title. Since punctuation between the main title and subtitle of a work is not usually shown, you may need to supply it. Always use a full colon followed by a single space to separate the main title and subtitle.

Underline the full title of a book, periodical, or other work published as an independent whole (e.g., a film, play, cassette recording, or other such work, as discussed later in this chapter). Note that these types of titles are underlined in the examples in this text. If your instructor agrees, you may use italics instead of underlining. Always place the title of a periodical article between quotation marks:

Book with subtitle	King, Stephen. <u>Everything's Eventual: 14 Dark Tales</u>. New York: Scribner, 2002.
Magazine article with subtitle	Vesilind, Priit J. "Once and Future Fury: California's Volcanic North." <u>National Geographic</u> Oct. 2001: 68-83.

(For the title of a work included in another work's title, see section 18 later in this chapter.)

Place of Publication, Publisher, and Date.   Since publishers for periodicals, unlike those for books, remain standard and are not essential to locating periodical material, do not include the names of publishers and places of publication for periodical entries on the Works Cited page.

For a book, consult the title page or the copyright page for publication facts. Give the place of publication first, followed by a colon, the name of the publisher, and the publication date:

Solomon, Susan. <u>The Coldest March: Scott's Fatal Antarctic Expedition</u>. New Haven: Yale UP, 2001.

Place of Publication.   Give the name of the city in which the book was published. If the city may be unfamiliar to your reader, add the postal abbreviation of the state or country (*Upper Saddle River, NJ; Darwin, Austral.*):

Palmer, Eve. <u>The Plains of Camdeboo: The Classic Book of the Karoo</u>. Rev. ed. Johannesburg, S. Afr.: 1986.

Sze, Arthur. <u>The Silk Dragon: Translations from the Chinese</u>. Port Townsend, WA: Copper Canyon, 2001.

When more than one city of publication is listed, give only the name of the first city mentioned.

Publisher's Name.   Give the publisher's name in shortened form, omitting articles, business abbreviations (*Inc., Co., Ltd.*), and descriptions (*Publishers, Library, & Sons*):

Full publisher's name	*Shortened form*
E. P. Dutton	Dutton
Harcourt Brace Jovanovich, Inc.	Harcourt
Harper & Row Publishers, Inc.	Harper
Houghton Mifflin Co.	Houghton
McGraw-Hill	McGraw
W. W. Norton and Co., Inc.	Norton
Prentice-Hall	Prentice
Simon & Schuster, Inc.	Simon

For university presses, abbreviate *University* as *U* and *Press* with *P.* Do not use periods after either letter:

Full publisher's name	*Shortened form*
Cambridge University Press	Cambridge UP
Oxford University Press	Oxford UP
University of Chicago Press	U of Chicago P
University Press of Florida	UP of Florida

(See Chapter 14 for other examples and further guidelines for shortening publishers' names.)

Page Numbers.   When citing part of a complete work (such as a chapter in a book or an article in a periodical), give the continuous page numbers on which the cited material is located.

For entries included in a book, give the page number(s) after the period following the work's publication date:

> Hardy, Thomas. "Channel Firing." <u>Selected Poems</u>. Ed. Andrew
>
> Morton. London: Dent, 1994. 75-76.

When listing a periodical article, give the inclusive page numbers for the entire article cited, listing the first page reference exactly as it is given in the source: *221–32; B2–4; Nov/6.* When the full article does not appear on consecutive pages (e.g., appears first on page 2 and then skips to page 8), give only the first page number followed by a plus sign:

> Burch, Audra. "A Street Named Desire." <u>Miami Herald</u> 14 Apr. 2002:
>
> 1M+.
>
> Landesman, Peter. "The Light at the End of the Chunnel." <u>New York</u>
>
> <u>Times Magazine</u> 14 Apr. 2002: 36+.

For an electronic source with page numbers, give the range of total pages, paragraphs, or other selections, if they are numbered. Abbreviate "pages" as *pp.* and "paragraph(s) as *par.* or *pars.*:

> Kent, Michael. "When Species Become Extinct." Environment 112.5
>
> (2002): 12 pp. 13 Oct. 2002 <http:enviro.com/spr267/112/html>.
>
> Miner, Cam. "Modernism." Early Modern Literary Studies 2.4 (2001): 24
>
> pars. 3 Dec. 2002 <http://www.humanities.ualberta.ca/emis/
>
> 02-4/minjan.html>.

No page numbers are necessary for articles from a reference book (such as an encyclopedia) in which entries are arranged alphabetically:

> "Chemical Warfare." Encyclopedia Britannica. 2003 ed.

Index to Works Cited Forms

The rest of this chapter outlines standard MLA forms for sources listed in the Works Cited section of a research paper. Use the list below as a quick index to these forms when compiling and editing your own paper.

Books

1. A Book by One Author
2. More Than One Book by the Same Author
3. A Book by an Author Whose Name Includes Initials
4. A Book by an Anonymous Author
5. A Book by a Pseudonymous Author
6. A Work by a Classical Author
7. A Book by Two or Three Authors
8. A Book by More Than Three Authors
9. More Than One Book by the Same Multiple Authors
10. A Book with an Editor
11. A Book with Two or Three Editors
12. A Book with More Than Three Editors
13. A Book by a Corporation, Committee, Institution, or Other Group
14. The Published Proceedings of a Conference or Meeting
15. A Book in Multiple Volumes
16. A Single Volume Included in a Multivolume Work
17. A Part of a Volume Included in a Multivolume Work
18. A Book That Is Included in Another Book
19. A Book That Is Part of a Series

20. A Book That Is an Anthology or Collection
21. A Work That Is Included in an Anthology or Collection
22. A Work That Is Cross-Referenced to an Anthology or Collection
23. A Book That Is a Later Edition, Revision, or Reprint
24. A Book That Has Been Republished
25. A Book That Has Been Printed by a Division of a Publisher
26. A Book That Was Printed before 1900
27. A Book That Has Been Published in a Foreign Language
28. A Book That Has Been Translated
29. A Book with an Introduction, Preface, Foreword, or Afterword
30. An Article or Entry in a Reference Book
31. The Bible
32. A Published Dissertation
33. An Unpublished Dissertation
34. A Government Publication
35. A Legal Citation

Magazines and Journals

36. An Article in a Journal with Continuous Yearly Pagination
37. An Article in a Journal with Discontinuous Pagination by Issue
38. An Article with No Author Named
39. An Article in a Weekly Magazine
40. An Article in a Monthly Magazine
41. An Article in a Series
42. A Published Interview
43. A Review in a Magazine or Journal
44. An Article Title That Includes Another Title
45. Letters, Comments, or Notes in a Journal or Magazine
46. A Dissertation or Article Abstract in an Abstract Journal

Newspapers

47. Standard Form for a Newspaper Article
48. An Unsigned Article in a Newspaper
49. Citing the Edition of a Newspaper
50. Citing the Pagination of a Newspaper

Other Sources

51. An Interview
52. A Public Address, Speech, or Lecture
53. A Letter
54. A Pamphlet
55. A Bulletin
56. An Article in a Microfilm Collection of Articles

57. An Advertisement
58. A Manuscript or Typescript
59. An Unpublished Paper
60. Material on a CD–ROM
61. Material on Diskette or Magnetic Tape
62. Material in Multiple Electronic Publication Forms
63. Material Accessed through the Internet or a Database
64. A Work of Art or a Photograph
65. An Illustration, Table, Chart, or Map
66. A Cartoon or Comic Strip
67. A Film, Video Tape, Video Disc, or Slide Program
68. A Television or Radio Program
69. A Recording

Works Cited Forms

Books

1. A BOOK BY ONE AUTHOR

Angelou, Maya. <u>A Song Flung Up to Heaven</u>. New York. Random, 2002.

Parenthetic citation form: (Angelou 26).

2. MORE THAN ONE BOOK BY THE SAME AUTHOR

List multiple works by the same author (or editor) alphabetically by title after the individual's name. Substitute three unspaced hyphens and a period in place of the author's name after citing the first work. If the author is the editor, add *ed.* following a comma after the name. When the author has written a work with another person, list such works as different entries:

Daiches, David, ed. <u>A Companion to Scottish Culture</u>. New York: Holmes and Meier, 1982.

- - -. <u>The Novel and the Modern World</u>. Chicago: U of Chicago P, 1984.
- - -. <u>The Scottish Enlightenment</u>. New York: State Mutual Bank, 1986.
- - -. <u>Two Worlds: An Edinburgh Jewish Childhood</u>. Tuscaloosa: U of Alabama P, 1989.
- - -, ed. <u>Wuthering Heights</u>. New York: Penguin, 1990.

Daiches, David, and John Flower. <u>Literary Landscape of the British Isles: A Narrative Atlas</u>. New York: Penguin, 1981.

Parenthetic citation forms: (Daiches, <u>Companion</u> 130); (Daiches, <u>Novel</u> 11); (Daiches, <u>Scottish</u> 334); (Daiches, <u>Two Worlds</u> 114); (Daiches, <u>Wuthering</u> 12); (Daiches and Flower 64).

3. A BOOK BY AN AUTHOR WHOSE NAME INCLUDES INITIALS

Always use the same form for an author's name as given on the title page of the work:

> Auden, W. H. <u>Collected Shorter Poems: 1927-1957</u>. New York: Random,
>   1964.
>
> Fitzgerald, F. Scott. <u>Tender Is the Night</u>. New York: Scribner's, 1951.
>
> *Parenthetic citation forms:*   (Auden 21); (Fitzgerald 91).

While it is not necessary to provide the full names of well-known authors, you may supply the full names in brackets, if you wish:

> Auden, W[ystan] H[ugh]. <u>Collected Shorter Poems: 1927-1957</u>.
>   New York: Random, 1964.
>
> *Parenthetic citation forms:*   (Auden 40).

4. A BOOK BY AN ANONYMOUS AUTHOR

> <u>Beowulf</u>. Trans. Michael Alexander. New York: Viking-Penguin, 1995.
>
> *Parenthetic citation form:*   (<u>Beowulf</u> 6).

5. A BOOK BY A PSEUDONYMOUS AUTHOR

> Molière. <u>Le Misanthrope and Other Plays</u>. Trans. Donald M. Frame.
>   New York: NAL, 1968.

To indicate the real name of an author published under a pseudonym, use square brackets followed by a period:

> Molière [Jean Baptiste Poquelin]. <u>Le Misanthrope and Other Plays</u>.
>   Trans. Charles H. Wall. Rosedale, NY: Players, 1993.
>
> *Parenthetic citation form:*   (Molière 51).

6. A WORK BY A CLASSICAL AUTHOR

> Sophocles. <u>Antigone, Oedipus the King, Electra</u>. Trans. H. D. Kitto.
>   London: Oxford UP, 1995.
>
> Virgil. <u>The Aeneid</u>. Trans. Robert Fitzgerald. New York: Random, 1983.
>
> *Parenthetic citation forms:*   (Sophocles 3.115-18); (Virgil 1.61).

7. A BOOK BY TWO OR THREE AUTHORS

Cite the first and last names of the first author in reverse order, separated by commas, and follow his or her name with the other authors' names in normal order. Use *and* before the last author's name:

Mayes, Linda C., and Donald J. Cohen. <u>The Yale Child Study Center
Guide to Understanding Your Child</u>. Boston: Little, Brown, 2002.

Silvers, Anita, David Wasserman, and Mary B. Mahowald. <u>Disability,
Difference, Discrimination: Perspectives on Justice in Bioethics
and Public Policy</u>. Lanham, MD: Rowan, 1998.

Parenthetic citation forms: (Mayes and Cohen 129);
(Silvers, Wasserman, and Mahowald 140).

8. A BOOK BY MORE THAN THREE AUTHORS

For books with more than three authors, you have several options. You
may cite all authors in the order in which they are listed on the source's title
page:

Andrews, Sam S., Morrison C. Bethea, Luis A. Balart, and H. Leighton
Steward. <u>Sugar Busters! for Kids</u>. New York: Ballantine, 2001

Parenthetic citation form: (Andrews, Bethea, Balart, and Leighton 115).

As you can see, however, citing all of the names could result in a lengthy parenthetic citation, which will interfere with your paper's text. To avoid such citations, you may also give only the first author's name (in reverse order), followed by a comma and the abbreviation *et al.* (meaning "and others"):

Andrews, Sam S., et al. <u>Sugar Busters! for Kids</u>. New York:
Ballantine, 2001.

Parenthetic citation form: (Andrews et al. 37).

9. MORE THAN ONE BOOK BY THE SAME MULTIPLE AUTHORS

Cite all the authors in the first citation only; use three unspaced hyphens, followed by a period, in place of the authors' names in succeeding
entries. List all works in alphabetical order by title (ignoring the words *A*,
An, and *The* at the beginnings of titles).

Note that three hyphens can be used for successive entries only when the
authors are *exactly* the same. Thus, the example below shows one work by
Richard Leakey, followed by three he coauthored with *Roger Lewin* (listed by
title in alphabetical order); the last entry shows a work by *Lewin* only:

Leakey, Richard. <u>The Origin of Humankind</u>. New York: Basic-Harper,
1994.

Leakey, Richard, and Roger Lewin. <u>Origins: The Emergence and
Evolution of Our Species and Its Possible Future</u>. New York:
Dutton, 1977.

- - -. <u>Origins Reconsidered: In Search of What Makes Us Human</u>.
    New York: Anchor-Doubleday, 1992.

- - -. <u>People of the Lake: Mankind and Its Beginnings</u>. New York:
    Avon, 1979.

Lewin, Roger. <u>The Origin of Modern Humans</u>. New York: Freeman, 1993.

Parenthetic citation forms: (Leakey 150); (Leakey and Lewin,
<u>Origins</u> 102); (Leakey and Lewin, <u>Origins Reconsidered</u> 14);
(Leakey and Lewin, <u>People</u> 20); (Lewin 82).

10. A BOOK WITH AN EDITOR

a. To Focus on the Work of the Editor

Bryant, John, ed. <u>Tales, Poems, and Other Writings</u>. By Herman
    Melville. New York: Modern Library, 2001.

Sontag, Kate, and David Graham, eds. <u>After Confession: Poetry as
    Autobiography</u>. St. Paul: Graywolf, 2001.

Parenthetic citation forms: (Bryant 110); (Sontag and
Graham 13).

b. To Focus on the Work of the Author

Melville, Herman. <u>Tales, Poems, and Other Writings</u>. Ed. John Bryant.
    New York: Modern Library, 2001.

Muske-Dukes, Carol. "Women and Poetry: Some Notes." <u>After
    Confession: Poetry as Autobiography</u>. Eds. Kate Sontag and David
    Graham. St. Paul: Graywolf, 2001. 281-304.

Parenthetic citation forms: (Melville 39); (Muske-Dukes 300).

11. A BOOK WITH TWO OR THREE EDITORS

Chafe, William H., Reymond Gavins, and Robert Korstad, eds.
    <u>Remembering Jim Crow: African Americans Talk about Life
    in the Segregated South</u>. New York: New Press, 2001.

Danziger, Sheldon H., Gary D. Sandefur, and Daniel W. Weinberg, eds.
    <u>Confronting Poverty: Prescriptions for Change</u>. Cambridge, MA:
    Harvard UP, 1994.

Parenthetic citation forms: (Chafe, Gavins, and Korstad 15);
(Danziger, Sandefur, and Weinberg 33).

12. A BOOK WITH MORE THAN THREE EDITORS

Again, you have several options here. You may cite a book with more than three editors by naming each editor in the order given on the source's title page:

> Ethridge, Paul, Marie Dowson, Michael Desserak, and Jane Kiel, eds.
> Laws for Tomorrow's Living: Essays on Right Order Politics.
> Newark, NJ: Plains, 1999.

> *Parenthetic citation form:*   (Ethridge, Dowson, Desserak, and Kiel 65).

As this example demonstrates, however, including numerous names in the parenthetic citation makes it cumbersome to read and distracts from the paper's content. Unless there is a reason for including all the editors' names in the parenthetic citation and in the Works Cited section, it is generally better to give only the first editor's name, followed by a comma, *et al.* (meaning "and others"), and *eds.:*

> Ethridge, Paul, et al., eds. Laws for Tomorrow's Living: Essays on Right
> Order Politics. Newark, NJ: Plains, 1999.

> *Parenthetic citation form:*   (Ethridge et al. 241).

13. A BOOK BY A CORPORATION, COMMITTEE, INSTITUTION, OR OTHER GROUP

> American Bar Association. The Official Guide to ABA-Approved Law
> Schools. Newton, PA: Law School Admission Council, 2001.
> National Geographic Society. National Geographic Atlas of the
> Middle East. Ed. Carl Mehler. Washington, DC: National
> Geographic, 2003.
> Parents for Children. Teach Them Well: A Parent's Guide to Educating
> Your Child. Berkeley, CA: Wren, 1999.

> *Parenthetic citation forms:*   (American 125); (National 44); (Parents 20).

Note that you should cite the editor of a corporate work when one is listed in the source (see the example for the National Geographic Society above), as well as shorten corporate authors' names to avoid lengthy citations in the text. (See related guidelines for citing government authors in section 34).

14. THE PUBLISHED PROCEEDINGS OF A CONFERENCE OR MEETING

Include the place, date, and nature of the conference or meeting if they are not provided in the title:

> Federal Bar Association Staff. Conference on Advertising Law:
> Proceedings of the Federal Bar Association. 12 Sept. 1998.
> Washington, DC: Federal Bar Assoc., 1998.

Preparing for Tomorrow: Communications in the Twenty-First Century.
35th International Communications Conference, Detroit, MI:
Society for International Communications, Oct. 20, 1999.

Parenthetic citation forms: (Federal 16); (Preparing 88).

15. A BOOK IN MULTIPLE VOLUMES

Shakespeare, William. The Complete Works of William Shakespeare.
Ed. Geroge T. Langley. 6 vols. New York: Westbrook, 1998.
Yehoshua, H. L., and T. R. Barry. A History of British Philosophy:
1890-1995. 2 vols. London: James Barrow, 1999.

Parenthetic citation forms: (Shakespeare 3:445-46);
(Yehoshua, vol. 2).

Give the inclusive publication dates if the volumes were published over a period of years (*1989 98*). If some volumes have been printed but others have not, include the phrase *to date* after the number of volumes (*4 vols. to date*) and leave a space after the hyphen following the beginning date (*1998–*):

Boyd, Julian P., et al., eds. The Papers of Thomas Jefferson. 25 vols. to
date. Princeton, NJ: Princeton UP, 1950- .

Parenthetic citation form: (Boyd 3:221).

16. A SINGLE VOLUME INCLUDED IN A MULTIVOLUME WORK

If you are using one volume of a multivolume work, cite only the number of the volume you are using (*Vol. 2*) and give the publication information for that particular volume, as well:

Atwater, Frederick C. Nuclear Arms Databook: America's Arsenal for
the Millennium. Vol. 2. Boulder, CO: Cress, 1999.

Parenthetic citation form: (Atwater 193).

17. A PART OF A VOLUME INCLUDED IN A MULTIVOLUME WORK

To cite a part of a volume in a multivolume work, give the volume number of the part you are citing before the place of publication (as shown in the preceding example). Cite the inclusive page numbers of the material after the publication date, followed by the total number of volumes:

Clader, Timothy D. The Settling of the American Southwest. Ed.
Harold Mann. Vol. 1. Carbondale: Southern Illinois UP, 1998. 89.
2 vols.

Morrill, Daniel. "From Hanoi and Back." <u>The Southeast Asian World</u>.
Ed. J. D. Booth. Vol. 2. London: Whiteside, 1999. 253-65. 3 vols.

Parenthetic citation forms: (Clader 29); (Morrill 260).

18. A BOOK THAT IS INCLUDED IN ANOTHER BOOK

Do not underline or italicize the title of a book when it is included within the title of another work. Make sure, however, that you underline or italicize the rest of the title:

Jaffe, Mare, ed. <u>Three Great Novels of the Civil War</u>: The Killer Angels
<u>by Michael Shaara</u>; Andersonville <u>by MacKinlay Kantor</u>; The Red
Badge of Courage <u>by Stephen Crane</u>. New York: Wings, 1994.

Swartz, Mark Evan. <u>Oz before the Rainbow: L. Frank Baum's</u> The
Wonderful Wizard of Oz <u>on Stage and Screen to 1939.</u> Baltimore:
Johns Hopkins UP, 2000.

Parenthetic citation forms: (Jaffe 222); (Swartz 120).

19. A BOOK THAT IS PART OF A SERIES

Include the series name and number (when given) before the place of publication. Use the standard abbreviation *Ser.* when the word *series* is part of the series name:

Eiseley, Peter M. <u>The Solar System</u>. Science Masters Ser. New York:
Basic-Harper, 1998.

Hunt, Everett, and Maxine Collier. <u>Vanishing Species of the Americas</u>.
Wildlife Ser. 3. New York: Glenn-Goldor, 1999.

Parenthetic citation forms: (Eiseley 33); (Hunt and Collier 110).

20. A BOOK THAT IS AN ANTHOLOGY OR COLLECTION

Augunbraum, Harold, and Margarite Fernandez Olmos, eds. <u>The Latino
Reader: From 1542 to the Present</u>. Boston: Houghton, 1997.

Stevens, Wallace. <u>Collected Poems</u>. New York: Random, 1982.

Parenthetic citation forms: (Augunbraum and Olmos 117);.
(Stevens 47).

21. A WORK THAT IS INCLUDED IN AN ANTHOLOGY OR COLLECTION

Give the name of the author of the work you are citing, followed by the work's title in quotation marks or underlined/italicized, depending upon how it is regularly indicated. Next, give the title of the anthology or collection, followed, if appropriate, by the editor's or translator's name in normal order, preceded by *Ed.* or *Trans.* After the publication information, give the page numbers on which the work appears in the anthology or collection:

> Allende, Isabelle. "The Argonauts." <u>Herencia: The Anthology of</u>
>
> > <u>Hispanic Literature of the United States</u>. Ed. Nicolos Kanellos. New
> >
> > York: Oxford UP, 2002. 483-87.
>
> Stevens, Wallace. "The Palm at the End of the Mind." <u>Collected Poems</u>.
>
> > New York: Random, 1982. 237.

Parenthetic citation forms: (Allende 485); (Stevens).

22. A WORK THAT IS CROSS-REFERENCED TO AN ANTHOLOGY OR COLLECTION

When you cite two or more works from the same anthology or collection, cross-reference them to the editor of the larger work, which you must also cite separately. Give only the editor's surname after the name of the author and title of the work you are citing. Use no punctuation between the editor's name and the page numbers for the cited work. Omit *ed.* or other descriptive words in the cross-reference:

> Haas, Robert, ed. <u>Best American Poetry 2001</u>. Series ed. David Lehman.
>
> > New York: Scribner, 2001.
>
> Kinnell, Galway. "The Quick and the Dead." Haas 128-31.
>
> Rich, Adrienne. "The Architect." Haas 198-99.

Parenthetic citation forms: (Haas 142-44); (Kinnell 129); (Rich 198).

23. A BOOK THAT IS A LATER EDITION, REVISION, OR REPRINT

Following the information on the title page or copyright page, indicate that a book is a later, revised, or reprinted edition by giving the edition number (*2nd ed.* or *3rd ed.*), a description (*Rev. ed.* for "Revised edition," *Abr. ed.* for "Abridged edition, or "*rpt.* for "reprinted"), or a year (*1972 ed*). For a work that has been revised by someone other than the original author, give the name of the reviser after the title (see the *Paden* entry below):

> Caruso, Enrico Jr., and Andrew Farkas. <u>Enrico Caruso: My Father</u>
>
> > <u>and My Family</u>. Abr. ed. Opera Biography Ser. 2. New York:
> >
> > Amadeus, 1997.
>
> Hine, Andrea, and James E. Martin. <u>The Alternative Health &</u>
>
> > <u>Medicine Encyclopedia</u>. 2nd ed. Detroit: Gale, 1998.
>
> Order, Stanley E., and Sarah S. Donaldson. <u>Radiation Therapy of</u>
>
> > <u>Benign Diseases: A Clinical Guide</u>. Rev. ed. New York: Springer
> >
> > Verlag, 1998.

Paden, Henry. <u>Sitting Bull: A Noble Life</u>. Rev. Gordon Adams. 2nd ed.
Stillwater, TX: Wilcox, 1999.

Reich, Warren Thomas, ed. <u>The Ethics of Sex and Genetics: Selections
from the Five-Volume MacMillan Encyclopedia of Bioethics</u>.
Rev. ed. New York: Simon & Schuster, 1998.

Parenthetic citation forms: (Caruso and Farkas 114); (Hine and Martin 33); (Order and Donaldson 82); (Paden 184); (Reich 9).

24. A BOOK THAT HAS BEEN REPUBLISHED

Cite a republished book by giving the original publication date after
the title and the recent date of publication at the end of the entry:

Cushing, Frank Hamilton. <u>Zuni Folktales</u>. 1901. Tucson, AZ: U of
Arizona P, 1992.

Parenthetic citation form: (Cushing 118).

You may also include supplementary information about the original or later
publication, as relevant to your purpose:

Cushing, Frank Hamilton. <u>Zuni Folktales</u>. Fwd. John Wesley Powell.
1901. Tucson, AZ: U of Arizona P, 1992.

Parenthetic citation form: (Cushing 86).

25. A BOOK THAT HAS BEEN PRINTED BY A DIVISION OF A PUBLISHER

Paperback versions of cloth-bound editions are often reprinted by divisions of the main publisher. If the title or copyright page carries a publisher's special imprint, list the division first, joined by a hyphen to the
name of the main publisher:

Fraser, Antonia. <u>Marie Antionette: The Journey</u>. New York: Nan A.
Talese-Doubleday, 2001.

Parenthetic citation form: (Fraser 297).

26. A BOOK THAT WAS PRINTED BEFORE 1900

Cite an early book as you would any other, but omit the publisher's
name:

Melville, Herman. <u>Redburn</u>. London, 1849.

Parenthetic citation form: (Melville 200).

Note that the lengthy and descriptive subtitle common to many older books is usually shortened. The full title of Melville's *Redburn*, for example, is *Redburn: His First Voyage, Being the Sailor-boy Confessions and Reminiscences of the Son-of-a-Gentleman, in the Merchant Service.*

27. A BOOK THAT HAS BEEN PUBLISHED IN A FOREIGN LANGUAGE

Maintain capitalization, spelling, and punctuation of names and titles exactly as in the original. Include any special symbols (e.g., accent marks, umlauts) required by the respective foreign language:

> Jaramillo, Maria Mercedes, Angelo Robledo, and Flor Maria Rodriquez-Arenas, eds. ¿Y las mujeres?. Medellin, Colombia: U de Antioque, 1991.
>
> *Parenthetic citation form:*　(Jaramillo, Robledo, and Rodriquez-Arenas 43).

28. A BOOK THAT HAS BEEN TRANSLATED

a. To Focus on the Translator

> Reck, Michael, trans. The Iliad. By Homer. New York: Icon, 1994.
>
> *Parenthetic citation form:*　(Reck 90).

b. To Focus on the Original Author

> Homer. The Iliad. Trans. Michael Reck. New York: Icon, 1994.
>
> *Parenthetic citation form:*　(Homer 202).

29. A BOOK WITH AN INTRODUCTION, PREFACE, FOREWORD, OR AFTERWORD

a. To Focus on the Author of the Supplementary Material

If the author of the introduction, preface, foreword, or afterword is also the author of the book you are citing, give only his or her last name after the word *By* (see the entry for *Stevenson,* below). List the page numbers on which the supplementary material appears in the book:

> Hancock, Herbie. Preface. Sonic Boom: Napster, MP3, and the New Pioneers of Music. By John Alderman. Cambridge, MA: Perseus, 2001. xvii-xviii.
>
> Harkin, Tom. Foreword. Tomorrow's Energy: Hydrogen, Fuel Cells, and the Prospects for a Cleaner Planet. By Peter Hoffman. Cambridge, MA: MIT, 2001. vii-viii.

Stevenson, Victor. Introduction. <u>The World of Words: An Illustrated History of Western Languages</u>. By Stevenson. New York: Sterling, 1999. 8-9.

Parenthetic citation forms: (Hancock xviii); (Harkin vii); (Stein vii-viii).

b. To Focus on the Author of the Work Cited

If you have referred in your paper to both the author of the work cited and the author of the supplementary material, you will need to include them each separately in the Works Cited list. For example, if you had cited both *Tom Harkin* and *Peter Hoffman* in your paper's text (see the example for *Harkin*, above), your Works Cited list would include entries for both: the *Harkin* entry shown above and the following entry for *Hoffman:*

Hoffman, Peter. <u>Tomorrow's Energy: Hydrogen, Fuel Cells, and the Prospects for a Cleaner Planet</u>. Fwd. Tom Harkin. Cambridge, MA: MIT, 2001.

Parenthetic citation form: (Hoffman 133).

As this example shows, when listing a work by its author, rather than by the author of the supplementary material, you should use the abbreviation *Introd.* ("Introduction"), *Fwd.* ("Foreword"), *Pref.* ("Preface"), or *Aftwd.* ("Afterword"), as appropriate, after the title of the work.

30. AN ARTICLE OR ENTRY IN A REFERENCE BOOK

Cite an article or entry in a reference book—such as a dictionary or encyclopedia—as you would a piece in an anthology or collection, but do not cite the editor of the work. If the article or entry has an author, begin with his or her name. If there is no author, begin with the title of the article or entry (in quotation marks). After the article or entry, cite the title of the reference book (underlined or italicized) followed by the edition number (if stated) and the year of publication. Separate all these elements with periods:

"Artificial Intelligence." <u>The Encyclopedia Americana</u>. 2001 ed.

"Morose." <u>The Oxford English Dictionary</u>. 2nd ed. 1989.

Nelson, Audrey M. "O'Connor, Sandra Day." <u>American Women in Politics</u>. 2nd ed. 1998.

"Stanton, Elizabeth Cady." <u>Merriam Webster's Biographical Dictionary</u>. 1995.

Parenthetic citation form: ("Artificial"); ("Morose"); (Nelson); ("Stanton").

Note that if the articles or entries in a reference book are arranged alphabetically (which is usually the case), you do not need to include the volume of the work or the page number of the article or entry. And for familiar reference books, like the examples above, you should also leave out the publisher and the city of publication. But for less common works (especially those that have only been published in one edition), give full publication information:

> Ward, John J. "Mark Twain." <u>Encyclopedia of American Authors</u>. Ed.
>   Susan N. Scott-Dale. 4 vols. New York: Ross, 1999.
>
> *Parenthetic citation form:*   (Ward).

31. THE BIBLE

Do not list the Bible on your Works Cited page if you are using the King James version. In the text of your paper, cite a book, chapter, or verse of the Bible parenthetically, using standard abbreviations (see the example below and on p 351–52). Cite other versions of the Bible as you would a book with an anonymous author:

> New American Bible: Revised New Testament. Grand Rapids:
>   Christian UP, 1988.
> The Revised English Bible with Apocrypha. London:
>   Oxford UP, 1990.
>
> *Parenthetic citation forms:*   (Gen. 2:11); (Matt. 1:2).

32. A PUBLISHED DISSERTATION

Underline or italicize the title of a published dissertation. Use the abbreviation *Diss.* for "Dissertation" after the title of the work and before the name of the degree institution. Include the year in which the degree was granted after the institution's name, followed by standard publication information (place, publisher, date). For works published by University Microfilms International (UMI), you may include the order number as supplementary material, if you wish:

> Harris, Rachel. <u>Picasso and the Evolution of Cubist Literature</u>. Diss.
>   U of Kansas, 1997. Austin, TX: Prairie, 1998.
> Mickle, Anne Robinson. <u>An Analysis of the Psychosocial Development
>   of College Student-Athletes</u>. Diss. U of Massachusetts, 2001. Ann
>   Arbor: UMI, 2001. 3000323.
>
> *Parenthetic citation forms:*   (Harris 23); (Mickle 98).

33. AN UNPUBLISHED DISSERTATION

For an unpublished dissertation, give the title in quotation marks, followed by the name of the institution granting the degree, a comma, and the date:

> Allen, Annette Marie. "AIDS and the Aging: Are the Elderly
>
> Becoming the New At-Risk Population?" Diss. U of North
>
> Texas, 1999.

Parenthetic citation form: (Allen 126).

34. A GOVERNMENT PUBLICATION

Government agencies generate a multitude of documents in varying forms. The citation examples shown here are representative of the most common types. Observe these guidelines:

a. In most cases, treat the major agency as the author, followed successively by the subagency or -agencies. For United States government documents, it helps to remember that *departments* (e.g., Department of Health and Human Services, Department of Justice) oversee *bureaus, administrations, offices,* and the like (e.g., National Bureau of Standards, Maritime Administration, Office of Justice Programs).

b. Note the standard abbreviations for certain items when citing U.S. government publications. For instance, the *Congressional Record* is abbreviated *Cong. Rec.*; its page numbers begin with *H* or *S* to stand for the *House* or the *Senate* sections of the publication. Most United States government materials are printed by the *Government Printing Office,* abbreviated *GPO*.

c. If you list more than one entry by the same agency, do not repeat the agency name. Use three hyphens followed by a period for each successive entry by the same agency/author. The example below uses hyphens to stand for *United States* and *Dept. of Commerce,* as given in the previous entry:

> Cong. Rec. 10 May 1999. S2966. Florida State. Joint Committee on
>
> Language Education. Standards for Elementary Grades Language
>
> Instruction. Tampa: Greydon, 1999.
>
> United Nations. General Assembly. Resolutions and Decisions. 42nd
>
> sess. 15-21 Dec. 1987. New York: United Nations, 1988.
>
> United States. Dept. of Commerce. Bureau of the Census. 1990 Census
>
> of Retail Trade: Pennsylvania. Geographic Area Ser. Washington,
>
> DC: GPO, 1998.

- - -. - - -. Bureau of Economic Analysis. <u>Selected Foreign Investment
Fluctuation: Analysis</u>. Washington, DC: GPO, 1993.

- - -. President. <u>Public Papers of the Presidents of the United States</u>. Bk.
2. 4 July-31 Dec. 1998. Washington, DC: GPO, 1998.

Parenthetic citation forms: Although you may cite the author of a
government publication parenthetically—for example, *(United Nations, General Assembly 65–81)*—it is best to avoid interrupting the
reader with a lengthy parenthetic citation. Whenever possible, name
the author in the text and cite the page numbers in parentheses:

The report from the United Nations General Assembly shows worldwide
crop yields have changed dramatically in the last seven years (225).

35. A LEGAL CITATION

Citations for sections of the United States Constitution, federal and
state codes, as well as court cases are usually heavily abbreviated. If your
paper requires several such citations, you may want to consult *The
Blue Book: A Uniform System of Citation,* published by the Harvard Law
Review Association.

Do not underline titles of laws, acts, and similar documents in the text
or in the Works Cited (Constitution of the United States, Declaration of In-
dependence, Interstate Commerce Act). You may abbreviate, add relevant
years, and cite sections of such titles as needed when citing them in the
text. Also do not include well-known historical documents and the United
States Code (USC) in the Works Cited. Cite such sources parenthetically in
the text (e.g., *US Const., art. 6, sec. 3* or *12 USC 2283, 1998*). Always begin
a reference to the United States Code with the relevant title number (*12* in
the preceding parenthetic example).

A Works Cited entry for an act should include the act title, its Public Law
Number, date of enactment, and its Statutes at Large cataloguing number. Abbreviate Public Law and Statutes at Large as *Pub. L.* and *Stat.* respectively:

Federal Financing Bank Act. Pub. L. 97-255. 1973. Stat. 879.

To cite a court case, give the name of the case, using the abbreviation
v. (for "versus") between the litigants' names. Next list the volume and page
numbers for the work cited, and the year of the case decision:

People v. Keith. 741 F 2nd 220 DC CA 3d 2002.

This entry shows that *People v. Keith* was decided in the Third District Court
of Appeals in 2002. The case is described in volume 741 of the *Federal Reporter*, second series, page 220. Note that you should underline or italicize
the name of a court case in your paper's text, but not in the Works Cited list.

Magazines and Journals

Magazines and journals differ in their contents and intended audiences as well as in the information you need to locate and document for use in your paper. While magazines are generally published monthly or weekly, journals are published less frequently and often irregularly. For this reason, the publication information needed for a magazine and a journal differ significantly. For example, a magazine will likely have a weekly or monthly publication date (e.g., *May 24, 2001* or *August 2002*), whereas a journal will have a publication date indicating a more general time period (e.g., *Winter 1998* or *Vol. 4, no. 3, 2001*).

Volume and Issue Numbers.   Volume and issue numbers are important for documenting journal articles. Each *issue* of a journal is usually numbered, and all the issues published in a single year make up one *volume* of that particular journal. Thus, the cover or title page of a particular journal may indicate that its contents comprise *Volume 2, number 2*. This information may be all that you have to locate the journal in the library or to document its contents in your paper. Although magazines also have volume and issue numbers, their more specific dates of publication make that information unnecessary for documentation purposes and for listing them in the Works Cited list.

Page Numbers.   Another difference in documentation information between magazines and journals is in how issues are paginated. Magazines use *discontinuous* pagination, whereby each issue starts with page 1 and ends with any given page number. Although some journals also use discontinuous pagination, most use *continuous* pagination, in which each issue continues the numbering of pages from wherever the previous issue stopped. For instance, the first issue in a given year of a continuously paginated journal might begin on page 1 and end on page 260; the next issue would begin with page 261; and so forth. Each successive issue would continue pagination from where the previous issue stopped.

The distinctions between information needed to document sources from magazines and journals will become increasingly clearer to you once you begin working with such periodicals and following these guidelines:

36. AN ARTICLE IN A JOURNAL WITH CONTINUOUS YEARLY PAGINATION

For an article in a journal with continuous pagination, give the author's name first, followed by the article title in quotation marks. Next give the journal title (underlined or italicized), the volume number, the publication year in parentheses, followed by a colon, and then the page numbers of the article, ending with a period. Do not include the issue number for a continuously

paginated journal, since the volume number and sequential pagination are
all that will be needed to locate the source:

> Teller, Sharon R. "What Huck Finn Did to the River: Ecology and
> Adventure at Odds." New Literary History 33 (1999):
> 529-38.

> Young, Suzanne. "The Simple Art of Detection: The Female Detective
> in Victorian and Contemporary Mystery Novels." Modern Fiction
> Studies 47 (2001): 448-57.

Parenthetic citation forms: (Teller 530); (Young 452).

37. AN ARTICLE IN A JOURNAL WITH DISCONTINUOUS PAGINATION BY ISSUE

For an article in a journal with discontinuous pagination, begin with the
author's name, the article title, and the journal title (formatted as just described for continuously paginated journals). Then give the volume number
and issue number, separated with a period (*9.3*). Use a hyphen to show
combined issues (*44.2-3*). Do not include the word *volume* or any abbreviations for it, such as *vol.* or *vols.* Following the volume and issue numbers,
add the date in parentheses, followed by a colon and the page numbers:

> Nochimson, Martha P. "Ally McBeal: Brightness Falls from the Air."
> Film Quarterly 53. 3 (2000): 25-32.

> Raston, Elizabeth. "Potentials in Teen Suicide Patterns." Social Issues
> 10.3-4 (1998): 76-82.

Parenthetic citation forms: (Nochimson 29); (Raston 80).

38. AN ARTICLE WITH NO AUTHOR NAMED

Begin the entry with the article title, and follow the format for a magazine or journal, as appropriate. List the article alphabetically by its title, but
ignore the word *A, An,* or *The* when it appears as the first word in the title:

> "Can We Save Antarctica?" Hemisphere Quarterly 16.4 (1998): 34-40.

> "The Rich Are Different." Economist 6 Apr. 2000: 47-48.

Parenthetic citation forms: ("Can" 36); ("Rich" 47).

39. AN ARTICLE IN A WEEKLY MAGAZINE

> Irion, Robert. "Did Life on Earth Come from Mars?" Discover Aug.
> 2001: 64-69.

Parenthetic citation form: (Irion 65).

Use a plus sign (+) after the first page number to indicate that the entire article does not appear on consecutive pages. Thus, the pagination for an article beginning on page 12 and continuing again on pages 17–19 would be indicated by *12+,* followed by a period to end the entry.

40. AN ARTICLE IN A MONTHLY MAGAZINE

Reiner, Yair. "Hate Radio." Lingua Franca Feb. 1999: 9-11.

Parenthetic citation form: (Reiner 9).

41. AN ARTICLE IN A SERIES

If the article in the series has the same title and author in each issue of a publication, list all bibliographic information, including serial publication dates, in one entry:

Frankel, M. H. "The Picasso Mystique." Fine Arts Journal 21 (1998):
88-93; 22 (1990): 115-20; 151-52.

Parenthetic citation form: (Frankel 22: 118).

If the series articles have different titles in various issues, list each separately. You may include a brief explanation at the end of the entry to indicate that the article is part of a series:

Manz, Joan. "Ladies of the Night." Stateside. Mar. 1999: 45-58. Pt. 2 of
a series.

Parenthetic citation form: (Manz 50).

42. A PUBLISHED INTERVIEW

Begin the entry with the name of the person interviewed, followed by a period, then add the term *Interview,* followed by the interviewer's name, if pertinent; end with a period. For the rest of the entry, include the information and follow the format used for a magazine or journal article, as appropriate:

Soderbergh, Steven. Interview with Gavin Smith. "Hired Gun." Film
Comment Jan./Feb. 2001: 26-31.

Parenthetic citation form: (Soderbergh 30).

43. A REVIEW IN A MAGAZINE OR JOURNAL

Follow the reviewer's name and the title of the review with *Rev. of,* followed by the title of the work reviewed, a comma, the word *by,* and the name of the work's author. Use appropriate abbreviations, such as *ed.,* ("editor"), *trans.* ("translator"), and *dir.* ("directed"), instead of *by,* as needed.

List a review for which no author's name is given by its title. Include the name of the magazine or journal, along with the remaining publication information, as appropriate:

> Davis, Francis. "I Hear America Scatting." Rev. of <u>Jazz</u>, television documentary, dir. Ken Burns. <u>Atlantic</u> Jan. 2001: 76-79.
>
> Strout, Cushing. "Books." Rev. of <u>Not Like Us: How Europeans Have Loved, Hated, and Transformed American Culture Since World War II</u>, by Richard Pells. <u>Partisan Review</u> 1 (1999): 81-83.

Parenthetic citation forms: (Davis 79); (Strout 81).

44. AN ARTICLE TITLE THAT INCLUDES ANOTHER TITLE

Put the title of the periodical article you are citing in quotation marks and underline or italicize any titles of whole works within it. Included titles that are usually written in double quotation marks should be cited with single quotation marks inside double:

> Inui, Karen. "Moments in Southern Time: Faulkner's <u>Sound and the Fury</u>. <u>American Literature</u> 82 (1998): 229-35.
>
> Peel, Robin. "<u>The Bell Jar</u> Manuscript: Two January 1962 Poems, 'Elm' and 'Ariel.'" <u>Journal of Modern Literature</u> 23. 3/4 (2000): 441-54.

Parenthetic citation forms: (Inui 234-35); (Peel 443).

45. LETTERS, COMMENTS, OR NOTES IN A JOURNAL OR MAGAZINE

> Bristol, David. Letter. <u>Chronicle of Higher Education</u> 29 June 2001: B17.
>
> Engle, Patricia. "Dickinson's 'Because I Could Not Stop for Death.'" <u>Explicator</u> 60. 2 (2002): 72-75.
>
> Walsh, Thomas, and Natasha Walsh. "Patterns of <u>Who/Whom</u> Usage." <u>American Speech</u> 64 (1998): 284-86.

Parenthetic citation forms: (Bristol); (Engle 73); (Walsh and Walsh 284-85).

46. A DISSERTATION OR ARTICLE ABSTRACT IN AN ABSTRACT JOURNAL

Abstract journals publish condensed versions of scholarly and professional works, such as articles and dissertations. When you list an abstract in the Works Cited portion of your paper, give the original publication information about the abstracted work first; follow this information with the underlined or italicized title of the abstract journal; then give the volume number, year (in parentheses), and item or page number of the abstract.

Whether you list an item number or page number will depend upon the journal source. Some journals, such as *Psychological Abstracts* and *Current Index to Journals in Education,* use an item number with each abstract entry; others, such as *Dissertation Abstracts* and *Dissertation Abstracts International,* use a page number.

If the title of the journal does not indicate that the item you are citing is an abstract, include the word *Abstract* (capitalized but not underlined, italicized, or in quotation marks) immediately after the original publication information (see the entry for *Love* below).

Use the abbreviation *DA* for *Dissertation Abstracts* and *DAI* for *Dissertation Abstracts International,* followed by the volume number and then the date in parentheses. Give the page number on which the abstract appears, including the series letter (*A* denotes "humanities and social sciences"; *B,* "the sciences"; *C,* "European dissertations"):

> Helms, Joseph. "Dyslexia and Social Integration in Adolescents." Diss. U of California, Los Angeles, 1998. <u>DAI</u> 61 (1998): 191A.
>
> Love, Taylor F. "Incentives for Change: The Politics of Child Care Policies." <u>Research in Higher Education</u> 42 (1999): 330-39. Abstract. <u>Current Index to Journals in Education</u> 40 (1998): item GT83627.
>
> Street, Evan. "Online Drug Affairs: Extreme Internet-User Addiction Patterns." <u>Journal of Psychology and Technology</u> 24 (1999): 23-25. <u>Psychological Abstracts</u> (44): item 11C6383.

Parenthetic citation forms: (Helms); (Love 330); (Street 24).

Newspapers

47. STANDARD FORM FOR A NEWSPAPER ARTICLE

For each newspaper article, provide the name of the author, the article title (in quotation marks), and the newspaper title (underlined or italicized), as well as the publication date, section (if appropriate), and page number(s). If the place of publication is not part of the title, supply it in square brackets after the newspaper name (but not underlined or italicized). When the pages on which an article appears are not continuous, give only the first page number and a plus (+) sign, with no intervening space:

> Hilliard, Constance. "Health Woes: Not So Black and White." <u>USA Today</u> 1 Feb. 2002, final ed.: A13.
>
> Witze, Alexandra. "DNA Testing Tames a Would-Be Monster." <u>Dallas Morning News</u> 18 Feb. 2002: C1+.

> Woods, Mark. "Major Leagues Seem Bent on Destruction." <u>Florida Times Union</u> [Jacksonville, FL] 7 Nov. 2001: E1+.

Parenthetic citation forms: (Hilliard); (Witze A13); (Woods E1).

Note that when a newspaper article is only one page, just the author's name is included in the parenthetic citation (see *Hilliard,* above). For an article without an author, just the shortened title is included in the parenthetic citation (see following example in section 48).

48. AN UNSIGNED ARTICLE IN A NEWSPAPER

When no author's name is given, list the article alphabetically in the Works Cited list by its title:

> "Weed Killer Found to Sexually Deform Frogs." <u>New York Times</u> 17 Apr. 2002, natl. ed.: A17.

Parenthetic citation form: ("Weed Killer").

49. CITING THE EDITION OF A NEWSPAPER

The front page, or *masthead,* of a newspaper indicates if the issue is a particular edition, such as a *national, final,* or *county* edition. Because different issues of newspapers contain different information, it is important to list the specific edition used, when one is given. When it is, designate the edition after the date:

> Lee, Jessica. "Senate Says No to Limits on Lawsuits." <u>USA Today</u> 5 May 1998, weekend ed.: 1A.
>
> Rohter, Larry. "A Witness Says He Lied, But the Execution Is On." <u>New York Times</u> 25 Oct. 1995, natl. ed.: sec. 1:9.

Parenthetic citation forms: (Lee); (Rohter).

50. CITING THE PAGINATION OF A NEWSPAPER

Newspapers vary in pagination practices, and some even change paginating formats for different editions of their own publications. A few have continuous paginations (see the entry for *Ritzen,* below), while many others have paginations that combine section letters or numbers with page numbers (*B3* or *4-2,* see *Correa,* below). If no section letter or number is included in the pagination, you must add the abbreviation *sec.* to show the "section" of the indicated page (see *Wallace,* below). As explained elsewhere, cite the first page number followed by a plus sign (+) for an article that does not appear in full on consecutive pages:

> Correa, Tracy. "Dying to Lose Weight." <u>Fresno Bee</u> 30 Dec. 2001: A1+.

Ritzen, Joseph. "Schooling for All." <u>International Herald Tribune</u> 9 Apr.
    2002: 10.

Wallace, David J. "High Tech Identity Checks." <u>New York Times</u> 7 Apr.
    2002: sec 5:5.

Parenthetic citation forms: (Correa A1); (Ritzen); (Wallace).

Other Sources

51. AN INTERVIEW

For an interview you have conducted yourself, list the name of the interviewee first. Indicate the type of interview (e.g., *personal, e-mail,* or *telephone*) and the date or dates on which it was conducted:

Banning, Linda. E-mail interview. 3 June 2003

Nguyen, Phan. Personal interview. 10-14 Feb. 2003.

To list a published or recorded interview, start with the name of the
interviewee, followed by *Interview* (unless a title makes it obvious; see
section 42). If there is a title for the interview, include it in quotation
marks:

Edwards, Robbie. "An Interview with Robbie Edwards." <u>Profile</u> 12 July
    1998: 34-35.

Soderbergh, Steven. Interview with Gavin Smith. "Hired Gun." <u>Film
    Comment</u> Jan./Feb. 2001: 26-31.

Parenthetic citation forms: (Edwards 34); (Soderbergh 30).

52. A PUBLIC ADDRESS, SPEECH, OR LECTURE

If the presentation has a title, place it in quotation marks and provide
information about the occasion, place, and date of the presentation. For
any presentation without a title, provide a descriptive phrase after the
speaker's name:

Brocket, Oscar G. Keynote Address. Southeastern Theatre Conference.
    Mobile, AL, 8 Mar. 2002.

Margon, Bruce. "Cosmic Recycling: We Are Made of Stars."
    Twenty-Fourth Annual Faculty Lecture. U of Washington,
    25 Jan. 2000.

Whitson, Carol. Address. City Council Meeting. Branning, MI, 24
    Feb. 1997

Parenthetic citations forms: (Brocket); (Margon); (Whitson).

53. A LETTER

a. For a Letter Published in Another Work

Cite the letter's author first, followed by the descriptive title of the letter in quotation marks. Next, add the date of the letter and, if the editor has assigned one, its number. After including standard information about the source in which the letter is reprinted, include the page numbers for the letter:

> Eliot, T. S. "To John Quinn." 13 Nov. 1918. In The Letters of T. S. Eliot.
>   Ed. Valerie Eliot. Vol. I. San Diego, CA: Harcourt, 1990. 177-79.

Parenthetic citation form: (Eliot 178).

b. For an Unpublished Letter

Describe the material, including the date on which it was written, the collection in which it was found (if any), and the place in which it is now located:

> Eliot, T. S. Letter to Bertrand Russell. [4] Jan. 1916. Mills Memorial
>   Library. McMaster University, Hamilton, OH.

Parenthetic citation form: (Eliot).

c. For a Letter Written to You

Cite as follows:

> Cheney, Sharon. Letter to the author. 4 Feb. 2002.

Parenthetic citation form: (Cheney).

54. A PAMPHLET

Pamphlets are listed the same as books:

> Nolan, Kenneth C. Gangs in Your Neighborhood. Sante Fe, NM: Trend,
>   1999.
> Places of Their Own: Carr, O'Keeffe, Kahlo. Toronto: McMichael
>   Canadian Art Collection, 2001.
> US Public Health Service. Healthy People in Healthy Communities.
>   Washington, DC: GPO, 2001.

Parenthetic citation forms: (Nolan 2); (Places); (US Public Health 75).

55. A BULLETIN

> Harding, Frederick. Marital Status and Employee Benefits. Bulletin 43.
>   Sacramento, CA: State Dept. of Employment, 1998.

US Bureau of Labor Statistics. Department of Labor. <u>Employment</u>
<u>Outlook 1998-2008</u>. Bulletin 2522. Sept. 2000. Washington, DC:
GPO, 2000.

Parenthetic citation forms: (Harding 102); (US Bureau of Labor Statistics 18).

56. AN ARTICLE IN A MICROFORM COLLECTION OF ARTICLES

Periodical articles available in microform versions may be accessed
through reference sources such as *Newsbank* or other services available at
the library. List such an article as you would any periodical entry (see sections 35–45), and then add relevant information about the microform source,
including its title (underlined or italicized), volume number, year (in parentheses), and identifying numbers and descriptions (*fiche 16, grids 2–3*):

Ruiz, Maria R. "B. F. Skinner's Radical Behaviorism." <u>Psychology of</u>
<u>Women Quarterly</u> 19.2 (1997): 161-79. <u>Newsbank: Welfare and</u>
<u>Social Problems</u> 10 (1997): fiche 1, grids B1-7.

Parenthetic citation form: (Ruiz 170).

57. AN ADVERTISEMENT

Begin with the name of the company or product that is the subject of
the advertisement or, if it is in print form, the title, heading, or first words of
the advertisement (without underlining/italics or quotation marks), followed by a period. Then add the word *Advertisement* and another period.
Add remaining information about where and when the ad appeared, as
shown here:

Biotechnology Researchers Call It "Golden Rice." Advertisement.
Council for Biotechnology Information. <u>Money</u> Dec. 2001: 39.
Ford Aerostar. Advertisement. NBC. 10 Mar. 2002.

Parenthetic citation forms: (Biotechnology); (Ford).

58. A MANUSCRIPT OR TYPESCRIPT

Bradley, Frederick. "Art and Science in the Nuclear Age." Unpublished
essay, 1998.
Hadley, Joyce. Notebook 7, ts. Hadley Collection. Trinity Coll., Hartford.
Joyce, James. "Penelope." Ts. Huntington Library, Pasadena, CA.

Parenthetic citation forms: (Bradley 4); (Hadley 23); (Joyce).

59. AN UNPUBLISHED PAPER

Brenner, William G. "The Good, the Wise, and the Ugly in Faulkner's
    World." Unpublished paper, 2002.

Parenthetic citation form: (Brenner 2).

60. MATERIAL ON A CD–ROM

a. For a Source from a Periodically Published Database

Many of the sources available on CD–ROM are simultaneously included
in databases for periodicals (newspapers, magazines, and journals) because
they are also available in print or microfilm versions. When this is the case
for a CD–ROM source you need to list in your Works Cited section (such as
a journal article), provide all of the information you would normally include
for such a work, along with information about the CD–ROM source.

To list CD–ROM material that also appears in another version, give the
author's name (if provided), followed by the publication information for the
other form of the material. Then provide the title (underlined or italicized)
of the database in which the other form of the source is listed followed by
the publication medium, vendor, and publication date of the CD–ROM, in
that order and separated by periods:

Hastie, Reid. "Is Attorney-Conducted Voire Dire an Effective Procedure
    for the Selection of Impartial Juries?" The American University
    Law Review 40 (1996): 703-26. InfoTrac: Magazine Index Plus.
    CD-ROM. Information Access. Nov. 1998.
"Number of Hospitals in Decline." New York Times 8 Mar. 1997: B2+.
    New York Times Ondisc. CD-ROM. UMI-Proquest. Sept. 1994.
Silby, Caroline Jane. "Differences in Sport Confidence among Elite
    Athletes with Different Perceived Parenting Styles." DAI 54
    (1995): 3145A. U of Virginia, 1994. Dissertation Abstracts Ondisc.
    CD-ROM. UMI-Proquest. Dec. 1995.

Parenthetic citation forms: (Hastie 720); ("Number" B4); (Silby).

If the CD–ROM gives no page numbers for a source, avoid parenthetic
citation by using the author's name in the text ("Carter has shown . . ."). If
all of the information needed for entries like those just listed (such as vendor name) is not given, cite what is available:

Mandell, Rachel, ed. The Complete Works of William Shakespeare.
    CD-ROM. New York: Anthem, 1999.

Parenthetic citation form: (Mandell).

b. For Material Not Indicated as Appearing in a Periodically Published Database

If the CD–ROM bears no information stating that its contents are available in another form and so listed in a periodically published database, provide only the necessary information about the CD–ROM itself. Give the author's name (if provided), followed by the title of the material accessed (in quotation marks), the date of the material, the title of the database (underlined or italicized), the publication medium, the vendor name, and the CD–ROM's publication date, in that order (separated by periods):

> Symonds, Terry L. "Marketing Analysis: Peterbrooks, Inc." 23 Jan.
> 1998. <u>Business Database Plus</u>. CD-ROM. Information Access.
> Dec. 1999.
>
> United States. Dept. of State. "Immigrant Population Centers." 1997.
> <u>National Trade Data Bank</u>. CD-ROM. US Dept. of Commerce. July
> 1998. "US Population by Age: Urban and Urbanized Areas." 1990
> <u>US Census of Population and Housing</u>. CD-ROM. US Bureau of the
> Census. 1998.

> *Parenthetic citation forms:*   (Symonds); (United States, Dept. of State).

c. For Material That Is Not Periodically Updated after Publication

Some information on CD–ROM is not intended to appear periodically or to be regularly updated. Cite such a source as you would a book, but include the publication medium after the title:

> <u>The Hispanic Legacy</u>. CD-ROM. Research International. 2001
>
> <u>The Oxford English Dictionary</u>. 3rd ed. CD-ROM. Oxford, Eng.: Oxford
> UP, 1992.

> *Parenthetic citation forms:*   (<u>Hispanic</u>); (<u>Oxford</u>).

If you are citing only part of a work, give the name of that part first:

> "Alcohol." <u>A Guide to Abusive Substances</u>. CD-ROM. New York: Clary,
> 2001.

> *Parenthetic citation form:*   ("Alcohol").

61. MATERIAL ON DISKETTE OR MAGNETIC TAPE

Cite a source located on diskette or magnetic tape as you would a book or part of a book, with a description of the medium following the title:

"Arthur Rimbaud." <u>The French Symbolist Poets</u>. Diskette. Berkeley,
CA: Western, 2001.

Pier, Robert. <u>The Expanding Universe</u>. Diskette. New York: Science,
2000.

"Weslin College." <u>Peterson's College Database</u>. Magnetic tape.
Princeton: Peterson's, 1998.

Parenthetic citation forms: ("Arthur"); (Pier); ("Weslin College").

If the source on diskette or magnetic tape has a printed version, give
information about that version first:

Kress, Martin M. <u>The Story of Philosophy: From the Greeks to Modern
Times</u>. Chicago: U of Chicago P, 1997. Magnetic tape. New York:
Eastend, 1999.

Parenthetic citation form: (Kress).

62. MATERIAL IN MULTIPLE ELECTRONIC PUBLICATION FORMS

When electronic publications are issued and packaged together as a
single product, include each medium in the Works Cited listing:

Smolan, Rick, and Jennifer Erwitt. <u>Passage to Vietnam: Seven Days
Through the Eyes of Seventy Photographers</u>. Sausalito, CA:
Eight Days, 1994. CD-ROM, video disc. International Research.
1995.

Parenthetic citation form: (Smolan and Erwitt).

63. MATERIAL ACCESSED THROUGH THE INTERNET OR A DATABASE

The basic citation form for an electronic source usually includes the
following five elements:

Author's name. "Document Title." Print publication information.
Electronic publication information. Access information.

Providing Access Information

Date of Access. Because information in an electronic document can
change, it is important to include the source's date for the content as well as
the date on which you accessed the source. If you accessed an online document more than once, give the last date you viewed it.

URL. Also include the Internet address or URL (for *uniform resource lo-
cator*) enclosed in angle brackets, immediately following the date of access.
If the URL runs into more than one line, you may divide it only at a slash.
Do not add or allow your computer to add a hyphen at the division point.
Give the complete URL, including the access mode (such as http, gopher, or
telenet). If the URL is so long or complicated that transcribing or using it

might present a problem, give instead the URL of the site's search page, if there is one. From that page, another researcher can locate the document by using relevant publication facts such as the author's name or document title. Or if citing a site's search page is not possible, you may give the URL of the site's home page. In such a case, follow the URL with the word *Path* and a colon; then list the sequence of links that would lead to the document being cited. Separate the links with a colon if there is more than one:

> "Persian Gulf War." History Channel.com. 2003. History Channel. 10
>
> April 2003. http://historychannel.com/. Path: Iraq; Persian Gulf War.

The following sections discuss MLA style for citing Internet-type electronic sources in the Works Cited section of a research paper. Note that citations for electronic sources should always be as complete as possible; however, if some information is not provided, include what is available.

a. An Entire Internet Site

To cite an information base, scholarly project, journal, or professional Internet site, list the site title (underlined), followed by the name of the site editor (if given), electronic publication information, including version number (if relevant and not part of the title), date of publication or latest update, and the name of the sponsoring institution. Conclude this information with the date of access and URL:

> Electronic Text Center. Ed. Michael Engle. 10 Dec. 2002. Cornell U. 10
>
> Jan. 2003 <http://www.library.cornell.edu/okuref7cet/cot.html>.

Parenthetic citation form: (Electronic).

b. A Home Page for a Course or Academic Department

To list the home page for a course, give the instructor's name first, reversed for alphabetizing, followed by the course title without underlining or quotation marks. Add a description such as *Course home page* (without underlining or quotation marks), the course dates, department and institution names, your access date, and the URL:

> Hoffman, Lynne. American Literature. Course home page. January-May
>
> 2003. Department of English, Orange Coast College. 19 Mar. 2003
>
> <http://www.hofflit.occ.edu/depart/litlang/index. html>.

For the home page of an academic department, begin with the department name, followed by a description, the institution name, your date of access, and the URL:

> American Indian Studies. Dept. home page. California State College,
>
> Long Beach. 3 June 2003 <http://www.csulb.edu/colleges/cla/ais/
>
> main.html>.

Parenthetic citation form: (Hoffman); (American).

c. A Personal Home Page

Begin with the name, reversed, of the home page's creator, followed by a description, access date, and URL:

Abbott, Cheryl. Favorites home page. 22 June 2002
<http://www.fallsapart.com/lists.html>.

Parenthetic citation forms: (Abbott).

d. An Online Book or Part of an Online Book

Cite an entry for an online book or part of an online book the same as its printed counterpart (see pages 271–181l), followed by the relevant information about the electronic version:

Quiller-Crouch, Arthur, ed. <u>The Oxford Book of English Verse</u>:
1250–1900. Oxford, Eng.: Oxford UP, 1919. <u>Bartleby Project
Archive</u>. Ed. Steven van Leeuwen. April 1997. Columbia U. 23 May
2003 <http://www.bartleby.com/101/>.

Santos, Carolyn. "A Beginning." <u>Strangers Never Prosper and Other
Stories</u>. New York: Bixby, 2001. 10 Nov. 2002
<http://www.books.com/ebooks/foreign/fiction/santos.txt>.

If some information is not given, include what is available. You may add in brackets relevant information not included in the source:

Zimmer, Gordon. <u>A Guide to Costa Rica's Plantlife</u>. [San Jose, Costa
Rica]: Sun P., 2002. 23 May 2003
<http://www.etext.com/costa/bot/246>.

Parenthetic citation forms: (Quiller-Crouch 213); (Santos); (Zimmer 21).

d. Material Appearing in an Online Periodical (Such as a Scholarly Journal, Newspaper, or Magazine)

To cite an article, letter, editorial, review or other material appearing in an online periodical, begin by giving the same information you would if the item appeared in a printed periodical such as a scholarly journal, newspaper, or magazine (see pages xxx-xxx). Include the range or number of total pages or paragraphs if they are given, abbreviating "pages" as pp. and paragraph as par. or pars. Follow this information with the access date and URL.

Borter, Daniel. "In Cochise's Footsteps." <u>Journal of Western History</u>.
4.2 (2002): 32 pars. 23 June 2003
<http://whon.org/jwh03/vol4/borter.html>.

Miklaszewski, Jim. "Wild Celebrations as Baghdad Falls." <u>Newsweek</u> 9
April 4 May 2003
<http://www.msnbc.com/site_elements/bantop_nwsfhidden.gif>.

Taylor, Jane L. "Students Want Education With Guarantees." <u>New
York Times on the Web</u>. 25 Nov. 2002: 2 pp. 5 Jan. 2003
<http://www.nytimes.com/2003/04/10/intemational/
worldspecial/10MILI.html>.

Parenthetic citation forms: (Borter, par. 4); (Miklaszcwski); (Taylor 1).

e. An Online Government Publication

State the relevant information for citing a printed government work
(see pages xxx), followed by the relevant facts about the electronic source:

United States. Dept. of the Treasury. Office of Foreign Assets Control.
<u>Terrorist Financing Rewards Program</u>. Dec. 2002. 25 May 2003
<http://www.ustreas.gov/offices/enforcement/ofac/articles/
index. html>.

Parenthetic citation forms: Avoid lengthy citation of a government
publication by naming the author and, if appropriate, source title in the
text of your paper.

f. An Article in a Reference Database

"Censorship." <u>Encyclopedia Britannica</u>. 2003. 15 July 2003.
<http://www.britannica.com/bcom/images/ home_featuring2.gif>.

Parenthetic citation form: ("Censorship")

g. A Work from a Library Subscription Service

Give the name of the database used (underlined), if known. Follow
this information with the name of the service; the name of the library or library system (including city or state abbreviation, or both if useful); date of
access; URL of the service's home page, or omit it if not known. If only the
starting page number of an article's original publication is given, give the
number followed by a hyphen, a space, and a period: 104-.

"War and the Economy." <u>Business Week</u> 18 May 2002: 3 1. <u>Academic
Search Premiere</u>. EBSCO. Citrus College Library, Glendora, CA. 2
Oct. 2002 <http://www.epnet.com>.

Parenthetic citation form: ("War").

h. A Work from a Personal Subscription Service

If you use a keyword or similar designation to access material from a personal subscription service, add *Keyword*, followed by a colon and the keyword itself, after the name of the service and access date.

> "Gasohol." Columbia Encyclopedia 6th ed. 2001. America Online. 20
>
> May 2003. <http://www.aol.com/>. Keyword: Gasohol.

When you have followed a series of steps to get to the online source, write the word *Path*, followed by a colon and the topics you followed to the source page. Separate multiple path topics with a semicolon.

> "What Is Karate?" Shokotan Karate of America 1998. America Online. 8
>
> Feb. 2003. <http://www.aol.com/>. Path: Karate; Shokotan Karate
>
> of America.
>
> *Parenthetic citation forms:*   ("Gasohol"); ("What").

i. An Online Posting

> Barnes, Hailey. "Internet and Addiction." Online Posting. 18 Jan. 2003.
>
> Online Addiction Page. 3 pars. 22 April 2003
>
> <http://www.oiap.com/reports/addict82/html>.
>
> *Parenthetic citation form:*   (Barnes, par. 2).

j. A Personal E-mail Communication

> Hanning, Lau. "Test Preparation." E-mail to Doug Norrs. 8 Oct. 2002.
>
> *Parenthetic citation form:*   (Hanning).

64. A WORK OF ART OR A PHOTOGRAPH

Give the name of the artist when known, followed by a period and the title; underline or italicize the title if the work is a painting or sculpture. For any art you view personally, list the proprietary institution and, if not indicated in the institution's title, the city in which the work is found:

> Rodin, Auguste. The Thinker. Metropolitan Museum of Art, New York.

Refer to such a work of art in your text, rather than in a parenthetical citation: *Rodin's* The Thinker *shows* . . .

Cite a photograph or another reproduction of a work of art the same as above, but also add publication information about the source of the reproduction:

> Moore, Henry. Recumbent Figure. Illus. 842 in History of Art. By
>
> Charles Minot. New York: Harper, 1992.
>
> *Parenthetic citation form:*   (Moore).

(These forms are acceptable, but you should normally name the artist and the work in the text.)

65. AN ILLUSTRATION, TABLE, CHART, OR MAP

Birds of California. Chart. San Diego, CA: Walson, 2001.

Mexico. Map. Chicago: Rand, 1999.

"Two Views of Modern Human Origins." Illus. in Richard Leakey, The Origin of Humankind. New York: Basic, 1994. 87.

Parenthetic citation forms: (Birds); (Mexico); ("Two").

66. A CARTOON OR COMIC STRIP

Cullum, Leo. Cartoon. New Yorker 7 April, 2003: 64.

Trudeau, Gary. "Doonesbury." Chicago Tribune 12 Apr. 2002: sec 2: 9.

Parenthetic citation forms: (Smaller); (Trudeau).

67. A FILM, VIDEO TAPE, VIDEO DISC, OR SLIDE PROGRAM

For a film, list the title (underlined or italicized), followed by the name of the director, the distributor, and the year of release, in that order. Add other information you feel is relevant. To focus on one person's involvement, cite him or her first, followed by a description of his or her role:

A Beautiful Mind. Dir. Ron Howard. Perf. Russell Crowe. Dreamworks SKG. 2001.

Foster, Jody, perf. The Panic Room. Dir. David Fincher. Writ. David Koepp. Sony Pictures, 2002.

Parenthetic citation forms: (Beautiful); (Foster).

For a video cassette, video disc, slide program, or filmstrip, begin with the title (underlined or italicized), followed by the medium, the distributor (including location, if available), and the release date (if available). Specify individual performances or roles as for film entries (see above):

Black Hawk Down. Dir. Ridley Scott. Video cassette. Columbia Tristar Home Video, 2002.

Climbing the Rockies. Sound filmstrip. Colorado Environments, 2000.

Coen, Joel, dir. O Brother, Where Art Thou? Video disc. Touchstone Pictures/Disney, 2001.

Shakespeare, William. All's Well That Ends Well. Prod. John Kendall. Video cassette. New York: Press, 1998.

Parenthetic citation forms: (Black Hawk); (Climbing); (Coen); (Shakespeare).

68. A TELEVISION OR RADIO PROGRAM

List the name of the episode or segment (in quotation marks), followed by the title of the program (underlined or italicized). Next give the title of the series (if any), the name of the network on which the program appeared, the call letters and city of the local station (if any), and the broadcast date, in that order. Cite the names of individuals and their roles after the program title, or list them first if your focus is primarily on their work:

> "Mom's at Work." <u>Dateline NBC</u>. Rpt. Karen Knolls. NBC. KNBC, Los
>
> Angeles. 19 June 1999.
>
> Springer, Jerry, host. "Spring Break." <u>Jerry Springer</u>. WMOR, Tampa.
>
> 19 Apr. 2002.
>
> *Parenthetic citation forms:*   ("Mom's"); (Springer).

69. A RECORDING

> London, Jack. <u>The Call of the Wild</u> and <u>Other Stories</u>. Audio tape. Read by
>
> Trent Williams and Jason Miller. Listening Library, CXL 634, 1999.
>
> Tchaikovsky, [Peter Ilyich]. <u>The Nutcracker</u>. Cond. Leonard Marx.
>
> St. Louis Symphony Orchestra. RCA, C684 B4. 2001.
>
> *Parenthetic citation forms:*   (London); (Tchaikovsky).

W O R K I N G   W I T H   O T H E R S

As with intext citations and the content notes for the paper, you will appreciate another reader's assurance that the Works Cited section is done correctly. Share the final draft of your paper with a friend or classmate in these ways:

- Ask your reader to assist in checking to see that every source cited intext or in the Notes section of the paper is also included on the Works Cited page(s). An easy way to do this is to list each author or work as you read the draft and then compare the list with the entries on the Works Cited page(s).

- Review your paper's citations for online sources with your classmate, and discuss any you are unsure about. Check these entries against the guidelines and examples presented in this chapter.

CHAPTER 13

Alternative Documentation Styles

Author-Date (APA and *Chicago*), Number-System, and CBE

Research papers written for most college English courses follow the Modern Language Association (MLA) author-page documentation style discussed in Chapters 11 and 12. Papers for other subjects, however, often require different documentation formats. Writers in the social, biological, medical, and applied sciences; education; fine arts; and humanities (excluding literature) follow formats recommended by their own professional associations or leading journals. Documentation in these disciplines differs from MLA style in the way sources are cited in the text and the References section.

In general, papers that do not use the author-page, MLA style of documentation follow one of three other basic formats:

1. *Author-date style:* This style is generally associated with the American Psychological Association (APA); in fact, it is often called *APA style.* However, author-date format is also recommended by *The Chicago Manual of Style,* a leading reference work for writers and editors, for papers in most of the sciences and humanities (see pp. 337–40).

In APA author-date style, sources are cited parenthetically in the text by the author's last name and the work's publication date:

> According to Cryer (2001), behavioral links between adolescent aggression and television viewing are greater than previous studies have shown (Adams, 1994; Metz, 1998).

All sources cited in the text are fully documented in a References section at the end of the paper.

2. *Number-system style:* This documentation format is often called *CBE style,* as it is used primarily by the Council of Biology Editors; it is appropriate for most papers in the applied sciences (see pp. 331–37).

In this style, raised superscript numerals in the text—like this[5]—refer to numbered sources listed at the end of the paper in a References, Literature Cited, or References Cited section.

3. *Footnote or endnote style: The Chicago Manual of Style,* 14th ed. (Chicago: University of Chicago Press, 1993), considers author-date style the most practical means of documentation for all papers in the natural sciences and most of those in the social sciences. For some papers in the humanities, however, the use of footnotes or endnotes is recommended. In sum, notes are appropriate for papers about subjects that may require numerous or extended explanations or definitions apart from the regular text; such papers are usually written for very specific and knowledgeable audiences.

In this style, raised superscript numerals in the text refer to explanatory notes and documented sources appearing either at the bottoms of pages as footnotes or at the end of the paper as endnotes in a Notes section. The advantage of using notes is that explanatory-type information can be presented along with source citations in the same place.

NOTE: Because the use of footnotes or endnotes is rarely recommended for student papers, this style will not be discussed in this chapter. See Chapter 11 (pp. 240–43) for more information on explanatory-type notes. Also see *The Chicago Manual,* Chapter 15, for specific guidelines on the use of note-style documentation. As always, you should check with your instructor regarding which documentation style to follow in your paper.

Understanding Various Styles

The various documentation formats discussed in this chapter and preceding ones provide emphases for writers and readers in what are often specialized fields of study. As bewildering as the variety of styles can often seem, however, try not to be intimidated by their differences. After all, you need only master one documentation style to write your own paper. Familiarity with different documentation styles, on the other hand, can aid you in locating and taking accurate notes from a variety of sources—or even in documenting them in your own paper. If necessary, use your knowledge of a particular documentation style to change your paper's intext citations and References list to conform to any of the formats used by other disciplines. Naturally, which documentation style you follow for your paper will depend upon its subject, the example of a particular journal, or the requirements of your instructor. As you pursue your research and writing, take care not to confuse variant forms appearing among discipline journals with the guidelines given here.

Author-Date Documentation

The author-date style of documentation is so named because it includes an author's last name and the date of publication whenever a writer *cites* a source:

> Blustein (2001) links the crisis in developing countries to the
> shortcomings of international investment. Other analysts (Engleman,
> Halwell, & Nierenberg, 2002), however, cite regional population
> explosions.

Intext citations such as these direct the reader to more complete descriptions of the named authors' works in the paper's References section. Placed at the end of the paper, the References list each source cited in the text alphabetically by the author's last name (or by a work's title when no author is given). In addition to the author's name, each entry also provides the work's title and publication information.

APA Style

Author-date documentation style is the form adapted by the American Psychological Association (APA) and recommended in its guide, *Publication Manual of the American Psychological Association*. Because it provides efficient intext citations of other researchers' work, APA documentation style predominates in papers for the social sciences and several other disciplines, including anthropology, biology, business, education, economics, political science, psychology, and sociology. Though they often practice slight variations, writers and journals in these disciplines follow basic APA style for intext citations and for listing sources in papers' References sections.

Abstracts

Papers written according to APA style or other formats for the sciences or social sciences often include *abstracts,* which are short, 100- to 150-word summaries of the papers. (Abstracts for theoretical papers are usually briefer, 75 to 100 words.) An abstract should state the purpose (thesis), findings, and conclusion of your research without commenting on or evaluating the paper itself. Put the abstract on a separate page, titled Abstract, after the title page. Use lowercase roman numerals for page numbers. The sample abstract for Steve Hanner's paper in Appendix A provides a model.

Headings

Headings function like brief titles to emphasize certain content and to indicate the main sections of the paper. Like an outline, textual headings indicate the organization of the paper's content and emphasize the importance of each section. Use indentation, upper- or lowercase letters, and italics to show the level of importance of each heading (i.e., the hierarchy, as in an outline). Topics with the same level of importance should have the same type of heading throughout the paper.

Many articles in APA journals use standard headings—such as Purpose, Method, Procedure, Results, and Conclusions—to organize the discussion. Most student research papers, however, use headings that reflect their individual subjects, as these sample headings for a paper on *drug testing* illustrate:

1st level—Type the   Rationale for Drug Testing
heading centered,
upper- and lowercase.

                              Procedures

              2nd level—Type the heading centered, upper- and
              lowercase, and italic.

Testing methods.

              Type the heading flush left, upper and lower case, and
              italic.

Although a paper may have as many as five levels of headings, student research papers seldom need more than two or three, if any. Check with your instructor as to the suitability of headings for your paper and his or her requirements for heading levels.

Intext Citation

APA form documents a paper's sources both by citing them in the text and describing them bibliographically in the paper's References list. When the work's author is named in the text, the publication date follows in parentheses:

> Ramirez (1999) has pointed out the disadvantages of postponing counseling until depression begins to curtail normal activities.

When the author is not named in the text, cite his or her name parenthetically, *followed by a comma* and the year of the work's publication:

> In many parts of Africa, disputes over the use of natural resources have led to violent civil conflict (Renner, 2002).

NOTE: You may find during your research that some journals omit the comma between the author's name and the publication date, such as (*Gross 2000*). APA style, however, requires punctuation. Unless your instructor approves omitting the comma, be sure that you include it.

The following method of citing a source is also acceptable:

Wilkins's 2001 study found considerable evidence that college students are more likely to give satisfactory evaluations to instructors who award higher grades.

As the above examples demonstrate, intext citation allows acknowledging sources with the least interruption of the reader's attention to the paper's content. You give immediate credit to an authority whose work you have drawn upon and support your own arguments in doing so. Including a work's publication date in the citation is also important. Because information changes rapidly in some disciplines, such dates allow the reader to assess the relevancy of data and to make comparisons.

The guidelines here and on the following pages conform to the *Publication Manual of the American Psychological Association,* 5th ed. (Washington, DC: APA, 2001).

AUTHORS' NAMES

1. CITING AN AUTHOR, EDITOR, GROUP, OR CORPORATE AUTHOR

Treat individuals, editors, corporate authors (e.g., associations, committees, and departments), and others who would normally be considered responsible for producing a work as *authors.* Cite personal authors or editors intext by their surnames only:

Individual author	Heimer (2001) suggests that people make decisions based on comparing external cases and by relying on internal biography and narrative.
Editor	Cohabitation is now so common among heterosexual adults in the United States that most couples who do marry start off by living together (Smock, 2001).

Spell out the full name of each group or corporate author the first time you cite it parenthetically in text. For subsequent citations, you may cite the full name or a shortened version, depending on whether the name will be readily recognized by the reader and whether the source can be easily found in the References list. For a recognizable, easily located source, give an abbreviated form of the name in brackets within the first intext parenthetical citation (see following example, *International Labor Organization*). But if the name is short or would not be readily understood as an abbreviation, spell out the full name each time you cite the source (see *Worldwatch,* below):

Group or corporate author	Bonded child labor is most prevalent in the countries of Southeast Asia (International Labor

Organization [ILO], 1999). While many governments in the region have passed laws forbidding child labor, they are not strictly enforced (Worldwatch, 2000).

Group or corporate author (subsequent citation)   Government harrassment of human rights activists is common (ILO, 1999). . . . Increasingly, consumers in the West are being encouraged to avoid goods produced by child labor (Worldwatch, 2000).

a. For a Work with Two Authors

Cite both names each time the source is mentioned in text:

First citation   Link and Phelan (2001) have done significant work on the concept of social stigma.

Subsequent citation   . . . while Link and Phelan (2001) identify five components of stigma.

b. For a Work with Three to Five Authors

Name each author the first time the work is cited, but in subsequent citations, give only the first author's last name, followed by a comma and *et al.:*

First citation   DiMaggio, Hargittai, Neuman, and Robinson (2001) believe that sociologists could do more extensive research on Internet usage.

Subsequent citation   The cultural impact of the Internet is of particular interest to DiMaggio et al. (2001).

NOTE: The phrase *et al.* comes from *et alii,* which is Latin for "and others." Since *al.* is an abbreviation for *alii,* it must always be written with a period after it. (Do not underline or italicize *et al.* in your paper.)

c. For a Work with Six or More Authors

Give only the first author's name, followed by a comma and *et al.* Include the date in parentheses:

Source authors   Brunnell, Lemoy, Massey, Freeman, Noser, Siegele, and White (2001)

All text citations   According to Brunnell et al. (2001), such recovery does not last.

If two of your sources with six or more authors happen to have the same first author (or several authors), include as many other names as needed to distinguish between the sources:

Two sources' **authors**	Brunnell, Lemoy, Massey, Freeman, Noser, Siegele, and White (2001)
	Brunnell, Lemoy, Ramirez, Noser, Kelly, and White (2001)
Text citations	Research findings vary: Brunnell, Lemoy, and Massey et al. (2001) found that . . . , whereas Brunnell, Lemoy, and Ramirez et al. (2001) found that . . .

NOTE: Be sure to spell out the names of all authors, regardless of how many, when listing a source in the References section of your paper.

2. CITING TWO AUTHORS WITH THE SAME LAST NAME

Differentiate between two authors with the same last name by including their initials in the running text or parenthetic citation. Cite the authors in alphabetical order by their initials:

L. R. Brown (2001) and S. Brown (2002) have reported an increase in worldwide hunger.

At least two experts (L. R. Brown, 2001; S. Brown, 2002) have reported an increase in worldwide hunger

3. CITING WORKS BY THE SAME AUTHOR, PUBLISHED THE SAME YEAR

Proceeding alphabetically by title, assign each individual work by the same author and published in the same year a lowercase letter (*a, b, c,* and so forth) after the publication date: (*Franz, 2001a*) or (*Franz, 2001a, 2001b*). Also add the assigned letter to the publication date of each work as it appears alphabetically by title in the References section of the paper (see Authors section, pp. 313–16).

4. CITING A WORK WITH NO AUTHOR

Cite the work by its title, using the first two or three key words in place of an author's name:

Full title—Book	*A Study of adults exhibiting stable behavioral patterns over a twenty-year period*
Book title cited **in text**	One 20-year study found a significant correlation between the way individuals behaved in high school and later as adults (*Study of Adults*, 1999).
Full title— **Journal article**	Fuel economy overview: evolution of the current policy"

Title cited in text   The popularity of SUVs is partly responsible for the drop in average fuel economy over the last ten years ("Fuel Economy," 2002).

List such works alphabetically by full title in the paper's References section.

NOTE: Cite a work's author parenthetically as *Anonymous* only if that is how the author is named in the source. The intext citation will look like this:

The cost of such programs (Anonymous, 1999) may account for . . .

If you do cite an anonymous source, also list the work alphabetically, with *Anonymous* as author, in the References section of the paper.

5.   CITING MORE THAN ONE AUTHOR

Separate multiple authors' names with *and* when the names are part of the running text. When you cite names parenthetically, separate them with an ampersand (*&*), not *and*:

Names in   Benford and Snow (2000) conclude that conceptual
running text   framing processes are relevant to social movements.

Green, McFalls, and Smith (2001) have reported a relationship between hate crimes and economic downturns.

Names cited   One pair of researchers (Benford & Snow, 2000)
parenthetically   have found that framing processes are relevant to social movements.

A relationship seems to exist between hate crimes and economic downturns (Green, McFalls, & Smith, 2001).

NOTE: Do not be confused by journal articles that use other ways to separate authors' names for intext citations. You may also find such parenthetic forms as (*Wells and Shorter, 2000*), (*Behrman 2001; Rankin 2001*) and (*Davis, Graton, 2000; Li, Brennan, Kohler, 2001*) used in journals you research. Unless your instructor tells you otherwise, follow the APA forms shown here.

6.   CITING UP TO SIX OR MORE AUTHORS

For works with two authors, use both names in every citation. For works with more than two authors but fewer than six, mention all names in the first reference:

Running text   Druss, Bradford, Rosenheck, Radford, and Krumholz
(first citation)   (2002) have linked mental disorders to some instances of heart attack.

Names cited   One study (Druss, Bradford, Rosenheck, Radford, &
in parentheses   Krumholz, 2002) has linked mental disorders to some in-
                      stances of heart attack.

After the first citation, give only the first name followed by *et al.* (not italic
or underlined) and the year:

> Druss et al. (2002) also found that . . .
>
> Further research (Druss et al., 2002) has shown that . . .

All of the authors' names should be spelled out in the References.

When a work has more than six authors, cite only the first author's
name, followed by *et al.*, for the first and succeeding intext citations. Spell
out the names of all authors when listing them in the References.

7. CITING AUTHORS OF TWO OR MORE SEPARATE WORKS TOGETHER

Cite such works parenthetically only, beginning in alphabetical order
with the first author's last name. Separate the citations with semicolons:

> It remains unclear whether a link can be established between diet
> and childhood attention deficit disorder (Berger, 2000; Gardner, 2002;
> Washington & Karen, 2001).

Each source should be listed fully in the References section of the
paper.

QUOTATIONS AND SPECIFIC PARTS OF SOURCES

APA documentation style uses the abbreviations *p.* and *pp.* for the
words *page* and *pages, ch.* for *chapter,* and *sec.* for *section* (respectively).
Use these and other standard abbreviations (see Abbreviations in Chapter
14) when citing specific parts of a work and whenever you use direct quotation or paraphrase. The following examples demonstrate common practices:

> Chaves and Gorski (2001) argue that religious pluralism does not
> contribute to religious practice in a country (cf. Perl, 2000, pp. 15-25).
>
> According to Blustein (2001, esp. ch. 10), the Federal Reserve
> responded too cautiously to Russia's 1998 economic collapse.
>
> French (2002) concludes that "the persistence of extreme poverty in the
> face of unprecedented plenty . . . calls into question the durability of
> our current globalization path" (p. 198).

People connected by the same religion often respond by "giving emergency help, loaning money, giving trusted advice or even therapeutic counseling" (McPherson, Smith-Lovin, & Cook, 2000, pp. 425-426), an observation that has also been made by Louch (2000, sec. 3).

LONG QUOTATIONS

Quotations of 40 words or more should be typed double-spaced and indented five spaces from the left margin. Indent the first line of each quoted paragraph five additional spaces. Place the page number of the source in parentheses after the period ending the quotation:

> Sheehan (2001) sums up the problem as follows:
>
> Roads . . . cause profound changes in ecosystems. . . . Water quality and quantity both suffer in proportion to the amount of paved roads and parking that cover a watershed. Plants and animals are killed during road construction, as well as by vehicles. And roads . . . divide populations of various species into smaller, less stable populations. (p. 111)

LEGAL REFERENCES

Include the date of a court case in parentheses with the name; if the case is mentioned in the text, put the date in parentheses immediately after the case name:

> *Fletcher v. Peck* (1810) established the right of the U.S. Supreme Court to declare a state law unconstitutional.

> The U.S. Supreme Court established its right to declare a state law unconstitutional more than a hundred years ago (*Fletcher v. Peck*, 1810).

Note that the names of court cases are italicized when cited in text but not when listed in the References section.

To cite a statute, give the name and year. Do not italicize the name in either the text or the References section:

> The Securities Exchange Act (1934) was designed to protect the public from fraud or manipulation in the sale of securities.

> Federal law requires the regulation and registration of securities exchanges (Securities Exchange Act, 1934).

PERSONAL COMMUNICATIONS

Unpublished letters, memos, telephone conversations, e-mail correspondences, interviews, and such are *personal communications*. Since they are not available to other researchers, you should use them sparingly in your research and only rarely include them in your paper. When you do use such sources, *cite them in the text only,* not in the References for your paper. Give the last name and initials of your personal source as well as the date on which you communicated with him or her (be as accurate as possible):

> One prominent interpersonal communication researcher, M. E. Cody
> (personal communication, February 3, 2002), has expressed the
> view that the Internet can, in many cases, actually enhance family
> relationships.

> Despite the claims of ETS officials, those who coach students in SAT
> preparation courses note an improvement in student scores after
> coaching (K. Owsley, personal communication, December 11, 2001).

References

Except for personal communications (such as letters, personal interviews, electronic mailings, online discussion groups, and the like), the References include all of the sources cited in the paper's text. Include no other works, no matter how useful they may have been to you at some point in the research. This means that the References will undoubtedly not include some, perhaps several, works that contributed background information or common knowledge to your research. You may have consulted 50 sources during your research and ended up paraphrasing, quoting, or naming only 10 of them in your paper. Only those 10 should be listed as references.

The following pages provide guidelines and sample entries for works included in the References section of an APA-style research paper. Note that APA form calls for indenting the second and succeeding lines of each entry five to seven spaces. (See the References pages of Steve Hanner's paper in Appendix A for an example.)

AUTHORS' NAMES

1. LISTING AUTHORS, EDITORS, AND GROUP AUTHORS

Treat the names of editors and group authors (i.e., associations, committees, corporations, councils) and editors the same as authors' names. Cite corporate authors by name, alphabetically. List personal authors and editors alphabetically by surname, followed by the initials of their first and (if given) middle names. For editors, use *Ed.* or *Eds.* in parentheses, followed by a period, after their names. Use an ampersand (&) between names of joint authors; separate the names by commas. For works by more than six authors, list only the first six, followed by "et al." Follow these examples:

Single author   Crouch, M. A. (2001). *Thinking about sexual harrassment:*
                       A guide for the perplexed. New York: Oxford UP.

Single editor   Lewis-Williams, J. D. (Ed.). (2000). *Stories that float from*
                       afar: Ancestral folklore of the San of southern
                       Africa. Galveston: Texas A&M UP.

Joint editors   Brown, L. R., Flavin, C., & French, H. (Eds.). (2002). *State*
                       of the world 2002. New York: Norton.

Two authors   Mayes, L. C., & Cohen, D. J. (2002). *The Yale Child Study*
                       Center guide to understanding your child. Boston:
                       Little, Brown.

Corporate author   New York State Medical Practices Board. (2001).
                       Guidelines for health facilities funding: 2000-2001.
                       Albany: Author.

Parenthetic citation forms: (Crouch, 2001); (Lewis-Williams, 2000);
Brown, Flavin, & French, 2002); Mayes & Cohen, 2002); (New York
State Medical Practices Board, 2001).

There should be a period at the end of the author's name (or the last author's name). If the last part of the name is an initial, as is often the case, do not add a second period (i.e., initial already ends with a period).

NOTE: In the last example, the corporate author is also the publisher. In such a case, the word *Author* should be used in place of the publisher's name.

2. LISTING A WORK WITH NO AUTHOR

Cite a work with no author alphabetically by title (ending with a period). Include the articles *a, an* and *the* at the beginnings of titles, but ignore them when ordering titles alphabetically:

Periodical   Fuel economy overview: Evolution of the current policy.
article cited   (2002, May). *Congressional Quarterly,* pp. 130-131, 160.
by title

Book cited   *Millennium politics: The stakes for tomorrow's*
by title   *future.* (1999). El Paso, TX: Stant.

Parenthetic citation forms: ("Fuel economy," 2002); (*Millennium,* 1999).

NOTE: When a source provides no author's name, do not use *Anonymous* unless that term is actually given in the source. If the author is named as *Anonymous* in the source, list the work alphabetically under that term.

3. LISTING WORKS PUBLISHED BY THE SAME AUTHOR(S) IN THE SAME YEAR

Proceed alphabetically by title, and assign lowercase letters (*a, b, c,* and so on) after the publication dates. List works in the alphabetical order of the letters assigned:

Jackson, L. P. (1999a). What thinking does to our sense of reality. *Scientific American, 283,* 49-55.

Jackson, L. P. (1999b). Where do memories reside? *Behaviorial Brain Science, 20,* 31-40.

Parenthetic citation forms: (Jackson, 1999a); (Jackson, 1999b).

4. LISTING MULTIPLE WORKS BY THE SAME AUTHOR(S)

List the works in chronological order of publication. Include each author's last name(s) and first and middle initials (if given) in each entry:

Single author   Pipher, M. (1999) *Another country: Navigating the emotional terrain of our elders.* New York: Riverhead.

Pipher, M. (2002). *The middle of everywhere: The world's refugees come to our town.* New York: Harcourt.

Joint authors   Leakey, R. E., & Lewin, R. (1977). *Origins: The emergence and evolution of our species and its possible future.* New York: Dutton.

Leakey, R. E., & Lewin, R. (1979). *People of the lake: Mankind and its beginnings.* New York: Avon.

Leakey, R. E., & Lewin, R. (1992). *Origins reconsidered: In search of what makes us human.* New York: Anchor-Doubleday.

Parenthetic citation forms: (Pipher, 1999); (Pipher, 2002); (Leakey & Lewin, 1977); (Leakey & Lewin, 1979); (Leakey & Lewin, 1992).

5. ORDERING SINGLE- AND JOINT-AUTHOR ENTRIES

Give the name of the first author in each entry. List personal works before edited works, single-author entries before multiple-author entries. Put joint-author entries in alphabetical order by the second and succeeding authors' names:

Author	Cotton, H. R. (1995). *Social reform and social politics: A review of our options.* Washington, DC: Brookings Institute.
Editor	Cotton, H. R. (Ed.). (1997). *When policies fail and politics survive.* New York: Harper.
Joint authors	Cotton, H. R., & Otrell, C. C. (1999). *Reforming child-care laws: Decisions for today.* Lansing, MI: Perron.
Joint editors	Cotton, H. R., & Parnelli, F. R. (Eds.). (1998). *Why is no one looking after health care?* New York: Basic.

Parenthetic citation forms: (Cotton, 1995); (Cotton, 1997); (Cotton & Otrell, 1999); (Cotton & Parnelli, 1998).

For ordering multiple works published under the same name(s), follow the guidelines given in section 4 (p. 315).

DATES OF PUBLICATION

Place the work's publication date in parentheses, followed by a period, after the author's name. For magazine or newspaper articles, give the month and date of publication in parentheses after the year, separated by a comma. Do not abbreviate the month. Follow these examples:

Journal article	Myers, S. Impact of religious involvement on migration. (2000). *Social Forces, 79*(2), 755-783.
Newspaper article	McNally, S. (2000, April 29). World's biggest building no skyscraper. *Washington Times,* p. E2.
Magazine article	Goold, S. D. (2001, November-December). Trust and the ethics of health care institutions. *The Hastings Report, 31*(6), 26-33.
Book	Deitcher, D. (2001). *Dear friends: American photographs of men together, 1840-1918.* New York: Harry N. Abrams.

Parenthetic citation forms: (Myers, 2000); (McNally, 2000); (Goold, 2001); (Dietcher, 2001).

TITLES

1. BOOKS

Capitalize only the first word of a work's title, the first word of its subtitle, and all proper nouns within it. Italicize (or underline) the complete title, and end it with a period:

McWhorter, J. H. (2002). *The power of Babel: A natural history of language.* New York: Freeman.

Parenthetic citation form: (McWhorter, 2002).

Note that this chapter conforms to APA-style guidelines in showing titles of books, magazines, journals, and newspapers in italic print rather than underlined. Unless you are writing your paper on a typewriter or unless your instructor prefers underlining, use the font selection function of your computer's software program to write book titles in italic.

2. PERIODICALS

As with a book title, capitalize only the first word of an article title (whether a magazine, journal, or newspaper article), along with the first word of its subtitle and all proper nouns within it. Do not underline or italicize the article title or put it in quotation marks; end it with a period. Type the name of the magazine, journal, or newspaper title in upper- and lower-case letters; italicize or underline it and the comma that follows:

Allerton, R. M. (1998). Are educators doing their jobs? <u>American Schools, 240,</u> 61-73.

Wolff, M. (2002, March 11). My dinner with Rupert. *New York,* 20-23.

Parenthetic citation forms: (Allerton, 1998); (Wolff, 2002).

PERIODICAL VOLUME AND ISSUE NUMBERS

For a journal, magazine, or newsletter article, always give the volume number, followed by a comma, after the title of the source. Extend the underlining or italics for the title to include the volume number and the comma (see examples below). Add the issue number in parentheses immediately after the volume number *only* when each issue of the journal or magazine begins with page 1. (Some periodicals paginate issues continuously throughout each year or volume; see Chapter 12, pp. 285–87.) Note that if a parenthetic issue number is given, no space or comma separates it and the volume number. There is, however, a comma following the parenthetic issue number. Follow the punctuation and spacing shown in these examples:

Journal with volume number only	Mays, G. (1998). What children know about sex. *American Demographics, 28,* 34-39.
Journal with volume and issue numbers	Heaton, G. T. (1998). Why the movies move us. *Film Quarterly, 56*(3), 30-35.
Magazine article with volume and issue numbers	Cartmill, M. (1999, March). Oppressed by evolution. *Discover, 19*(3) 78-83.

Parenthetic citation forms: (Mays, 1998); (Heaton, 1998); (Cartmill, 1999).

PAGE NUMBERS

Use *p.* or *pp.* before the page number(s) for parts of books or articles in newspapers but not for journal, magazine, or newsletter articles. The page numbers for part of a book (such as a chapter) are added in parentheses after the book's title (see *Wogrin* example following). The page numbers for an article in a periodical are added at the end of the entry, following the volume and issue numbers. Give inclusive page numbers in full: *361–382; 130–133.* Separate discontinuous page numbers with commas: *pp. A5, A12.* Follow these examples:

Magazine article	MacKenzie, D. (2002, February). The science of surprise. *Discover, 23*(2), 59-62.
Chapter in book with several volumes	Miller, R. D. (1999). Life in Vienna. In G. Rosen (Ed.), *Freud: The man and the legacy* (Vol. 2, pp. 404-432). New York: Harper.
Chapter in book	Wogrin, C. (2001). The dying process. In *Matters of life and death* (pp. 57-84). New York: Broadway Books.
Signed newspaper article	Steinberg, P. (2002, April 21). Focus on bingers, not all campus drinkers. *Washington Post,* pp. B1-B2.
Unsigned newspaper article	Neurosis finds a cure. (1998, March 13). *San Francisco Chronicle,* p. C3.

Parenthetic citation forms: (Mackenzie, 2002); (Miller, 1999, p. 410); (Wogrin, 2001); (Steinberg, 2002); ("Neurosis," 1998).

Note that the period that ends the title goes after the parenthetic information about page numbers, not before it, as shown in these and the following examples (see *Miller* and *Wogrin* above).

AN EDITION OR REVISION OF A BOOK

Indicate an edition or revision of a book in parentheses after its title:

Esposito, J. L. (2001). *Women in Muslim family law* (2nd ed.). Syracuse, NY: Syracuse UP.

Wasserman, K. (Ed.). (1998). *Guide to mental health* (Rev. ed.). New York: Cresent.

Parenthetic citation forms: (Esposito, 2001); (Wasserman, 1998, pp. 130-132).

A TRANSLATION OR REPRINT OF A BOOK

Indicate that a book has been translated or reprinted by adding the publication date of the original work in parentheses at the end of the entry (after the end period). For a translation, also include the name of the translator in parentheses after the title:

Vernant, J. (2000). *The universe, the gods, and men* (L. Asher, Trans.). New York: HarperCollins. (Original work published 1999)

Conforte, C. (1999). *A brief history of mental pathology.* New York: Scholars' Facsimiles and Reprints. (Original work published 1941)

Parenthetic citation forms: (Vernant, 1999/2000); (Conforte, 1941/1999).

A VOLUME IN A MULTIVOLUME WORK

Give the number of the volume(s) you consulted in parentheses after the title. Use *Vol.* or *Vols.* before the volume number(s). The number itself should be an arabic number, not a roman:

Schama, S. (2001). *A history of Britain* (Vol. 2). New York: Hyperion.

Parenthetic citation form: (Schama, 2001).

If particular volumes are published over more than a one-year period, indicate the span of dates:

Rowlands, C. C., & McColley, N. (Eds.). (1995-1999). *A handbook of contemporary addiction treatment* (Vols. 2-4). Washington, DC: Center for Addictive Behavior.

Parenthetic citation form: (Rowlands & McColley, 1995-1999).

A WORK PUBLISHED IN AN EDITED BOOK

List the work by its author's last name, followed by first and (if given) middle initial(s). Then give the publication date (in parentheses), followed by the work's title (no underlining or italics). Next, give the editor's initials and last name, followed by the abbreviation *Ed.* in parentheses (or *Eds.*, if more than one editor). After a comma, state the title of the book (underlined or italicized). Include the volume number (if applicable), followed by a comma and the page number(s) for the included piece in parentheses:

Christensen, J. R. (2001). What is traumatic brain injury? In L. Schoenbrodt (Ed.), *Children with traumatic brain injury* (pp. 1-22). Bethesda, MD: Woodbine House.

Parenthetic citation form: (Christensen, 2001).

A TECHNICAL OR RESEARCH REPORT

List a published report the same as a book. If the issuing agency has assigned a number to the report, you may if you wish include it in parentheses after the title:

Bird, J., & Gaston, P. R. (1999). *Youth gangs and the new mythology of manhood* (Social Research Monograph No. 23). Los Angeles: U of California P, 1999.

Parrot, D. M. (1998). *Acquaintance rape and college responses in New York State* (Open File Report 43-748). Washington, DC: U.S. Department of Education.

U.S. Congress, Office of Technology Assessment. (1999). *Electronic delivery of public assistance benefits: Options for policy issues* (F/N053-004-01221-3). Washington, DC: U.S. Government Printing Office.

Parenthetic citations forms: (Bird & Gaston, 1999); (Parrot, 1998); (U.S. Congress, 1999).

THE PROCEEDINGS OF A MEETING

For published proceedings, treat the work the same as a book:

Bumiller, T. C., & Forer, J. (1999). *Proceedings of the Atlanta Conference on Health and Technology.* Atlanta: National Health Association.

Parenthetic citation form: (Bumiller & Forer, 1999).

For unpublished proceedings, cite when and where the meeting was held (as accurately as possible), as no publisher can be cited:

World Food Conference. (1998, December). *Proceedings of the World Food Conference.* Conference held at University of Virginia, Charlottesville, VA.

Parenthetic citation form: (World Food Conference, 1998).

ELECTRONIC SOURCES

Electronic sources include material found through the Internet as well as on CD-ROM, diskette, and magnetic files. To list electronic sources in the References section of your paper, you should include standard bibliographic elements along with whatever information another researcher would need to locate and retrieve the material. Electronic communications, such as e-mail and bulletin board postings, should be cited in the text as personal communications (see p. 313).

ONLINE SOURCES

In general, include the same basic information as for print sources. For articles retrieved from Internet-only journals, conclude the entry with the date that you retrieved the article and its electronic address, or URL. If an online article is a duplicate of that found in the print version of the journal, then include *Electronic version* in brackets following the article title. For such articles, you need not include the URL and date retrieved, unless you believe the online version has been changed from the print version in terms of format, paging, or the inclusion of additional commentary, data, and the like. For all other online sources, include the retrieval date and URL.

When possible, the URL should link directly to the article. When a citation concludes with a URL, do not follow it with a period. If a URL goes to another line in the citation, break the address after a slash or before a period. Do not hyphenate URL line breaks.

1. **ONLINE ARTICLE BASED ON A PRINT SOURCE**

   Nagel, J. H., & McNulty, J. E. (2000). Partisan effects of voter turnout in presidential elections [Electronic version]. *American Politics Quarterly 28*(2), 335-350.

   Parenthetic citation form: (Nagel & McNulty, 2000)

2. **ONLINE ARTICLE MODIFIED FROM A PRINT SOURCE**

   Lawler, E. J. (2001). An affect theory of social exchange. *American Journal of Sociology, 107*(2), 707-722. Retrieved January 15, 2002, from http://www.journals/uchicago.edu/AJS/journal/contents/ v107n2.html

   Parenthetic citation form: (Lawler, 2001)

3. **ARTICLE IN AN INTERNET-ONLY JOURNAL**

   Turner, J. W. (2001). Telepsychiatry as a case study of presence: Do you know what you are missing? *Journal of Computer-Mediated Communication, 6*(4). Retrieved February, 2, 2002, from http://www.ascusc.org/jcmc/vol6/issue4/turner.html

   Parenthetic citation form: (Turner, 2001)

4. **A PERSONAL OR PROFESSIONAL SITE**

Lorenzen, M. (n.d.). *A brief history of library instruction in the United States.* Retrieved May 1, 2002, from http://www.libraryreference. org/lihistory/html

Tobacco use among youth (n.d.) Retrieved December 15, 2001, from http://tobaccofreekids.org/research/factsheets/pdf/0002.pdf

Indicate sites that are not dated with the abbreviation "n.d." in parentheses. If no author is named, begin with the title of the document.

Parenthetic citation forms: (Lorenzen, n.d.); ("Tobacco use," n.d.)

5. **DOCUMENT RETREIVED FROM A UNIVERSITY PROGRAM OR DEPARTMENT WEB SITE**

Powell, A. D., & Kahn, A. S. (2001). Racial differences in women's desire to be thin. Retrieved February 13, 2002, from University of Maryland, Women's Studies Database Reading Room Web site: http://www.inform.umd.edu/EdRes/Topic/WomensStudies/ ReadingRoom/AcademicPapers/race+body-image

When a document is part of a large, complex site (such as that of a university or government agency), identify the sponsoring organization and program or division, followed by a colon and the URL.

Parenthetic citation form: (Powel & Kahn, 2001)

6. **ARTICLE IN AN ONLINE NEWPAPER OR NEWSWIRE**

Michaud, A. (2001, July 31). The computer gender gap. *Boston Globe.* Retrieved September 30, 2001, from http://www.boston.com/ dailyglobe2/212/science/The_computer_gender_gapP.shtml

Study: Kids can get tobacco as easily as ever. (1999, October 14). *APBnews.com.* Retrieved August 31, 2001, from http://www.apbnews. com/safetycenter/family/1999/10/14/tobacco1014_01.html

Parenthetic citation forms: (Michaud, 2001, July 31); ("Study: Kids can," 1999, October 14)

7. **ARTICLE IN AN ONLINE MAGAZINE**

Mayfield, K. (2001, June 6). The push to push women higher. *Wired.* Retrieved August 2, 2001, from http://www.wired.com/news/ print/0,1294,44519,00.html

Parenthetic citation form: (Mayfield, 2001, June 6)

8. AN ONLINE ABSTRACT

Shanahan, M. (2000). *Forging men and manufacturing women.* Abstract retrieved June 27, 2001, from http://www.lib.umich.edu/dissertions/29355

Parenthetic citation form: (Shanahan, 2000)

9. ELECTRONIC MAILING LIST MESSAGE

Wilson, C. (2002, February 15). New research on starch and cancer. Message posted to CANCERGROUP Updates, archived at http://www.cangroup.org/archive/updates/5005.html

Parenthetic citation form: (C. Wilson, personal communication, February 15, 2002)

10. DISCUSSION GROUP MESSAGE

Singh, V. (2001, November 11). Hypnotherapy for Internet addicts [Msg. 298]. Message posted to http://www.groups.google.com/group/addictions/message/298

Note that for online postings to mailing lists and discussion groups, only those that are archived (that is, that can be retrieved by a reader via a URL) should appear on the References list. Nonarchived postings and other nonarchived electronic communications, such as personal e-mail, should be noted parenthetically in the body of paper as *personal communication* (see page 313) but not included on the References list.

Parenthetic citation form: (V. Singh, personal communication, November 11, 2001)

OTHER ELECTRONIC SOURCES

Include the medium, in square brackets, after the title, with no period separating the title and medium. Next include the location and name of the producer or distributor or both, as appropriate, in parentheses:

1. A PERIODICAL SOURCE ON CD-ROM OR DISKETTE

Irion, Robert. (2001, August). Did life on earth come from Mars? *Discover, 67*(8), 64-69. Retrieved from *General Periodicals Ondisc-Magazine Express* [CD-ROM], UMI-Proquest.

Parenthetic citation form: (Irion, 2001, August)

2. A NONPERIODICAL SOURCE ON CD-ROM OR DISKETTE

Ainsley, V. H., & Norton, B. (1999). *Sigmund Freud: A lifetime of inquiry* [CD-ROM]. New York: Research Associates [Producer].

Parenthetic citation form: (Ainsley & Norton, 1999)

3. DATA FILE

Studies in dream-consciousness and psychic ordering, 1997-98 [Data file]. (1998). San Francisco, CA: Center for Health and Living [Distributor].

Parenthetic citation form: ("Studies in dream-consciousness," 1998)

LEGAL SOURCES

Give the information needed for a reader to locate the source. Using the source itself or a referent to it as your guide, give the information indicated in the following examples. If you are working on a computer, you should be able to insert the symbol for *section* (§). If you are working on a typewriter or computer that does not have this symbol, use the abbreviation *Sec.* As mentioned earlier, do not italicize or underline the names of court cases in the References, but do italicize or underline them in text citations (see p. 312). Do not italicize or underline the names of laws, acts, codes, or documents in either the text or References (such as the *U.S. Constitution*).

1. A FEDERAL DISTRICT COURT OPINION

Name   Volume   Source   Page   Region   Date

Hazard v. Kinola, 554 F. Supp. 927 (S.W. Ark. 1998).

This 1998 case was tried in federal district court for the Southwestern District of Arkansas. It appears in volume 554, page 927, of the *Federal Supplement.*

Parenthetic citation form: (Hazard v. Kinola, 1998).

2. A CASE APPEALED TO THE U.S. SUPREME COURT

Name   Volume   Source   Page   Date

Baker v. Carr, 369 U.S. 186 (1997).

This case was tried in 1997 before the U.S. Supreme Court. It appears in volume 369 of the *United States Reports*, page 186.

Parenthetic citation form: (Baker v. Carr, 1997).

3. A FEDERAL LAW

Name   Title number   Source   Section   Date

Voting Rights Act, 42 U.S.C. § 1973 (1965).

Passed into law in 1965, this act appears in title 42, section 1973, of the *United States Code*.

Parenthetic citation form: (Voting Rights Act, 1965).

Many federal laws are cited by title number rather than by name. Note that the *United States Code* (cited above) may be abbreviated as *U.S.C.:*

15 U.S.C. sec. 221 (1983).

For more information about the forms of legal references, see *The Bluebook: A Uniform System of Citation,* 17th ed. (Cambridge, MA: Harvard Law Review Association, 2001).

NONPRINT SOURCES

1. MOTION PICTURE (FILM OR VIDEO)

Give the principal contributors' names, followed by their function(s) in parentheses. Specify the medium (*Motion picture*) in brackets after the title, followed by the location and name of the distributor:

> Choate, H. R. (Producer), & Kimbel, M. M. (Director). (1998). *Marriage and commitment* [Motion picture]. Chicago: Academy Productions.
> Intercultural Relations Institute (IRA). (1996). *Take two* [motion picture]. Palo Alto, CA: Author.

Parenthetic citation forms: (Choate & Kimbel, 1998); (IRA, 1996).

2. AN AUDIO RECORDING

Give the principal contributors' names, followed by their function(s) in parentheses. Specify the medium (*Audio recording*) in brackets after the title. If a recording number is given on the source, include that information with the medium specification—for example, (*Audio recording No. 71*). List the publisher's location and name last:

> Jacobs, M. L. (Ed.), & Reese, J. (Narrator). (1998). *The child as storymaker* [Audio recording]. Columbus, OH: Ohio State University.

Parenthetic citation form: (Jacobs & Reese, 1998).

Sample References List: Psychology

Though variations occur among some journals, the author-date style recommended by the American Psychological Association (APA) predominates in papers in psychology, education, and a number of other fields. The examples shown in Figure 13.1 conform to the guidelines discussed in

Public Therapy 19

References

Group author/ publisher

Amercian Psychiatric Association. (1994). *Diagnostic and statistical manual of mental disorders* (4th ed.). Washington, DC: Author.

Bander, H. (1998). Listening to your friends: The new rules. In K. M. Modrell & G. T. Joad (Eds.), *Conversation as therapy* (pp. 93-106). New York: Contour.

Selection included in another work

Journal article

Carly, F. (1998). "Transatlantic communication and culture." *Quarterly Journal of Speech, 86*(4), 143-153.

Hardin, D. (1997). *Abnormal psychology.* New York: HarperCollins, 1997.

Book/ single author

Magazine article

Kotlowitz, A. (1999, February 8). The unprotected. *New Yorker, 76,* 43-53.

Lindberg, D., & Numbers, R. L. (Eds.). *God and nature: Essays on the encounter between Christianity and science.* Berkeley: U of California P, 1986.

Book/joint editors

Markowitz, W. (2001). Early childhood intervention and impulse control [Electronic version]. *Journal of Child Behavior, 38* (1), 198-210.

Online article based on a pr source

Unsigned newspaper article

"People at Risk." (1999, May 11). *USA Today,* p. D-2.

Potter, J. Y. (2002). "Reality" television: Reinforcing or shattering cultural stereotypes? *Contemporary Media Studies, 5*(2). Retrieved April 18, 2002, from http://www.icms.org/journal/cms/v5n2/potter.html

Article in an Internet-only journal

Report/ corporate author

Psychiatry and the Community Committee. (1998). *A family affair: Helping families cope with mental illness* (GAP Report: No. 183). New York: Kunn-Bates.

Stiller, J. D. (1999, October 4). As the child, so the adult. *The News and Observer,* pp. 1A, 10A.

Newspaper article

FIGURE 13.1   Sample References page: APA style

previous sections and the recommendations of the *Publication Manual of the American Psychological Association,* 5th ed. (Washington, DC: American Psychological Association, 2001).

Discipline Practices: APA Variations

Disciplines that follow APA, author-date documentation cite sources in the text, as described earlier in this chapter. For entries in the References list, however, many of these disciplines employ variations of APA form, modifying punctuation, spacing, capitalization, and other details. You may discover that adapted versions of APA references forms are common in papers or journals written for agriculture, anthropology and archaeology, the biological sciences, business and economics, education, geology, and home economics. Many papers in linguistics follow LSA style, a version of APA recommended by the Linguistics Society of America. In political science and sociology, writers often use APSA style, a variation of APA adopted by the American Political Science Association. (See the section on Discipline Style Manuals near the end of this chapter for guides on LSA and APSA documentation.)

Be alert to modifications of APA style (or any other major documentation style) as you read and record notes from all your research sources. Make sure such notes are accurate and that your own paper follows precisely the documentation style recommended by your instructor.

Number-System Documentation

The majority of authors, editors, and journals in the applied sciences (chemistry, computer sciences, mathematics, and physics) as well as the medical sciences employ the number-system style of documentation. This style uses arabic numerals in the text to cite sources correspondingly numbered and listed in the References section of the paper.

Intext Citation

The intext citation numerals appear in the text either (a) between parentheses, (b) between brackets, or (c) as raised superscript numerals, as shown here:

a. Harland (3) has shown that traditional comparisons of cigarette smoke yields have been reliable. On the other hand, it is important to remember that the chemical composition of nontobacco cigarette smoke is very different from that of ordinary tar (4,5).

b. Despite the endorsement of Nobel laureate Paul Berg [3], some scientists [1,7,12] maintain that the genome project is unnecessary or that it will produce only what Ayala [4, p. 10] calls "indecipherable junk."

c. Oxygen affects yeast viability and is essential to any yeast ethanol production process.[4-6] The Pasteur effect[12] demonstrates the influence of oxygen and respiration on the ability of the cell to produce ethanol.

(See the instructions for typing brackets and superscript numerals in Chapter 14.)

As these example show, it is not unusual for a citation to refer to more than one source at a time with the number-system method. In addition, note that the citation numerals do not necessarily appear in sequential order. The numeral sequence depends upon the method by which each discipline or publishing journal prefers to list and number sources in a paper's References.

References

For ordering sources in the References section, papers that employ the number-system style follow one of two widely used methods:

1. Numbering sources listed in the References section by their order of appearance in the text
2. Numbering sources according to their alphabetized order in the References

Disciplines and journals vary as to their practices. Which numbering method you use will depend upon the discipline or journal you are following or the directions of your instructor.

1. NUMBERING SOURCES BY ORDER OF APPEARANCE IN THE PAPER

In this method, citation numbers proceed sequentially throughout the text (1, 2, 3, and so on) until they are repeated when a source is cited again. Corresponding sources in the References section are listed and numbered in the order they are cited in the paper, rather than alphabetically by author or title:

Parenthetic citation form

While the effects of aging on the brain can differ dramatically among individuals (1), most structural and chemical differences become apparent in late middle life, usually around the fifties and sixties (2,3). Encouragingly, studies have shown that the brain is also capable of dynamic remodeling of its neuronal connections, especially when exposed to new environments (4). Experiments with placing laboratory rats in visually stimulating environments (1) and altering their DNA (5) have produced apparently substantial increases in cognitive function.

References

1. Finch, C. E. *Longevity, senescence, and the genome.* Chicago: U of Chicago P, 1990.

2. Coleman, P. D., Flood, D. G. Neuron numbers and dendritic extent in normal aging and Alzheimer's disease. *Neurobiol of Ag* 8 (1987): 521-45.

3. Davis, E. M. *Neural aging and the brain.* New York: Hight, 1992.

4. Weindruch, R., Walford, R. L. *The retardation of aging and disease by dietary restriction.* Springfield, IL: Thomas, 1997.

5. Shule, N., Watts, J. S. *Genetics and cognitive growth.* Chicago: Wayley, 1998.

Given that the order of sources is likely to change as you write the first draft of your paper, using the number-by-appearance method can be troublesome. To avoid numbering and renumbering sources, put each author's name in parentheses as you write the draft. Once you have completed the paper in draft form, with all sources entered and in final order, then substitute numbers for the authors' names. The numbering of citation sources by order of appearance in the References is common for papers written in computer science, engineering, mathematics, and nursing.

2. NUMBERING SOURCES BY ALPHABETIZED ORDER

Begin by alphabetizing all sources for the paper according to the author's last name (or the work's title, if no author is given). Next, number each source sequentially, as shown below:

References

1. Coleman, P. D., Flood, D. G. Neuron numbers and dendritic extent in normal aging and Alzheimer's disease. *Neurobiol of Ag* 8 (1987): 521-45.

2. Davis, E. M. *Neural aging and the brain.* New York: Hight, 1992.

3. Finch, C. E. *Longevity, senescence, and the genome.* Chicago: U of Chicago P, 1990.

4. Shule, N., Watts, J. S. *Genetics and cognitive growth.* Chicago: Wayley, 1998.

5. Weindruch, R., Walford, R. L. *The retardation of aging and disease by dietary restriction.* Springfield, IL: Thomas, 1997.

As you write the paper, cite these sources parenthetically by number (or raised superscript) as they appear in the text. Remember that a number should be repeated in the text each time the source it designates is cited:

> While the effects of aging on the brain can differ dramatically among individuals (3), most structural and chemical differences become apparent in late middle life, usually around the fifties and sixties (1,2). Encouragingly, studies have shown that the brain is also capable of dynamic remodeling of its neuronal connections, especially when exposed to new environments (5). Experiments with placing laboratory rats in visually stimulating environments (3) and altering their DNA (4) have produced apparently substantial increases in cognitive function.

Note that sources are *not* cited in numerical order. The citations above for *Finch (3), Coleman (1), Davis (2),* and *Weindruch (5),* for example, correspond to the order in which those authors appear in the References section.

Listing sources alphabetically by their authors' last names and then numbering citations accordingly is the usual method for papers in biology, mathematics, and psychology.

Other Features

Abstracts.   A paper following the number-reference style generally includes an *abstract,* or brief summary, of the paper. (Reviews of the literature, however, do not include abstracts.) An abstract informs the reader of the paper's contents and serves as a useful review once the paper has been read. If your instructor wishes you to include an abstract with your paper, see the general discussion in the section Abstracts, earlier in this chapter.

Headings.   Headings serve as short titles for various sections of the paper. They are helpful in organizing the discussion and emphasizing important ideas for the reader. See the section titled Headings earlier in this chapter if you plan to include headings in your paper.

Journal Abbreviations.   Disciplines following the number-system style of documentation consistently abbreviate titles of journals listed in a paper's References section. For example, the *Scandinavian Journal of Clinical Laboratory Investigations* and the *International Journal of Epidemiology* are abbreviated as follows (respectively):

Scand J Clin Lab Invest
Int J Epidemiol

(Remember that titles of works are not underlined or italicized in number-system style references.)

Exceptions to the practice of abbreviating titles are journals whose titles are only single words (e.g., *Biochemistry, Geology, Science*). While such one-word titles should not be abbreviated in your paper, you will need to abbreviate others.

Make certain the abbreviations you use conform to accepted practices for the discipline you are writing about. The major source for all discipline abbreviations is the *American National Standard for Abbreviation of Titles of Periodicals, Z39.5-1985* (New York: American National Standards Institute, 1985). In addition to consulting the discipline style guides listed on page 341–42, you can find most standard abbreviations for journal titles in the biological and medical sciences in the two following sources:

> *List of Journals Indexed in Index Medicus*. Bethesda, MD: National Library of Medicine (annual).
> *Serial Sources for the BIOSIS Data Base®*. Philadelphia: BIOSIS, 1989–date (annual).

CBE Style

The Council of Biology Editors (CBE) recommends documentation styles for papers in anatomy, genetics, physiology, and zoology. A research article or paper written to conform to CBE standards cites sources in the text and documents them fully in a References section at the end of the work. In its most recent publication, *Scientific Style and Format: The CBE Manual for Authors, Editors, and Publishers,* 6th ed. (Cambridge: Cambridge UP, 1994), the CBE also describes two other acceptable methods of intext documentation: the *citation-sequence* and *name-year* systems. Each of these citation systems is described in a following section; then CBE practices for preparing the References list are summarized and a sample CBE References page is given. Follow your instructor's advice about which CBE recommended style—citation-sequence or name-year—you should use in documenting your research paper.

Name-Year Intext Citation Form

The CBE name-year method is similar to APA style (see the beginning of this chapter) in that each source is cited parenthetically in the text by the author's last name and the work's publication date. Note that, whereas APA style inserts an ampersand between two authors' names, CBE name-year method uses *and*:

> The cost of using solar energy to heat homes has fallen by as much as 65 percent in the last 10 years (Bradshaw and Awerbach 1998).
> *or*
> Bradshaw and Awerbach's work (1998) shows that the cost of using solar energy to heat homes has fallen by as much as 65 percent in the last 10 years.

As in APA style, full bibliographic information for all sources cited in-text is provided in the paper's References section. Note, however, that unlike an APA-style intext citation, a CBE citation does not use a comma between the author's name and the publication date (e.g., *Blay 1999*).

Citation-Sequence Intext Citation Form

The citation-sequence system is essentially a number-system style of documentation: Sources are numbered in the order in which they are cited in the text of the paper and listed in the same order in the References section. Subsequent citations of the same source use the same number as its initial citation. Proper CBE style calls for citation numbers to appear as superscripts—that is, positioned above the regular line of text and in type one or two sizes smaller than that used for the text. (If your typewriter or computer lacks the ability to do superscripts, you may print the numerals in your paper by hand or use one of the alternate number-citation styles described on p. 327–28, if your instructor agrees.) As the following example illustrates, a multiple citation is made by using a dash between three or more sequential numbers; a comma separates nonsequential citation numbers:

> It is estimated that by the year 2000, scientists working on the Human Genome Project will have identified more than 99 percent of all active human genes[1] and found ways to use them for medical purposes. Medical experts predict, for example, that future advances in gene therapy will allow doctors to inject needed genes directly into the bloodstream. Once there, the genes will seek out targeted cells and unload material that will eventually produce helpful disease-killing proteins.[2-5] Since the majority of diseases originate from gene imperfections,[1,3,5] such therapy will be useful in treating conditions ranging from AIDS to cystic fibrosis and even high cholesterol.

The sources represented by the numeral citations in this paragraph would be correspondingly numbered and listed in the paper's References, as follows:

1. Walters LR. The ethics of human gene therapy. Nature 1996; 320:225-227.
2. Lyon J, Gordon P. Altered fates: Gene therapy and the retooling of human life. New York: Norton; 1995. 245 p.
3. Green RD, Richards MA. Recent gene therapy: Applications and results. J Intl Genet 1997;168:1254-1262.
4. Mason TH. Medical research: practice and promise. Chicago: Hartley; 1998. 285 p.

5. Culver KW. Gene therapy: A handbook for physicians. New York:
    Liebert; 1998. 361 p.

References Forms

The preceding examples conform to CBE citation-sequence requirements for the most common types of sources (i.e., books and periodicals)
appearing in research papers in the sciences. Whether done according to
name-year or citation-sequence style, CBE reference entries are precisely
stated and punctuated to present only the most essential information about
sources. The following sections summarize the major elements of CBE form
(including proper punctuation) required for most entries in the References
list. To familiarize yourself with CBE references style, study each section
carefully and refer to the sample References list (Figure 13.2) for relevant
examples of the topics discussed. Review these sections and examples
again later, as you write the References section of your paper. Unless
specifically stated otherwise, the procedures described apply both to CBE
name-year and citation-sequence documentation styles.

1. AUTHORS' NAMES

For name-year style, list authors alphabetically by their last names; for
citation-sequence style, list authors in the order in which they are named in
the text. For both styles, follow each author's last name with the initials of
his or her first and (if given) middle names; there is no comma between the
last name and initials and no space and punctuation between initials (*Her-
rick RW*).

For More Than One Author

For both styles, list two or three authors as just described for a single
author, using commas to separate the individual authors' names (*Graham
HW, Shaw K*). For more than three authors, list only the first three; then add
a comma after the third name, and follow it with the phrase *and others*
(*Roberts JD, Brookline AM, Groot ST, and others*). Note that CBE style does
not use the Latin phrase *et al.*

For Group or Corporate Authors

Cite a group or corporate author alphabetically by its abbreviated
name, which is placed in brackets at the start of the entry (e.g., *[WHO]
World Health Organization*).

For an Anonymous Author

For any work not attributed to a specific author, use the term *Anonymous* in brackets at the start of an entry (e.g., *[Anonymous] How Americans
can . . .*).

Advances in Health

References

Abstract Beller HJ. Changes in concentration of selected chemical
pollutants in wet-soil sytstems [abstract]. In:
American Environmental Association 8th annual
meeting program; 1998 Mar 5-9; San Francisco.
Chicago (IL): Science Associates; Abstract nr KL211.

[Anonymous]. The Komodo Monitor dragon is real enough   Unsigned
[editorial]. New York Times 1998 Sept 12:C4.   newspaper
editorial

Book with Grutz HD, Limmer JO, Thomas BF, editors. The
editors pharmacology of East Borneo forest people. New
York: Aston, 1999. 360 p.

Journal Grieman PT. Biology recycled. Online J of Therap [serial
article article online] 1998 Mar 20; Doc nr 15[3740 words;
accessed 10 paragraphs]. 3 figures; 1 table.
online

Miller DA, Pensley AT, editors. Stages in human embryos: Conference
Including a survey of the Carnegie collection.   proceedings
Conference on Community Health and Services; 1998
April 4-7; Chicago. Chicago: West; 1999. 92 p.

Selection Konner TT, George MC. Cell biomass yield. In: Collins KA.
included in Biothermodynamics. Chicago: Haley, 1998. p 329-34.
another
work Labb RE. Ending death with disease. N Eng J Med 1998;   Journal
332:1055-57.   article

Magazine Lammer O. Can science survive? Sci Am 1998 Sep 5:
article 136-44.

Modayu AR, Hopper K, Roberts MH, and others.   Book with
Molecules. 4th ed. Menlo Park: Benjamin/Cummings;   multiple
1998. 453 p.   authors

Group [WHO] World Health Organization. Our planet, our health.
author Report to the United Nations Health Conference.
Paris, France; 1998 December.

23

FIGURE 13.2   Sample References page: CBE citation-sequence style

For an Editor

In both the citation-sequence and name-year systems, place the term *editor* or *editors* (lowercase) after the author's name or after the last author's name, if there is more than one (e.g., *Trevitt CK, Hearter LD, editors*). Note that you should not use the abbreviations *Ed.* or *Eds.*

2. TITLES

Capitalize only the first word of a work's title, the first word in its subtitle (i.e., after the colon), as well as all proper nouns within the title and subtitle (*Educational reform: A means of providing for America's children*). Note that CBE style does not underline or italicize titles.

3. PLACE OF PUBLICATION AND PUBLISHER

CBE guidelines for the form and content of publication information for books and similar sources are the same as those for MLA and APA papers (both discussed earlier in this chapter). For a book, give the place of publication following the work's title, followed by a colon. Next, state the publisher's name, shortened to avoid unnecessary details (*Hope for our side. New York: Croft*).

4. DATE OF PUBLICATION

Where the date of publication is placed will depend upon which style of CBE documentation you are using.

For Citation-Sequence Form

For a book, list the publication date following a semicolon after the publisher's name (*New York: Croft; 2001*). For a periodical, give the year after the title of the work, with no punctuation (*Amino acid nomenclature 2002*). For a journal article, follow the year with the abbreviated month (*2001;Mar*), and for a newspaper article, include the day (*2001,Nov 10*).

For Name-Year Form

Place the publication date after the author's name, followed by a period (*Hanes TC. 1998*). For a magazine or newspaper article, include the month (abbreviated, with no period after) and the day, as applicable (*Jones G. 1998 Aug 2*).

5. PAGE NUMBERS

As with the publication date, how you handle the page numbers depends upon which style of CBE documentation you use.

For Citation-Sequence Form

For a book, after the publication date, add a period and two spaces (unless your word processing program automatically adjusts such spacing after a period); then state the number of pages the book contains, followed by a space and the letter *p* (*2002. 241 p.*). For a journal article, add a semi-colon after the publication date, followed by the volume number (with no space between), the issue number (if included) in parentheses, and a colon; then list the inclusive page numbers (with no space after the colon), like this: *2001 Feb;83(2):455-461*. For a magazine article, give the page numbers after the colon following the date (*2001 July 12:28*). For a news-paper article, give the section number after the date, followed by a colon and then the page number(s) (*2002 May 3;Sec 4:A2*).

For Name-Year Form

Do not give the numbers of pages for books listed in the References sec-tion. But if you are citing a source that is included in another work, give the page numbers of where the source appears in that work; to do so, add a pe-riod after the date, followed by the letter *p* (with no period) and the inclusive page numbers (*New York: Croft; 2001. p 45–51*). Give the page numbers for a periodical article after the colon following the volume or issue number of a journal (*2000; 74:311–2*); after the date and a colon for a magazine article (*2002 Nov:23-29.*); and after the section number (abbreviated *Sec* with no pe-riod) and a colon for a newspaper article (*Aug 25;Sec A:2*). If you give the number for the newspaper column (abbreviated *col* with no period) in which a source appears, it should follow the page number, as in *Sect A:2(col 3)*.

6. ELECTRONIC PUBLICATIONS

A references entry for a source published electronically should include the same information usually given for its printed equivalent, plus information relevant to how it was accessed electronically. The latter re-quirement includes adding a description of the medium (*CD–ROM* or *serial online*) in square brackets following the title of the work as well as a state-ment of availability, which documents how and when the work was ac-cessed. For an online source lacking a date or page numbers, give as much information as you can, including descriptions of the document number (ab-breviated *Doc nr*), the number of words (bracketed) or paragraphs, plus the number of illustrations (if relevant). Use the following examples as models:

> Grieman PT. Biology recycled. Online J Therap [serial article online] 2001 Mar 12; Doc nr 2 [3720 words; 10 paragraphs]. 3 figures; 1 table.
>
> Rowley LK. Better health gets easier. Time [serial article online] 2000 April 9; 12 paragraphs. Available from: CompuServe. Accessed 2001 Nov 3.
>
> THE MERCK INDEX ONLINE [monograph online]. 14th ed. Rahway (NJ): Merck; 1997. Adsorption chromatography; monograph nr 87. Available from: Dialog Information Services, Palo Alto, CA. Accessed 2000 Aug 5.

Also refer to Figure 13.2 for additional examples of CBE-style references.

NOTE: Many standard reference works are better known by their titles than their editors' names. In such a case, list the work under its title; if the editor's name is included, place it after the title:

1. Annual review of cell biology. 4th ed. James A. Spudich and others, editors. Palo Alto, CA: Annual Reviews; 1994.
2. Dictionary of genetics. 4th ed. Robert C. King and William D. Stansfield, editors. London: Oxford University Press; 1990. 416 p.

Discipline Practices: CBE Variations

Like basic author-date (APA) documentation style, number-system style includes varying practices in both citation and references forms. Papers in the applied sciences—chemistry, mathematics, physics, and the medical sciences, for example—often follow documentation styles recommended by discipline associations. (See the list of style manuals for various disciplines near the end of this chapter.) By consciously noting such variations, you should have no trouble understanding the application of number-system documentation to your own research paper.

As you take notes during reading or prepare your own paper's references, do not confuse standard CBE documentation form with modified versions. Be certain that your paper follows your instructor's requirements.

Chicago-Style Documentation

As mentioned at the beginning of the chapter, writers in the fine arts (art, music, dance, and philosophy) and in certain areas of the humanities and some sciences follow documentation standards recommended by *The Chicago Manual of Style* (Chicago: The University of Chicago Press, 1993), now in its 14th edition. The style currently recommended by the editors of the *Chicago Manual* for most publications* is essentially author-date, like APA style, in which sources are cited parenthetically in the text by their authors' last names and dates of publication. Sources are then listed alphabetically by authors' last names and described bibliographically in a References section at the end of the paper. There are some relatively minor but distinctive differences between the two styles; nonetheless, students following *Chicago*-style author-date documentation would do well to study the APA practices described earlier in this chapter and apply those practices to the few differences discussed in this section.

Note that this chapter conforms to *Chicago*-style guidelines in showing titles of books, magazines, journals, and newspapers in italic print rather than underlined. Unless you are writing your paper on a typewriter or unless your instructor prefers underlining, use the font selection function of your computer's software program to write book titles in italic.

*See p. 304 for an explanation of which types of documentation *Chicago* recommends for certain subject areas.

Intext Citation

Although *Chicago*-style author-date documentation forms agree in most ways with those recommended for APA-style papers, note the following differences in basic citation elements:

1. AUTHORS: SINGLE AND MULTIPLE

Cite each source parenthetically within text, including the author's last name and the publication year. It is preferable to place these parenthetic citations at the ends of sentences or at natural syntactic breaks near the content being cited. For a work with two or three authors, give all three names in the citation; state only the first author's name, followed by *et al.* or the phrase *and others* for a work with more than three authors. Follow these examples:

(Johnson 2001)

(Parrish and Davidson 2002)

(Wilkins, Nguyen, and McGuire 2002)

(Berzoli et al. 2001)

Note that unlike APA style, *Chicago* style uses the word *and* between authors' names, instead of an ampersand (*&*), and no comma is used between the last (or only) author's name and the date. Editors are cited by their names only, with no *Ed., Eds., editor,* or other such descriptor included.

Group or corporate authors should be cited by their full names or recognizable shortened versions, which correspond to the alphabetized listing in the References. Cite a work for which no author is named by its title or a similarly recognizable shortened version. Do not use *Anonymous* to cite an unknown author:

(Huntington Library 2000)

(Western Philosophical Society 2002)

(*Transitions in Thinking* 2001)   *or*   (*Transitions* 2001)

("Dancing on Air" 2002)   *or*   ("Dancing" 2002)

2. PARTS OF A WORK

When it is necessary to include page numbers or other specific parts of a work in the source citation, add the information (preceded by a comma) after the date. Use a colon between the volume number of a work and the relevant page numbers:

(Bui and Wesson 2002, 46)

(Hassel 2001, 213-20)

(Winter 2002, 3:116)

(Fruehan, King, and Farrar 2000, 2:91)

3. MULTIPLE SOURCES

Separate two or more sources in the same parenthetic citation using a semicolon. Works by the same author or authors should be identified by their publication dates only; add an alphabetical identifier (*a, b, c*) to distinguish works by the same author or authors published in the same year. The page numbers can be included after a comma in entries with multiple sources:

(Crane and Lessing 2001; Stuart and King 2002)

(Jessup 2000a, 2000b)

(Harrison and Waters 2000, 92-97; Cruz and Mitchell 2002)

Notes

A separate section labeled Notes can follow the text of the paper to explain or amplify points made within it. Number each note consecutively to correspond to a superscripted number (one or two types sizes smaller than text type) in the text. In the Notes section, however, the note number should be typed in normal-size type and aligned with the rest of the text:

Citation in text	Russell's objection to Descartes[1] was based on his dislike of ambiguity.
Entry in Notes section	1. Russell describes his objections in his *Autobiography*, 221-24.

References

The entries for a *Chicago*-style References section are similar in format to those for an APA-style list. One fairly important difference, however, is how authors' first names are cited: While APA style lists authors' first names by their initials only (and their middle initials, too, if available), *Chicago* style prefers that authors be listed by their first names in full, with or without middle initials (although using initials for both names is also acceptable in *Chicago* style):

Maccay, Robert L. 2001. *Mind and Mind-Games: New Turns in Philosophy*. New York: Burton.

or

Maccay, R. L. 2001. *Mind and Mind-Games: New Turns in Philosophy*. New York: Burton.

Figure 13.3 shows a sample *Chicago*-style References page. Use this example as a model for listing various kinds of works in a research paper

20

References

Book with 2 authors Butler, David, and Francis Mall. 1998. *Arbitration in South Africa: Law and Practice.* New York: Harbor.

Cavetts, Marsha. When times were good. In *Best stories for 1997,* eds. Kelly R. Monroe and Francis Nguyen, 119-25. Boston: Houghton. **Work included in another work**

Book with single author Doll, Michael L. 1998. *War, but Never Peace.* Chicago: University of Chicago Press.

Haverstock, Nathan A. 1993. *Cuba in Pictures.* New York: Lerner. **Multiple works by same author**

- - -. *Fifty Years at the Front: The Life of War Correspondent Frederick Palmer.* New York: Lerner.

Unsigned journal article Iraq and the modern world. 1998. *Journal of History and Ideas* 4: 110-115.

Mustajuk, Marru, ed. 1993. *Law and Poverty in the United States.* Vol. 2. New York: Greyley. **Volume of book**

Journal article with 3 authors Piner, Gary, David Ferr, and Dina Sanjet. 1997. Civil rights for immigrants. *Popular Culture* 56: 43-49.

Possack, Margo. 1998. *Teaching the History of Other Lands and Cultures.* (Alabama State Department of Education, September 1997), Dialog, ERIC, ED 18253. **Online source**

U.S. House of Representatives. 1997. Committee on Ways and Means. *1997 Greenbook: Background Material and Data on Programs Receiving Federal Funding.* Washington, DC: GPO. **Government document**

Book with more than 3 editors Walsh, Peter E., et al., eds. 1998. *The Structure of a Federal System.* Princeton: Princeton University Press.

Wo, Joyce, and Robert Edwards, eds. 1997. *Holdouts for Peace.* New York: Banner. **Book with 2 editors**

FIGURE 13.3   Sample References page: *Chicago* author-date style

written according to the author-date documentation standards of *The Chicago Manual of Style*. (See Chapter 16 in *The Chicago Manual* for more information on these standards.)

Discipline Style Manuals

As discussed earlier in this chapter, documentation practices between and among discipline journals vary greatly. The most comprehensive guide is *The Chicago Manual of Style* (14th ed.); however, as previously noted, it is written more for professional writers and editors than for students working on course papers. The style manuals in the following list recommend the basic documentation forms for their respective disciplines. If you need more information than is provided in this text about a particular discipline or journal documentation style, consult one of these sources:

Biological Sciences
Council of Biology Editors. *Scientific Style and Format: The CBE Manual for Authors, Editors, and Publishers.* 6th ed. Bethesda, MD: Council of Biology Editors, 1994.

Chemistry
Dodd, Janet S., ed. *The ACS Style Guide.* 2nd ed. Washington, DC: American Chemical Society, 1998.

Geology
United States Geological Survey. *Suggestions for Authors of Reports of the United States Geological Survey.* 6th ed. Washington, DC: GPO, 1990.

Linguistics
Linguistics Society of America. *LSA Bulletin* Dec. issue, annually.

Literature and Languages
Gibaldi, Joseph. *MLA Handbook for Writers of Research Papers.* 6th ed. New York: Modern Language Association of America, 2003.
MLA Style Manual and Guide to Scholarly Publishing. 2nd ed. New York: Modern Language Association of America, 1998.

Mathematics
American Mathematical Society. *The AMS Author Handbook.* Providence, RI: American Mathematical Society, 1994.

Medical Sciences
American Medical Association. *American Medical Association Manual of Style: A Guide for Authors And Editors.* 9th ed. Baltimore: Lippincott, 1997.

Physics
American Institute of Physics. *AIP Style Manual.* 5th ed. New York:
American Institute of Physics, 1995.

Political Science
American Political Science Association. *Style Manual for Political Science.* Rev. ed. Washington: American Political Science Association, 1993.

WORKING WITH OTHERS

The complex documentation styles for the various disciplines discussed in this chapter require close attention to details of form, punctuation, and spacing. Review the Notes and References pages of your draft with another person to see that you have handled such details correctly. A close review of the paper's documentation now will help you avoid errors and omissions when you prepare the final copy.

- Begin by asking a classmate or friend to review your paper's author-date or number-system citations for accuracy and correct form. Next, read the notes and the works named in them aloud while your classmate checks to make sure each work named is also included in the References list.

- Point out any unusual or complicated entries included in the References page(s). Ask your reader to verify the form and punctuation for entries such as multiple authors or editors, works included in volumes, and articles in journals. Check such entries together to make sure they appear in correct form.

- Compare your reader's References list with your own. Note any differences in the way you each have listed similar kinds of sources, and discuss reasons for the differences. Make changes as necessary.

- Ask your reader to review the References list for omissions or unwanted inclusions of underlining or italics, quotation marks, colons, or periods. Check to see that you have spaced correctly between volume and issue numbers. Also review any special formats required by your instructor or discipline.

CHAPTER 14

Preparing the Final Manuscript

The thoughtful work you have done researching and writing the completed draft of your paper should continue through preparation of the final manuscript. Plan time for production—including revising, editing, typing, and proofreading—of the final copy well in advance of the paper's due date. Your instructor undoubtedly views your taking responsibility for matters of correct formatting and technical details as an important part of the research paper assignment. Careful preparation of the manuscript will enhance its contents and ensure his or her appreciation of your efforts.

Reviewing and Strengthening the Final Draft

Like most writers, you have undoubtedly made changes, additions, and deletions throughout developing several drafts of the research paper. Having now composed a final version, you should carefully review the draft before typing or printing a final copy. As you review, be prepared to (1) *revise* the paper as needed for overall focus and organization; (2) *edit* for style and correctness; and (3) *proofread* for omissions and other small errors.

Revising

Revise by making any necessary changes to the whole paper, taking into account such broad qualities as completeness, organization, unity, and purpose. Expect to add or delete content, but do not interpret *revising* to mean *rewriting* the paper. Your goal in revising is to assess the general flow of ideas and to rearrange content for more effectiveness.

**THINKING CRITICALLY
ABOUT YOUR FINAL MANUSCRIPT**

Particularly with a project as large in scope as a research paper, student writers—having concluded the complicated process of gathering and organizing sources, creating several drafts, and inserting citations along with a Works Cited page—may understandably feel ready to "put the baby to bed." Because of the complexity of the process, however, it is easy for writers, while drafting, to overlook details that would not have escaped their attention when working on a shorter paper.

In mapping your schedule for completing a research paper, be sure to allow some time—a day or two, at least—between your completion of a "final" draft and the date the paper is due. Most writers find they need to get away from the draft for a while in order to approach it again with a fresh eye. In this final stage of the research and writing process, you need to consider your work with as much critical detachment as possible. Read over your draft several times, first evaluating larger content issues of development and support, then considering the unity and coherence of individual paragraphs, and later looking at individual sentences for effectiveness and grammatical correctness. Finally, proofread carefully for matters of format, punctuation, spelling, and so forth; seemingly minor errors can seriously undermine the authority of your work.

How to Revise

Begin by carefully reading the draft several times to determine if the content flows smoothly and, on the whole, presents a complete discussion. Pay particular attention to and note any areas that appear underdeveloped, out of place, or irrelevant (see following). Mark changes right on the draft itself (see Figure 14.1, p. 347). If you wrote the draft of your paper on a typewriter, use scissors and tape to rearrange sections to achieve the best order for the content. If you wrote the draft on a computer, use its word-processing functions to add content and move or delete whole sections of text as needed. But before making these changes on the computer, mark them on a printed copy to provide a record of your changes. (Some word processing programs can track changes and multiple revisions to a document.) Also make a backup copy of your paper on computer following each work session. It is a good idea to keep a master of the paper on your hard drive and a backup on a disk.

What to Revise

As you review the draft for revision, follow these suggestions:

1. Make sure the paper's content is unified around a clearly stated main idea. The content of Steve Hanner's paper in Appendix A, for example, develops and supports this thesis:

EQ does matter more but in different ways than just rivaling intellect as a measure of ability.

Look for content in your draft that strays from the research topic or is not clearly related to the paper's thesis. You may need to change inappropriate content or, if it is a significant amount, revise the thesis statement to include it.

2. Identify the paper's introduction, body, and conclusion. Does the introduction state a thesis and introduce the paper's topic effectively? Do paragraphs in the body of the paper illustrate and support the thesis? Study the conclusion of the paper to be certain that it clearly reasserts your position and has developed logically from the rest of the paper.

3. If you made an outline of the paper during the planning stage, compare the outline with the final draft. Note any differences in content and organization, and determine whether they are appropriate.

4. Consider the flow of content in the paper to determine whether ideas proceed in a logical fashion. Does the content develop and support the paper's thesis? Look for recognizable patterns of development, such as cause-and-effect, comparison-and-contrast, and chronological order. Are these patterns clear and handled effectively? If the content does not follow any of these patterns, should it be revised to do so?

5. Decide whether the discussion is complete. Do any significant ideas, arguments, supporting examples, or issues seem to be missing? Does the paper answer your original research question? Make any changes or additions necessary to ensure that the paper's discussion is complete.

6. Determine whether your paper has achieved an argumentative or informative purpose (see Chapter 3). Would any changes in content or wording of the thesis accomplish your purpose more effectively?

Editing

Editing focuses upon details that influence the quality of a paper's content and expression. As in revising, the object here is not to rewrite the paper (though some additional writing may be called for). Rather, the goal is to strengthen the paper's argument by sharpening expression and bolstering supporting evidence and documentation.

How to Edit

Work directly on the draft copy with a pen or pencil to add, delete, or modify the content and writing. Keep a dictionary at hand to check spelling. Consult a handbook as necessary for matters of grammar, punctuation, and style. If you write on a computer, use the "spellcheck" and "search" functions to identify errors for editing. Depending on the capabilities of your software, you may be able to check points of style and grammar, as well. In most cases, however, careful reading of the printed draft, with pen or pencil in hand, will produce the best results as well as a permanent record of the changes made.

Edit with an eye to improving the text, rather than recreating it, but do not hesitate to eliminate weaknesses or outright errors. Figure 14.1 (p. 347) demonstrates common techniques as well as the thoroughness that may be required for effective editing.

What to Edit

As Figure 14.1 shows, editing occurs at the paragraph and sentence levels to correct spelling, grammar, and punctuation errors and to strengthen the paper's thesis support and documentation. In general, edit the paper with close attention to these and the following matters of style and correctness:

1. Edit the paper for redundant, repetitious, or ineffective word choices:

Wordy	Several of the earliest and first settlers in the area made immediate friends with the Apaches.
Edited	Several early settlers made friends with the Apaches.
Vague	Some crimes are punished by very long sentences in prison.
Edited	Capital crimes such as murder and kidnapping are punishable by life imprisonment or death.

2. Strengthen weak or faulty sentences. Reduce any that are too long to be effective by eliminating unnecessary words, clauses, and phrases:

Too long	It is people with AIDS who are demanding more and more access to new treatments.
Edited	People with AIDS are demanding increased access to new treatments.

3. Correct sentences that are incomplete or incorrectly punctuated:

Sentence fragment (bold)	Global warming will have varying effects. **Because of the changes it will create in drought and rainfall frequencies.**
Revised	Global warming will have varying effects because of the changes it will create in drought and rainfall frequencies.
Comma splice	Most of these ruins have been looted, even the villagers have helped themselves to saleable antiques.

in 1935.

wrote Ernest Hemingway ~~once wrote that~~ "All modern literature

comes from one book by Mark Twain called <u>Huckleberry Finn</u>," He

~~claimed,~~ *most* "It's the best book we've had" (22). Although ~~it appears~~

~~that a large number of~~ literary critics and scholars, as well as the

general ~~reading public, would agree with Hemingway's~~ *assessment,* ~~statement;~~

Mark Twain's <u>The Adventures of Huckleberry Finn</u> is also one of

the most ~~debated and~~ controversial works on American

bookshelves.~~today.~~

FIGURE 14.1   An example of editing

Revised   Most of these ruins have been looted. Even the villagers
           have helped themselves to saleable antiques.

4. Eliminate discriminatory language. Stereotyping individuals by race or ethnicity, gender, age, exceptionality, or any other characteristic is as inappropriate in a research paper as it is in life. Avoid using language that perpetuates an inaccurate and unfair perception of any person or group of people. Writing a sentence such as *An airline pilot has to be a mechanic as well as a navigator if **he** wants to survive,* for example, implies that only men are airline pilots. Eliminate gender bias by rewriting such sentences:

Make pronoun   An airline pilot has to be a mechanic as well as a
unnecessary   navigator to survive.

Make subject and   Airline pilots have to be mechanics as well as
pronoun plural   navigators if they want to survive.

5. Examine each paragraph for a topic sentence or unifying idea that supports or develops the thesis statement. Check to see that the paragraph includes enough examples, reasons, or facts to support the topic sentence. Make sure that you have integrated your sources into the text in an effective way and that you present ideas of your own in each paragraph.

Technical Editing Guidelines

The following guidelines apply to research papers using the documentation style of the Modern Language Association (MLA). Certain subjects or the requirements of an individual instructor may call for variation. For conventions of manuscript preparation for APA-, CBE-, or *Chicago*-style papers, consult publication guidelines for the particular discipline (e.g., physics, history, or chemistry). (See the list of style manuals in Chapter 13.)

ABBREVIATIONS

The majority of abbreviations should appear in the paper's documentation to save space and add precision to the entries. In the paper's text, generally spell out all words except those commonly abbreviated between parentheses, such as *e.g.* ("for example") and *cf.* ("compare"). Otherwise, use abbreviations for major, recurrent terms in the paper only after first giving the full names in the text, with the abbreviations following in parentheses:

> Magnetic resonance imaging (MRI) offers several improvements over x-ray diagnosis. With MRI, for example, doctors can distinguish blood vessels from malignant tissue.

> One organization, Mothers Against Drunk Driving (MADD), has been particularly vocal on this issue. According to MADD, . . .

As these examples demonstrate, many abbreviations are written today without periods or other punctuation marks. Use periods or spaces in an abbreviation as common use suggests (in your sources, for example).

Avoid creating your own abbreviation for any term in the paper. When necessary and useful, employ the standard abbreviations listed here for parenthetical comments in the text, for Works Cited (or References) entries, and for content notes, endnotes, or footnotes. Note the punctuation and use indicated for each abbreviation listed.

1. COMMON ABBREVIATIONS AND REFERENCE WORDS

Use the following abbreviations throughout your paper's documentation (Works Cited, References, and any notes), but employ them only parenthetically in the text:

abbr.	abbreviated, abbreviation
abr.	abridged, abridgment
acad.	academy
adapt.	adapted by, adaptation
anon.	anonymous
app.	appendix
assoc.	association
b.	born
bibliog.	bibliography, bibliographer, bibliographic(al)
biog.	biography
bk.	book

bull.	bulletin
c.	*circa* ("about": use with approximate dates: *c. 1492*)
cf.	*confer* ("compare")
ch.	chapter
col.	column
coll.	college
comp.	compiled by, compiler
cond.	conducted by, conductor
Cong.	Congress
Cong. Rec.	*Congressional Record*
Const.	Constitution
(contd.)	continued
d.	died
DA, DAI	*Dissertation Abstracts, Dissertation Abstracts International*
dir.	directed by, director
ed.	edited by, editor
e.g.,	*exempli gratia* ("for example": see also the section on this term later in the chapter)
et al.	*et alli* ("and others")
etc.	*et cetera* ("and so forth")
facsim.	facsimile
fig.	figure
fwd	foreword, foreword by
GPO	Government Printing Office
HR	House of Representatives
i.e.,	*id est* ("that is")
illus.	illustrated by, illustration, illustrator
intl.	international
introd.	introduction
jour.	journal
LC	Library of Congress
ms., mss.	manuscript, manuscripts
narr.	narrated by, narrator
n.d.	no date of publication
n.p.	no place of publication; no publisher
n. pag.	no pagination
p., pp.	page, pages
perf.	performed by, performer
pref.	preface by, preface
prod.	produced by, producer
pseud.	pseudonym
pt.	part
rept.	reported by, report
rev.	revised by, revision, reviewed by, review
rpt.	reprint

sec.	section
sess.	session
sic	"thus, so" (see the discussion of this term later in the chapter)
trans.	translated by, translator, translation
ts., tss.	typescript, typescripts
UP	University Press
vol., vols.	volume, volumes

2. ABBREVIATIONS OF TIME

Spell out the names of all months in the text. Except for *May, June,* and *July,* abbreviate the names of months in notes and documentation. Abbreviate some standard time designations—*a.m., p.m., BC, AD*—but spell out most other units of time—*minutes, hours, years*—when they appear in the text.

AD	*anno Domini* ("in the year of the Lord": used before year date: *AD 1100*)
Apr.	April
Aug.	August
BC	Before Christ (used after year date: *65 BC*)
BCE	Before the Common Era
cent., cents.	century, centuries
Dec.	December
Feb.	February
hr., hrs.	hour, hours
Jan.	January
Mar.	March
min., mins.	minute, minutes
mo., mos.	month, months
Nov.	November
Oct.	October
sec., secs.	second, seconds
Sept.	September
wk., wks.	week, weeks
yr., yrs.	year, years

3. ABBREVIATIONS OF GEOGRAPHICAL LOCATIONS

Except for common abbreviations of some countries (*USA, UK*), spell out the names of cities, states, territories, provinces, and countries when they appear in the text. Abbreviate such locations in the paper's documentation, however. Designate U.S. states by their ZIP code abbreviations: *AZ* for *Arizona; MA* for *Massachusetts; OH* for *Ohio.* A list of common abbreviations for other geographical locations follows. For places not given here, follow the practice of your research sources, an unabridged dictionary, or a standard atlas:

Aus.	Austria
Austral.	Australia
BC	British Columbia
Braz.	Brazil
Can.	Canada
DC	District of Columbia
Eng.	England
Gt. Brit.	Great Britain
Jap.	Japan
Isr.	Israel
Leb.	Lebanon
Mex.	Mexico
Neth.	Netherlands
Norw.	Norway
NZ	New Zealand
Pan.	Panama
PR	Puerto Rico
S. Afr.	South Africa
Sp.	Spain
Swed.	Sweden
Switz.	Switzerland
UK	United Kingdom
US, USA	United States of America

4. ABBREVIATIONS OF BOOKS OF THE BIBLE

Follow a quotation from a book of the Bible with a parenthetical citation in the text; separate chapter and verse by a period with no space after it: *Acts 16.6* or *2 Kings 4.27.* Except for most one-syllable titles (*Job, Luke, Mark*), abbreviate books of the Bible when citing them in the text: *Eccles. 6.3, Matt. 11.12.* Do not underline or italicize the title of the Bible or place quotation marks around the names of Biblical books (regardless of whether they are abbreviated).

A list of standard abbreviations for books of the Bible follows. For those not given here, devise unambiguous forms of your own, or consult the list of abbreviations found at the fronts of most editions of the Bible:

Old Testament (OT)

1 and 2 Chron.	1 and 2 Chronicles
1 and 2 Sam.	1 and 2 Samuel
Dan.	Daniel
Deut.	Deuteronomy
Eccles.	Ecclesiastes
Esth.	Esther
Exod.	Exodus
Gen.	Genesis
Jer.	Jeremiah

Judg.	Judges
Lev.	Leviticus
Num.	Numbers
Prov.	Proverbs
Ps.	Psalms
Song Sol. (also Cant.)	Song of Solomon (also Canticles)

New Testament (NT)

1 and 2 Cor.	1 and 2 Corinthians
1 and 2 Thess.	1 and 2 Thessalonians
1 and 2 Tim.	1 and 2 Timothy
1 and 2 Pet.	1 and 2 Peter
Eph.	Ephesians
Jas.	James
Gal.	Galatians
Heb.	Hebrews
Matt.	Matthew
Phil.	Philippians
Rev. (also Apoc.)	Revelation (also Apocalypse)
Rom.	Romans

5. ABBREVIATIONS OF WORKS OF LITERATURE

Spell out the names of all sources, including literary works, listed in the Works Cited or References page(s) of your paper. You may abbreviate a work occurring frequently in the text or notes after first using the full title in the text, followed by the abbreviation in parentheses:

<u>The Merchant of Venice (MV)</u> is one of the earliest of Shakespeare's attempts to mix comedy and tragedy.

For well-known authors and their works, use standard abbreviations, such as those in the following list for Shakespeare. For other Shakespearean works or works by other authors, follow the practices of your research sources or devise easily understood abbreviations of your own: *GW* for *The Grapes of Wrath; SL* for *The Scarlet Letter; MD* for *Moby Dick,* and so forth:

Shakespeare

Ant.	*Antony and Cleopatra*
AWW	*All's Well That Ends Well*
F1	First Folio ed. (1623)
F2	Second Folio ed. (1632)
Ham.	*Hamlet*
1H4	*Henry IV, Part 1*
2H4	*Henry IV, Part 2*
H5	*Henry V*
JC	*Julius Caesar*
Lr.	*King Lear*

Mac.	*Macbeth*
MM	*Measure for Measure*
MND	*A Midsummer Night's Dream*
MV	*The Merchant of Venice*
Oth.	*Othello*
R2	*Richard II*
R3	*Richard III*
Rom.	*Romeo and Juliet*
Shr.	*The Taming of the Shrew*
TGV	*The Two Gentlemen of Verona*
TN	*Twelfth Night*
Tro.	*Troilus and Cressida*
WT	*The Winter's Tale*

ABSTRACTS

An abstract is not usually part of an MLA-style paper. Research papers in the sciences and social sciences, however, generally include abstracts as part of the frontmatter (i.e., the preliminary pages before the actual text, including the title page, outline, etc.). (If your instructor requires an abstract with your paper, see the sections on Abstracts and Headings in Chapter 13.)

ACCENT MARKS

For both English and foreign words, include all accent marks necessary for accurate quotation and correct spelling (e.g., *résumé, mañana, tête-à-tête*). If your typewriter or computer does not have the necessary accent marks, print them in neatly by hand.

AMPERSANDS

Do not use the ampersand symbol (&) to replace the word *and* in the text or in MLA style citations. (Note that the ampersand is correct in APA-style papers only to cite authors parenthetically in the text [*Harriston & Brown, 2002*] and References [*Harriston, R. M., & Brown, L. L.*].)

ANNOTATED BIBLIOGRAPHIES

If your instructor requires, you may annotate the paper's list of references by providing two or three descriptive sentences at the end of each entry in the Works Cited section. Characterize the work's subject, purpose, strengths or weaknesses, and general usefulness to the reader:

Trenton, Patricia, and Patrick T. Houlihan. <u>Native Americans: Five Centuries of Changing Images</u>. 2nd ed. New York: Harry N. Abrams, 1998. This work compares 500 years of historical information and artifacts with drawings, paintings, and photographs depicting Native Americans and their cultures.

The historical information provided is useful, but the book provides no art revealing how Native Americans have viewed themselves.

"BARS" (/)

Use a *virgule,* commonly known as a *bar* or *slash,* to indicate division or separation. When quoting up to three lines of poetry in the text, use this mark (with a space on each side) to show the original beginnings and endings of lines:

William Blake's poem "A Poison Tree" asserts the value of dealing openly with one's feelings: "I told my wrath. / My wrath did end," says the speaker.

Typed without a space before or after, the bar is also used to separate parts of a date expressed in digits (*3/12/02*) and the elements of fractions (*1/2, 1/3*). Avoid using expressions such as *and/or* and *his/her,* which require the bar and are generally too informal for precise writing.

CAPITALIZATION OF TITLES

For papers in MLA form, capitalize the main title and subtitle of all publications such as books, magazines, journals, and newspapers as well as the titles of works published in them (stories, essays, articles, chapters, appendixes, most poems, and plays). Capitalize the first and last words in such titles along with all other words except prepositions, conjunctions, articles, and the word *to* before verbs.

Follow these general examples even if a title's original capitalization differs (as when letters are variously capitalized for visual effect):

Books	A Tale of Two Cities
	Zen and the Art of Motorcycle Maintenance: An Inquiry into Values
Short stories	"A Rose for Emily"
	"I Stand Here Ironing"
Periodicals	Modern Fiction Studies
	New York Daily News
	TV Guide Magazine
Articles and essays	"Clinton Will Try Again"
	"It Is Time to Stop Playing Indians"
	"Motherhood: Who Needs It?"
Short poems	"Theme for English B"
	"The Fish"

Plays   A Midsummer Night's Dream
                           Death of a Salesman

When referring in the text to a poem without a title, use the first line as the name of the work. Do not alter the punctuation or capitalization of the original:

> The imagery of Dylan Thomas's poem "Do not go gentle into that good night" suggests . . .

> The last stanza of Dickinson's "I died for Beauty—but was scarce" compares . . .

The paper's reference list should cite the anthology or other work in which an untitled poem (usually short) appears.

Ordinarily, do not capitalize the initial article in the name of a periodical (the *New York Times*). Nor should you write a title in all capital letters—except for the names of some journals when their titles include capitalized initials (e.g., *PMLA: Publications of the Modern Language Association of America*).

For disciplines following other than MLA style, see the examples in Chapter 13.

CONTENT NOTES

See the discussion and examples of content notes in Chapter 11.

COPYRIGHT LAW

Federal copyright law protects most published works and even unpublished manuscripts from commercial use or reproduction without permission. For the purpose of criticism or research, however, you may reproduce certain amounts of published or unpublished material without permission from the author or copyright holder. The amount you reproduce without permission cannot exceed *fair use*—that is, an amount considered reasonable for your purposes and in fair proportion to the copyrighted work as a whole. As long as your use is noncommercial and in an amount not exceeding fair use, you may copy or quote substantial amounts or even all of a chapter, a short story, article, short essay, short poem, or any drawing or illustration. Naturally, you must give credit in the paper to the source of any ideas or language you include in the text.

DATE OF PUBLICATION

Include the date of publication for each work listed in the Works Cited section of the paper. Dates for articles in magazines or journals usually appear on the cover or table of contents page. Locate the publication date of a book on the title page or the copyright page following it. If no printing date is given, use the latest copyright date. If there is no publication or copyright date given, use the abbreviation *n.d.* ("no date"), as in *New York: Atlas, n.d.*

Whenever possible, get the publication date from the work itself. If you must learn the date of publication from another source, enclose the date in brackets: *[2002]*. Place a *c*. (for *circa*, "around") before a date in brackets if you can only approximate the date: *[c. 2002]*. Follow the date with a question mark if you are not certain of its accuracy: *[2002?]*. (See Chapter 11 for the formats for listing publication dates of revised or reprinted material as well as volumes published over a period of years.)

DATES

Use the same form throughout the paper for dates—that is, writing either *18 April 2002* or *April 18, 2002*. When the month and day precede the year, separate the day and year with a comma, as in the preceding example. An additional comma also follows the year if the date appears other than at the end of the sentence:

On May 1, 2002, Congress debated the bill again.

When the day is not included in the date, do not put a comma between the month and year: *July 2002*. To list daily, weekly, or monthly periodicals in the Works Cited section, abbreviate all months except *May, June,* and *July,* as in *4 Oct. 2002.*

Place the abbreviation *BC* after the year, but use *AD* before it: *450 BC,* but *AD 1100.* Write the names of centuries in lowercase letters—*the nineteenth century*—making certain to hyphenate them when used as adjectives—*nineteenth-century beliefs, seventeenth- and eighteenth-century poetry.* Write the names of decades without capitalization—*the sixties*—or use numbers *1960s* or *the '60s.* Indicate full dates for a range of years from AD 1000 o unless they are in the same century: *1794–1802* or *2001–02.* Give the full for ranges of years beginning before AD 1: *349–343 BC* or *136 BC–AD 1*

DEFINITIONS

Define terms that are central to your topic and may not be familiar to your audience. At the same time, also avoid defining terms that may be unfamiliar only to you. Be consistent in the form for definitions.

Underline or italicize a word you are discussing as a word:

A <u>periodical</u>, as intended here, is a regularly published magazine, journal, or newspaper.

Set off a technical term the first time you mention it with a definition by underlining or italicizing it; thereafter, use the term without an underline or italics:

An <u>iconic image</u> is a visual pattern that persists in the viewer's experience after the image source terminates. The remarkable completeness of an iconic image suggests . . .

NOTE: In this text, example terms are underlined, rather than italicized, in keeping with the recommended style of the Modern Language Association (MLA). Although either form is acceptable, students wishing to use italics should check first with their instructors and follow their preferences. Regardless of whether you are writing on computer or typewriter, the principles behind highlighting terms are the same as those outlined here. (See also the section on Underlining, later in this chapter.)

If you are translating a foreign term, underline or italicize it, and then define it in one of two ways:

1. If the definition follows immediately after the term, with no intervening words or punctuation, put the definition between single quotation marks:

Gorbachev's defense of the new <u>glasnost</u> 'openness' gained wide support in the West.

2. If the definition is separated from the term by words or punctuation, put the definition between double quotation marks:

Gorbachev's defense of the new <u>glasnost</u>, or "openness," gained wide support in the West.

Use accurate terminology as required by your subject, but avoid overloading the paper with terms needing definition. In many instances, the substitution of a more common term or phrase may be just as effective. For example, use *ordered* rather than *enjoined* when describing instructions given by a court of law.

Also see the discussion about defining terms in Chapter 10.

e.g.

Use this abbreviation for *exempli gratia* ("for example") without capital letters and usually in parentheses to introduce an example (*e.g., as shown here*). Use a period after each letter, and do not space between the first period and the second letter. The term is set off by commas, *e.g.,* as here, or set within parentheses. Do not confuse *e.g.* with the abbreviation *i.e.,* which means "that is."

ENDNOTES/FOOTNOTES

As discussed in Chapter 13, the use of endnotes or footnotes for *documentation* is recommended for only a limited selection of topics and papers (i.e., those requiring numerous or extended explanations or definitions apart from the regular text and written for specific, knowledgeable audiences). The use of *content* notes, however, is a separate matter (see Chapter 11). That is, you may use footnotes or endnotes for explanatory information yet cite sources using another form of documentation (e.g., author-date or number-system). In this case, you will have both Notes and Works Cited pages at the end of your paper. Always check with your instructor regarding the use of notes for either content or documentation purposes.

et al.

When referring to a single work by three or more authors, cite all of their names or that of the first author followed by *et al.* ("and others"). An intext citation would follow either of these formats: *(Cage, Andre, and Rothenberg 163)* or *(Cage et al. 163).* In the Works Cited section, either of the following formats would be correct:

Cage, John, Michael Andre, and Erika Rothenberg. <u>Poet's</u>

<u>Encyclopedia</u>. New York: Unmuzzled Ox, 1997.

Cage, John, et al. <u>Poet's Encyclopedia</u>. New York: Unmuzzled Ox, 1997.

Although either format—citing all authors' names or using *et al.*—is correct according to MLA style, you should select one and use it consistently in your paper. (Papers written according to CBE style should use the phrase *and others* instead of *et al.*)

Note that *al.* is an abbreviation and must be followed by a period. For parenthetic intext citations, no punctuation appears between the author's name and *et al.* Do add a comma before *et al.* in a Works Cited entry, however. (See also Chapter 13 for examples and use of *et al.* in other documentation styles.)

FOREIGN LANGUAGES

Indicate foreign words or phrases with underlining or italics in the text:

Instead of the <u>Zeitgeist</u>, he discovered only <u>la belle dame sans merci</u>.

For a work published in a foreign language, follow the capitalization, spelling, and punctuation exactly as given in the original. (See also the section on Accent Marks, earlier in this chapter.) If necessary for your particular audience, provide a translation of the title in brackets, along with the place of publication:

Sand, George. <u>La Petite Fadette</u> [Little Fadette]. Paris: Garnier-Flammarion, 1998.

ITALICS

To avoid misreading, MLA guidelines recommend underlining as preferable to italics for indicating titles and highlighting terms (but allow either, in accordance with instructors' preferences). Consult with your instructor before deciding to use italics, and follow his or her preference. (See Definitions, earlier in this chapter, and Underlining, later.)

NAMES OF PERSONS

State a person's full name the first time you use it in text—*Ernest Hemingway, Joyce Carol Oates, Percy Bysshe Shelley*. Thereafter, refer to the individual by last name only—*Hemingway, Oates, Shelley*—unless your paper mentions more than one person with the same last name, such as *Robert Browning* and *Elizabeth Barrett Browning*. Famous individuals may be referred to by their commonly known names, rather than pseudonyms or seldom-used names—*Voltaire* instead of *Francois-Marie Arouet; Mark Twain* rather than *Samuel Clemens; Vergil* instead of *Publius Vergilius Maro*.

Do not use formal titles when referring to authors or other actual persons. Use *Ernest Hemingway* first, and thereafter *Hemingway*, but not *Mr. Ernest Hemingway* or *Mr. Hemingway*. This also holds true for women: *Emily Dickinson*, then *Dickinson*, but not *Miss Dickinson*. Refer to characters in literary works by their fictional names: *Goodman Brown, Huck, Hester, Gatsby*.

NAMES OF PUBLISHERS

Use shortened forms of publishers' names for sources in the Works Cited or References page(s) and in content notes, footnotes, and endnotes. In general, shorten publishers' names by omitting the following elements:

- Articles (*a, an, the*)
- First names (*Abrams* for *Harry N. Abrams, Inc.*)
- All but the first name listed (*Allyn* for *Allyn and Bacon*)
- Business abbreviations (*Inc., Co., Ltd.*)
- Descriptors (*Publishers, Library, Press, & Sons*)

For a university press, abbreviate *University* as *U* and *Press* as *P*. Do not use a period after either letter.

The following list provides examples of shortened names for many major publishers. For those not listed, devise abbreviated forms of your own following the guidelines and examples given here:

Shortened Form	Full Publisher's Name
Abrams	Harry N. Abrams, Inc.
Allyn	Allyn and Bacon
Appleton	Appleton-Century-Crofts
Barnes	Barnes and Noble Books
Bowker	R. R. Bowker Co.
Cambridge UP	Cambridge University Press
Columbia UP	Columbia University Press
Dell	Dell Publishing Co., Inc.
Dutton	E. P. Dutton, Inc.
Feminist	The Feminist Press at the City University of New York
Harcourt	Harcourt Brace Jovanovich, Inc.

Harvard UP	Harvard University Press
Harvard Law Rev. Assoc.	Harvard Law Review Association
Houghton	Houghton Mifflin Co.
Harper	Harper and Row Publishers, Inc.
Holt	Holt, Rinehart and Winston, Inc.
Macmillan	Macmillan Publishing Co., Inc.
McGraw	McGraw-Hill, Inc.
NEA	The National Education Association
Norton	W. W. Norton and Co., Inc.
Oxford UP	Oxford University Press, Inc.
Prentice	Prentice-Hall, Inc.
Putnam's	G. P. Putnam's Sons
Simon	Simon and Schuster, Inc.
UMI	University Microfilms International
U of Chicago P	University of Chicago Press
UP of Florida	The University Presses of Florida

NUMBERS

In most cases and except as described here, use arabic numerals (*1, 2, 3*) rather than roman (*iv, v, vi*) for all numbers in your paper. The following general guidelines apply to most uses of numbers in an MLA-style research paper:

1. Write as words the numbers from *one* to *nine: six people, three restrictions.* Always write any number beginning a sentence as a word: *Nineteen hundred votes* . . . or *Three constellations* . . .

Use figures to express the numbers *10* and higher: *nearly 300 species, 88 pounds.* Also use figures to express any number requiring more than two words to write: *2¹/3, 3.477.*

2. To indicate count, place commas between the third and fourth digits from the right or, for larger numbers, between the sixth and seventh, and so on: *4,000; 44,000; 81,723,000.* Do not use commas with figures that indicate line or page numbers, four-digit year numbers, or addresses, including ZIP codes: *lines 1037–67, page 1201, before 1990* (but *50,000 BC*), *25322 Shadywood Rd., Atlanta, GA 30304.*

3. Express related numbers in the same style (i.e., digits or words): *four of the thirty-two students, fewer than 100 of the 3,000 men and women.* To indicate a range of numbers, give the second number in full when it is *99* or lower: *5–10, 12–21, 75–86.* For a number with three digits or more, give only the last two figures unless the third is needed for clarity: *91–102, 221–31, 998–1007, 5468–71, 5588–600.* Use a combination of words and figures for very large numbers: *2.5 million, 150 billion.*

4. When typing numbers, do not substitute the small letter *l* ("el") for the figure *1* ("one") unless your typewriter lacks the number key. Also, do not type the capital letter *O* for the figure *0* ("zero").

(See related sections for guidelines on uses of numbers: Dates; Percentages and Money; and Roman Numerals.)

PERCENTAGES AND MONEY

If your discussion includes only a few figures and each can be written in no more than two words, spell out numbers to indicate percentages and amounts of money: *six percent, one hundred percent, thirty-five cents, twelve dollars.* It is also acceptable to use numerals and the appropriate symbols to express such amounts: *4%, 85%, 18¢, $45.15, $3,670.* The latter is typical of papers involving many figures, such as those in the applied sciences. (See other guidelines in the section Numbers.)

ROMAN NUMERALS

Use capital roman numerals whenever they are part of established terminology (*a Class III missile*), a name (*Elizabeth I, John Paul II*), or headings in a formal outline (*IV. Major Influences*). Use small roman numerals to cite or to number the pages preceding the regular text of a book or other printed source: *page vii.* Your instructor may also prefer that you use both capital and small roman numerals to designate acts and scenes of plays: *Hamlet, III.ii.* Write inclusive roman numerals in full: *xii–xvi.*

Sic

Use the Latin word *sic* (meaning "thus," "so") to indicate that a quotation is accurate, despite an apparent error in spelling, sense, or logic. Place the term, without quotation marks or underlining/italics, between parentheses whenever it follows a quotation (as when included in your own sentence) or between brackets whenever it must be added in the middle of a quotation:

Following a quotation	Rollins considers "the rascal Huckleberry Fin" [sic] too resistant to authority to be an acceptable role model for children (12).
In the middle of a quotation	Rollins insists that "the rascal Huckleberry Fin [sic] is likely to be a bad example for all children" (12).

Note that *sic* is not accompanied by a correction of the quotation. Changes or corrections of quotations should appear in brackets, without *sic.* (See the discussion of *sic* in Using Quotations in Chapter 10.)

SPELLING

Check the accuracy as well as the consistency of spelling throughout the paper. Give extra attention to unfamiliar or complex terms, names of individuals, and foreign words. If you use a computer program to check spelling, do not overlook the need to proofread the manuscript carefully yourself, as well. The "spellcheck" function may register repeated words but not omitted words, misused homonyms (e.g., *it's* vs. *its*), or misspelled words that are still words (e.g., *form* vs. *from*).

As noted earlier, correct spelling means including accents or other marks for some words, such as those from foreign languages. Put the marks in place by hand if your typewriter or computer printer lacks them (see Accents).

Use a complete, college-level dictionary to check words you are unsure about. If more than one spelling is listed for a word, use the first form given or the one with the most complete definition.

SUPERSCRIPTS

Use superscript numbers—like this[2]—for content notes or documentation using footnotes/endnotes or number-system style. Avoid splintering a sentence with numerous superscript numerals or placing numerals where they interfere with reading the text. As with text citations, place the numeral nearest the material to which it refers. Note how the varying placement of superscript numerals in the following examples might direct a reader to different commentary or sources:

> Several critics[3] have pointed out that Kaplan's earliest work was realistic, a view that Davidson apparently ignored.

> Several critics have pointed out that Kaplan's earliest work was realistic,[3] a view that Davidson apparently ignored.

> Several critics have pointed out that Kaplan's earliest work was realistic, a view that Davidson apparently ignored.[3]

Type superscript numerals a half space above the line. If you are writing on a typewriter, turn the roller slightly to move the paper up; type the numeral, and then return the roller to its original position. If you are using a computer, use the formatting function for typing superscripts.

No punctuation or other marks should accompany superscript numerals. Type the numeral so that it follows all punctuation marks, like this.[2] Exceptions include dashes and parentheses when the superscript refers to material inside parentheses (such as here[4]).

TABLES AND ILLUSTRATIONS

Illustrative material included in your research paper should be genuinely helpful and presented as simply as possible. Use tables and illustrations to summarize, illustrate, simplify, or otherwise clarify the paper's content. Place such material as near the text referring to it as possible or in an appendix at the end of the paper.

1. *Tables:* Arrange information for a table in columns, and use the arabic-numbered label *Table 1* as a title (then *Table 2, Table 3,* and so on). Below

the title, include a caption explaining the subject of the table. Type the caption and the title both flush left and above the table data. Immediately below the table, list the source and below it, any notes. Identify each note by a superscript letter (to distinguish the note from text). Double-space the title, caption, table data, source information, and notes throughout. Figure 14.2 provides a model for most kinds of tables.

2. *Illustrations:* Nontabular materials—such as drawings, graphs, charts, maps, and photographs—are considered illustrations. Label each illustration as *Fig.* (for *Figure*), and assign it an arabic number, as in *Fig. 3*. Number all illustrations consecutively throughout the text. Place the figure label, *along with a caption or title to explain the material,* below the illustration. Below the caption, give the source of the material. Begin all entries flush left, and double-space throughout the text accompanying the illustration. Figure 14.3 shows a plotted-line graph, one of several kinds of illustrations.

Always refer to specific tables and illustrations in the text by their labels: *Figure 2, Table 3, col. 1,* or *Fig. 4.* Sources for illustrations should be cited in the text like those for any other works (see Figures 14.2 and 14 3) as well as fully documented in the Works Cited section of the paper.

TITLES

Other than the exceptions that follow, a title in an MLA-style paper should appear either between quotation marks or underlined/italicized. (See Chapter 13 for various forms for other documentation styles and disci plines.) A general rule is to use quotation marks around the title of a work

Table 1
4th Week Student Enrollment Profile, 1998-2002

Ethnicity	1998	1999	2000	2001	2002
Native American	208	209	220	227	233
Asian	2,220	2,245	2,472	2,860	3,164
Black	340	356	390	397	412
White	11,667	11,120	11,131	11,315	11,461
Hispanic	426	451	479	475	494
Filipino	49	58	61	88	99
Other	238	278	345	222	314
Unknown	2,774	2,338	1,463	1,110	901
Total	17,922	17,055	16,561	16,694	17,078

Source: Census System Files, Westfall Community College.

FIGURE 14.2 A sample table

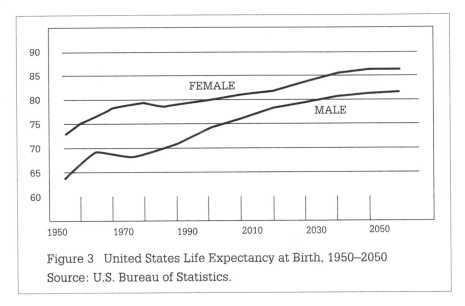

Figure 3   United States Life Expectancy at Birth, 1950–2050
Source: U.S. Bureau of Statistics.

FIGURE 14.3   A sample illustration

not published or produced as a whole, such as a short story ("The Tell-Tale Heart") or an essay ("A Defense of Reason"). Also put quotation marks around the titles of chapters, short poems, unpublished works like dissertations or speeches, and individual episodes of radio or television programs.

The titles of works that are published independently should be underlined or italicized, including those of books (*The Heart of Darkness*), plays (*Hamlet*), and long poems (*The Waste Land*), as well as newspapers, magazines, journals, record albums, ballets, operas, films, and radio or television programs. Also underline or italicize the titles of works of art (Rodin's *The Thinker*) and names of ships, aircraft, and space vehicles (*Challenger*). (See also the section on Underlining, following.)

An underlined or italicized title may include the name of a work that should normally be set in quotation marks: *Twain's "Jumping Frog" and American Humor.* Conversely, a work whose name is underlined or italicized may also be part of a title normally set in quotation marks: "The Sea in Virginia Woolf's *To the Lighthouse*." When a title that is normally set in quotation marks is part of another title in quotation marks, the included title appears within single quotation marks: "Another View of Twain's 'Jumping Frog'." Finally, when one underlined or italicized title includes another, the incorporated title appears without underlining, italicizing, or quotation marks: *Character and Art in Virginia Woolf's* To the Lighthouse.

Do not underline, italicize, or put quotation marks around titles of sacred writings (*the Bible, Genesis, New Testament, Koran, Talmud*) or the names of editions (*Centennial Facsimile Edition, New Revised Edition*), series (*American Poets Series*), societies (*The Thoreau Society*), or academic courses (*philosophy*, or *Philosophy 100*).

UNDERLINING

To avoid misreading, MLA guidelines recommend underlining as preferable to italics for indicating titles and highlighting terms, while APA guidelines recommend italics (but allow either in accordance with instructors' preferences). You should use one or the other exclusively in your paper. Note that the same guidelines (as explained throughout this book) apply both to underlining and italicizing.

When typing your paper, keep in mind that a continuous underline is usually easier to read than a broken one and also faster and more accurate to type. Avoid separate underlining of words and punctuation to show titles. That is, avoid this: A Feast of Words: The Triumph of Edith Wharton.

WORD DIVISION

A word divided or hyphenated at the end of a line can make for ambiguous interpretation and interfere with the reader's concentration on the text. Rather than break up such a word at the end of a line, start a new line and leave the preceding one short. If you choose to hyphenate, consult a dictionary and break words syllabically. If your computer has a "hyphenate" function, use it but do so cautiously, verifying the accuracy of word breaks by checking them in a dictionary.

Producing the Final Manuscript

You may elect to type your paper or produce it using a computer and word-processing program. Whichever method you use, print the paper's contents on one side of the paper only. Follow the guidelines given here to prepare the final copy of the paper.

PAPER

Use standard $8^1/2$- by 11-inch white paper between 16- and 20-pound weight, or thickness. Do not use onionskin or erasable paper, which often smudges. If you must use either of these for typing or printing the final draft of the paper, submit a photocopy of the finished manuscript on plain, uncoated paper.

TYPE STYLE

Use a common, easily readable type size and style such as 10-point (elite) or 12-point (pica) throughout the manuscript. Use roman type; do not use script, bold, or italic (except for the uses of italic discussed). If your computer or typewriter offers a choice of fonts, Times Roman and Palatino are good options.

TYPE QUALITY

If you are using a typewriter to prepare the final draft of your paper, use a fresh black ribbon to ensure the best results. Watch for smudging or fading, and replace the ribbon if the type becomes difficult to read.

If you are writing the paper on computer, output it using a printer with letter-quality capability. In general, a daisywheel, ink jet, or laser printer will produce the most readable and visually impressive manuscript. Replace the printer's ribbon or cartridge (whether ink or toner) as needed to avoid faint or uneven print quality.

MARGINS

A one-inch margin at the top and bottom, as well as on both sides of the text, is standard for MLA-style papers.

SPACING

Except for footnotes, double-space the paper throughout, including the title, outline, indented quotations, captions, notes, appendixes, and Works Cited entries. You need only space once after a concluding punctuation mark unless your instructor prefers that you space twice for more clarity.

INDENTING

Except for single, quoted paragraphs, indent each paragraph of text five spaces from the left margin. Indent quotations of four or more lines ten spaces from the left margin, but do not indent the first sentence of a single indented paragraph (even if it is indented in the original). When quoting two or more paragraphs, however, indent the first line of each paragraph an additional three spaces (a total of thirteen indented spaces; see Chapter 10, Using Quotations).

To type entries in the Works Cited list, begin each flush left, but indent the second and succeeding lines five spaces. (See Chapter 13 for indentation requirements for APA, CBE, and other styles.)

For typing endnotes and footnotes, indent each first line five spaces, beginning with the raised superscript numeral. Type succeeding lines flush left.

PAGE NUMBERS

Except for the title page, number all pages preceding the first page of text consecutively with lowercase roman numerals (*ii, iii, iv,* and so on). Count but do not put a number on the title page, if it appears as a separate page. If the title page is also the first page of text (as for a short paper), number it as page *1.*

Following the preliminary pages numbered with roman numerals (i.e., the frontmatter), begin on the first page of text to number all pages consecutively with arabic numerals (*1, 2, 3,* and so on) throughout the manuscript. Count and put a number on every page, including the first page of text. Place each page number one-half inch down from the top of the paper and one inch in from the right edge.

RUNNING HEADS

If your paper is in MLA style, begin on page *2* to include your last name, followed by a space, before each page number: *Kramer 2.*

MAKING CORRECTIONS

After carefully proofreading the final printed paper, make any necessary corrections or revisions by hand in ink. Place all corrections or additions above the text line, never below it or in the margins. Indicate where inserted words or punctuation marks should go in the line of text with a caret (^).

You should reprint any page on which numerous revisions or corrections interfere with the readability or neat appearance of the paper. The finished paper should be submitted with as few errors and corrections as possible.

ORGANIZING AND BINDING

Organize the main parts of a completed research paper in this order:

1. Title page*
2. Outline*
3. Abstract*
4. Text
5. Content Notes
6. Appendix*
7. Works Cited

Before turning in the finished paper to your instructor, make a photocopy for yourself, in case the original gets lost or damaged. In addition, if you have written the paper on computer, keep a copy of it on your system or a disk. (Actually, making a backup copy is a good idea, too.)

Your paper needs no special cover or binding. Add a blank page at the front and back to help keep it neat. Secure all pages with a paperclip or staple in the upper-left corner. Do not put the paper in a folder or other type of cover unless your instructor approves.

If your instructor agrees, you may submit the paper electronically as a file attachment to an e-mail or by FAX.

*Not always required. Check with your instructor.

W O R K I N G   W I T H   O T H E R S

Many instructors believe students take more responsibility for revising, editing, and proofreading the final drafts of their research papers when they perform these tasks by themselves. Before beginning to work with another person to review your own or each other's final draft, check with your instructor about working cooperatively. If he or she agrees to your sharing the draft with others, use the following suggestions to guide you through this important final process.

- Before printing the final version of your paper, exchange final drafts with another student in your class. Carefully read each other's draft at least twice to share general impressions about the content and writing. Review the suggestions for revision, and offer helpful opinions about organization and unity of content. Check to see that the thesis statement is clearly stated or supported and developed throughout the paper's introduction, body, and conclusion. Is each of these sections effectively handled in the paper?

- Point out parts of your own draft that were improved by editing. Discuss the changes you made with your classmate. Ask his or her opinion about the effectiveness of sentence and paragraph structures and the use of language. If necessary, review the section on editing together.

- Without making corrections on the other person's draft, offer any helpful advice you can about problems in grammar, punctuation, or style. Encourage the author to review the draft to give these matters further attention. Point out any sentences in which the language may be discriminatory, sexist, or otherwise inappropriate. Discuss these problems and ways to resolve them.

- Check general technicalities such as the uses of underlining/italics, numbers, abbreviations, and so forth in each other's draft. Identify anything that you may be unsure about, and discuss its use. Make changes or corrections as necessary.

- After you have printed the final copy of the paper, exchange papers with your partner. Read to catch any glaring omissions or mistakes, and bring any problems to the attention of the author. Before turning the papers in to your instructor, take a few moments to congratulate each other on the work you have done.

APPENDIX A

Sample Research Papers

APA (Author-Date) and CBE (Citation-Sequence System) Documentation Styles

Sample Paper 1: APA (Author-Date) Documentation Style

The following research paper, Emotional Intelligence: Is EQ More Important Than IQ?, uses the author-date style of documentation recommended by the American Psychological Association (APA). The *Publication Manual of the American Psychological Association* (5th ed., 2001) was written for authors intending to submit their papers for publication; it suggests that students alter guidelines as needed in order to meet the requirements of instructors. In a format consistent with other papers for college courses, for example, the title page of the sample research paper that follows does not include an abbreviated title as the running head, although APA style calls for one if the paper is intended for publication. (Note that the running head *Emotional Intelligence* appears on all other pages.) All other features of the paper—including the abstract, intext citations, and entries in the References—conform to APA style.

Annotations in the margins of the paper describe important APA style features, which are discussed more fully in Chapter 13. Also consult your instructor regarding any special requirements he or she may have.

**Type paper's
title and other
necessary
information
double-spaced
and centered**

Emotional Intelligence:

Is EQ More Important Than IQ?

Steve Hanner

Bay State College

Professor Jane Ismond

English 102

May 9, 1999

**Check with instructor
about listing course
information**

Number all pages consecutively with arabic numerals, beginning with title page

Emotional Intelligence 2

Center heading at top of page

Abstract

The importance of emotional intelligence in contributing to success at school, on the job, and in everyday life continues to attract interest and debate. Emotional intelligence, or *EQ* (for "Emotional Quotient"), is important but does not necessarily rival IQ in measuring ability or predicting success. Although the concepts underlying interest in emotional intelligence have been around for several years, Daniel Goleman's ideas are central to how EQ is understood and applied today. Citing recent research, Goleman has shown that emotional intelligence does indeed influence the levels of happiness and satisfaction people achieve. School districts across the nation have instituted curricula based upon his ideas, and employers are increasingly making measures of EQ standard in hiring and evaluating employees. While EQ is not the sole measure of people's abilities in life, it is clearly an important component of our success in dealing with others and in better understanding ourselves.

Type abstract as single paragraph, block format

For running head, use short title or your
last name, as instructed; first page of
text is page 3

Emotional Intelligence 3

Emotional Intelligence:

Is EQ More Important Than IQ?

People who count on a PhD or high SAT score
to guarantee their success on the job may be a little
disappointed by the results of recent research on
intelligence. A study reported by university researchers
in Manila has found that cognitive intelligence--the
kind measured on IQ tests and thought to decide one's
fate in school and career--takes second place to
emotional intelligence as a predictor of success at
work; separate studies elsewhere had the same results
("EQ More," 1998). Although there is little new in
finding out that what may sound like common "people
skills" matter at work or elsewhere, the research
reflects today's widespread interest in whether
someone's emotional quotient, or *EQ*, might matter
more than his or her IQ. The fact is, EQ does matter
more but in different ways than just rivaling intellect
as a measure of ability.

The basic concepts underlying most people's
current idea of emotional intelligence dates back
to 1920 and the concept of *social intelligence* first
espoused in the work of psychologist E. L. Thorndike
(Young, 1996). Later, during the 1980s, the theories of
Howard Gardner, a psychologist at the Harvard School
of Education, spurred interest in the concept of *multiple
intelligences*[1] and what he termed "access to one's
own feeling life" (1983, p. 239). The term used today,
however, was coined by Yale psychologist Peter
Salovey and colleague John Mayer at the University
of New Hampshire in 1990. They defined *emotional*

Margin annotations:

- For running head, use short title or your last name, as instructed; first page of text is page 3
- Center title at top of page
- Cite source with no author given by shortened title; include date
- Thesis statement announces paper's main idea
- Raised superscript directs reader to Notes section
- Give page number when quoting source; use *p.* or *pp.* for page(s)

Emotional Intelligence 4

intelligence as the "ability to monitor one's own and others' emotions, to discriminate among them, and to use the information to guide one's own thinking and actions" (Mayer & Salovey, 1997, p. 4).

It was not until the publication of Daniel Goleman's best-selling book, *Emotional Intelligence: Why It Can Matter More Than IQ*, in 1995 that the concept of emotional intelligence per se gained general popularity and wide acceptance. Goleman took Gardner's ideas and those of Salovey and Mayer a few steps further, defining emotional intelligence as self-motivation and persistence, control of one's impulses, regulation of one's mood and ability to think clearly, and the ability to empathize and to hope (Goleman, 1995a, p. 34). As Goleman states in his book, human beings have "two brains, two minds--and two different kinds of intelligence. rational and emotional. How we do in life is determined by both--it is not just IQ, but *emotional* intelligence that matters" (p. 28). Goleman's ideas about emotional intelligence (or *EQ*, as others have come to call it[2]) have become so influential that they form the foundation for the popularity and widespread application of emotional theory today.

Goleman's argument for emotional intelligence derives from numerous studies that show people who score highly on intelligence tests are not always as successful in life as their lower-scoring peers. Research on male Harvard students from the 1940s, for example, found that 40 years after graduating, those who had received the highest test scores when they were in college ended up less happy with their lives and less

Italicize titles of books in text; capitalize significant words

Use *a* and *b* to identify two sources published in same year by same author

Use an ampersand between names of joint authors

Do not cite author, date, or title when stated in text; include page number(s) for quotations

Emotional Intelligence 5

Extended examples illustrate and support ideas

successful than their peers who had received lower scores (Goleman, 1995a, p. 35). Another study, this one of valedictorians and salutatorians (all students with high grade points), found that 10 years after high school, only one in four were at the highest level of people their age in their chosen professions, and some were much lower (Goleman, 1995a). Cases like these, of course, may be welcome news to those who believe it takes more than good grades to succeed in life. As a professor of education at Boston University points out, to know "a person is a valedictorian is
to know only that he or she is exceedingly good at achievement as measured by grades. It tells you nothing about how they react to the vicissitudes of

Include full range of page numbers

life" (Goleman, 1995a, pp. 35-36).

Giving the page number when paraphrasing for a long work helps the reader, but is optional.

Goleman argues for the importance of emotional intelligence in people's daily lives by citing research indicating the evolutionary precedence of emotions and their superior role in survival. The emotional part of the human brain is older than the rational part, which is why the emotional brain takes over and controls the thinking brain during emergencies, Goleman says. When people feel and act before they think, it is because the emotional brain circuitry has allowed the sensation of an experience to bypass the neocortex, or thinking part of the brain (1995a, pp. 5-9). This is what happens, for instance, when someone acts out of anger and then later thinks about the consequences and regrets his or her action.

But unthinking, emotional responses such as these are essential, claims Goleman, because without them,

Emotional Intelligence 6

people would not be able to act in any situations,
even normal ones. Without the impetus provided by
emotions, cognitive reflection, or thinking, paralyzes
people by offering too many choices. To illustrate,
Goleman cites the work of neurologist Antonio
Damasio, who made a study of cases involving patients
with damage to the emotion-based areas of their brains.
Although all the patients were clearly intelligent, the
damage to their emotional circuitry left them unable to
make quick decisions, react to warnings, or feel regret
or shame (1995, pp. 27-28). They could think, but they
could not feel; they analyzed every situation over
and over for its variable outcomes, thereby delaying
responsive action and feeling. Such cases, according
to Goleman, demonstrate that people should not try to
suppress or elliminate emotions but only to control
them Properly understood and exercised, he says,
emotions are the basis of people's feelings about
themselves and others and thus the basis for a
successful and satisfying life (1995a, p. 63).

  Proponents of EQ agree that it plays an unquantified
but central role in people's success in life, and they also
recognize that its presence, diminishment, or absence
can profoundly affect the society at large. They argue
that what Goleman calls "emotional literacy" (1995b,
p. 6) and others commonly refer to as "people skills"--
such as graciousness and amiability as well as the
ability to "read" social situations--are becoming
increasingly important and more highly valued today.
This is likely due in part to the fact that American
society is characterized by an increasing loss of

**Example
illustrates
point about
importance
of emotions**

**Type long
dash as two
unspaced
hyphens**

Emotional Intelligence 7

traditional values and concern for other human beings.
According to Goleman:

**Format
quotation of 40
words or more
as double-spaced
block; indent
5 to 7 spaces
from left margin
(but not right);
do not use
quotation marks**

> An abundance of the qualities that make for emotional
> intelligence lead to greater drive and self-discipline,
> caring and cooperation--all of which make our lives
> better and our streets safer. But deficiencies in
> emotional intelligence--impulsivity, a lack of empathy
> and emotions like anxiety or rage run amok--can
> destroy lives and communities. (1995b, p. 4)

**Cite source
of quote in
parentheses
after end
punctuation;
if author is
named in text
cite only date
and page(s);
use *p.* or *pp.*
before page
number(s)**

Empathy, for instance, is an innate quality and
expression of emotional intelligence, and it is shaped
by an individual's experiences. Very young babies get
upset at the sound of another infant crying, and their
innate empathy is reinforced as they grow up watching
how others react to people in distress (Gibbs, 1995,
p. 67). On the other hand, research also shows that the
life experiences of cruel criminal types, such as child
molesters and psychopaths, may have left them devoid of
any capacities for empathy (Goleman, 1995a, pp. 109-110).

Most importantly, because empathy and other
behaviors associated with emotional intelligence are
shaped by experience, they can be taught, say Goleman
and others. Grade school curricula have included the
elements of emotional intelligence since the late 1970s,
and Goleman believes they are more important today
than ever in education:

> As family life no longer offers growing numbers of
> children a sure footing in life, schools are left as the
> one place communities can turn to for correctives
> to children's deficiencies in emotional and social
> competence. That is not to say that school alone
> can stand in for all the social institutions that too

Emotional Intelligence 8

Use ellipsis to indicate omitted content in quotation

often are in or nearing collapse. But . . . it offers a place to reach children with basic lessons for living that they may never get otherwise. (1995a, p. 279)

Many agree. By 1997, only two years after Goleman's book came out, over 700 school districts across the United States had formally adopted emotional intelligence-based models of teaching and learning into their curricula (Ratnesar, 1997). In New Haven, Connecticut, for example, children throughout the district and in all grade levels take part in its Social Development Program. Classroom lessons revolve around "emotional learning"--activities that reinforce values such as kindness and people skills. Children are taught to consistently compliment each other and to take active roles in dealing with their own and others' emotions, including openly discussing their feelings with teachers and classmates. Although some parents object to what they see as a curriculum overly devoted to therapy, educators defend the approach. "We are teaching them values that are universal," says a second-grade teacher. "Being kind to a person--that's something all people need to do" (Ratnesar, 1997, p. 62).

Use numerals to express numbers 10 and above; spell out numbers less than 10

Spell out ordinal numbers such as *second* and *tenth*

Results say they may be right: Educators in districts where "emotional literacy" is part of the curriculum report that student attitudes are more upbeat because of emotional learning, and personal and academic problems are fewer

Cite multiple sources alphabetically by authors' last names; separate with semicolons

(Kelly & Moon, 1998; Ratnesar, 1997). Indeed, researchers are uncovering increasing evidence of a relationship between emotional intelligence and other skills such as leadership, group and individual performance, interpersonal relationships, managing change, and conducting evaluations (Young, 1996).

Emotional Intelligence 9

As a result, teachers and administrators are beginning to rethink the importance of traditional lessons and standardized tests. "We have gone from teaching information for its own sake to teaching kids to appreciate how information can be used to enhance their understanding of themselves and others," says a tenth-grade teacher in California (Wells, 1998, p. 35). Peter Relic, president of the National Association of Independent Schools, even favors getting rid of the SAT and replacing it with EQ-based standards, despite the expense of doing so:

Introduce indented quotation with colon or comma

> Yes, it may cost a heck of a lot more money to assess someone's EQ rather than using a machine-scored test to measure IQ. But if we don't, then we're saying that a test score is more important to us than who a child is as a human being. That means an immense loss in terms of human potential because we've defined success too narrowly. (qtd. in Gibbs, 1995, p. 167)

Not everyone agrees with the proponents of emotional intelligence, however. While researchers in the field welcome all the attention given to feelings, they also fear that popularization will lead to misuse of what is known about it. Some parents, for example, disagree that the EQ-based emotional learning their children receive in school is appropriate. At its worst, they say, emotional learning verges on therapy sessions, and many complain that teaching about more than one kind of achievement ability has lead schools to "dumb down" the meaning of the word *intelligence*. According to one teacher of emotional literacy, the new emphasis has schools saying that all children are intelligent in

Emotional Intelligence 10

one way or another--although, as she insists, "They are
not all academically intelligent" ("Signs," 1997, p. A4).

Quotation
integrated
into text

One of the biggest concerns about emotional
intelligence is that there is currently no accepted
method of measuring it. As early emotional intelligence
researcher John Mayer points out, there is no rational
basis for saying that emotional intelligence can
outpredict IQ, because there "is no single entity called
EQ"; too much depends upon the situation and culture
involved (Jimenez, 1999, p. 8). Proponents respond that
not enough is yet known about emotional intelligence
or how it influences thinking and behavior.

Indeed, IQ tests measure precisely--and only--
what they are intended to measure: academic
aptitudes, not aptitudes for living. Most researchers
agree that IQ predicts only about 20% of academic and
occupational success; what accounts for the other 80%
remains undetermined (Gibbs, 1995). It is clear, however, that intellectual and emotional intelligence develop independently of each other and may influence
academic outcomes differently. Thus, the children who
score highest on nonverbal sensitivity tests do better
in school than those who score lower on such tests,
despite the fact that the high scorers do the same or
even worse on IQ tests (Cohen, 1998).

**Use numerals
and percent
signs for
percentages**

Despite the unknowns that remain, one area in
which the value of emotional intelligence is becoming
more widely accepted all the time is in business and
industry. Studies of the workplace show that the skills
people need to do their jobs effectively or to advance in
their careers seem, as often as not, to be those defined
by EQ and its related elements. Optimism, for example,

is an "emotionally intelligent attitude," according to Goleman (1995a, p. 88), that has been shown to correlate highly with success in one's career. That is why it is not surprising to EQ advocates that in a study by the Metropolitan Life Insurance Company, salespeople who scored the highest on a test for optimism when they were hired later outsold test-identified pessimists by 21% the first year and 57% the second year of their employment (Gibbs, 1998). Other research has found that the three capabilities most desired by employers are communication skills, interpersonal skills, and initiative--all elements of emotional intelligence. The same research showed that the further an individual went up the corporate ranks, the more these things seemed to matter (Daniel, 1998).

In keeping with such findings, more people seeking jobs today are finding out that, as one writer has expressed, "IQ gets you hired, but EQ gets you promoted" (Gibbs, 1995, p. 63). Nice guys do, it seems, finish first in many businesses, but those who are not perceived as nice may not last long enough to succeed. Thus, research studying the careers of corporate executives who had lost their previous jobs found that perceived weaknesses in their interpersonal skills, rather than any lack of knowledge or business savvy, was often a deciding factor in their firing (Gibbs, 1995).

Businesses today, in fact, are beginning to evaluate employees using "360 degree" performance measures-- rating not only productivity and technical skills but also how well an employee works with others (Gibbs, 1995).

Emotional Intelligence 12

Many employers want to use evaluation instruments like the new, as yet unproven, Bar-On Emotional Quotient Inventory. Its makers say the test can measure emotional quotient and discriminate between employees with high and low emotional skills (Wells, 1998, p. 35). As Goleman rightly insists:

> The rules for work are changing, and we're all being judged, whether we know it or not, by a new yardstick--not just how smart we are and what technical skills we have, which employers see as givens, but increasingly by how well we handle ourselves and one another. (qtd. in Daniel, 1998, p. 293)

Few would argue today that emotional intelligence, in one form or another, is not highly valued in society generally and in the classroom and the workplace especially. In some ways, the embracing of EQ has been due in large part to a backlash: There seemed to be a need to rebalance the single-focused respect for IQ and to reexamine the value of the skills, insights, and intelligences that make people successful in their own lives and in living and working successfully with others. Even so, IQ is only one measure of one kind of ability. "There are hundreds and hundreds of ways to succeed," Howard Gardner has said, "and many, many different abilities that will help get you there" (qtd. in Goleman, 1995a, p. 37). Today, emotional intelligence is surely recognized as one of the most important of those ways. EQ does matter in society, just as much and perhaps more than IQ, if only because valuing it brings people back to valuing their own feelings and those of others.

Conclusion summarizes thesis and general content

Use *qtd. in* to show quote from secondary source

Emotional Intelligence 13

Begin section on new page after regular text; center title

Notes

[1]Gardner identified seven kinds of intelligence: musical, spatial, verbal, mathematical, kinesthetic, intrapersonal, and interpersonal. Later, he expanded the list to include naturalistic intelligence (appreciation and understanding of the natural world) and (with great qualification) spiritual intelligence. See Gardner, 1983, p. 36; Goleman, 1995a, pp. 37-43.

[2]EQ, or *emotional quotient*, was not originally a term that Goleman used or proposed. He first used it in a 1995 article for *USA Weekend*. See Goleman, 1995b.

Notes provide information not immediately relevant to discussion; sources cited parenthetically

Begin section on new page after Notes (or regular text, if no notes); center title; list entries alphabetically by authors' last names or, if no author given, by title

References

Cohen, L. (1998, August 8). Back to school, and to basics. *Jerusalem Post, 65*(9). Retrieved March 12, 1999, from: http:www.elibrary.com/id/120/200/getdoc ...docid=1698741@library_k&dtype+)-0&dinst=0

Daniel, A. (1998, 26 October). Success secret: A high emotional IQ. *Fortune, 145,* 293.

EQ more important than IQ for work success: First scientific study compares IQ and actual work performance. (1998). *Business Wire.* Retrieved March 12, 1999, from http://www. elibrary.com/id/120/200/getdoc...docid =e&type=0~0&dinst=0

Gardner, H. (1983). *Frames of mind: The theory of multiple intelligences.* New York: Basic.

Gibbs, N. (1995, October 2). The EQ factor. *Time, 262,* 60-68.

Goleman, D. (1995a). *Emotional intelligence: Why it can matter more than IQ.* New York: Bantam.

Goleman, D. (1995b, September 8). EQ: Why your emotional intelligence quotient can matter more than IQ: The new thinking on smarts. *USA Weekend,* pp. 4-7.

Jimenez, R. (1999, February 2). Don't go overboard about EQ. *New Hampshire Weekly,* p. 8.

Kelly, K. R., & Moon, S. M. (1998, June). Personal and social talents. *Phi Delta Kappan, 124,* 743.

Weekly periodical; capitalize first word of title and subtitle and all proper nouns; no quotation marks around title

Online newspaper; include year, month, and day of publication

Online source with no author given; include retrieval date and URL

Book with single author; include place published and publisher

Newspaper article; use *p.* or *pp.* before page numbers

List multiple works by same author chronologic-ally; add *a* and *b* to dates

Use an ampersand to separate two authors' names; for journal, include volume number (underlined) after title and before page numbers

Emotional Intelligence 15

Mayer, J. D., & Salovey, P. (1997). What is emotional intelligence? In P. Salovey & D. Sluyer (Eds.), *Emotional development and emotional intelligence: Implications for educators* (pp. 3-31). New York: Basic Books.

Include month and day in date of weekly magazine; underline volume number

Ratnesar, R. (1997, September 29). Teaching feelings. *Time, 156,* 62.

Signs of intelligence: Do new definitions of smart dilute meaning? (1997, January 4). *USA Today,* p. A4.

Wells, K. (1998, September 6). Why teachers love EQ. *California Educator, 100,* 34-40.

Young, Cheri A. (1996). *Emotions and emotional intelligence.* Retrieved March 15, 1999, from: http://trochim.human.cornell.edu/gallery/young/emotion.htm.

For source included in another work, use *In* before editor's name(s) and *Ed.* or *Eds.* in parentheses after; include page numbers parenthetically

Web site; include retrieval date and URL

Sample Paper 2:
CBE (Citation-Sequence System)
Documentation Style

The following sample paper presents a selected review of literature published in 1998 on alcohol consumption among college and university students. The intext citations and References section of the paper follow the citation-sequence system of documentation recommended by the Council of Biology Editors (CBE) (see Chapter 13) and described in its publication *Scientific Style and Format: The CBE Manual for Authors, Editors, and Publishers* (6th ed., 1994).

Note that sources in the References section are listed and numbered in their order of appearance in the text. Each author's last name is followed by a space and then his or her initials, with no intervening periods or spaces between the initials. There is no comma between the author's last name and initials, but commas are used to separate individual authors' names. Titles of sources are not underlined or italicized; titles of journals may be abbreviated. The publication date, journal and issue numbers, and page numbers are added at the end of each entry, separated with punctuation marks but no spaces.

Sources are cited in the text by corresponding superscripted numbers, following the content they reference. Intext citations include page numbers after quotations or whenever sources are lengthy. (See also discussion of CBE style in Chapter 13).

Annotations in the margin explain certain stylistic and documentation features of the CBE citation system. You should also consult your instructor regarding any special requirements he or she may have.

1

**Center title,
your name,
and other
relevant
information**

Research on Alcohol Consumption among
College and University Students:
A Selected Review of 1998 Literature

Carol Nguyen
Psychology 202
March 29, 1999

Running head is optional, unless paper to be submitted for publication; use short title or your last name (as instructed), plus page number as shown

Research on Alcohol Consumption

2

Abstract

A selected review of research reported during 1998 demonstrates ongoing concern about the relationships among alcohol consumption and various health aspects of college and university students' lives, particularly as these may relate to risky sexual activity and contraction of the human immunodeficiency virus, or HIV. The literature reviewed shows that membership, and especially leadership, in a campus fraternity or sorority associates significantly with high levels of alcohol consumption and permissive sexual attitudes. Levels of religious conviction also influence levels of student alcohol consumption, with perceived amounts of control over their drinking differing among Catholics and Protestants; religious conviction levels among men and women students in general correlate differently in regard to risky sexual behavior and alcohol consumption. Alcohol's role in coercive sexual strategies among men shows that such behavior correlates with women victims' behavior and with alcohol consumption levels of both sexes. Finally, the research indicates significant associations between fewer risk-taking behaviors and low alcohol consumption levels among female student athletes and students with high self-esteem.

Abstract defines paper's focus and summarizes content

Research on Alcohol Consumption

3

A selected review of research reported during 1998
demonstrates ongoing concern about the relationships
among alcohol consumption and various health aspects
of students' lives, particularly as these may relate to
risky sexual activity and contraction of the human
immunodeficiency virus, or HIV. The literature
reviewed here examines the influence of alcohol use in
its association with student memberships in campus
fraternities or sororities, levels of religious conviction,
risky sexual behavior, and coercive sexual strategies.

FRATERNITY AND SORORITY MEMBERSHIP

Higher Consumption Levels

In a study involving 25,411 college students (15,100
females), participants from 61 academic institutions
completed the Core Alcohol and Drug Survey.[1] Results
of the survey showed that students involved in fraternity
or sorority life consumed significantly more alcohol on a
weekly basis and suffered significantly more negative
consequences as a result of such consumption than other
students. The study also showed a significantly higher level
of drinking and negative consequences among the leaders
of fraternities and sororities than among other Greek
members. To a greater extent than non-Greeks, fraternity
and sorority members indicated they believed alcohol was
a vehicle for friendship, social activity, and sexuality. The
findings corroborate earlier research on fraternity and sorority
drinking as well as indicate that Greek leaders participate in
setting heavy-drinking norms among their peers.

Campus Regulations

Following the death of a student that resulted
from binge drinking at a Massachusetts Institute of

Research on Alcohol Consumption

4

Technology fraternity initiation party, MIT and other
campuses across the United States are imposing new,
stricter rules to regulate drinking, especially among and
fraternities and sororities. MIT has increased its alcohol
education programs for students and beginning in 2001
will require all students to live on campus. The need is
apparent: A recent Harvard University study shows 43
percent of college students binge drink.[2]

LEVELS OF RELIGIOUS CONVICTION

Affiliation Levels

A survey of 263 alcohol-using students showed that
those with no religious affiliation reported significantly
higher levels of alcohol consumption than did students
with either Protestant or Catholic religious affiliation.[3]
Protestants believed they exercised higher levels of
control over their drinking than Catholics, according to
the study, but no differences across groups were found
regarding problems with alcohol use. Concern for
responsibility toward the tenets of one's religion appeared
to play a more important positive role regarding drinking
behavior for Protestants than for Catholics.

Convictions and Unsafe Practices

A second study[4] examined the relationships among
alcohol use, strength of religious convictions, and
unsafe sexual practices among 210 public university
students. The study found that women with strong
religious beliefs consumed less alcohol and were less
likely to engage in unsafe or risky sexual practices than
women with weaker religious convictions. The strength
of religious conviction had little influence on alcohol
consumption by the men in the study; however, levels

**Superscript
citation
numbers
should be
1 or 2 type
sizes smaller
than text**

Research on Alcohol Consumption

5

of alcohol consumption correlated significantly with unsafe or risky sexual practices among the men. Men consumed more alcohol and participated in more unsafe sexual practices than women, although the two groups did not differ in the overall frequency of their sexual activity. The authors of the study indicate that future research is needed to identify more fully the relationships among religious convictions, sexual activity, and alcohol use, especially among students in different geographical areas.

COERCIVE SEXUAL STRATEGIES

Victimization Patterns

Two studies reported on the use of alcohol as a strategy for coercing sexual participation from female partners. In the first,[5] a survey conducted by Synovitz and Byrne of 241 female college students elicited information about demographics, dating history, sexual history, personality characteristics, and associated factors in order to discriminate between victims and nonvictims of sexual assault. Following analysis of the data, variables found to be related to women's being sexually victimized were (a) number of different lifetime sexual partners, (b) provocative dress, and (c) alcohol use.

Coercive Strategies

A study regarding women sexual victims and alcohol use examined coercive sexual strategies used by men and their effects on the behavior of women.[6] The study gathered information from 541 male and female college undergraduates. The men were asked about their use of three types of coercive sexual strategies and the women about their experiences with

Authors may be named in text; give numbers for locating sources in References

these strategies. For women, the results showed an association between high levels of sexual activity and permissiveness, drinking alcohol, and being a victim of certain types of coercive strategies. Among the men, permissiveness about sex and attitudes toward rape were shown to be significant predictors of their use of verbal coercion. An association with being in a fraternity and using verbal and physical coercion as a sexual strategy, as well as membership in a sorority and being a victim of alcohol/drug coercion and physical force, was also found. The research corroborated other studies indicating use by college males of alcohol as means of sexual coercion.[1,7,8]

HIV AND ALCOHOL USE

Self Esteem and Risk Taking

A study relating the influence of alcohol use and self-esteem on risky sexual behavior among college students found that students with low levels of alcohol use and high self-esteem reported less sexual risk taking.[9] Such students used condoms more often during sex than their low self-esteem peers reported using. Women and students with low self-esteem indicated greater perceptions of themselves and their partners at risk.

Female Athletes

Associating alcohol and other drug use with HIV risk, another study compared risky health behaviors among college female athletes and their nonathlete peers.[10] The study included 571 female university athletes (109 athletes and 462 nonathletes peers) and matched each athlete with nonathletes to account for

Form for citing multiple sources at same time

dichotomous outcome variables. An HIV risk scale was developed to identify factors, including alcohol and drug use, associated with increased HIV risk for all of the participants. The results of the study showed that female athletes engage in significantly fewer risk-taking behaviors than nonathletes and were less at risk for HIV infection.

Contrasting Results. A different study[11] found contrasting results, however, about college athletes and drinking. A survey of over 51,000 students at 125 institutions indicated that male and female athletes consumed alcohol at excessive levels and suffered adverse consequences to a greater degree than their nonathlete peers.

Third-level heading indented, followed by period; significant words capitalized

CONCLUSION

Conclusion summarizes paper's major findings

Research demonstrates the ongoing concern by health and educational authorities to understand more fully how alcohol use among college and university students relates to other important aspects of their lives. Particular attention is given to the negative consequences of student drinking, especially as it relates to sexual victimization of female students and to risk-taking sexual behavior. Current health literature demonstrates significant concern about how alcohol consumption, sexual risk taking, and contraction of HIV associate with student belief systems and the activities they engage in while attending college. In all the literature reviewed, authors recognized the need to relate their findings to larger studies of student attitudes and behaviors regarding alcohol.

Research on Alcohol Consumption

8

**References section begins
new page; center title at top**   References

1. Cashin JR, Presley CA, Meilman PW. Alcohol use   **Sources**
in the Greek system: follow the leader? J Stud Alcohol   **listed in**
order of
1998;59(1):63-70.   **appearance**

Article in   2. Hammel S. Cooling it on campus. Newsweek   **in text**
monthly
1999 November 9:34.
magazine

3. Patock-Peckham JA, Hutchinson GT, Cheong J,
Nagoshi CT. Effect of religion and religiosity on alcohol
use in a college student sample. Drug Alcohol Depend
1998;49(2):81-8.

4. Poulson RL, Eppler MA, Satterwhite TN,   **Use authors'**
Wuensch KL, Bass LA. Alcohol consumption, strength   **initials instead**
of first names;
of religious beliefs, and risky sexual behavior in college   **no spaces or**
students. J Am Coll Health 1998;46(5):227-32.   **periods**

Capitalize   5. Synovitz LB, Byrne TJ. Antecedents of sexual
first words
victimization: factors discriminating victims from
and all
proper   nonvictims. J Am Coll Health 1998;46(4):151-8.
nouns in   6. Tyler KA, Hoyt DR, Whitbeck LB. Coercive
book and
sexual strategies. Violence Vict 1998;13(1):47-61.
article titles;
capitalize all   7. Johnson TJ, Wendel J, Hamilton S. Social
significant   anxiety, alcohol expectancies, and drinking-game
words in
participation. Addict Behav 1998;23(1):65-79.
journal titles
8. Smeaton GL, Josian BM, Dietrich UC. College   **Do not**
students' drinking binge at a beach-front destination   **underline/**
italicize
during spring break. J Am Coll Health 1998;46(6):   **journal titles**
247-54.   **or volume**
numbers
9. McNair LD, Carter JA, Williams MK. Self-esteem,
gender, and alcohol use: relationships with HIV risk
perception and behaviors in college students. J Sex
Marital Ther 1998;24(1):29-36.

Research on Alcohol Consumption

9

Article in journal

10. Kokotailo PK, Koscik RE, Henry BC, Fleming MF, Landry GL. Health risk taking and human immuno-deficiency virus risk in collegiate female athletes. J Am Coll Health 1998;46(6):236-8.

Journal titles abbreviated according to standard practice

11. Leichliter JS, Meilman PW, Presley CA, Cashin JR. Alcohol use and related consequences among students with varying levels of involvement in college athletics. J Am Coll Health 1998;46(6):257-62.

Reference Sources for Selected Subjects

This appendix is composed of lists of commonly found reference sources, first, by subject and next, within each subject, by type. Use these resources and others located near them in the library to find materials for general reading about a subject and for establishing a preliminary bibliography for research. Also consult the general reference sources listed throughout Chapter 4.

Index to Subjects

Reference Sources by Subject

Anthropology and Archaeology

Bibliographies, Guides, and Indexes

Anthropology of Minority Groups: Index of New Information With Authors and Subjects. Washington, DC: ABBE, 1998.

Barrett, Stanley R. *Anthropology: A Student's Guide to Theory and Method.* Toronto, Canada: U of Toronto P, 1996.

International Bibliography of Social Sciences: Social and Cultural Anthropology 1996. London: British Library of Political and Economic Science, 1996

Week, John M. *Introduction to Library Research in Anthropology.* Westview Guides to Library Research. Boulder, CO: Westview, 1998.

Encyclopedias, Dictionaries, and Handbooks

Ancient Americas: A Brief History and Guide to Research. Trans. Hans J. Prem and Kornelia Kurbjuhn. Salt Lake City: U of Utah P, 1997.

Archaeology of Prehistoric Native America: An Encyclopedia. Eds. Guy E. Gibbon and Kenneth M. Ames. New York: Garland, 1998.

Cambridge Encyclopedia of Human Paleopathology. Eds. Arthur C. Aufderheide, Conrado Rodriguez-Martin, and Odin Langsjoen. New York: Cambridge UP, 1998.

Companion Encyclopedia of Anthropology. Eds. Tom Ingold and Tim Ingold. New York: Garnet, 1997.

Dictionary of Anthropology. Ed. Thomas Barfield. Cambridge, MA: Blackwell, 1997.

Dictionary of Archaeology. Eds. Ian Shaw and Robert Jameson Cambridge, MA: Blackwell, 1999.

Encyclopedia of Social and Cultural Anthropology. Eds. Alan Barnard and Jonathan Spencer. New York: Routledge, 1998.

Abstracts and Digests

Abstracts in Anthropology. Farmingdale, NY: Baywood, 1970–date. Quarterly.

Art and Architecture

Bibliographies, Guides, and Indexes

Applied and Decorative Arts: A Bibliographic Guide. Ed. Donald L. Ehreshmann. 2nd ed. Littleton, NJ: Libraries Unlimited, 1993.

Art Books: A Basic Bibliography of Monographs on Artists. Ed. Wolfgang M. Freitag. New York: Garland, 1997.

Art Index. New York: Wilson, 1929–date. Quarterly.

Avery Index to Architectural Periodicals: 1995. New York: Hall, 1996.

Davies, Martin. *Romanesque Architecture.* New York: Macmillan, 1993.

Landscape Architecture Sourcebook: A Guide to Resources on the History and Practice of Landscape Architecture in the United States. Ed. Diana Vogelsong. New York: Omnigraphics, 1996.

Langer, Cassandra. *Feminist Art Criticism: An Annotated Bibliography.* New York: Hall, 1994.

McCracken, Penny. *Women Artists and Designers in Europe Since 1800: An Annotated Bibliography.* 2 vols. New York: Hall, 1998.

Museum of Modern Art. *Annual Bibliography of Modern Art: 1997.* New York: Hall, 1998.

Wiebenson, Dora, Gerald Beasley, Nicholas Savage, Robin Middleton, and Gerard Beasley. *The Mark J. Millard Architectural Collection: British Books: Seventeenth through Nineteenth Centuries.* 2 vols. New York: Braziller, 1998.

Encyclopedias, Dictionaries, and Handbooks

Bullfinch Guide to Art History: A Comprehensive Survey and Dictionary of Western Art and Architecture. Ed. Shearer West. Minnetonka, MN: Bullfinch, 1996.

Ching, Francis D. K. *A Visual Dictionary of Architecture.* New York: Wiley, 1996.

Colvin, Howard. *A Biographical Dictionary of British Architects 1600–1840.* New Haven, CT: Yale UP, 1998.

Concise Oxford Dictionary of Art and Artists. Ed. Ian Chilvers. New York: Oxford UP, 1997.

Dictionary of Architectural and Building Technology. Ed. Henry J. Cowan, Peter R. Smith, and Jose Carlos Damski. New York: Sabin, 1998.

Dictionary of Twentieth-Century Art. Ed. Ian Chilvers. New York: Oxford UP, 1998.

Encyclopedia of American Acrchitecture. Eds. Robert T. Packard and Balthazar Korab. 2nd ed. New York: McGraw, 1994.

Biographical Dictionaries and Directories

American Art Directory. New York: Bowker, 1952–date.

Cumming, Paul. *A Dictionary of Contemporary American Artists.* 5th ed. New York: St. Martin's, 1988.

Databases

ARCHITECTURE DATABASE (RILA)   ART LITERATURE INTERNATIONAL
ART BIBLIOGRAPHIES MODERN

Biological Sciences

Bibliographies, Guides, and Indexes

Bell, George H., and Diane B. Rhodes. *Guide to the Zoological Literature: The Animal Kingdom.* Englewood, CO: Libraries Unlimited, 1994.

Baumer-Schleinkofer, Anne. *Bibliography of the History of Biology/Bibliographie Zur Geschichte Der Biologie.* New York: Lang, 1997.

Bibliography of Bioethics. 8 vols. Detroit: Gale, 1975–date.

Biological and Agricultural Index. New York: Wilson, 1978–date.

Hailman, Jack Parker, and Karen B. Strier. *Planning, Proposing and Presenting Science Effectively: A Guide for Graduate Students and Researchers in the Behavioral Sciences and Biology.* New York: Cambridge UP, 1997.

Information Sources in the Life Sciences. Ed. H.V. Wyatt. Stoneham, MA: Butterworth, 1987.

McNally, Bruce. *Animals in Wildlife – Biology, Behavior, and Vectorisms for Disease: Index for New Information.* Washington, DC: ABBE, 1995.

Encyclopedias, Dictionaries, and Handbooks

American Men and Women of Science 1998–1999: A Biographical Directory of Today's Leaders in Physical, Biological, and Related Sciences. New Providence, NJ: Bowker, 1998.

Cambridge Encyclopedia of Human Growth and Development. Eds. Stanley J. Ulijaszek, Francis E. Johnston, and Micha Preece. New York: Cambridge UP, 1998.

Encyclopedia of Animal Rights and Animal Welfare. Eds. Marc Bekoff and Carron Meaney. Westport, CT: Greenwood, 1998.

Encyclopedia of Environmental Biology. Ed. William Aaron Nierenberg. Orlando, FL: Academic, 1995.

Encyclopedia of Human Biology. Ed. Renato Dulbecco. 9 vols. Orlando, FL: Academic, 1997.

Ethics of Sex and Genetics: Selections from the Five-Volume MacMillan Encyclopedia of Bioethics. Ed. Warren Thomas Reich. Rev. ed. New York: Simon, 1998.

Martin, Elizabeth. *A Dictionary of Biology.* New York: Oxford UP, 1996.

McGraw-Hill Dictionary of Bioscience. Ed. Sybil P. Parker. New York: McGraw, 1996.

Notable Women in the Life Sciences: A Biographical Dictionary. Eds. Benjamin F. Shearer and Barbara S. Shearer. Westport, CT: Greenwood, 1996.

Ridley, Damon D. *Online Searching: A Scientist's Perspective.* New York: Wiley, 1996.

United States Department of Agriculture. *Yearbook of Agriculture.* Washington, DC: GPO, 1894–date.

Abstracts and Digests
Biological Abstracts. Philadelphia: Biological Abstracts, 1926–date.

Databases
AGRICOLA

AGRIS INTERNATIONAL

AQUACULTURE

BIOSIS

LIFE SCIENCES COLLECTION

SCISEARCH

ZOOLOGICAL RECORD

Business

Bibliographies, Guides, and Indexes
Accountant's Index. New York: American Institute of Certified Public Accountants, 1921–date.

Business Index. New York: Wilson, 1958–date. Microfilm.

Business Periodicals Index. New York: Wilson, 1958–date.

1999 Index of Economic Freedom. Eds. Bryan T. Johnson and Kim R. Holmes. New York: Dow Jones, 1998.

Pagell, Ruth A., and Michael Halperin. *International Business Information: How to Find It, How to Use It.* 2nd ed. Phoenix, AZ: Oryx, 1997.

Prentice Hall Directory of Online Business Information, 1998. Eds. Christopher Engholm and Scott Grimes. Needham Heights, MA: Prentice, 1997.

Encyclopedias, Dictionaries, and Handbooks
Blackwell Encyclopedic Dictionary of Accounting. Ed. A. Rashad Abdel-Khalik. Cambridge, MA: Blackwell, 1999.

Blackwell Encyclopedic Dictionary of Business Ethics. Eds. Patricia Werhane and R. Edward Freeman. Cambridge, MA: Blackwell, 1998.

Dictionary of Accounting Terms. Eds. Joel G. Siegel and Jae K. Shim. Hauppauge, NY: Barron's, 1995.

Dictionary of Business. Eds. Jack P. Friedman and J. Downs. Hauppauge, NY: Barron's, 1997.

Databases
ABI/INFORM

ACCOUNTANTS INDEX

D&B DUN'S FINANCIAL RECORD

D&B ELECTRONIC YELLOW PAGES

DISCLOSURE

ECONOMIC LITERATURE INDEX

LABORLAW

MOODY'S CORPORATE NEWS

PTS F&S INDEXES

STANDARD & POOR'S NEWS

TRADE AND INDUSTRY INDEX

Chemistry and Chemical Engineering

Bibliographies, Guides, and Indexes
Applied Science and Technology Index. New York: Wilson, 1958–date.

Chemical Titles. Washington, DC: ACS, 1998.

Essential Guide to Analytical Chemistry. Trans. Georg Schwedt and Brooks Haderlie. New York: Wiley, 1997.

How to Find Chemical Information: A Guide for Practicing Chemists, Teachers, and Students. Ed. Robert Maizell. 2nd ed. New York: Wiley, 1987.

Introducing the Chemical Sciences: A CHF Reading List. Philadelphia: Chemical Heritage, 1997.

Encyclopedias, Dictionaries, and Handbooks

CRC Handbook of Chemistry and Physics. 79th ed. Ed. David R. Lide. Boca Raton, FL: CRC, 1998.

Chemical Engineering Handbook. Piscataway, NJ: Research and Education, 1996.

Dictionary of Inorganic Compounds: Dictionary of Inorganic Compounds. Vol 9. Ed. F. McDonald. New York: Chapman, 1996.

King, R. B. *Encyclopedia of Organic Chemistry.* New York: Wiley, 1997.

McGraw-Hill Dictionary of Chemistry. Ed. Sybil P. Parker. New York: McGraw, 1996.

Macmillan Encyclopedia of Chemistry. Ed. J. J. Lagowski. New York: Macmillan, 1997.

Abstracts and Digests

Annual Reviews of Industrial and Engineering Chemistry. Washington, DC: ACS, 1972–date.

Chemical Abstracts. Washington, DC: ACS, 1907–date.

General Science Index. New York: Wilson, 1978–date.

Databases

CA SEARCH	COMPENDEX
CHEMICAL ABSTRACTS	INSPEC
CHEMICAL INDUSTRY NOTES	NTIS
CHEMIS	SCISEARCH
CHEMNAME	

Computer Science

Bibliographies, Guides, and Indexes

Applied Science and Technology Index. New York: Wilson, 1958–date.

Bibliographic Guide to the History of Computer Applications, 1950–1990. Comp. James W. Cortada. Westport, CT: Greenwood, 1996.

Computer Literature Index. Phoenix, AZ: ACR, 1971–date.

Computer-Readable Bibliographic Data Bases: A Directory and Data Sourcebook. Washington, DC: ASIS, 1976–date.

Liu, Lewis-Guodo. *The Internet and Library and Information Services: Issues, Trends, and Annotated Bibliography 1994–1995.* Westport, CT: Greenwood, 1996.

Encyclopedias, Dictionaries, and Handbooks

Dictionary of Computer and Internet Terms. Eds. Douglas Downing, Michael Covington, and Melody Mauldin Covington. Indianapolis, IN. IDG, 1998.

Encyclopedia of Computer Science and Technology. Ed. Jack Belzer. 20 vols. New York: Dekker, 1975–date.

Freedman, Alan. *Computer Desktop Encyclopedia.* New York: AMACOM, 1996.

Greenia, Mark. *History of Computing: An Encyclopedia of the People and Machines That Made Computer History.* Danbury, CT: Lexicon, 1998.

Sheldon, Tom. *Encyclopedia of Networking: Electronic Edition.* New York: McGraw, 1997.

Abstracts and Digests

Artificial Intelligence Abstracts. New York: Bowker, 1983–date. Annually.

Databases

BUSINESS SOFTWARE DATABASE   INSPEC
COMPUTER DATABASE   MICROCOMPUTER INDEX

Ecology

Bibliographies, Guides, and Indexes

Bibliographic Guide to the Environment 1995. New York: Macmillan, 1996.

Dumanski, J, S. Gameda, J. M. Christian, and G. Pieri. *Indicators of Land Quality and Sustainable Land Management: An Annotated Bibliography.* Lanham, MD: Worldbank, 1998.

Environmental Index. Ed. M. Pronin. New York: Environmental Information. Annual.

Environmental Periodicals Bibliography. Santa Barbara, CA: Environmental Studies Institute, 1972–date.

Encyclopedias, Dictionaries, and Handbooks

Dictionary of Ecology, Evolution and Systematics. New York: Cambridge UP, 1998.

Encyclopedia of Ecology & Environmental Management. Ed. Peter Calow. Cambridge, MA: MIT, 1998.

Environment Encyclopedia and Directory 1998. 2nd ed. Detroit: Europa, 1998.

General Science Index. New York: Wilson, 1978–date.

Handbook of Environmental Data on Organic Chemicals. Ed. Karel Verschueren. New York: Wiley, 1997.

Abstracts and Digests

Biological Abstracts. Philadelphia: Biological Abstracts, 1926–date.

Ecology Abstracts. Bethesda, MD: Cambridge Scientific Abstracts, 1975–date. Monthly.

Energy Abstracts for Policy Analysis. Oak Ridge, TN: TIC, 1975–date.

Environment Abstracts. New York: Environment Information Center, 1971–date.

Pollution Abstracts. Bethesda, MD: Cambridge Scientific Abstracts, 1970–date.

Databases

APTIC   ENVIRONMENTAL PERIODICALS BIBLIOGRAPHY
BIOSIS PREVIEWS   POLLUTION ABSTRACTS
COMPENDEX   WATER RESOURCES ABSTRACTS
ENVIRONLINE

Education

Bibliographies, Guides, and Indexes

Academic Advising: An Annotated Bibliography (Bibliographies and Indexes in Education). Comp. Virginia N. Gordon. Westport, CT: Greenwood, 1994.

Africa: Africa World Press Guide to Educational Resources from and about Africa. Lawrenceville, NJ: Red Sea, 1998.

Bibliography of Jewish Education in the United States. Comp. Norman Drachler. Detroit: Wayne State UP, 1996.

Children's Nonfiction for Adult Information Needs: An Annotated Bibliography. Ed. Rosemarie Riechel. New York: Linnet, 1998.

Gall, Joyce P., Meredith D. Gall, and Walter R. Borg. *Applying Educational Research: A Practical Guide.* New York: Longman, 1998.

1998 Guide to the Evaluation of Educational Experiences in the Armed Services. 3 vols. Washington, DC: American Council on Education, 1998.

Olive, J. Fred. *The Educational Technology Profession: A Bibliographic Overview of a Profession in Search of Itself: A Selected Bibliography.* Englewood Cliffs, NJ: Educational Technology Publications, 1997.

Public School Restructuring: A Selected Bibliography. Eds. Jeannette R. Olson, Diana F. Ryan, and Charles M. Reigeluth. Englewood Cliffs, NJ: Educational Technology Publications, 1996.

Research Methods in Language and Education. Vol. 8. Ed. Nancy H. Hornberger and David Corson. Norwell, MA: Kluwer Academic, 1998.

Encyclopedias, Dictionaries, and Handbooks

Encyclopedia of Educational Research. Ed. Marvin C. Alkin. Old Tappan, NJ: Macmillan, 1998.

Handbook to Education. Ed. Robert Base. Westport, CT: Greenwood, 1998.

Historical Encyclopedia of School Psychology. Ed. Thomas Fagan and Paul G. Warden. Westport, CT: Greenwood, 1996.

Index to AV Producers & Distributors, 1997: A Nicem Reference Directory to Resources in Educational Media. 10th ed. Albuquerque, NM: National Information Center for Educational Media, 1996.

Taylor, Bonnie B. *Education and the Law: A Dictionary.* Santa Barbara, CA: ABC-CLIO, 1997.

Abstracts and Digests

Digest of Educational Statistics. Washington, DC: United Sates Department of Education, National Center for Educational Statistics, 1962–date.

Education Abstracts. Paris: UNESCO, 1949–date.

Educational Documents Abstracts. New York: Macmillan, 1966–date.

Databases

AIM/ARM	ERIC
A-V ONLINE	EXCEPTIONAL CHILD EDUCATIONAL RESOURCES

Ethnic Studies

Bibliographies, Guides, and Indexes

African American Newspapers and Periodicals: A National Bibliography. Eds. James Philip Danky and Maureen E. Hady. Boston: Harvard UP, 1999.

Black American Women Fiction Writers. Eds. Harold Bloom and William Golding. Broomall, PA: Chelsea, 199

Black/White Relations in American History: An Annotated Bibliography. Ed. Leslie Vicent Tischauser. Lanham, MD: Scarecrow, 1998.

Craig, Haynes. *Ethnic Minority Health: A Selected, Annotated Bibliography.* Lanham, MD: Scarecrow, 1997.

Guide to Native American Music Recordings. Ed. Greg Gombert. Summertown, TN: Book, 1996.

Lassiter, Sybil M. *Cultures of Color in America: A Guide to Family, Religion, and Health.* Westport, CT: Greenwood, 1998.

Mitchell, Robert. *Multicultural Student's Guide to Colleges: What Every African American, Asian-American, Hispanic, and Native American Applicant Needs to Know.* Newport Beach, CA: Noonday, 1996

Racism in Contemporary America. Bibliographies and Indexes in Ethnic Studies. Ser. Ed. Meyer Weinberg. Westport, CT: Greenwood, 1996.

Ryskamp, George R. *Student's Guide to Mexican American Genealogy.* Phoenix, AZ: Oryx, 1996.

She, Colleen. *A Student's Guide to Chinese American Genealogy.* Phoenix, AZ: Oryx, 1996.

Sonneborn, Liz. *A to Z of Native American Women.* New York: Facts on File, 1998.

Wells, Robert J. *Native American Resurgence and Renewal: A Reader and Bibliography.* Lanham, MD: Scarecrow, 1994.

Woodtor, Dee Parmer. *Finding a Place Called Home: An African-American Guide to Genealogy and Historical Identity.* New York: Random, 1999.

Encyclopedias, Dictionaries, and Handbooks

Biographical Dictionary of Hispanic Americans. Ed. Nicholas E. Meyer. New York: Facts on File, 1996.

Dictionary of Native American Mythology. Eds. Sam D. Gill and Irene F. Sullivan. New York: Oxford UP, 1994.

Dictionary of Race and Ethnic Relations. Eds. Ernest Cashmore, Michael Banton, James Jennings, Barry Troyna, and Ellis Cashmore. New York: Routledge, 1997.

Encyclopedia of Native American Biography: Six Hundred Life Stories of Important People, from Powhatan to Wilma Mankiller. Eds. Bruce E. Johnsen, Bruce Elliott Johansen, Donald A. Grinde, Jr. New York: Da Capo, 1998.

Gale Encyclopedia of Multicultural America. 2 vols. Eds. Rudolph J. Vecoli, Judy Galens, and Robyn V. Young. Detroit: Gale, 1995.

Herbst, Philip H. *Color of Words: An Encyclopaedic Dictionary of Ethnic Bias in the United States.* New York: Intercultural, 1997.

Illustrated Dictionary of the Gods and Symbols of Ancient Mexico and the Maya. Eds. Mary Miller and Karl Taube. New York: Thames, 1997.

International Encyclopedia of Racial and Ethnic Relations. Ed. Joseph B. Gittler. Greenwich, CT: J A I P, 1998.

Multi-Ethnic Handbook and Guide. Ed. Landus Marry. New York: Polk, 1998.

Abstracts and Digests

Sage Race Relations Abstracts. San Mateo, CA: 1976–date.

Sociological Abstracts. La Jolla, CA: 1952–date.

Databases

AMERICA: HISTORY AND LIFE SOCIAL SCISEARCH
ERIC SOCIOLOGICAL ABSTRACTS
PAIS

Film

Bibliographies, Guides, and Indexes

Armour, Robert A. *Film: A Reference Guide.* Westport, CT: Greenwood, 1980.

Film Literature Index. New York: Film and Television Documentation Center, 1973–date. Quarterly with annual indexes.

Halliwell, Leslie. *Halliwell's Film Guide.* 4th ed. New York: Scribner's, 1983.

International Index of Film Periodicals. New York: Bowker, 1975–date.

Oxford Companion to Film. Ed. Liz-Anne Bawden. New York: Oxford UP, 1976.

Performing Arts Research: A Guide to Information Sources. Detroit: Gale, 1976.

Ross, Harris. *Film as Literature, Literature as Film: An Introduction to and Bibliography of Film's Relationship to Literature.* Westport, CT: Greenwood, 1987.

Whalon, Marion K. *Performing Arts Research: A Guide to Information Sources.* Detroit: Gale, 1976.

Encyclopedias, Dictionaries, and Handbooks

Film and Television Handbook, 1994. Ed. David Leafe. Bloomington: Indiana UP, 1994.

Film Encyclopedia. Ed. Phil Hardy. New York: Morrow, 1983–84.

Abstracts and Digests

New York Times Film Reviews. New York: Times, 1970–date.

Geography

Bibliographies, Guides, and Indexes

Geographers: Bio-Bibliographical Studies. Ed. T.W. Freeman et al. London: Mansell, 1977–date. Annually.

Geography and Local Administration: A Bibliography. Ed. Keith Hoggart. Monticello, IL: Vancy, 1980.
Geologic Reference Sources: A Subject and Regional Bibliography. Ed. Dedrick C. Ward, Marjorie Wheeler, and Robert A. Bier. 2nd ed. Metuchen, NJ: Scarecrow, 1980.
Guide to Information Sources in the Geographical Sciences. London: Croom Helm, 1983.
International List of Geographical Serials. 4th ed. Chicago: U of Chicago, 1995.
Social Sciences Index. New York: Wilson, 1974–date.

Encyclopedias, Dictionaries, and Handbooks
Encyclopedia of Geographic Information Sources. Ed. J. Mossman. 4th ed. Detroit: Gale, 1986.
Encyclopedia of World Geography. North Bellmore, NY: Cavendish, 1993.
Longman Dictionary of Geography. Ed. Audrey N. Clark. London: Longman, 1989.

Abstracts and Digests
Geo Abstracts, A–G. Norwich, Eng.: Geo Abstracts, 1972–date. Bimonthly.

Databases
GEOBASE   SOCIAL SCISEARCH

Geology

Bibliographies, Guides, and Indexes
Bibliographical Index of Geology. Boulder, CO: American Geological Institute, 1933–date. Monthly with annual indexes.
Bibliography of North American Geology. 49 vols. Washington, DC: Geological Survey, 1923–71.
Guide to the Geology of North America. Ed. William Sylvester. New York: Planet, 1998.
Research in Geology, 1997–98. Ed. Kay Thomas. Indianapolis, IN: Seven Point, 1997.
Sierra Range: An Index to Published Sources. Eds. Mary Cedam and John Cassidy. Orlando, FL: Gaven Institute, 1998.

Encyclopedias, Dictionaries, and Handbooks
Challinor's Dictionary of Geology. Ed. Anthony Wyatt. Aberystwyth: U of Wales P, 1998.
Encyclopedia of Field and General Geology. Ed. C. W. Finkle. New York: Van Nostrand, 1988.
Handbook to Geology. Ed. Kenneth H. Longman. New York: Wiley, 1998.
McGraw Hill Dictionary of Earth Sciences. Ed. Sybil P. Parker. New York: McGraw, 1998.

Databases
COMPENDEX   GEOBASE
GEOARCHIVE   GEOREF

Health and Physical Education

Bibliographies, Guides, and Indexes
Anabolic Steroids and Sports and Drug Testing 1991–1997: An Annotated Bibliography. Comp. Ellen R. Paterson. Troy, NY: Whitson, 1998.
Consumer Health Information Source Book. Ed. Alan M. Rees. 4th ed. New York: Bowker, 1994.
Current Index to Journals in Education. Phoenix, AZ: Oryx, 1969–date.
Griffin, Attrices Dean. *Directory of Internet Sources for Health Professionals.* Albany, NY: Delmar, 1998.

Medical and Scientific Reports and Research on Eficiency in and Performance in the Health Sciences. Annandale, VA: American Health Research, 1993.

Physical Education Index. Cape Giradeau, MO: Oak, 1978–date.

Physical Fitness and Sports Medicine. Washington, DC: GPO, 1978–date.

U.S. Health Law and Policy 1999: A Guide to the Current Literature. Ed. Donald H. Caldwell. Chicago: American Hospital, 1998.

Zeigler, Earl F. *A Selected, Annotated Bibliography of Completed Research on Management Theory & Practice in Physical Education & Athletics to 1972.* Champaign, IL: Stipes, 1995.

Encyclopedias, Dictionaries, and Handbooks

Dictionary of Nutrition and Dietetics. Ed. Karen Eich Drummond. New York: Wiley, 1997.

Encyclopedia of Healing Therapies. Eds. Anne Woodham and David Peters. New York: DK, 1997.

Encyclopedia of Human Nutrition. Eds. Michele J. Sadler, Benjamin Caballero, and J. J. Strain. New York: Academic, 1998.

O'Brien, Teri. *The Personal Trainer's Handbook.* Champaign, IL: Human Kinetics, 1997.

Panik, Michael, and Jamie C. Paz. *Acute Care Handbook for Physical Therapists.* Newton, MA: Butterworth, 1997.

Abstracts and Digests

Nutrition Abstracts and Reviews. New York: Wiley, 1931–date.

Databases

ERIC
MEDLINE
MEDOC

SOCIAL SCISEARCH
SPORT AND RECREATION INDEX

History

Bibliographies, Guides, and Indexes

Africa, Asia and South America Since 1800: A Bibliographical Guide. Comp. A. J. H. Latham. New York: Manchester UP, 1995.

Arts and Humanities Citation Index. Philadelphia, PA: Institute for Scientific Information, 1976–date. Annually.

Benjamin Rush, MD: A Bibliographic Guide. Eds. Claire G. Fox, Gordon L. Miller, and Jacquelyn C. Miller. Westport, CT: Greenwood, 1996.

History Atlas of Asia. Eds. Ian Barnes, Bhikhu Parekh, and Robert Hudson. Indianapolis, IN: Macmillan General Reference, 1998.

Russian Revolution, 1905–1921: A Bibliographic Guide to Works in English. Comp. Murray Frame. Westport, CT: Greenwood, 1995.

Social Sciences Citation Index. Philadelphia, PA: Institute for Scientific Information, 1979–date. Annually.

Encyclopedias, Dictionaries, and Handbooks

American Heritage Encyclopedia of American History. Ed. John MacFaragher. New York: Holt, 1998.

Biographical Dictionary of World War II. Eds. Mark M Boatner and Mark A. Boatner. Novato, CA: Presidio, 1996.

Dictionary of Amercian History. Eds. Michael Martin and Leonard Gelber. New York: Dorset, 1990.

Encyclopedia of World History. New York: Oxford UP, 1999.

Abstracts and Digests

Recently Published Articles. Washington, DC: American Historical Association, 1976–date.

Writings on American History. Washington, DC: American Historical Association, 1903–date.

Databases

AMERICA: HISTORY AND LIFE   SOCIAL SCIENCES CITATION INDEX
HISTORICAL ABSTRACTS

Journalism and Mass Communications

Bibliographies, Guides, and Indexes

Cates, Joel A. *Journalism: A Guide to the Reference Literature.* 2nd ed. New York: Libraries Unlimited, 1997.

Gale Directory of Publications and Broadcast Media. An Annual Guide to Publications and Broadcasting Stations Including Newspapers, Magazines, Journals, Film, and Communications Media. Ed. Carolyn A. Fischer. Detroit: Gale, 1998.

Greenberg, Gerald S. *Tabloid Journalism: An Annotated Bibliography of English-Language Sources.* Westport, CT: Greenwood, 1996.

Houston, Brant. *Computer-Assisted Reporting: A Practical Guide.* New York: St. Martin's, 1996.

Mass Communications Research Resources: An Annotated Guide. Eds. Christopher H. Sterling, James K. Bracken, and Susan M. Hill. Mahwah, NJ: Erlbaum, 1998.

Sloan, William David. *American Journalism History: An Annotated Bibliography.* Westport, CT: Greenwood, 1989.

Encyclopedias, Dictionaries, and Handbooks

Encyclopedia of Television News. Ed. Michael D. Murray. Phoenix, AZ: Oryx, 1998.

History of the Mass Media in the United States. An Encyclopedia. Ed. Margaret A. Blanchard. Chicago: Fitzroy, 1998.

Reporter's Handbook: An Investigator's Guide to Documents and Techniques. Ed. Steve Weinberg. New York: St. Martin's, 1995.

Abstracts and Digests

Communications Abstracts. San Mateo, CA: Sage, 1978–date.

Databases

AP NEWS   REUTERS
MAGAZINE INDEX   SOCSCI SEARCH
NATIONAL NEWSPAPER INDEX   UPI NEWS
NEWSEARCH

Language

Bibliographies, Guides, and Indexes

Annual Bibliography of English Language and Literature. Cambridge, Eng.: Cambridge UP, 1921–date. Annual.

Critical Bibliography of English Language Studies. Cambridge, MA: Blackwell, 1998.

Higginson, Roy, and Brian McWhinney. *An Annotated Bibliography of Child Language and Language Disorders, 1997.* Baton Rouge, LA: Erlbaum, 1997.

Key, Mary Ritchie. *Male/Female Language: With a Comprehensive Bibliography.* Lanham, MD: Scarecrow, 1996.

MLA International Bibliography of Books and Articles on the Modern Languages and Literatures. New York: MLA, 1993. Annual.

Rogers, Bruce. *Complete Guide to TOEFL.* Boston: Heinle, 1997.

Encyclopedias, Dictionaries, and Handbooks
Crystal, David. *Cambridge Encyclopedia of Language.* New York: Cambridge UP, 1997.
————. *Cambridge Encyclopedia of the English Language.* New York: Cambridge UP, 1997.
Parker, Philip M. *Linguistic Cultures of the World: A Statistical Reference.* Westport, CT: Greenwood, 1997.
Sternberg, Martin L. A. *American Sign Language Dictionary.* New York: Harper Reference, 1998.

Abstracts and Digests
Language and Language Behavior Abstracts. Chicago: Sociological Abstracts, 1967–date.

Databases
LANGUAGE AND LANGUAGE BEHAVIOR ABSTRACTS
MODERN LANGUAGE ASSOCIATION BIBLIOGRAPHY

Literature

Bibliographies, Guides, and Indexes
American Women Fiction Writers, 1900–1960. 3 vols. Eds. Harold Bloom and William Golding. Broomall, PA: Chelsea, 1997.
Bibliography of American Literature. New Haven: Yale UP, 1995–date.
Concise Oxford Companion to English Literature. Ed. Margaret Drabble. New York: Oxford UP, 1996.
Contemporary Authors: A Bio-Bibliographical Guide to Current Writers in Fiction, General Nonfiction, Poetry, Journalism, Drama, and Motion Pictures. Detroit: Gale, 1998.
Critical Theory Today: A User-Friendly Guide. New York: Garland, 1998.
Directory of Literary Magazines 1998. Emeryville, CA: Moyer, 1998.
Doyle, Robert P. *Banned Books: 1998 Resource Guide.* Chicago: American Library, 1998.
Garland Shakespeare Bibliographies. 18 vols. New York: Garland, 1980–date.
MLA International Bibliography of Books and Articles on the Modern Languages and Literatures. New York: MLA, 1921–date.
Morris, Evan. *The Book Lover's Guide to the Internet.* New York: Fawcett, 1998.
Nineteenth-Century Literature Criticism. 2 vols. Detroit, IL: Gale, 1998.
Rand, Donna, Toni Parker, and Sheila Foster. *Black Books Galore! Guide to Great African American Children's Books.* New York: Wiley, 1998.

Encyclopedias, Dictionaries, and Handbooks
American Folklore: An Encyclopedia. Ed. Jan Harold Brunvand. New York: Garland, 1998.
Book Review Index. Detroit: Gale, 1965–date.
Cumulative Index. Vol. 9. Ed. Elizabeth Kniss. Woodbridge, CT: Blackbirch Marketing, 1998.
Dictionary of Cultural and Critical Theory. Eds. Michael Payne, Meenakshi Ponnuswami, and Jennifer Payne. Cambridge, MA: Blackwell, 1998.
Encyclopedia of Science Fiction. Eds. John Clute and Peter Nicholls. New York: St. Martin's, 1995.
Encyclopedia of World Literature in the 20th Century. 3rd ed. Ed. Steven Serafin. Detroit: St. James, 1998.
Essay and General Literature Index. New York: Wilson, 1934–date.
Handbook of Critical Theory. Ed. David M. Rasmussen. Cambridge, MA: Blackwell, 1996.

Miller, R. H. *Handbook of Literary Research.* Lanham, MD: Scarecrow, 1995.
Reader's Encyclopedia of Shakespeare. Eds. Oscar Campbell and George Quinn. New York: Fine Communications, 1998.
Shakespeare Dictionary. Ed. Sandra Clark. Orlando, FL: NTC, 1996.

Abstracts and Digests
Abstracts of English Studies. Urbana, IL: NCTE, 1958–date.
Book Review Digest. New York: Wilson, 1905–date.

Databases
BOOK REVIEW INDEX   MLA BIBLIOGRAPHY

Mathematics

Bibliographies, Guides, and Indexes
Brief Bibliography of Selected Periodical Sources in Mathematics. Ed. Hunter Evans. New York: Adelphi, 1998.
Integer Programming and Related Areas: A Classified Bibliography. New York: Springer, 1999.
Mathematical Journals: An Annotated Guide. Ed. Diana F. Laing. Lanham, MD: Scarecrow, 1992.

Encyclopedias, Dictionaries, and Handbooks
Cambridge Dictionary of Statistics. New York: Cambridge UP, 1998.
CRC Concise Encyclopedia of Mathematics. Ed. Eric W. Weisstein. New York: CRC, 1998.
Encyclopedic Dictionary of Mathematics. Ed. Kiyosi Ito. Cambridge, MA: MIT P, 1993.
Harris, John W., and Horst Stocker. *Handbook of Mathematics and Computational Science.* New York: Springer, 1998.
Spiegal, Murray R., and John M. Liu. *Mathematical Handbook of Formulas and Tables.* New York: McGraw, 1998.

Abstracts and Digests
General Science Index. New York: Wilson, 1978–date.
Mathematical Reviews. Providence, RI: American Mathematical Society, 1940–date. Monthly.

Databases
MATHSCI

Medical Sciences

Bibliographies, Guides, and Indexes
Amercian Drug Index 1999. Eds. Norman F. Billups and Shirley M. Billups. Maryland Heights, MO: Facts and Comparisons, 1998.
Bartone, John C. *Medical Anatomy and Clinical Research: Index of Modern Authors and Subjects, with Guide for Rapid Research.* Annandale, VA: ABBE, 1991.
Cumulative Index to Nursing and Allied Health Literature. Glendale, CA: Glendale. Adventist Medical Center, 1977–date. [Formerly *Cumulative Index to Nursing Literature,* 1956–1976.]
Fisher, J. Patrick. *Medical Terminology.* 4th ed. New York: Macmillan, 1993.
Hospital Literature Index. Chicago: American Hospital, 1945–date.
Index Medicus. Washington, DC: National Library of Medicine, 1960–date.
Medical and Scientific Reports and Research on Efficiency in and Performance in the Health Sciences. Annandale, VA: American Health Research, 1993.

Medical Reference Works, 1679–1966: A Selected Bibliography. Eds. John B. Blake and Charles Roos. Chicago: Medical Library, 1967. Supplements 1970–date.

Medical Research Report: What's Going On in the U.S.A? Index of New Information and Research Bible. Annandale, VA: ABBE, 1995.

Encyclopedias, Dictionaries, and Handbooks

AIDS Crisis in America: A Reference Handbook. Eds. Eric K. Lerner and Mary Ellen. Santa Barbara, CA: ABC-CLIO, 1998.

Black's Medical Dictionary. Ed. Gordon McPherson. Lanham, MD: Barnes, 1996.

Encyclopedia of Medical Organizations and Agencies. 5th ed. Detroit: Gale, 1993.

Merriam-Webster's Medical Desk Dictionary. Springfield, MA: Merriam, 1998.

Databases

BIOSIS PREVIEWS   NURSING AND ALLIED HEALTH
EMBASE   SCISEARCH
MEDLINE

Music

Bibliographies, Guides, and Indexes

Bibliographic Guide to Music. Boston: Hall, 1976–date.

Music Article Guide. Philadelphia: Information Services, 1966–date.

Music Index. Warren, MI: Information Coordinators, 1949–date.

Music Reference and Research Materials: An Annotated Bibliography. Eds. Vincent H. Duckles, Ida Reed, and Michael A. Keller. New York: Schirmer, 1997.

Pollock, Bruce. *The Rock Song Index: Essential Information on the 7,500 Most Important Songs of Rock and Roll.* New York: Schirmer, 1997.

RILM (Repertoire Internationale de Litterature Musicale). New York: City U of New York, 1967–date.

Encyclopedias, Dictionaries, and Handbooks

Baker's Biographical Dictionary of Twentieth-Century Classical Musicians. Eds. Nicolas Slonimsky, Laura Kuhn, and Dennis McIntire. New York: Schirmer, 1997.

Larkin, Colin. *The Billboard Illustrated Encyclopedia of Rock.* New York: Billboard, 1998.

New Grove Dictionary of Music and Musicians. Ed. Stanley Sadie. New York: Grove, 1995.

Whitsett, Tim. *The Dictionary of Music Business Terms.* New York: Leonard, 1998.

Databases

RILM ABSTRACTS (Repertoire Internationale de Litterature Musicale)

Philosophy and Religion

Bibliographies, Guides, and Indexes

Fischer-Schreiber, Ingrid, Franz-Karl Ehrhard, and Kurt Friedrichs. *The Encyclopedia of Eastern Philosophy and Religion: Buddhism, Hinduism, Taoism, Zen.* Boston: Shambhala, 1994.

Hugo, T. W. *Morals and Dogma Index.* Kila, MT: Kessinger, 1997.

Navia, Luis E. *The Philosophy of Cynicism: An Annotated Bibliography.* Westport, CT: Greenwood, 1995.

Philosopher's Index: An International Index to Philosophical Periodicals and Books. Bowling Green, OH: Bowling Green U, 1966–date.

Religion Index One: Periodicals. Chicago: American Theologian, 1978–date.

Encyclopedias, Dictionaries, and Handbooks
Baker Bible Encyclopedia. Ed. Baker Book House Staff. Ada, MI: Baker, 1998.
Diamant, Anita. *Choosing a Jewish Life: A Handbook for People Converting to Judaism and for Their Family and Friends*. New York: Schocken, 1998.
Encyclopedia of Apocalypticism. Eds. Bernard McGinn, John Joseph Collins, and Stephen J. Stein. New York: Continuum, 1998.
Encyclopedia of Classical Philosophy. Eds. Donald J. Zeyl, Daniel T. Devereux, and Phillip Mitsis. Westport, CT: Greenwood, 1997.
Routledge Encyclopedia of Philosophy. 10 Vols. Eds. Edward Craig and Luciano Floridi. New York: Routledge, 1998.

Abstracts and Digests
World Philosophy: Essay Reviews of 225 Major Works. Ed. Frank Magill. 5 vols. Englewood Cliffs, NJ: Salem, 1982.

Databases
PHILOSOPHER'S INDEX

Physics

Bibliographies, Guides, and Indexes
Applied Physics and Technology Index. New York: Wilson, 1958–date.
Current Papers in Physics. London: IEE, 1966–date.
Particle Physics: One Hundred Years of Discoveries: An Annotated Chronological Bibliography. Eds. V.V. Ezhela et al. Woodbury, NY: American Institute of Physics, 1996.
Princeton Guide to Advanced Physics. Ed. Alan C. Tribble. Princeton, NJ: Princeton U Dept. of Art & Archaeology, 1996.
Smith, Roger. *Popular Physics and Astronomy: An Annotated Bibliography*. Lanham, MD: Scarecrow, 1996.

Encyclopedias, Dictionaries, and Handbooks
Cassell Dictionary of Physics. Ed. Percy Harrison. New York: Academic, 1998.
Macmillan Encyclopedia of Physics. Ed. John S. Rigden. Indianapolis, IN: Macmillan, 1998.
Physically Speaking: A Dictionary of Quotations on Physics and Astronomy. Eds. Carl C. Gaither, Alma E. Cavazos-Gaither, and Andrew Slocombe. Chicago: Hayes, 1998.

Abstracts and Digests
Physics Abstracts. Surrey, Eng.: IEE, 1898–date.
Science Abstracts. London: IEE, 1898–date.

Databases
SCISEARCH   SPIN

Political Science

Bibliographies, Guides, and Indexes
ABC: Pol Sci. Santa Barbara, CA: ABC-Clio, 1969–date.
Foreign Affairs Bibliography. New York: Council on Foreign Relations, 1933–date. Published every 10 years.
Guide to the American Left: Directory and Bibliography. Comp. Laird Wilcox. Washington, DC: Library Alliance, 1998.
International Bibliography of Politics and Political Science. Paris, France: UNESCO, 1953–date. Annually.

Parker's 1999 Larmac Consolidated Index to the Constitution and Laws of California. n.p.: Lexis Law, 1998.

Public Affairs Information Service. *Bulletin.* New York: PAIS, 1915–date. Semimonthly.

Social Sciences Citation Index. New York: Wilson, 1973–date.

Social Sciences Index. New York: Wilson, 1974–date.

Encyclopedias, Dictionaries, and Handbooks

Dictionary of Political Biography. Ed. Dennis Kavanagh. New York: Oxford UP, 1998.

Encyclopedia of American Government. Eds. Joseph M. Bessette and R. Kent Rasmussen. Englewood Cliffs, NJ: Salem, 1998.

Encyclopedia of Governmental Advisory Organizations 1999. 13th ed. Detroit: Gale, 1998.

Handbook of Latin American Studies. Gainesville: U of Florida P, 1936–date.

Kravitz, Walter. *American Congressional Dictionary.* Washington, DC: Congressional Quarterly, 1997.

New Handbook of Political Science. Eds. Robert E. Goodin and Hans-Dieter Klingemann. New York: Oxford UP, 1998.

Abstracts and Digests

International Political Science Abstracts. Oxford, Eng.: Blackwell, 1951–date.

Political Science Abstracts. New York: Plenum, 1967–date.

Sage Urban Studies Abstracts. San Mateo, CA: Sage, 1973–date.

United States Political Science Documents (USPSD). Pittsburgh: U of Pittsburgh P, 1975.

Databases

ASI	PAIS
CIS	U.S. POLITICAL SCIENCE
CONGRESSIONAL RECORD ABSTRACTS	DOCUMENTS
GPO MONTHLY CATALOG	WASHINGTON PRESSTEXT
NATIONAL NEWSPAPER INDEX	WORLD AFFAIRS REPORT

Psychology

Bibliographies, Guides, and Indexes

Bartone, John C. *Consumers' Reference Book and Index about Sex Counseling and Diseases.* Washington, DC: ABBE, 1996.

Gay and Lesbian Issues: Abstracts of the Psychological and Behavioral Literature 1986–1996. Eds. Clinton W. Anderson and Amanda R. Adley. Washington, DC: APA, 1997.

Jacobson, Neil S., and Andrew Christensen. *Acceptance and Change in Couple Therapy: A Therapist's Guide to Transforming Relationships.* New York: Norton, 1998.

Mental Health Services in Criminal Justice System Settings: A Selectively Annotated Bibliography, 1970–1997. Eds. Rodney Van Whitlock and Bernard Lubin. Westport, CT: Greenwood, 1998.

Science Citation Index. Philadelphia: Institute for Scientific Information, 1961–date. Annually.

Social Sciences Citation Index. Philadelphia: Institute for Scientific Information, 1969–date. Annually.

Encyclopedias, Dictionaries, and Handbooks

Biographical Dictionary of Psychology. Eds. Noel Sheehy, Antony J. Chapman, and Wendy Conroy. New York: Routledge, 1997.

Cambridge Encyclopedia of Human Growth and Development. Eds. Stanley J. Ulijaszek, Francis E. Johnston, Michael Preece, and J. Stanley Ulijaszek. New York: Cambridge UP, 1998.

Concise Dictionary of Psychology. New York: Routledge, 1998.
Handbook of Personality Psychology. Eds. Robert Hogan, John Johnson, and Stephen Briggs. Orlando, FL: Academic, 1997.

Abstracts and Digests
Annual Review of Psychology. Palo Alto, CA: Annual Review, 1950–date.
Child Development Abstracts and Bibliography. Chicago: U of Chicago P, 1927–date.
Psychological Abstracts. Washington, DC: APA, 1927–date.
Sage Family Studies Abstracts. San Mateo, CA: Sage, 1979–date.

Databases
CHILD ABUSE AND NEGLECT
ERIC
MENTAL HEALTH ABSTRACTS

PSYCHOLOGICAL ABSTRACTS
SOCIAL SCISEARCH
SOCIOLOGICAL ABSTRACTS

Sociology and Social Work

Bibliographies, Guides, and Indexes
Dickson, Donald T. *Confidentiality and Privacy in Social Work: A Guide to the Law for Practitioners and Students.* New York: Free Press, 1998.
Humanities Index. New York: Wilson, 1974–date.
International Bibliography of Social and Cultural Anthropology 1993. New York: Routledge, 1994.
International Bibliography of Social Sciences: Social and Cultural Anthropology 1996. Vol. 42. New York: Routledge, 1998.
Social Science Index. New York: Wilson, 1974–date.

Encyclopedias, Dictionaries, and Handbooks
Blackwell Encyclopedia of Social Psychology. Eds. Antony S. R. Manstead and Miles Hewstone. Cambridge, MA: Blackwell, 1999.
Dictionary of Sociology. Ed. Gordon Marshall. New York: Oxford UP, 1998.
Roberts, Carolyn S., and Martha Gorman. *Euthanasia: A Reference Handbook.* Santa Barbara, CA: ABC-CLIO, 1997.
Social Science Encyclopedia. Eds. Adam Kuper and Jessica Kuper. New York: Routledge, 1996.

Abstracts and Digests
Social Work Research and Abstracts. New York: NASW, 1964–date.
Sociological Abstracts. New York: Sociological Abstracts, 1953–date.

Databases
CHILD ABUSE AND NEGLECT
FAMILY RESOURCES
NCJRS (National Criminal Justice Reference Service)

SOCIAL SCISEARCH
SOCIOLOGICAL ABSTRACTS

Speech

Bibliographies, Guides, and Indexes
Bibliography of Composition and Rhetoric. Eds. Erika Lindemann and Sandra Monroe Fleming. Carbondale, IL: Southern Illinois UP, 1990.
Knapp, Triscia Goodnow, and Lawrence A. Galizo. *Elements of Parliamentary Debate: A Guide to Public Argument.* Reading, MA: Addison, 1998.
Speech Index: An Index to Collections of World Famous Orations and Speeches for Various Occasions. Lanham, MD: Scarecrow, 1996.

Encyclopedias, Dictionaries, and Handbooks

Augmentative and Alternative Communication: A Handbook of Principles and Practices. Ed. Lyle L. Lloyd. Needham Heights, MA: Allyn, 1997.

Terban, Marvin. *Scholastic Dictionary of Idioms.* Madison, WI: Demco Media, 1998.

World Book 1999 Encyclopedia of Speech. Chicago, IL: World Book, 1997.

Databases
ERIC
LLBA (Language and Language Behavior Abstracts)
MLA BIBLIOGRAPHIES
SOCIAL SCISEARCH

Women's Studies

Bibliographies, Guides, and Indexes

Beddoe, Deidre. *Discovering Women's History: A Practical Guide to Researching the Lives of Women Since 1800.* 3rd ed. White Plains, NY: Longman, 1998.

Index Directory of Women's Media. Washington, DC: Women's Institute for Freedom of the Press, 1975–date.

Index to Women's Studies Anthologies. 2 vols. Ed. B. Dickstein. Indianapolis, IN: Macmillan, 1997.

Oldfield, Sybil. *Collective Biography of Women in England, 1550–1900: A Select Annotated Bibliography.* Herndon, VA: Mansell, 1999.

Reader's Guide to Women's Studies. Ed. Eleanor Amico. Chicago: Fitzroy, 1998.

Ryan, Barbara. *The Women's Movement: References, and Resources.* Thorndike, ME: Hall, 1996.

Sherman, Aiza. *Cybergirl! A Woman's Guide to the World Wide Web.* New York: Ballantine, 1998.

Social Sciences Index. New York: Wilson, 1974–date.

Encyclopedias, Dictionaries, and Handbooks

Cullen-DuPont, Kathryn. *The Encyclopedia of Women's History in America.* New York: Facts on File, 1996.

Facts on File Encyclopedia of Black Women in America: Education. Vol 6. Ed. Darlene Clark Hine. New York: Facts on File, 1997.

From the Goddess to the Glass Ceiling: A Dictionary of Feminism. Ed. Janet K. Boles. Lanham, MD: Madison, 1996.

Know Your Rights: A Legal Handbook for Women Only. Eds. Patricia Phillips and George Mair. Indianapolis, IN: Macmillan General Reference, 1997.

Abstracts and Digests

Women Studies Abstracts. New York: Rush, 1972–date.

Databases
ERIC   SOCIOLOGICAL ABSTRACTS
SOCIAL SCISEARCH

INDEX